When Humans Stop Shopping

Consumers, Technology and the Future of Retail

by David Kerrigan

Preface

My most recent visit to a convenience store took just 9 seconds. I didn't have my wallet or any cash with me, didn't queue to checkout, didn't speak to any staff member, yet received an itemized receipt on my phone as I left the store with my purchases.

A box of new clothes, chosen for me by a computer, arrived on my doorstep the other day. My microwave oven just ordered more popcorn, my printer just ordered more ink by itself and I asked my smart speaker to find me the best price on some replacement batteries.

The result of all this is that I don't visit stores anywhere near as much as I used to, but I still have all the products I want. Algorithms have taken over much of my decision making to ensure I have what I need, at the time I need it, without having to even think. This is the brave new world of contemporary retail - shopping is no longer about stores and malls, or even websites; brands and retailers need to prepare for new consumers, new technologies and the end of shopping as we've known it.

Acknowledgements

My thanks firstly to family, and my friends who encourage my writing including Aideen, David, Caroline, Lorraine, Susan, Sylvia, Fergal, Sinead, Louise, Phelim, Orlagh, Adam, Matt, Karolina, Paula, Sudha, Henning, Trish, Rob, Luke, Simon and Marie.

Special thanks to the retailers and experts, as well as my clients, who gave me their time and thoughts as I researched this book, especially Kevin, Lisa, Husani, Pat, Paula, Sedge, Jeff and Ken for the cover design.

Accompanying Material

All images in the book are available in full color via the accompanying website at https://david-kerrigan.com/whss. You can also contact the author via the website.

Also by The Author

Your Phone Can Save Your Life (2015)
Life As A Passenger (2017)
The New Acceleration (2018)

All trademarks mentioned and images reproduced are the property of their respective owners.

© David Kerrigan, 2020. All Rights Reserved.

Contents

Chapter 1: Introduction 1

Chapter 2: Contemporary Shoppers 15

Chapter 3: Contemporary Shopping 69

Chapter 4: Faster Stores 115

Chapter 5: New Ways to Shop: Channels 151

Chapter 6: New Ways to Shop: Interfaces 175

Chapter 7: Removing The Humans 223

Chapter 8: Demanding Delivery 277

Chapter 9: What does the Future have in Store(s) ... 321

Chapter 10: Retail Futures 365

Appendix 1: Grocery & Restaurants 383

Appendix 2: Further Reading 395

References 397

Glossary of Terms

AI - Artificial Intelligence
AOV - Average Order Value
API - Application Programming Interface
AR - Augmented Reality
AV - Autonomous Vehicle
BFCM - Black Friday/Cyber Monday (Discount sales period, last weekend of November)
BLS - Bureau of Labor Statistics
BOPIS - Buy Online Pickup In Store
BORIS - Buy Online Return In Store
CPG - Consumer Packaged Goods
EDLP - Every Day Low Prices
FBA - Fulfilment by Amazon
FMCG - Fast Moving Consumer Goods
JIT - Just In Time
ML - Machine Learning
POS - Point of Sale
RTLI - Real Time Local Inventory
SFS - Ship From Store
SMB - Small and Medium Businesses
SKU - Stock Keeping Unit - a unique identifier for a product
VR - Virtual Reality

Chapter 1: Introduction

"One thing I love about customers is that they are divinely discontent. Their expectations are never static – they go up. It's human nature. We didn't ascend from our hunter-gatherer days by being satisfied. People have a voracious appetite for a better way, and yesterday's 'wow' quickly becomes today's 'ordinary'.

I see that cycle of improvement happening at a faster rate than ever before. It may be because customers have such easy access to more information than ever before – in only a few seconds and with a couple taps on their phones, customers can read reviews, compare prices from multiple retailers, see whether something's in stock, find out how fast it will ship or be available for pick-up, and more."

Jeff Bezos, CEO, Amazon[1]

How, where and what we buy matters. Why we shop matters. In fact, it's probably hard to overstate the importance of retail and wider consumer spending to the economy and, by extension, to society overall. Retail is key to much of the wealth generated and employs more people than any other sector - the retail sector is in fact North America's largest employer, as it is also in many other countries. Retail in the US directly and indirectly supports 42 million jobs, providing $1.6 trillion in labor income[2]. A drop in consumer spending can tilt a country into recession, political upheaval and societal change. So, when the retail sector changes as dramatically as it has, it's important to be aware of it; when it faces changes as dramatic as it does, it's vital to plan for it. I've spoken to many people who have seen the decline of the main street and dismiss it as irrelevant to them. Yet, when I point out that retail investment may be crucial to their pensions, they are suddenly more interested. There's no escaping the importance of retail - our towns and cities, transport infrastructure and many other industries are built on the concept of retailing - it's no exaggeration to say the pattern of our lives is tied very closely to how we trade goods.

But if the how, where, why and what we buy matter, the who also matters. As we'll see in the following Chapters, the how, where and when has already been changing dramatically over the last 10-20 years. But perhaps more significantly, *who* does the buying is going to change in the next 10 years. The who that is, not only in terms of changing demographics but also the who as in non-humans starting to make purchasing decisions on our behalf. Selling to non-humans, however, is a very different prospect - one that today's retailers are not prepared for.

All efforts to date in retail have focused on acquiring human customers - targeting people to buy things, with increasingly sophisticated (some might say invasive) techniques. And while changes in consumer behaviors between generations are important, the arrival of non-human purchasers is something completely new. As we'll see in this book, there are now numerous examples of humans handing growing amounts of control - up to and including full decision making - to artificial intelligence. Coupled with other changes in technology and in consumers, retail in the years ahead is still yet to feel the full force of its biggest upheaval ever, even if it feels like it's been under attack for years already.

The last decade has seen unprecedented upheaval, with tumbling employment in bellwether sectors, liquidation of stalwart names and growing concern about the future of traditional outlets in the face of competition, especially from online shopping. Although there has already been much coverage of "the end of retail" or "the death of the main street", I believe we're actually only at the beginning of a period of extreme change that will affect the entire sector. While physical stores may continue to bear the brunt of the changes, even newer online only or omni-channel retailers (ones that trade both digitally and from physical stores) are facing a further daunting wave of change. A 2017 study from Cornerstone Capital Group[3] predicted that up to 7.5 million existing retail jobs are at risk over the next decade from automation.

High Profile Retail

Retail is very relatable for most people - it's very visible; it touches on society, jobs, property, leisure, basic needs, transport/logistics, entrepreneurship, payments and myriad other aspects of economic activity and living. Most of us interact with retail in some form every day. It already provides good examples of early applications of new technologies such as Artificial Intelligence (AI), Computer Vision, Voice Recognition and more. It's also a confluence point for both online and offline examples of high-tech developments that raise several ethical questions, especially relating to jobs and privacy.

Major retailers have played an outsize role in the stock market for decades, but incumbents can't expect to stay successful by going about business as usual. Retail has become a very public battleground for the world's leading technology companies trying to innovate their way to a position of dominance in consumers' daily lives. As both Alphabet and Amazon's market value exceeds one *trillion* dollars, they have the R&D funds to experiment with countless innovations simultaneously and we'll refer to them frequently throughout this book. For Google, any shift away from web-based shopping, to voice-led or subscriptions, could severely impact its bottom line, given its dependence on advertising. Amazon, the world's most high-profile e-commerce company, as you'll see in the many examples throughout this book, is innovating and experimenting, having invested over the last two decades to build a dominant platform.

Continuum of Change

It's important to note that the term "retail" covers a broad, sometimes barely related set of experiences. Picking a $2 jar off a shelf in a discount grocer is a far cry from having a personal shopper escort you around a luxury showroom looking at $1,000 handbags, yet both are technically considered retail. So "retail" isn't a singular thing and different sectors will have different priorities and will move at different paces. You will see from the impacts discussed here, some innovations are clearly more focused on selling convenience than luxury, while others obviously make more sense when deployed in an elongated, high-cost purchase journey. Even within the same sector, you'll see variations in approach, outlook, and speed of adoption.

In many sections in this book, you'll see possibilities to take a cautious approach or a more ambitious adoption of new trends and technologies. For example, we'll talk about how Dollar General is just recently bringing basic mobile features to its shoppers, as 7-Eleven embrace mobile checkout, while Amazon launch convenience stores with no checkouts.

Trends

There are several key trends to look at in retail that relate both to shoppers and the technologies that are shaking up the sector. From the migration of previously offline sectors to online operation, to the invasion of technology into physical stores, to the plethora of new interfaces for shopping, there are many steps on the road to the ultimate evolution we'll see in many areas of retail: the removal of the human component. Among the major trends (the majority of which are built on new technologies) we'll explore are:

- Consumers' environmental concerns
- New retail business models
- Faster physical shopping
- More sectors moving online
- More technology applied to offline stores
- New ways to shop
- Humans delegating shopping

From Buying Technology to Technology Buying

With the seemingly endless media coverage of the decline of the main street/mall and the impact of online shopping, it may feel that the sector is already at the peak of change. But I contend it's only just beginning. While technology-enabled buying has already had an impact - online accounts for nearly 20% of spending on average (much higher in some verticals) and rising - we'll see more changes to how commerce works in the next 10 years than we have in the preceding 50.

Technology, both visible and invisible, is changing *how*, *where* and *when* we buy things. But next up, it's going to change *who* is buying things. Since the ancient agora in Greece, the common thread across all forms of retail has been a human final decision maker. But we are seeing the early signs of humans being relegated to a smaller role or even removed from the process. And this will have massive implications for everyone. *Who is doing the buying will matter more in the coming years as it will totally redefine many of the relationships between brands, retailers and buyers.*

The next decade will see a further massive shift of power, a concentration towards fewer retailers, powerful online marketplace aggregators/platforms and especially towards newly empowered and technologically augmented consumers and their digital agents.

Technology & Tastes

You could be forgiven for thinking, from reading reports about the future of retail, that technology is the only factor driving change. But it's not that simple. There are generational shifts in consumer attitudes to consider too, as we'll see in detail in the next Chapter. It's dangerous to look purely at the technology – failing to understand peoples' motivations, along with the technologies available to enhance the relationship, will doom many businesses. While retailers of the future may be selling to, and dealing via, non-human intermediaries, their ultimate target of customer satisfaction has to remain the primary focus and basis for survival.

Believe what you haven't seen

The pace of technological innovation, customer adoption and changes in expectations are dizzying. With so much going on, it's easy to miss out. New technologies can "go viral" and gain a worldwide audience of millions virtually overnight (consider the spread and influence of apps like Snapchat or TikTok) while regional differences in the adoption of technology can surprise global operators who don't localize their operations effectively. It's also important to adopt a willingness to believe what you haven't seen. Having travelled extensively to visit some of the most advanced concept stores and technology developers - I can provide multiple examples of technologies that may seem far-fetched - or plain unreal - to people who haven't seen them. But it's important to be aware that those developing new concepts now tend first to test them in a discreet location before rapidly rolling them out to gain competitive advantage – so just because you haven't seen it working in your locality doesn't mean it's not coming to a competitor near you soon! I'm not pushing a specific agenda or solution, but I strongly urge anyone involved in retail or marketing to *consider* the innovations discussed here - and keep a watching brief even if they don't seem relevant right now.

Retail Complexity

The contemporary retailer faces an unprecedented environment. Never before has there been a comparable series of concomitant developments - from macro socioeconomics to demographics to technological breakthroughs. Retailers and the brands they represent are fast losing their historic grip on consumers; those that fail to acknowledge and respond to these changes will fail. Even a quick look at a main street or mall shows technology, people, and policies are visibly moving at different paces. Consumers today have thousands of equally compelling stores, websites, products, brands and services right at their fingertips. There is change at every stage of retail - from discovery to purchase to payment to delivery to returns. Brands are trying new approaches to the market, as retailers struggle to adapt in the face of recalcitrant landlords, planning restrictions and outdated taxation regimes. Those that can't quickly find a way to navigate these complexities will soon be out of business.

If you've never worked in retail, you likely won't be familiar with the complexity of retail operations - voluminous handbooks and training courses for store staff, covering everything from rosters to cash handling, cleaning, stock management, merchandising, discounting and so much more. This is typically hidden from customers but is the reason why things work or don't work well for the customers. The retailers who have good people, with good processes and good technology have a head start that is likely to help keep them afloat. But even good operators need to be aware of the changes and respond to them.

This book summarizes much of the current thinking in the industry, and much of the current experimentation. Many of the experiments will fail, and some of the companies mentioned here may no longer exist by the time you read this. But lessons will have been learned, concepts will have been tried and even those that fail will feed into future decisions. There isn't a retailer in existence that needs to implement all of the ideas in this book. So don't be afraid to dismiss things if they're not relevant to you, but don't dismiss everything. There may be a bewildering array of ideas, trials and concepts that can make things confusing to the point of switching off. But I want to create informed awareness and give you every chance to compete if you're a retailer or brand and every chance to have the best shopping experience if you're a consumer.

Objective

The aim of this book is to explore how retail is changing as well as how these trends may continue to affect this hugely important sector in society. I want to look at changes to how, where and why we buy things; changes driven by evolving consumer preferences and emerging technologies. The book offers advice for retailers on how to prepare for what's coming and outlines how consumers can utilize technology to find and interact with retailers with transparency, convenience and value.

For consumers, I'll cover changes that will directly impact you - changes that will determine the makeup of your neighborhood, what products are available to buy, and at what price. If you don't think it's immediately relevant to you, remember that your ability to regulate or determine the amount of technology you want in your life may be diminishing. I also hope to explain some technologies you're not even aware of that you might benefit from in terms of time and/or money saved. But I also cover changes that could maybe lead to increased prices or reduced choice - something we're not used to after decades of the opposite.

Given the importance of consumer spending to the economy and the environment, I believe it's vital we are all aware of how our decisions and actions will shape the future. Some of the impacts are obvious, but many are not yet apparent or understood. There has been much oversimplification of retail's challenges, with sensationalist coverage blaming online shopping as the only culprit. But we need to understand the broader trends, challenges and opportunities; I think some of the biggest changes are yet to come and haven't been widely discussed, what with the commentators' fixation on Amazon or "Online" rather than addressing broader systemic issues.

The next generation of technology-powered shopping is fast arriving and it's going to have a bigger impact than first-generation online technologies. Coupled with the emerging spending power of younger cohorts of shoppers raised with a different outlook, technology changes and consumer shifts mean nobody will escape the impact of this new retail revolution.

Outline

The rest of this Chapter sets the scene and scope for the remainder of the book, with a reminder of just how important shopping is, how much time we devote to it and the trends that provide context for the following discussion.

Chapter 2 begins with a look at how marketers have historically categorized and understood consumers, before focusing on the new values that define contemporary consumers more than their age. Then it looks at dramatic changes in attitudes to ownership, second-hand goods and the importance of sustainability - changes that will upend the centuries-old dynamics between consumers and retailers.

Chapter 3 starts by looking at our current retail situation and talks about how the recent changes, large as they might seem, are only the first act in a much longer process. By assessing adoption in the last 10-20 years, we'll see how we got to now. There has been much change already and it gives useful context to set the scene, identify emerging and accelerating trends and likely scenarios.

Chapter 4 looks at efforts to make physical shopping faster - the removal of "friction" in stores through technology in a world hungry for more speed. Understanding the trajectory we're on in that regard will give context to the emergence of further new developments.

Chapter 5 describes some of the myriad new ways to shop, away from physical stores and in many cases away from what are now "traditional" online shopping sites. From social shopping to shopping everywhere, these technologies change our relationship with vendors, making everything shoppable with minimal effort.

Chapter 6 examines the emerging new interfaces we'll use to shop - text, voice and visual shopping.

Chapter 7 explores how humans are reducing their involvement in the purchase journey by automating ordering where possible. With the growth of subscriptions and automated replenishment, we may no longer make many purchase decisions, and that may create a winner-takes-all scenario for some retailers. Taking the removal of humans from shopping to its logical conclusion, we soon see a time where retailers can predict what we want and provide it to us before we even ask.

Taken together, Chapters 4, 5, 6 and 7 show clearly that our relationship with shops and shopping is changing in significant ways, potentially leading to our removal from large parts of the process. While many will undoubtedly be uncomfortable with this, others will embrace the potential time savings and efficiencies

In Chapter 8, I want to spend time discussing some of the technologies that are changing how products reach us - the logistics behind the new shopping, the devices to bring ever more convenience but also the costs of feeding our shopping convenience habits.

In Chapter 9, we'll look at some of the innovations that will shape the stores of the future, the main streets and malls of the future and how brands, retailers and policy makers can prepare.

Chapter 10 concludes the discussion with a summary and provides some final questions to consider.

Appendix 1 provides an in-depth look at the Food/Grocery sector as a microcosm of the effects of many of the changes discussed throughout the book.

Context

I noted earlier that retail is a huge and vitally important sector of the economy. So, let's take a few minutes to look at the scope of the discussion and at just how much time and money we spend on shopping.

Buying things is, of course, not a new habit. Ancient Greece and Rome had the Agora and the Forum respectively as marketplaces where citizens went to purchase goods. Trajan's market in Rome grew to over 150 stores, creating the world's first "shopping mall". Richer citizens could even expect home deliveries from merchants, or simply send their slaves to the market on their behalf. Retailing has grown a lot more complex since ancient times, especially in the last few decades. Advances in communication, trade and transportation mean that we now take for granted that we can purchase goods from all over the world. Shopping has also come to be a leisure activity for many, unlike the purely utilitarian nature of acquisition in historic times.

Though the term "retail" dates back to the 1400s and describes the concept of selling small pieces, what's commonly referred to nowadays as retail is a broad topic. So it's important to clarify here what I mean when I say retail - in most cases, I'm referring to consumer expenditure on goods or services that people buy for their own use or that of a family member, bought from a manufacturer/brand or a retailer. In some cases, I will also point out examples of changes impacting other consumer spending on services - things like financial products that aren't considered retail or aren't usually found in the mall, but nonetheless form an important portion of individual and household budgets and are also undergoing major changes.

For the purposes of this book, I'm not going to talk specifically about corporate purchasing - what's more commonly referred to as procurement, although this too, I believe, will see big changes. But for most people it's not as relatable as retail; it's not visible on the main street or in your social media feeds. In some ways though, procurement practices such as Requests for Proposal (RFP) and a market where the consumer defines their requirements with suppliers vying for business, are concepts that may become more common in a consumer context.

Spending is Big Business

Global consumer spending is enormous. At around $40 trillion dollars annually, it includes categories such as housing and transportation that are largely outside the scope of this book (which is not to say there isn't massive technologically and demographically driven change to explore there) but also areas such as food, household and clothes shopping that have formed the backbone of the retail sector for generations. An incredible amount of money is spent on personal consumption — more than $1 trillion every month. A little less than half of that is spent on products at retail stores and online. Everyone interacts with retail to some extent. It's difficult to go for any extended period without buying something. Whether it's food, medicine or leisure activities, the average person in the US makes 70 transactions per month. Even when you don't think you're engaging in retail, a subscription you have may be renewing in the background.

Spending Time Spending Money

As well as the large quantities of money we spend in retail, we also devote a lot of *time* to the pursuit of material acquisition. While much of this is for essential purchases, much more of it is optional - many people enjoy a good browse and delight in the serendipitous discovery of something unexpected (while others loathe the chore of acquiring items in stores when they could be watching sports or Netflix).

Although online shopping has removed or reduced the need to spend time in shops, the amount of time people spend shopping is still significant. According to the EU, Europeans spend between 17 and 35 minutes every day on shopping and personal services.

Figure 1 Shopping takes a lot of our time. Source: Eurostat

The BLS estimates that the average US citizen spends 0.72 hours per day every day on shopping and related activities. These 2017 BLS statistics cover browsing, waiting in line, paying, returning goods (there's even still a category for returning video tapes!) but don't include putting shopping away when you get home - that's classified as a household activity and measured separately from actual purchasing. Making shopping lists and picking up packages is also considered household management.

Buying vs Shopping

Some people already bemoan the loss of the human touch and the lack of pleasure in online shopping compared to tactile browsing and discovery in a traditional store. Our time is under pressure and people are more and more considering if it is preferable to visit a store and search, perhaps fruitlessly, for items which could be found quickly on a mobile website whilst binging on the latest must-watch show?

A crucial consideration is our motivation - are we shopping with a clear objective to buy or is it a more leisurely shopping trip where the trip is as important as whether we actually purchase? If we're in buying mode, it's primarily transactional - we'll seek the fastest possible and most convenient option. It's about efficiency. Buying mode is ideal for online. A shopping trip, on the other hand, is far more experiential. The exploration and discovery may be highly social, with an emphasis on slow, subjective considerations rather than clinical comparisons.

When Humans Stop Shopping

As we come to the end of the introduction, I'd like to pause for a moment to make an important point - although I believe that adopting the right amount of technology will be crucial to survival for retailers in the coming years, no amount of technology can save you if you fail to provide what customers want. Just as consumer behavior is a mixture of rational (needs) and irrational (wants/impulses), retailers too rely on a mixture of the art and the science of retail. These lines will be redrawn as technology plays an increasing role in every aspect of the sector but it cannot overcome bad retailing.

In the coming Chapters, we'll examine the perfect storm of change, with technologies maturing and the dominant cohort of consumers also changing. There have always been changes in store formats as well as changes in consumer habits, but the relentless advance of technology and changing demographics are combining to create the most volatile trading environment ever, and it's one that most retailers are ill equipped to handle. This matters not just because of the impact on main streets and on retail staff, but of the underlying importance of consumer spending to the economy.

We're about to see more automation of shops, shopping and even shoppers against a backdrop of changing consumers. This has massive implications for the world we live in, socially and economically. Most people have responded favorably to technology that makes shopping cheaper and more convenient - but where do you draw the line? Is it useful if you never run out of orange juice, but creepy if your fridge buys your food on Amazon, having noticed what you liked on Facebook and Instagram?

Consumers will stop shopping in the ways we're familiar with, in the places we expect, at the times we're used to. They'll stop shopping in the ways that our stores, supply chains and cities are built for. In some cases, the stark reality of the future is that humans won't shop anymore. They'll delegate shopping to their digital assistants. The future of retail will be about understanding and meeting consumer needs on their terms, rather than stacking items and hoping they find and buy them. Cumulatively, it's the biggest change ever to face the consumer industries.

Chapter 2: Contemporary Shoppers

"By all accounts, the retail sector in most of the world is struggling. Rising competition from online shopping has hit bricks-and-mortar retailers hard. Environmental concerns have led customers to question traditional packaging and farming practices. And the growing preference of many consumers, particularly younger ones, to favor 'experiences' over 'stuff' has eaten into overall demand."

The Financial Times[4]

While much of the change discussed in this book is enabled, or even driven, by technology, it would be a foolish brand or retailer that expects to survive without understanding the evolving role that humans still play in the ongoing retail revolution - their changing priorities and preferences, attitudes and expectations; their imminent total withdrawal from some sectors of retail and their reduction of involvement in others. Anyone who thinks good retail is a purely technological challenge will struggle - much technology is emerging to help better understand and serve customers, but comprehending wider market trends and customers' values is crucial not only in terms of retailing but even in terms of choosing which technologies to prioritize and what marketing channels to optimize.

In this Chapter, I want to focus on some key trends shaping consumers' approach to consumption, retail and brands. We'll examine who is shopping and what's important to them, before we look, in the next Chapter, at how and where they are shopping. Even though a core theme of this book is the prediction that humans will, in many cases, spend less time shopping, that's not to say that they won't still determine the priorities for what they consume, even if they delegate the actual purchasing to technology.

Retail is changing because the consumer is changing. New shopping channels are popping up nonstop on both the physical and digital planes. Consumers are now more informed than ever when it comes to the products retailers sell—and that's before they even set foot in a store, if they do so at all. In today's world, a retailer may never see the consumer - in fact they may be on the other side of the planet and may not even be human. Everything is shoppable, all the time, from anywhere, with near-perfect knowledge about price, competitive products and availability. The new consumer is more demanding, experiential and discerning, yet often still price oriented. They expect total convenience and personal service at discount prices.

There is a litany of change for retailers and brands to contend with. Not just the more obvious changes like the emergence of online shopping, but wider societal trends such as urban migration, an ageing population in many markets, as well as sustainability concerns. In later sections of this book, we'll talk about technologies for personalization and customer insight - solutions designed to target individual customers rather than generic segments. But before we get to that kind of detail, I want to start with a higher-level view of general consumer groupings that are most frequently used in discussions of retail and marketing at present.

Categorizing the Consumer

"All models are wrong - some are useful"

George Box

I've never been a huge fan of the broad marketing approach of grouping of people into "generations". I don't particularly like the rather sweeping labels of "Millennials" or "Gen X", etc., but there is undoubtedly some measurable generational change in shopping habits whether you agree with the specific monikers or not. With age as the baseline factor, the generations are largely assessed by marketers in terms of their life stage shopping requirements, and their attitudes to technology rather than considering more individual factors. But where I do find this approach useful is as a reminder that tastes change over time but also across and within cohorts. Human consumers are not always rational, nor are they always consistent. Having benchmark cohorts to assess consumer behavior against can prove useful.

There are, of course, some shared tendencies, values and preferences that describe each generation, but the favored rather blunt denominator of age doesn't take into account variations in gender, socio-economic conditions or outlook - for example older people who take the time to learn new technologies, can see very real benefits from the convenience it offers. Conversely, you may have younger generations who spend so much of their time connected that they will actively seek disconnected or retro experiences - like the minority who eschew music streaming services for the authenticity of vinyl. Although brands and retailers are moving towards more granular ways of targeting consumers, the nomenclature of generations remains very prevalent in the thinking of many marketers.

As a business owner, you must know both the current trends and what is on the horizon. This will help you navigate the continuously evolving market and at the same time help to provide a relevant shopping experience for your customers. "Segmentation" and "Marketing" may be alien to many small businesses who rely on instinct and precedent to trade, but even if you think you don't need to appeal to a certain segment, I would caution that behaviors have a habit of leaking between segments. It's useful to remember that Gen X, Y Z etc. are broad brush generalizations, not solid cohorts without variations or intermingling.

Keeping In Touch

While I mentioned in the previous Chapter my belief in the importance of open-mindedness about technologies that you haven't yet seen, I also want to stress the importance of learning about behaviors in cohorts that you may not be personally directly familiar with. If this is the only learning you take from the generations model, then it can be useful. For example, I am frequently shocked, but unfortunately no longer surprised, by the number of my older friends and acquaintances that do not appreciate the reach and influence of YouTube. Even though it's now a veritable senior citizen in tech circles, there seems to be a widespread tendency to dismiss it as a home of unimportant frivolous video uploads. For many consumers, it's a vital resource they turn to in order to research products, looking for video reviews that bring far more detail than static web pages. To put its reach in context, the most popular network television shows in the US may manage 20 million viewers per episode, but the top 10 YouTube channels all have at least 40 million subscribers[5]. Those viewers are undoubtedly skewed towards younger people but there are also active niche interest groups of all ages to be found on YouTube. As a Millennial might say, YMMV (Your Mileage May Vary).

The Generations

Traditionally, companies have used demographics to understand consumers. This allowed the development of concepts, such as Baby Boomers, Generation X and Millennials. But remember those catch-all terms are exactly that - making generalizations commonplace, missing the nuance of the individual customer and their particular wants, needs, expectations and values.

Given how widely used this approach is, we'll use it here as a basis to start the discussion on consumers before moving on to more current considerations. Despite some differences in the details, most marketing people agree on 4 major cohorts (with one emerging) when trying to categorize consumers. I'll use the US market for this discussion, but the relative size of each group does vary by country, so it's important to consider your local targets if operating/focused in another region.

Group	Born	Age	Size (USA)	Technology View
Baby Boomers	1945-1965	55-75+	70m	Many have adopted online shopping but not as mobile-centric as younger generations
Gen X	1965-1980	40-54	65m	Remember a time without connectivity but have largely adopted tech
Gen Y (Millennials)	1981-1994	25-39	90m	Grew up with computers, cell phones & iPods
Gen Z (Post Millennials)	1995-2010	10-24	75m	Cannot imagine a world without smartphones
Alpha	2010+	<10	48m	Will grow up with widespread voice, robotics and AI

Born since 2010 are Alpha Gen - obviously this group are not yet displaying any personal spending power but may already be a target for brands seeking to hook early behaviors via their Gen Y and Gen Z parents. And remember, there are influencers under the age of 10 that are millionaires thanks to YouTube!

For decades, marketers have sought to define and serve markets that are internally consistent on some common ground, yet externally different from other market segments. Understanding customers and better catering to their needs has been a key tenet of the consumer industry since the rise of marketing in the 1970s. As competition, differentiation and choice all grew - as a consequence of growth in manufacturing capability and capacity - the number of products available has increased dramatically. This has led to more specialist and niche solutions allowing for more precise targeting of consumers' needs.

Much industry discussion is obsessed with advising businesses (typically run by older generations) on how to understand and target the younger generations. And while it's crucial for most businesses to keep up with changing tastes, new consumer segments should ideally be additive rather than coming at the cost of your existing customers. It can be challenging for a brand or retailer to appeal simultaneously to diverse generations. When faced with the proliferation of articles and opinion pieces purporting to unlock the 'lucrative mysteries' of Millennials or Gen Z, it's important to take a balanced view of the market and be aware that older segments are growing in size and spending power in many markets.

Let's review each segment in terms of scale and their attitude to technology and shopping.

Baby Boomers

Born around the end of World War II in a favorable US economic climate, the youngest Boomers are now in their mid-fifties, the eldest in their mid-seventies. Thanks to the healthcare advances of the last few decades, Boomers are healthier than previous generations, though still spend large amounts on healthcare products and services. Numbering over 60 million in the US, Baby Boomers are a formidable consumer segment, controlling in excess of half of the nation's disposable income. They are also responsible for more spending growth over the past decade than any other generation, including the much-coveted Millennials. This is happening for two reasons: demographics—there are simply more consumers over 60 than there were 10 years ago (each day, 10,000 U.S. Baby Boomers turn 65[6])—and behavior: Baby Boomers, compared to generations that preceded them, are retiring later, holding on to more debt and maintaining budgets for travel and other discretionary spending. The ways Boomers are living and spending are changing; for instance, many Boomers are downsizing from larger homes and moving into smaller spaces. Those trends alone have implications for retailers that sell furniture and accessories, as well as for home-improvement stores. As homes shrink, so may the stores that serve the homeowners. As urban locations gain new residents such as Boomers, smaller-format grocery stores are becoming a popular option for customers who make multiple trips to the supermarket rather than to larger out of town locations. Stores catering to Boomers are also working to become more physically accessible by updating signage, layouts, and other features to make the shopping experience easier to navigate. For instance, some chains have lowered shelf heights or increased the font size on pharmacy labels. Retailers that fail to react to these trends will find Boomers won't shop with them.

Technology

Unlike subsequent generations, Boomers were not born with technology, yet somehow have managed to incorporate it into their daily lives and shopping habits. Despite the stereotypes of them as being unfamiliar with recent technologies, they are avid users of online shopping, with over 9 out of 10 Baby Boomers shopping online, with over 50% in the 65+ sub-group. Although there is high usage of online shopping among Baby Boomers, it is notable that they are more likely to use a laptop or PC than a mobile device.

According to research conducted by Google and Ipsos, the Internet "is the top source [Baby Boomers use] for gathering information on topics of interest, outpacing TV and print media by a substantial margin". Significantly, 71% of Baby Boomers use social media platforms on a daily basis, with Facebook being the most popular. After all, many Baby Boomers are retired, and have more time to devote to searching for products and reviews. As a group, they are also strongly influenced by peer opinion, with half of these shoppers researching products extensively ahead of purchase, so retailers should ensure they collect and surface testimonials and reviews. While a whopping 82% of Millennials make purchasing decisions influenced by the opinions of family, social media, and friends, the same is only true for just over half of Baby Boomers, who tend to be more influenced by retail websites themselves. Although members of this group enjoy shopping in physical stores, they do gravitate to online retailers as well, but tend to lean toward sites of retailers they already know, according to data from NPD Group. For example, Baby Boomers are likely to visit the websites of QVC or Macy's, since they are familiar with those sellers and may lack awareness or trust of newer retailers and brands.

Shopping

Members of the Baby Boomer generation have passed through endless malls and stores over the years, and they've seen it all in terms of selling strategies. The generation that grew up shopping on Main Street later saw the rise of malls and, more recently, online shopping, with all the associated changes in physical store formats, product selection, and technology over the decades.

Although they now regularly make purchases online, Baby Boomers are typically highest amongst all surveyed in expressing their preference to shop in-store. The root of Boomers' brick-and-mortar preference is tied to their high expectations of customer service. According to a LoyaltyOne survey[7] on generational consumer habits, Boomers were the most likely demographic to take their business away from retail chains following a subpar exchange with one of their sales associates or if the store is untidy. They still crave a personalized sales experience and they want personalized attention. Stores can help deliver this through new technology to empower better service from store staff, but retailers also need to consider how they train staff to communicate with Boomers in store - clienteling tools (software that helps store associates recognize and serve customers) are also great conversation starters that are very likely to impress Boomers. Boomers place immense value in brands based on their interactions with sales associates, and retailers can capitalize on this by offering the same emphasis on experience through digital channels. Similar to the physical store layout, retailers who hope to appeal to the Baby Boomer generation need to ensure that their website looks classic, neat, and uncluttered by too many colors or complicated categories.

Forgotten?

In the context of this book, Boomers are a slightly paradoxical cohort - the group least likely to stop shopping in traditional ways but surveys show that this is a group of humans that is starting to spend more! Yet although they are one of the easiest groups to retain as in store shoppers, they are very open to the convenience of online shopping, influenced by younger generations and also the attraction of new shopping and delivery services if they are facing health or mobility constraints.

While following the traditional marketing bias of aggressively courting the 18-49 target audience – being lured in by the prospect of a younger consumer, ripe with lucrative, long-term potential – retailers are neglecting an arguably more valuable source of business: Baby Boomers. Figures show[8] that as this generation began aging out of the popular 18-49 cohort, retailers started losing interest and now spend less than 5% of their advertising budgets toward them.

Brands and retailers need to re-embrace this older demographic and take their needs and behaviors into consideration in order to retain and expand access to a large market. Millennials may represent the bigger long-term opportunity, but Baby Boomers shouldn't be alienated. The changes to make the retail journey suitable for Boomers are not prohibitively expensive - all it takes is an awareness and recognition that this wealthy and growing older generation represents a big opportunity for consumer businesses and retailers, and one they should continue to pursue with interest.

In the UK, according to a study by Hitachi Consulting[9], almost three-quarters (74%) of stores are increasingly focusing their services on 19-38-year-olds, in a bid to capitalize on mobile and digital spending, as well as capturing the long-term loyalty of the next generation of shoppers. This means that brands and retailers are ignoring or irritating more than a third of the UK population, with more than 23 million people aged over-50 according to the Office for National Statistics (ONS). This is a generation who over the last decade has increased consumer spending on an average of 4.4% a year – faster than any other demographic.

Gen X

Gen X accounts for about 1 in every 5 people in the USA - Pew Research projects that Gen X will outnumber the Boomer population by 2028. Gen X members were born between 1965 and 1976 and are currently aged in their early 40s to mid-50s; they have considerable spending power as many of them now occupy high-paying jobs. On a global basis, Gen X now dominates workplace leadership, already accounting for half of all business management roles. About two thirds of the CEOs of Fortune 500 corporations are currently Gen Xers, and that number will only grow in coming years. Generation X's current high-earning period in their lives, coupled with especially high brand loyalty and affinity for nicer things, makes them an optimal target for luxury brands and more discretionary items. The youngest Gen Xers may still have kids in school or college, but older Gen Xers are becoming empty nesters. Many are moving into a phase of their lives where they have more discretionary dollars to spend on housing, consumables, travel and entertainment.

Gen-X has spawned a whole generation of innovators, including Elon Musk, founder of Tesla and SpaceX; and Jeff Bezos, founder and CEO of Amazon. Some 35% of the Time's 100 Most Influential People of 2019 are Gen-X, too. So Gen-X are making a considerable number of the decisions about the types of technologies being deployed and need to remain aware of the requirements and preferences of other cohorts. In their personal lives, as the bridge between Boomers and Millennials, Gen Xers have more influence than marketers realize, particularly if they are financially supporting both aging parents as well as young adults (Gen Z). According to Pew Research, nearly half (47%) of adults in their 40s and 50s have a parent age 65 or older and are either raising a young child or financially supporting a grown child (age 18 or older). From digital devices to clothing brands, and retirement homes to healthcare options, Generation X holds the majority of decision-making power over many individuals in the Boomer and Millennial generations. It's worth noting that Gen Xers not only make their own purchase decisions and influence many for the Boomers and Millennials, they also control, for now at least, the majority of their Gen Z progeny's spending intent.

Technology

Although like Boomers, they were not born into a world of widespread consumer technology, Gen X have seen and largely embraced the arrival of PCs, the Internet and mobile technologies. However, they remember a time before technology and many are still straddling the analog/digital divide - Gen X may be more aware of the compromises involved in opting for digitally-driven commerce, compared to younger generations who have no familiarity with a world without online shopping.

Mobile and social media usage are major elements of Gen X's digital activity, and technology also figures in their shopping habits. eMarketer/Bizrate Insights polling[10] early in 2019 identified a preference among Gen X for mobile apps to find information about a product or service (61%) or to transact a purchase (54%). While 18% of Gen Xers said they use mobile apps to keep up with brands, many more said they do so by visiting a retailer's website regularly (44%), subscribing to its emails (40%) or receiving direct mail (28%). In a Millward Brown Digital survey[11], 67% use a laptop/PC daily. Gen Xers frequently go online for activities like shopping, banking, researching products, finding the best deals, and reading the news. Additionally, they prefer laptops to shop for products/services in all sectors studied, although smartphones are gaining traction in some categories, like CPG and Consumer Electronics. It's important to know why and how Gen X uses laptops and smartphones in order to allocate resources efficiently across the path-to-purchase. We'll come back to talk about the customer journey a bit later, but this is an early reminder that as consumers' shopping behaviors change, ad campaigns and marketing efforts must follow them across technologies to maintain reach and relevance.

Shopping

To avoid regretting their expenditures, Xers won't purchase a product until they've researched it thoroughly, which is why they make extensive use of search engines, online reviews, and social media networks before making a purchase. They rely heavily on reviews from other customers but also on product detail pages from manufacturer websites. According to eMarketer, across all generations, brand loyalty is highest among Gen-X consumers. Once they find a brand they like and trust, they are less likely than any other group to change to a competitor brand. This group is willing to pay a premium for the products they love and may exhibit an irrational inertia.

Gen X outpace younger generations in buying groceries online for at-home delivery. Sixty percent of the Gen Xers surveyed[12] have ordered groceries via a laptop or computer with at-home delivery. Digitally, email is one of the best channels for reaching out to this generation - Xers check emails on a regular basis and are more likely to respond well to personalized offers based on their previous purchases.

Gen Y (Millennials)

Consumers born between the early 1980s and mid 1990s fall into this group, which includes about 90 million people in the U.S., making it a significantly bigger demographic than Boomers or Gen X. Though Baby Boomers and Gen X tend to think of Millennials as "young people", globally, Millennials have outnumbered Baby Boomers since around 1990 and with the oldest of the cohort approaching 40, they're not kids anymore. Millennials are maturing, having children and creating a powerful wave of employees, consumers and citizens. Millennials have reached what the financial sector calls "the most important age range for economic activity", when households are formed, babies are born and money is spent not just on going out but on settling down[13]. With spending power projected at $1.4 trillion in 2020, they are poised to be the most powerful consumers in the next 10 years and the timeline of how they stop shopping or change how they consume will be a key determinant of the speed of the next retail revolution.

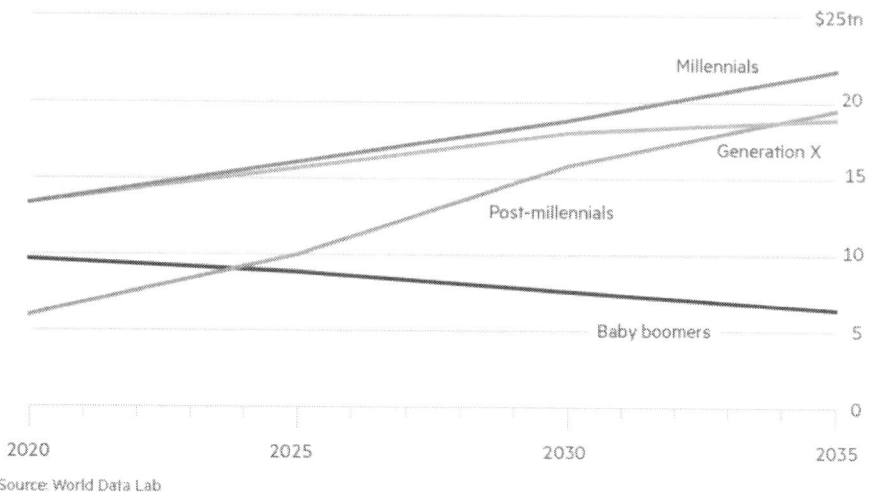

Figure 2 The relative spending power of generations. Source: World Data Lab

Compared to their predecessors, especially Boomers, Millennials live differently, buy differently and use technology differently. Most Millennials are in developing countries such as China and India rather than the US or Europe. This mobile, demanding, educated group of young adults is already having a huge impact on many industries and there is more disruption to come. Millennials are a challenge and at times a mystery, to companies that built their brands, distribution channels and stores for Baby Boomers.

Technology

Millennials have grown up and matured with mobile technology and expect to be able to use it in every aspect of their life. The youngest Millennials were 11 when the Apple iPhone was launched in 2007. They are used not only to communicating online but being able to buy most things there. They want to be able to make purchases, use social media, chat with friends, do online research and pay for products on their mobile, without compromise. They turn to their handheld devices to meet all their needs. Whether it be hailing a ride through the Uber app or ordering a breakfast burrito on the

Doordash app, technology is how they get things done, severely disrupting traditional purchasing patterns; the convenience and ubiquity of the mobile device is paramount to this group. This new generation is savvier and more educated, with a greater awareness of world affairs and a greater propensity towards activism.

Whether for social media, research, or purchases, Millennials rely on connected devices in nearly every aspect of their life, even while shopping in physical stores. Millennials demand the convenience of omnichannel accessibility during their shopping journey, which challenges retailers to have an integrated experience that can effortlessly transition their consumer data from their smartphone, to laptop, to local store, and back again. Improving the payment experience through self-checkout kiosks and advanced digital payment technologies is essential to keeping the Millennial shopper. They use multiple devices to make purchases and have started turning their mobile device into a handheld wallet, replacing cash, printed receipts and plastic loyalty cards.

Shopping

Millennials expect a customer-centric experience in which they feel valued. Showing interest in these shoppers creates loyalty - whether it is in-store or through social media channels. In order to do this, retailers need to closely examine what they're currently doing with customer data - this can include where customers shopped last, what was purchased, and their preferences - and ensure this information is being utilized to deliver a more personalized shopping experience.

It has been suggested that Generation Y individuals put little effort, emotions and time into low-involvement decisions, such as the choice of electricity or home insurance supplier, but a lot of effort, energy and emotions into high-involvement decisions[14]. Perhaps more than purchase decisions, this young generation especially values *experiences*. They shop, but they also want activities such as movies and dining. They utilize social media in real time, posting photos of their whereabouts and purchases, affording retailers instant social traction (or damage) while sharing their experiences with others. But a 2018 report from Nielsen[15] says that compared with other generations, Millennials are making on average 43 fewer trips to stores annually.

To encourage consumers to spend, brands have gotten creative in integrating experiences into shopping. For example, a number of fitness brands including popular athleisure brand Lululemon, offers complimentary in-store fitness classes. Stores are evolving into entertainment spots for Millennials who share similar interests, allowing them to spend time together, while also enabling consumers to engage with the brand. This group doesn't turn to social media only to share their experience, but also to be engaged with. Retailers are capitalizing on this emerging trend, leveraging the consumer-generated content of photo shares and hashtags to create word of mouth marketing. This sort of authenticity resonates with Millennials more effectively than traditional scripted adverts.

While many Millennials have shown a willingness to invest in premium brands such as iPhones, when it comes to consumer goods like groceries, they're much more likely to pick cheaper generics than brand-name products, with Walmart "seeing more private label acceptance maybe with this generation"[16]. In addition, Millennial consumers lean toward shopping in specialty stores rather than department stores, with word-of-mouth and social media key influencers of their purchase decisions. Like Gen X, Gen Y is also skeptical of overbearing marketing tactics. Millennials tend to reject retailers who constantly push products through messaging and instead prefer authentic interactions with sales associates who happen also to be consumers of their retailer's products. Millennials are also likely to interact with brands and retailers through social media sites such as Twitter and Facebook for their voices to be heard. In a trend we'll explore more in the rest of this Chapter, 65% of Millennials find it unacceptable to be silent on important societal issues according to Carolyn Tastad, Group President of P&G North America[17].

Gen Z

The generation born after Millennials, often referred to as Generation Z (though sometimes known as post-Millennials), was born after 1995 and are now entering their teenage years or early 20s. This means they are not only a new generation of consumers, but are also entering the workforce, even if primarily still on a part-time or entry-level basis. 77% of Gen Z, who are between 14 and 21 years old, currently earn their own money through freelance work, a part-time job, or earned allowance[18]. As employees, Gen Zs expect technology at their fingertips and won't understand why they are doing something manually when they don't have to. As digitally-savvy, entrepreneurial-minded workers, they will be disappointed if an employer is not keeping up with the latest digital trends and devices. Thus, for retailers hiring Gen Z, technology needs to be part of the recruitment and retention strategy. Recently in a Starbucks, I noticed they were using an app called 'Recroot' to reach young applicants, while many other retailers are using apps for shift sign-up and staff communications.

As their earning power grows, members of this group of consumers, who already control at least $50 billion in spending power, will soon make up one of the largest blocs of consumers in the world. And If you recall the discussion about Gen X and how they bridge the gap between the Baby Boomers and Gen Y, it's similarly true that Gen X turn to the young Gen Z for advice from this hyperconnected younger generation. Up to 70 percent of parents turn to their Generation Z children for help in making a buying decision. So not only are Gen Z impacting their own buying decision, but also those of their family.

Technology

Gen Z is the generation of fully digital natives that can't remember a time before the Internet, and as such, the platform has become the foundation of their buying process - they far higher and different expectations when it comes to the types of digital experiences they will engage with. For example, research found that 67 percent of Gen Z believe websites will know what they're looking for before they do anything[19]. Forty percent said they would stop visiting a website altogether if it didn't anticipate what they needed, liked or wanted. This means a huge majority of Gen Z expects predictive personalization to be part and parcel of the websites they interact with. If it's not, many of them will take their business elsewhere. Today, marketers only have seven seconds to get the attention of Gen Z before they move on to something else—with Millennials, it's 12 seconds. Because they've been digital natives throughout their lives, Gen Z has almost no patience when it comes to slow websites or mobile applications. They have infinite choice at their fingertips, and they will move on quickly.

Gen Z use their plethora of online resources to compare prices, styles, availability, and ratings of products to make the most educated purchase decision possible. They're a generation very comfortable with collecting and cross-referencing many sources of information. Being savvy with price-checking tools also makes Gen Z more selective when making big expenditures with many often buying products only when they're on sale or even delaying gratification by waiting for newer products to become available - products they know are coming thanks to extensive research. As digital natives, Gen Z are natural information-seekers. They know how to locate the information they're looking for – so if they can't find it, that's a big turn off. This means that e-commerce must be easily searchable to ensure that the most relevant products are displayed. Visual search technology (as we'll discuss in Chapter 6) was an innovation made for Gen Z. If a Gen Z consumer is struck with inspiration – a celebrity outfit, a product on screen, or on another real-life person – they want to be able to shop it instantly and visual search enables that.

When surveyed, Gen Z prefer brands like ASOS, that sell multiple brands in one place, with a powerful search function that uses AI and recommendations to present exactly what Gen Z are looking for, negating the need to visit multiple stores individually. Retailers must plan for the fact that Gen Z can start shopping in one channel, browse in another, and complete the journey in either, with their basket history and previous purchases remembered.

Although Gen Z admit being glued to their smartphones, 74% of them do not have their favorite retailer's app installed[20]. There are subtleties to be considered with Gen Z: just because they browse for products on their smartphones and devices, this doesn't mean they desire an app to complete a purchase. The reason? Many of this age range have limited data allowances for their phones or have cheaper phone models with limited storage.

Shopping

Despite being inundated with digital content, Gen Z still prefer to shop in-store versus online, but they crave a store that can keep up with their tech. Companies need to understand that technology drives Gen Z's shopping experience—an established social media presence should complement touchscreens in brick and mortar stores if retailers want to keep tech-savvy Gen Zers eager to interact with their brand. Like Gen Y, Gen Z is also likely to contribute to consumer-generated content for brands by voicing their comments and concerns online. Gen Z consumers sharing brand content on social media can easily be considered unofficial brand ambassadors. Gen Z are impatient - if their expectations are not met, then they will move on. They rarely give second chances and when they have a poor experience, they usually share it on social media. Their expectations of a retailer are more demanding and higher than any other generation. They are not as price conscious - while other generations were all about the "deal" Generation Z tends to be more about the experience and they are willing to pay for it.

While much of their research is digital, Gen Z still enjoys visiting stores as a social excursion. In fact, 84% of Gen Zers intentionally structure their shopping trips around a social activity; for the younger Gen Z members, having social freedom to venture into their nearby town is often new and exciting, and they combine retail experiences with socializing. The shopping trend of buying online and picking up in-store is quickly gaining traction with this group as they shortlist products online and then want to go and pick up the item for instant gratification.

Authenticity

How a company behaves is of more importance to Gen Z than any previous generation and ranks as a key factor in whether or not they will buy from or associate with a brand. Gen Z wants to know what impact a brand's choices have on people and the planet, all the way from employees' experience in the supply chain to what happens to the clothes that aren't sold. In Irregular Labs' 2018 Gen Z consumer report[21], 65% of young people interviewed agreed that authenticity was one of their top values. It doesn't take much for politically charged, social-savvy Gen Z consumers to recognize when companies fall short or are tone deaf.

Moving Beyond The Generations

Although it's been a staple of marketing for a couple of decades now for brands and retailers, looking at consumers through the lens of "generations" is likely to go out of fashion as technology now enables far more granular targeting - and consumers expect better than generic assumptions about their requirements. It will also be impacted by the most fundamental change in consumers in the history of retail - the emergence of non-human surrogate consumers.

While they may have been a useful framework over the years, I expect classifications by generation will start to fade from marketing toolkits, replaced by AI-powered personalization. Age-related factors, coupled with socio-economic conditions and life stage pressures will continue to influence needs, wants and shopping habits, but so too will a range of broader trends that will cut across generations as technology augments our ability to research and then offers to make decisions for us. Non-human shopping will level the playing field between generations as it can meet stated or data-inferred individual needs rather than generic, assumed preferences.

Macro Trends

While generations provide one element of context, brands and retailers of course don't exist in a vacuum. Larger global trends can provide challenges and also opportunities for those that can align with the prevailing consumer mood.

Meeting the challenge and benefitting from the opportunities won't be easy - not only have the relevant trend(s) to be identified, along with their relevance to your product/service, applicable reforms must be identified, designed and implemented all at the *right time*, whilst still delivering the product/service on a *commercially viable* basis. If you are ahead of a trend, you may not have a big enough target segment, while if you are behind, you may be too late to persuade consumers of the authenticity of your offering compared to competitors.

McKinsey & Company[22] have identified the following five dominant forces to consider in the consumer sector over the next ten years:

Trend	Examples
Changing Face of the Consumer	Ageing Population Urbanization
Geopolitical Dynamics	Climate Change The rise of Asia
New patterns of personal consumption	Increase in Convenience Focus on Health & Wellness Demand for Personalization and Customization Sharing Economy Shopping Experience Buying Local Simplification of Choice
Technological advancements	Mobile, 3-D, Robotics, Autonomy, AI, IoT, VR, Data
Structural industry shifts	D2C Activist Investors Consolidation

And if that list doesn't look daunting enough, each sector has its own specific challenges to consider. For example, if you're in the apparel sector, macro trends such as subscriptions and the rise of second-hand will weigh heavily on your mind, but so too will trends such as less demand for formal clothes as workplaces go casual - something retailers can't blame on geopolitics, Amazon or online shopping.

Brand Values

"Brand has never been more valuable for upstarts. Never been less valuable for incumbents"

D'Arcy Coolican, Investment Partner, A16Z[23]

Consumers are now less inclined to make their purchase decisions based solely on product attributes or price; they're frequently considering what a brand says, what it does and what it purports to stand for. Consumers will prioritize organizations whose brand purpose aligns with their personal beliefs.

As their information and choice expands, humans will stop shopping with brands and retailers they don't like, trust or agree with. They'll stop shopping with brands who don't provide the level of service they expect and believe they are entitled to, on their terms. They will gravitate towards organizations that champion a set of values that aligns with their own. Putting your mission at the center of your brand gives audiences something deeply personal to connect to and is highly influential in developing long-term loyalty and advocacy.

It simply isn't enough to tout the economic, societal and environmental issues brands claim to champion – purpose, mission, and values need to translate to action. In today's digital landscape, consumer patience for "lip-service purpose" is non-existent. Accenture Strategy's most recent global survey[24] of nearly 30,000 consumers in 35 countries—including more than 2,000 consumers in the United States—found that 62% of them want companies to take a stand on current and broadly relevant issues such as sustainability, transparency and fair employment practices. Companies that don't align with customer beliefs pay the price with serious loss of patronage – 42% of consumers walk away from the brand in frustration. One in five (21%) never come back.

There is however a notable difference across the generations according to this YouGov study:[25]

Get Up, Stand Up
Consumers were asked to respond to the statement "I like brands that are willing to get involved in societal issues." Younger consumers were more likely to agree, while older ones were more likely to disagree

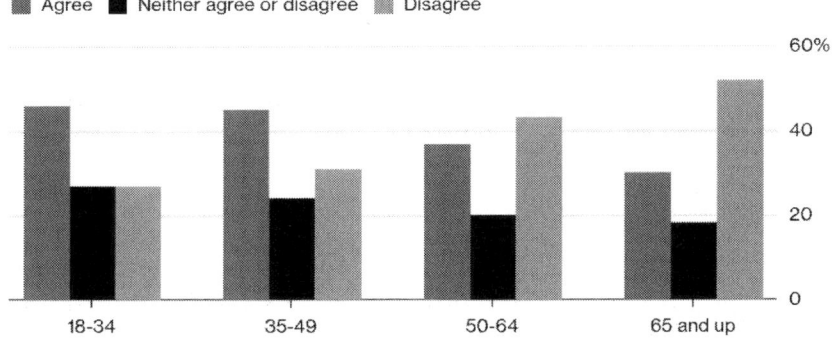

Source: YouGov Plan & Track

Figure 3 Consumer interest in brand stance on issues

For many consumers, it's no longer sufficient for a company to simply persuade them to buy a product on the basis of price or quality. Now, it can require the creation of a real brand affinity based on a belief in the producer's values. *"The traditional buy-sell model doesn't fly anymore"*, according to Americus Reed, a marketing professor at the University of Pennsylvania's Wharton School[26]. Younger generations weaned on the web demand a new kind of interaction—and much more attention.

The following table from Accenture's study shows how important issues other than price and quality are to consumers:

What attracts you to buy from certain brands over others (beyond price and quality)?	%
The brand has a great culture—it does what it says it will do and delivers on its promises	66
The company is transparent—with where it sources its materials, how it treats employees fairly, etc.	66
The company treats its employees well	65
They believe in reducing plastics and improving the environment	62
The brand has ethical values and demonstrates authenticity in everything it does	62
The brand is passionate about the products and services it sells	62
The brand stands for something bigger than just the products and services it sells, which aligns with my personal values	52
They stand up for societal and cultural issues they believe in	50
The brand supports and acts upon causes we have in common (e.g. social, charitable)	50
The brand connects me to others like me and gives me a sense of community	38
The brand takes a political stance on issues close to my heart	37

This trend for humans to shop not based solely on product or price marks a dramatic shift in consumer behavior and is forcing companies to react - and not just with press releases. Jane McDaid, founder of Irish youth marketing agency THINKHOUSE, says she sees businesses who are fundamentally rethinking how they do things so as to be more responsible and sustainable[27]:

"I think the days of 'greenwashing' are over – young people are far too smart and when they witness greenwashing, they're motivated to call it out which ends up being a huge embarrassment to brands/organizations. Brands know that younger consumers are voting with their wallets and they are supporting brands and businesses that are truly aligned with their values."

Firms that think being greener could add to their margins are unlikely to find sustainability is a sustainable profit booster.

"Consumers, especially Millennials, are indeed more loyal to sustainable brands, and indicate some willingness to pay a green premium. However, this premium may fade, as sustainability has moved beyond niche to mainstream, and becomes a basic expectation for consumers. It is critical that brands are authentic here: simple greenwashing can easily be exposed and backfire, and consumers are certainly ready to punish 'bad' brands that violate their trust."

Pei Yun Teng, A.T. Kearney Global Director of Social Impact[28]

New vs Nostalgia

As consumers research brands more than ever before, the consumer's perception of what a brand is has changed. The time it takes to establish a brand has been cut dramatically (as has the time to damage a brand), and younger consumers are especially open to new brands that meet their needs on their terms. Gen Z in particular are used to new brands appearing and gaining widespread awareness via social media and so heritage is far less important than alignment and convenience. For consumers, as long as it reaches a quality threshold, convenience, price, good reviews and authenticity or ethical compatibility outweigh long standing brand affiliations. The relative lack of importance of brand heritage will accelerate as decisions are delegated to a rational evaluator in the form of an AI assistant.

As the way humans shop for brands changes, there will be winners and losers. According to Kellogg on Marketing, for the top Consumer Packaged Goods (CPG) categories, from 1923-1983, 20 of the top 25 brands held the number 1 position in their category for the entire time. In contrast, since 1983, only 4 of the top 25 retained the number one position. This should give pause for thought to anyone planning to rest on their brand laurels! From apparel to razors to beauty products, the big "enduring" brands seem to be able to rely less and less on their brand equity.

Unique branding is essential for entering a market and gaining attention, but it's a short-term tactic not a long-term strategy. To succeed in the long term, you need something else to support the core product and brand - network effects, scale, better distribution. It's also worth pointing out that selling your product via Amazon cedes control over much of the consumer experience. The number of brands in most categories is immense. They won't all survive, but the ones that will understand a simple truth: you need a quality product that's actually relevant to today's consumer *and* in keeping with their values. Brands and retailers that don't align clearly with these current trends will struggle. For incumbents, a good way of thinking is to consider if an existing brand would be launched today. If not, then it's time to consider if nostalgia or inertia are the only things keeping it alive as neither of those forces are likely to be sustainable.

New entrants with strong branding that resonates with consumer values can quickly undermine decades of expensive brand building - consumers will not, just for cost benefits, forgive unpalatable stances on diversity, sustainability or human rights. When people find a young brand they identify with, they shout it from the rooftops and become brand ambassadors on social media, even without being paid influencers.

The emergence of new brands poses a unique challenge to physical retailers with limited shelf space. It's very difficult for smaller retailers to cope with microbrands where the sales volume may not justify the cost of stocking an item, training staff and contending with returns. Their previous defining role as curator of goods offered for sale is being replaced by self-service curation (research) and social media curation.

New Consumer Values

Coupled with technological advances, and in some cases accentuated by technology, this shift to consider and evaluate their choices on a non-price, non-product basis is transforming the consumer landscape in a way that cuts across all socioeconomic brackets and extends beyond any single generation, permeating the whole demographic range (although unevenly). As consumers reassess their values, their very relationship with consumption is changing.

In this section, we'll look at three major challenges for brands and retailers as they look to understand the future priorities of their consumers, their employees and their shareholders:

- Ownership (Access vs Possession)
- Ethics & Authenticity
- Sustainability

We'll explore further shifts in business models later and you'll see these issues recur in further Chapters as we look at the confluence of technology and consumer behaviors.

Ownership

I've already noted the change in emphasis among younger consumers towards favoring experiences over material accumulation. This also applies to the very concept of consumption, with a range of sectors being disrupted by a move to access rather than ownership—consumption means having access to products or services, not necessarily owning them. Consumers are shifting from buying individual items (CDs, DVDs) and instead choosing access on demand to a library of content (Spotify, Netflix). Companies historically defined by the products they sell as single transactions face a very different world if their consumers now want on-demand access to a range of products instead. We'll examine the impact of this change and the growth of rental in more detail later in this Chapter.

Peak Stuff?

Part of the attraction of rental models we're about to discuss derives from the fact that people no longer aspire merely to material accumulation. Younger age groups tend to prefer to spend on experiences, gyms, healthcare and services, not just retail products. As spending shifts to experiences over things, certain sectors are particularly hard hit: the fashion retail sector proved the most likely to call in administrators over the last decade, accounting for 41% of all business administrations[29]. The emergence of the mobile phone has all but eliminated the need to purchase dedicated music players, cameras or DVD players. As we'll see, the new emphasis on the circular economy and responsible use of resources means that accumulating material goods is no longer necessarily seen as desirable.

Ethics, Diversity & Staff Well-Being

Better informed consumers will not only align themselves with brands and retailers who share their environmental concerns but will also challenge those who are not actively addressing workers' rights, gender and diversity issues. Moves such as the announcement by Goldman Sachs in early 2020 that it would not provide IPO services to firms that did not have at least one 'diverse' Board member illustrate the level of visibility these issues now command. Across the US and Europe, over two-thirds of main Board and executive committee members are white and male, according to a study conducted by recruitment group Green Park, law firm DLA Piper and the World Retail Congress[30]. All 30 chairs were male and white, the study found, while women make up just 26% of US and 27% of European retail leaders.

In another example of how consumers now evaluate the organizations they do business with, shoppers are showing increasing concern for the well-being of retail staff. Walmart faced calls for boycotts when details spread on social media of their use of staff discounts instead of extra pay for working on holidays, while Instacart's changes to pay structures led to a backlash that saw them reversed.

Authenticity

We talked above about brand values and the importance of authentic positions. A company's actions must match its ideals, and those ideals must permeate the entire stakeholder system. Some 65% of shoppers try to learn the origins of anything they buy— where it is made, what it is made from, and how it is made. About 80% say they refuse to buy goods from companies involved in scandals.

For consumers, marketing and brand ethics are converging. Companies must therefore not only identify clearly the topics on which they will take positions but also ensure that everyone throughout the value chain gets on board and acts consistently. For the same reason, companies ought to think carefully about the agents who represent their brands and products. Marketing in the digital age is posing ever-more complex challenges as channels become more fragmented yet open to greater scrutiny.

Sustainability

"Last year, nearly half (49%) of consumers under the age of 24 stated that they had avoided a product or service due to its negative environmental impact in the last year. In addition, consumers now expect more from businesses - with 81% of them saying it is the responsibility of companies to help improve the environment."[31]

Consumers are now more aware of the wider impacts of consumption and are becoming much more conscientious. Common across all generations to varying degrees is a concern about the provenance of the goods and the environmental footprint along the way. Interestingly, it's not just consumers - workers are also voicing their concerns regarding the ethics of their firms, with staff pressuring to make bigger strides in reducing emissions from the organizations they work for. Customers may expect the currently impossible in terms of low-impact produce that meets current established price and convenience standards - but retailers and brands will have to invest heavily to try to stay on the right side of consumer and worker sentiment as they seek ways to understand their environmental impact and communicate their mitigation strategies to a skeptical public.

With endless information at their fingertips, consumers are more educated than ever before about the entire supply chain and its impact on the environment and humanity. They are keen to support the most sustainable retailers with their wallets and are pushing governments to pass laws that encourage sustainable practices. Sustainability manifests in different ways for different sectors - grocery retailers are primarily focused on reducing food waste and optimizing packaging, while fashion retailers are grappling with demand for recyclable or less resource-intensive materials. Each step in the retail chain — sourcing, manufacturing, packaging and transportation — has a potential impact on the environment. Many brands and retailers are starting to make concentrated efforts to implement sustainable practices e.g. brewing giant AB InBev's efforts to develop a variety of barley that needs less water and Unilever adjusting its detergent formulas so they work at the lower "eco" temperature settings on modern washing machines or, in the case of start-ups, to build their businesses with the environment in mind and use that as the brand foundation - e.g. Allbirds, which makes more environmentally friendly footwear. To remain successful in the face of this changing consumer mindset, brands must place greater focus on telling the story of what they stand for and stating their environmental or sustainability policies, as simply marketing and selling a product will no longer appeal to many. Consumers are also demanding a wider range of products to cater for vegan or gluten-free diets, for example. As mentioned earlier, this range of more niche products is very challenging for a local convenience store to cope with.

Fast Fashion

"It's a responsibility Nordstrom takes seriously, and we're proud of the progress we've made in reducing our carbon footprint and conserving resources across our global supply chain and we're continuing to make this a top priority for the company"

Gigi Ganatra, VP of corporate affairs and PR, Nordstrom

The trend in recent years towards fast fashion - inexpensive clothing, with quick turnover that encourages disposal and repurchasing - has created a juxtaposition where consumers seek frequent outfit updates to post on Instagram, while they worry about climate change. Textile waste has increased 811% between 1960 and 2015 making the sector one of the most polluting, and the vast majority of this is heading to the landfill, according to data from the US Environmental Protection Agency. The utilization of clothing — the average number of times a piece of clothing is worn before being discarded — has decreased 36% in the last 15 years, according to a landmark 2017 report[32].

The industry is responding to consumer concern with leaders such as H&M, despite being a pioneer in fast fashion, now taking ethical fashion seriously by committing to becoming 100% circular by 2030. The company's "100% Fair & Equal" program aims to ensure that their employees and suppliers have fair compensation and a safe workplace. The H&M website now includes information about the garment production process while consumers can access this information in store, using the H&M app to scan the price tag which brings up the product detail page. In the US, Nordstrom has joined the G7 Fashion Pact, a coalition of 32 global retailers and has created a web page for each of more than 2,000 products from 90 brands that are made from sustainably sourced materials, manufactured in factories that meet higher social or environmental standards, or that give back to their local communities.

Packaging

If fashion is an example of a specific sector attracting attention for its environmental impact, packaging is an area affecting a wide variety of categories. Excess and hard to recycle packaging is weighing heavily on consumers' minds. Consumers may stop shopping for products they perceive to be excessively packaged. Retailers who take action to reduce packaging will appeal to eco-conscious shoppers and it may be a vital differentiator in an otherwise commodity market. For example, in the grocery sector, several merchants are trialing initiatives such as reducing packaging on some products, improving the recyclability of packaging for others and offering refill stations where consumers bring their own containers to fill and pay by the weight. US electronics retailer BestBuy[33] has installed new cardboard packaging machines in its warehouses that can produce a package, made to fit an order, every 4 seconds but still reduce cardboard waste by 40%.

For anyone skeptical of consumers' desire to jump on the environmentally aware packaging bandwagon, New York University's Stern Center for Sustainable Business offers persuasive statistics, with the creation of the 'sustainable share index (SSI)'. The 2019 SSI[34] reviewed consumers' purchasing habits from 2013-2018 and found that products marketed as sustainably packaged experienced 5.6x faster growth than those that weren't, across 36 CPG categories.

Refills

"You simply have to start somewhere to test it and see what the barriers are and who actually buys into the model"

David Blanchard, Unilever Research and Development

One interesting trend for brands and retailers to watch is the consumer response to refills. Rather than consumers purchasing new containers with every purchase, several retailers globally are experimenting with the practicality of encouraging consumers to stop shopping for new packaging with every purchase and to reuse existing containers.

Figure 4 A Carrefour hypermarket Refill Station at the Mall of the Emirates in Dubai

Refilling containers actually harks back to the origins of the word retailer (from the French word 'retaille' - a piece cut off) where stores typically received large blocks of e.g. butter and then cut off pieces for customers, rather than the individually packaged produce we're more familiar with today. Refillables once dominated industries such as beer and soft drinks but lost out to convenient, affordable single-use containers. In 1947, refillables made up 100% of soft-drink containers by volume and 86% of beer containers, according to the Container Recycling Institute, a non-profit. By 1998 those figures dropped to 0.4% and 3.3%, respectively[35].

In the UK, beauty chains The Body Shop and Lush are both experimenting with refill stations in stores as well as "naked" products sold without packaging. UK supermarket Waitrose offers up to 15% discount on bulk products for consumers to refill into their own containers, while Asda (owned by Walmart), has announced a trial refill station including tea, coffee, cereal and pasta sold by weight.

In the US, some of the world's largest makers of CPGs such as shampoo, detergent and packaged food have embarked on tests selling their products in reusable containers, adopting a somewhat old-style mode. In a high-profile trial with recycling firm TerraCycle, P&G, Unilever and others are selling products such as Shampoo, Orange Juice and Deodorant in glass, steel and aluminum containers in place of existing plastics. Consumers on the trial can order the products via a special website. Products are distributed in a reusable tote bag. Once finished, users schedule a pickup for empty containers to be cleaned, refilled and reused. Unlike the trials mentioned above where consumers bring containers to a supermarket, the TerraCycle experiment will test consumer response to the refillable paradigm but with the convenience of home delivery.

Less is More

The role of packaging itself is changing as buying behaviors evolve - shoppers traditionally are influenced by packaging when it comes to purchasing decisions in a store. Yet, online shoppers don't see packaging. They instead see an image or a video of a product and make a decision based largely on that without any significant influence from the design or information placed on the product's container.

We'll talk frequently in this book about the singular power of Amazon, but one space in which it is making its muscle felt in particular is packaging. In late 2018, Amazon directed that their suppliers must reduce the size of their packaging or face a surcharge. Amazon has also worked with large suppliers such as Tide detergent to create product packaging more suited to delivery than retail presentation - The Tide package below uses 60% less plastic and reduces shipping weight from the previous 12 lbs. (5.4 kg) to 7.9 lbs. (3.6 kg).

Figure 5 P&G Tide packaging is a "bag in a box" for lighter shipping and less plastic than previous containers. Source: P&G

Although consumers say they dislike excessive packaging, it will be interesting to see how this plays out against another major trend in shopping that we'll discuss in Chapter 4 - the push for convenience and faster shopping. When faced with a choice between grabbing a bag from a shelf, or refilling a carton from a larger container – an operation that is virtually certain to take longer – what will they do? A packaging-free trial of some produce at UK grocer, Iceland, was halted after the company saw a 30% drop in sales[36].

Unboxing - The Packaging Paradox

Unboxing has become one of the most popular video trends of recent years, with a video of an iPhone X unboxing receiving a staggering 14+ million views[37]. However, while intricate packaging may help to create viral product demand, ornate packaging may soon turn from a positive brand statement into a negative.

Consumers and the Environment

"Everything we put in our shopping basket comes at an environmental cost"

World Economic Forum

The growing influence of environmental concerns on purchase decisions cannot be ignored by brands and retailers looking to survive. Market Research firm Euromonitor International now tracks a specific eco-conscious consumer segment. Comprising shoppers who try to have a positive impact on the environment and are worried about climate change and look for three or more green product features, such as recyclable packaging or made from recycled materials, when shopping - these account for about 14% of Western European shoppers[38].

The impetus for change is not coming only from consumers. Regulators are responding to public pressure and legislating to reduce waste; the European Circular Economy Action plan (2015) and European Strategy for Plastics (2018) aim to promote, and even require, recycling.

Health/Well Being

As well as caring about the impact of commercial activity on the planet, many consumers are also concerned about their own well-being. Healthier alternatives such as "organic" products have been gaining market share and this trend is likely to continue, driven by consumers but also by regulators keen to improve public health in order to reduce the strain put on healthcare services by obesity.

We'll talk more about augmented shoppers using apps in a later Chapter, but now is a good time to talk about technology empowering consumers interested in their own well-being. Consider Yuka, an app that lets consumers scan food and personal care product labels to get a recommendation about the healthiness of the ingredients. Covering over 700,000 food products and 300,000 cosmetics, the app recommends alternative products when a consumer scans an unhealthy item. With over 11 million downloads in France alone[39], Yuka's creators are expanding their operations internationally.

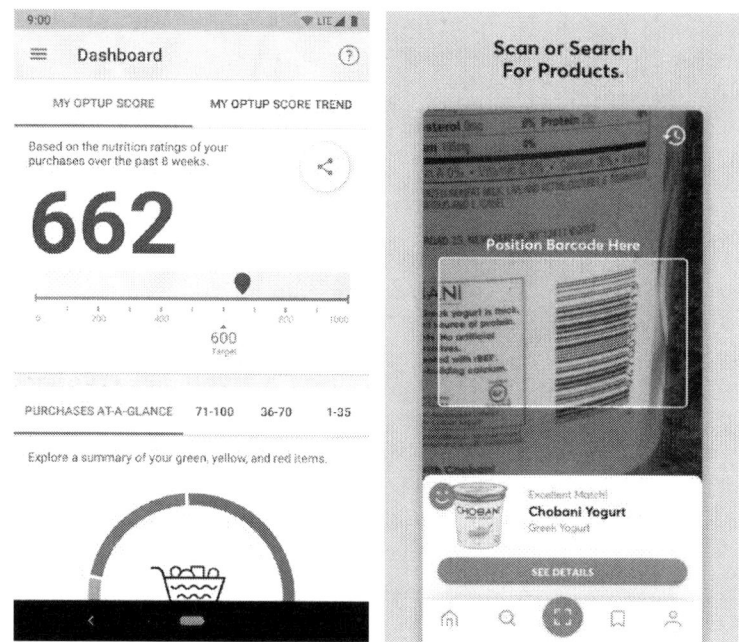

Figure 6 Kroger's OptUP (L) and ShopWell (R)

An app called ShopWell aims to help consumers find food that better meets their individual needs. Users can scan nutritional information on goods to get a personalized suitability score, including information on allergies and diets. Likewise, an app called OptUP from US grocer Kroger uses scores to show consumers their household nutrition dashboard, with the option to connect to a dietitian for personalized counseling.

Second Hand

"As the line between new and used apparel blurs for consumers, a powerful transformation in retail will unfold."

James Reinhart, CEO, thredUP

Following on from, and related to, concerns about sustainability, another major trend impacting consumer spending is the emergence of the second-hand sector, particularly in apparel. If people stop shopping for new items, this clearly has a major impact on brands producing new products, and on the entire supply chain, all the way to retailers. Once stigmatized, the second-hand market (also known as resale) has now grown to exceed the value of the previous major trend in consumer apparel - fast fashion. The resale clothing industry is expected to nearly double from $28 billion today to $51 billion by 2023. Growing concern over the impact of materialism has led from the conspicuous consumption of fast fashion to proud sustainability of repaired and "pre-loved" clothes.

Attitudes toward second-hand shopping first started shifting during the 2008 recession, when it became smart/necessary to make your money go further, but environmental and economic conditions are now converging to push younger shoppers to secondary markets. Waste in the clothing and textile industries is becoming a top concern for younger shoppers - nearly three-quarters of shoppers under 30 say they prefer to buy from sustainability-conscious brands, according to GlobalData - more than one in three Gen Z shoppers will buy second-hand clothes this year, compared to just 19% of Boomers. Resale appeals to younger shoppers on two fronts - they not only prefer sustainable brands, but they also like retailers who frequently offer new items, not just the more traditional seasonal ranges.

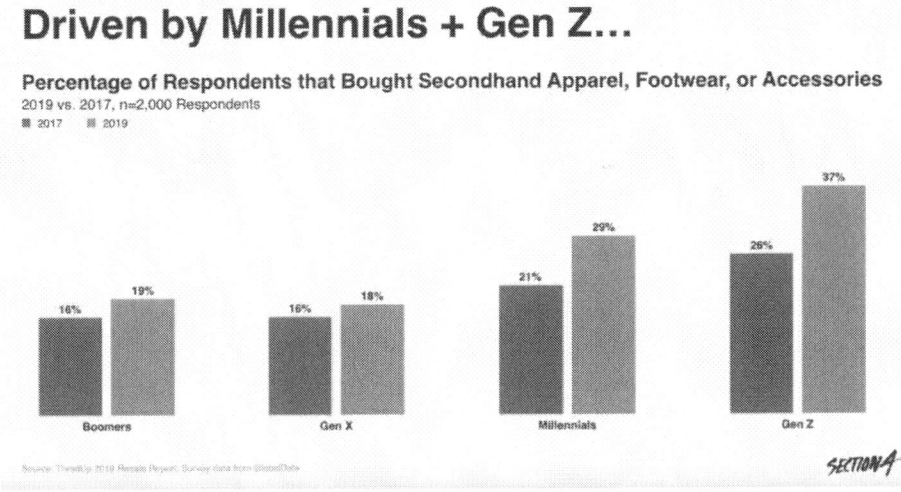

Figure 7 There's growing interest in second hand across all age groups. Source: thredUP via Section 4

Consumers on average buy 60% more clothing today than they did 15 years ago, but keep the items only half as long, according to

McKinsey & Co. That has resulted in more waste. Nearly 60% of the more than 100 billion garments produced annually end up in incinerators or landfills, McKinsey estimates. The production of one kilogram of fabric generates an average of 23 kilograms of greenhouse gases, the consulting firm says, making the fashion industry a big polluter.

40% of consumers now consider the resale value of an item before buying it. Although second-hand has been around for decades, what's different this time is the role of technology and the scale/reach apps bring. Start-ups now collect, curate, clean and list second-hand items for sale. According to a survey of 12,000 consumers by Boston Consulting Group, one-third of respondents said they sold items to empty their wardrobe and finance new purchases. At luxury goods consignment service, The RealReal, 53% of consignors were also buyers as of March, according to securities filings. A growing number of shoppers also sell their clothes and accessories on second-hand websites and in thrift shops, creating a virtuous circle that clears out their closets so they can buy more.

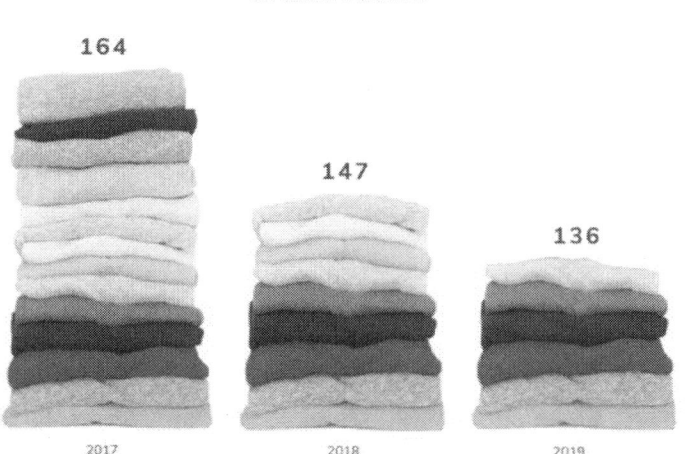

Figure 8 Declining Apparel ownership – average items per closet. Source: thredUP

The sale of second-hand goods—or recommerce—accounts for a tiny fraction of the $3.8 trillion in U.S. retail sales, but it is growing fast. 56 million U.S. women bought second-hand products in 2018, up from 44 million who did so in 2017 - that's almost half of the entire female adult population in the US. As more shoppers buy used products, they are spending less at traditional chains, from fast-fashion retailers to department stores. As discussed below, some established players are fighting back via partnerships or by launching their own resale programs, including Macy's and Levi.

The Second-hand Players

Vintage and second-hand stores have long been a niche sector of retail, and a staple of markets. But online is breathing new life into the sector, quickly becoming a key platform for buying and selling second-hand items. The online second-hand market breaks down primarily into two types of transaction - Consignment and Peer to Peer - and highlights a rapidly expanding interest among consumers in becoming (re)sellers.

- Sellers who don't want to handle transactions themselves can ship goods to companies that operate as virtual consignment stores. At the luxury end, The RealReal deals in authenticated luxury goods, while thredUP accepts a wide range of brands found at a typical mall.
- Other solutions let customers buy and sell directly from each other, e.g. general sites eBay or Facebook Marketplace, while new sites dedicated to second-hand apparel include Poshmark and Depop.

Second-hand - Consignment

A key consideration in the operation of second-hand at scale is, of course, the supply of the clothes. Unlike traditional retail, you can't contract a factory to make and send you the items you want. Instead, items are sourced from members of the public who are looking to sell or donate. Let's look at two consignment services that have risen to prominence in recent years to sell items on behalf of people looking to dispose of the clothes in a beneficial but hassle-free manner: mass market thredUP and luxury player The RealReal.

thredUP

thredUP proclaims itself as the world's largest online thrift store where you can buy and sell high-quality second-hand clothes. Aimed at a mainstream audience, thredUP has 500 assessors who add some 40,000 new items to its site each day, with brands from Gap to Gucci.

When users consign items to thredUP, it takes between 1-3 weeks from receiving items to listing them. By ordering a "Clean Out Kit", consignors send a bag of clothing for free to thredUP who inspect, photograph, and list the items, as well as providing details about estimated payouts. thredUP pays from 5% to 80% of the sale price to consignors depending on the value of the items. Consignors can set the selling price (up to a maximum 80% of the original retail value, though most accept the thredUP suggestion), while they choose to receive payment via PayPal/Discover Card or shopping credit for use on thredUP, or alternatively use a "Donation Kit" to turn their clothes into cash for charities - thredUP gives $5 to a nominated charity and gives the donor a donation tax receipt. Consignors can reclaim unsold items after the listing period has expired, but items not reclaimed within 14 days become the property of thredUP. Items that don't meet thredUPs quality threshold for resale are put into "Rescue boxes" and sold at discount.

thredUP trades heavily on the environmental benefits as much as the cost savings, claiming that if everyone bought just one used item instead of new this year, it would save almost 6 billion pounds of carbon emissions. That's the equivalent of taking half a million cars off the road for a year. On the sales side, the site continues the sustainability theme with a "Buy & Bundle" feature that consolidates multiple purchases into a single shipment by waiting for 7 days from a purchase before shipping.

If second-hand selling online sounds slightly low-tech, consider the growing use of technology by thredUP - it offers customers the chance to add items to their cart for up to 12 hours before committing to purchase them - during this time, other customers can flag their intention to purchase the item, if the original customer chooses not to proceed, using a feature called Autobuy. thredUP also offers an auction-style bidding process before items are listed for sale - all incoming arrivals have a 12-hour bidding window before they can be purchased directly. Bids must be higher than the opening price. As a loyalty bonus for returning customers, items in the bidding window are only accessible to customers who have previously made purchases. For those who don't have time or interest to brose the site and select items, thredUP offers a "Goody Box" which is a customized assortment of curated items that match your style profile. For a $10 deposit, each box contains 10 items, but customers can return any unwanted items for free and are only charged for those they keep.

ThredUp has also announced partnerships with Macy's and J.C. Penney totaling around 100 stores, giving the online player instant wider reach. According to thredUP CEO, James Reinhart, "Resale and retail working together is the future of fashion"[40].

The RealReal

The RealReal is an online marketplace that sells luxury goods (consigned clothing, jewelry, watches, art and home decor), on behalf of its members. A team of professionals authenticates submissions, determines the price and lists the items for sale via the RealReal web site, app or at one of its 10 physical stores.

Consignors can only submit items for sale by designers on the approved designers directory, which reads like a who's who of top luxury fashion, jewelry and watch brands. They are warned to submit only top-quality items that do not have any non-professional alterations, larger than pin-size holes or missing/broken zippers or buttons. The RealReal aims to sell the items "at the highest possible price within 30 days". According to their web site, pricing is based on four factors:

- Designer & Item Type
- Age
- Condition
- Color (Pieces in classic colors or on-trend, seasonal colors will earn more)

Consignors can view estimated prices before sending items and can expect to receive higher commission based on how much they sell - ranging from 55% on the first $1,500 of sales to 70% on over $10k.

Buyers browsing the RealReal site can expect to find items graded from pristine, excellent, very good and good. As a site very much aimed at bargain hunters, users can watch items for reductions and get notified by adding them to their Obsessions list. Buyers are warned that items sold at 40% or more off the list price, and items sold in the end-of-month "Real Big Sale" cannot be returned. Having gone public in 2019, The RealReal was valued at over $2bn, proving there's plenty of value involved, even when people stop shopping for new goods. The trend for second hand has also reached the luxury segment of physical retail with prestige London store Selfridges opening a space to buy and sell second-hand items.

Second Hand - Peer to Peer

While consignment services offer great convenience to people looking to quickly offload items in a single transaction, there are other options that remove the costs of using these services. Start-ups dedicated to the private sale of second-hand apparel have become particularly popular in specific segments. We'll look at two examples of how the way people are shopping (and selling) is changing: Poshmark and Depop.

Poshmark

Postmark is a social commerce marketplace, with an emphasis on social selling and on "Seller Stylists", who not only sell their personal items, but also curate looks for their shoppers by sharing recommended items. Poshmark is believed to have some 50 million users, with over 4 million sellers and over 25 million new and second-hand items for sale at any time.

Selling on Poshmark is as simple as uploading a photo of an item for sale, completing a description and setting a price via the free app. Once an item is sold, the lister prints a label from Poshmark and dispatches the item to the buyer. While individuals can sell one or two items to make some money or clear their closet, Poshmark is also home to active, trusted users called "Posh Ambassadors" who must meet all of the following criteria:

- Community Shares: Share (in the app) at least 5,000 items from other Poshers' closets
- Self-Shares: Share your own items at least 5,000 times to the community
- Available Listings: Have at least 50 available listings in your closet
- Listings Sold: Make at least 15 sales
- Average Rating: Have an average rating of at least 4.5 stars
- Average Ship Time: Have an average ship time of less than 3 days

These ambassadors' listings have higher visibility in the app and some of them are full-time sellers making their living on Poshmark. Poshmark buyers are protected by a money back guarantee, as the seller doesn't receive payment from Poshmark until the buyer has confirmed receipt of the goods expected. The guarantee doesn't cover change of mind or items that don't fit, and, in such cases, the buyers are recommended to relist the item and attempt to sell it on. A scheme called Posh Authenticate allows for luxury items over $500 to be shipped via Poshmarks' authentication team to confirm their authenticity before onward shipping to the buyer.

With its social emphasis, buyers are asked to rate/review a purchase as soon as they mark it received, but Poshmark also encourages users to host meetups in local communities, called Posh N Sips. Poshmark supplies hosts with branded merchandise and frequent hosts can earn credit for use on the site.

Poshmark offers a number of features to help buyers find deals - users can 'like' items to be notified if the seller reduces the price, while the Make an Offer feature is to privately negotiate the price of an item directly with the seller. Like thredUP, Poshmark also enables its sellers to bundle multiple items sold to a single buyer. As you might expect from a modern service, it supports the latest in-app and web payments features from Apple Pay and Google Pay.

Depop

Depop is part social network, part second-hand clothing marketplace and is very popular with the younger generation. Its user base of over 13 million users (as at Summer 2019) is predominantly (90%) under 25, smartphone users and highly engaged. As well as allowing for easy listing of items for sale, as you'd find on somewhere like eBay, it also offers the features you'd expect to find on a social network like Instagram, with the ability to message users, as well as to like or comment on listings. There's no fee to list items and Depop takes just a 10% commission on sales - which means it can be a lucrative source of extra income for young people. Depop is a fast and simple way for young people to (re)sell clothes, perhaps after only one wear or even just a photo on Instagram, rather than sending them to landfill. Gross Merchandise Value (GMV) sold through the platform in 2018 was reportedly nearly a quarter of a billion dollars, with a lifetime total of over half a billion dollars.

On Depop, anyone can setup a virtual storefront - each user creates a virtual store where they can upload photos of clothes items they wish to sell. Selling something on Depop is as easy as posting photos on a social app. You enter a description, a location, a brand and a price and you're good to go. After that, other users can buy stuff directly from the app. You can then ship your items and get your money in your PayPal account.

Users can also follow their favorite sellers and discover interesting new listings via curated feeds and hashtags. Popular influencers on platforms such as YouTube are using Depop to host their stores, but within Depop, the mixture of social network and shopping has hit a sweet spot for entrepreneurial and attention-craving Gen Z.

According to a 2015 study by Ernst & Young, Gen Z is more cost-conscious, more environmentally aware and more entrepreneurial than previous generations. That positions a resale app like Depop well in the youth market. The focus on the sale of used items unlike the new items you find on Instagram leaves Depop with a claim to a valuable on-trend segment of the influencer sector. With a large user base, Depop is gathering valuable data - the site has become a barometer of fashion trends, with the Depop shopping community identifying trends two to three months before they hit mainstream fashion.

"We have access to millions of young people in the UK and US and what they are searching for and what they want," she said. "A lot of people want to know what Gen Z is up to at the moment, what they are thinking, and what they are searching for so it is definitely something that a lot of brands would love to get their hands on."

Rachel Swidenbank, VP of Marketplace, Depop[41]

The New Fast Fashion

The growth of second hand is not just a US phenomenon - between 2014 and 2018, China's second-hand market grew by more than 450%, to $100 billion[42]. One recent survey found that 51% of urban Chinese were willing to rent products or buy second hand to help the environment. Young, educated consumers were more likely to opt for sustainable goods, suggesting a significant generational shift. Chinese Internet giants Alibaba and Tencent are investing in sites like Idle Fish and Zhuanzhuan that combine e-commerce for second-hand goods and social networking to build trust. There are other examples - if you're especially interested in this sector, also check out Vinted, a European second-hand marketplace start-up now valued at over $1bn[43].

At closer to 50 than 40, I may be one of very few Gen X in the world to have Snapchat, TikTok, Depop and Poshmark on my phone, but the lack of barriers to entry is one of the defining features of social selling. Regardless of consumer demographics, this is the ultimate empowered consumer-retailer. I was able to setup a virtual store on Depop in just under 5 minutes. With just my phone, name, email, logo, link to my PayPal account, I was good to start listing items and selling to Depop's 13 million users. Sadly, not much in my wardrobe would appeal to Gen Z (though they might view most of what I wear as vintage!) so I'm unlikely to make a huge income from Depop, but the point is how low the barrier to entry is. Similarly, I set up an account and listed my first item on Poshmark in less than 4 minutes. I had eleven followers less than 20 minutes after my first listing. This is the new "fast fashion" - rapidly listing, selling outfits and buying new ones without visiting a store, brand or retailer app. Brands and retailers that are unaware of this shift in behavior risk obsolescence. Second-hand clothes and peer to peer selling aren't necessarily new concepts but as younger generations embrace vintage fashion and environmentally friendly clothes, Depop and similar platforms offer a ready replacement for retailers that seem stuffy and outdated to the mobile-first generation.

Incumbents

"72% of secondhand shoppers shifted spend away from traditional retailers to buy more used items"

thredUP[44]

Terms like 'Clean Up Kit', and 'Posh N Sip' may seem miles from traditional retail but the numbers show that large numbers of people have already stopped shopping in the ways we've come to expect. In a sure sign that the move by consumers to stop shopping exclusively for new clothes has reached a significant level, traditional brands and retailers are joining too. Upmarket outdoor clothing outlet Patagonia now offers a service where customers can bring used clothes in good condition back to store (or freepost it in) receive store credit if it's in good enough condition to resell, where it appears on a dedicated "Worn Wear" section of their website. This has helped the brand appeal to younger customers - According to Phil Graves, Patagonia's Director of Corporate Development, shoppers who buy used clothes from the outdoor brand are typically a decade younger than those who purchase new gear from the chain[45].

As mentioned earlier, veteran US retailers Macy's and J.C. Penney both inked deals in 2019 with thredUP to feature some thredUP merchandise in stores in a pilot. Partnerships such as these enable thredUP to reach customers who want to touch and feel the merchandise before buying it, overcoming any reluctance to buy second-hand sight-unseen. For the retailers, it brings welcome extra footfall (due to the rapid turnover and arrival of new items at a faster pace than is common in department stores) and the hope that browsers will pick up other items when in store.

In early 2019, high end department store Neiman Marcus invested in Fashionphile, a resale site that offers pre-owned luxury handbags and accessories for up to 80% below their original price. Shoppers can also drop off their used shoes and bags at Neiman Marcus stores to ship back to Fashionphile.

As a fast-fashion retailer and pioneer of the throwaway-clothing trend, H&M isn't usually top of mind when it comes to sustainability, despite the initiatives mentioned earlier, but the Swedish chain has been working to change that. Back in 2013, they launched a program that lets shoppers drop off used clothes at H&M's nearly 4,500 stores world-wide. The items, which can be from any brand, are collected by a recycling company. Roughly 60% are resold through local thrift shops and markets; the rest are turned into other products or fibers for new garments.

Rental

"In fashion, the shift to new ownership models is driven by growing customer desire for variety, sustainability, and affordability. In 2019, we predict more consumers will see growing proportion of their wardrobes made up of pre-owned or rented products."

McKinsey x Business of Fashion, "The State of Fashion 2019"

Alongside the emergence of second-hand as a major trend, we are also seeing the simultaneous rise of interest in Rental. As consumers move away from shopping new for permanent ownership, they are also increasingly open to renting in categories where rental was not previously significant. There are already long-established markets for rental of things we need for short times (U-Haul or power tools) or can't justify buying. But it's moving into areas that were previously firmly for consumers to buy outright, use and replace.

This is a dramatic change. The consumer sector has been built on the sale of items - traditionally understood as the lasting transfer of possession and ownership. However, the digital economy and ultra-efficient supply chains have facilitated the emergence of a rental model. Rental offers ways to access products that suit at a given moment or life stage without owning them. Today's consumer being more willing to simply experience something, even temporarily, rather than owning it, represents a sea-change in consumption.

If consumers open an app, browse to select items they want for a short period, wait a couple of days for them to arrive, use them for a month or two and then return them, this represents a monumental challenge to traditional brands and retailers. Although it can be thought of as "online shopping" because the interface is a website or mobile app, the impacts go far deeper. If a few rental services curate what products are offered to customers, this changes the entire dynamic. Brands may need to look at producing more durable items that better survive having multiple "owners", while rental services may become the ultimate try-before-you buy approach that avoids buyer's remorse but eliminates or significantly reduces the market size for some items.

Apparel

Clothing rental isn't new, but it was traditionally limited to very distinct niches, such as wedding suits, especially for men. As peoples' spending on clothes decreases, they are turning to rental to ensure they have access to the clothes they want, when they want them.

Rent the Runway

The most high-profile firm in this space is Rent the Runway (RTR). It has grown from its origins offering designer dresses and accessory rentals to now include 6 main categories - Wedding, Kids, Gala,

Work, Night Out or Weekend. Sizes range from 0 to 22, and pricing depends on whether you want a piece for a special occasion or want to refresh your wardrobe on a regular basis.

RTR is designed for an era of less shopping. For any apparel retailer, a visit to the RTR site starts with a frightening headline:

> Everything to Wear.
> No Shopping Required.

Figure 9 renttherunway.com - October 2019

Scroll down the website and it doesn't get any better - you're greeted by a graphic showing 89% of the millions of RTR customers report spending less time and money on shopping for clothes – not what apparel brands and retailers want to hear.

RTR Reserve allows customers to rent an item for 4 or 8 days starting from $30 per item, or typically 10 - 20% of the retail price of the item. At the end of the rental period, customers return the item via UPS. RTR has a strict policy for non-returns, charging customers a late fee of $50 per day after a 24-hour grace period, up to the maximum price of the item.

RTR also offers two monthly subscription plans - RTR Update ($89, 4 items) or RTR Unlimited ($159, unlimited items). Used items can be sent back at the end of the month or purchased at a discount. In order to make it as painless as possible for subscription customers, they don't pay for dry cleaning or item insurance - so they can simply send back an item if they spill something on it and get a replacement item with 2-day shipping. However, items damaged beyond repair will be charged to the customer.

Valued at over $1 billion dollars following an early 2019 funding round, RTR operates the biggest dry-cleaning facility in the world - 2,000 items per hour and 75 seamstresses to carry out running repairs at their New Jersey facility[46]. A recent partnership with WeWork allows for drop-offs to select WeWork offices instead of UPS stores. Nearly three-quarters of its 9m US customers use RTR for work clothes but RTR has recently announced the addition of a range of West Elm brand bedding items, which leads directly onto the next topic regarding furniture rentals.

LeTote

Wear, Return, Repeat is LeTote's catchphrase. Offering an online women's clothing rental business using a subscription box model, prices start at $69/month for 5 items and $109 for 10 items. Users pick out the items they wish to wear, which are then delivered in a tote box. Customers can wear the items as often as they wish until they are due to be returned, at which point they can pay for items they wish to keep or can rent favorite pieces again.

LeTote offers a wider range than RTR, with Professional, Business Casual, Casual, Night Out, Event and Athleisure categories, as well as accessories and maternity wear. They even match recommended items to the weather in your Zip code!

As well as the convenience of not having to shop for your clothes and the benefit of frequent refreshes, LeTote, says their customers wear each clothing item one and a half to two times per rental on average, and that same clothing item gets shipped out on average 10 times before it gets to an end-of-life stage[47]. That suggests each piece of clothing gets worn around 20 times before it becomes trash - much better than the number of times most clothing is worn, which is two to three times per owned item before it's discarded.

In a symbol of the growing power of new retail models such as LeTote, it was announced in August 2019 that it was purchasing venerable (and vulnerable) retailer Lord & Taylor.

Furniture and More

As the popularity of renting more general apparel is growing, there are also a number of start-ups in other areas seeking to appeal to the trend away from ownership. Chief among these is home furnishings. With home ownership in the US at the lowest level for 30 years among Americans in the 20s and 30s, many people are renting the contents of their homes, not just the dwelling. This allows for flexibility to move to a new apartment or city easily, as well as the ability to swap items regularly compared to long term ownership.

Fernish

With a tagline of "Get the furniture & décor you've always wanted, for as long as you need, at a low monthly fee", Fernish is aimed at people who want nice brands but don't necessarily want to commit to buying them outright. Fernish users can subscribe to furniture (curated by room) for three to 12 months. At the end of a year, they can return, extend, swap or buy items (at retail price less the rental amount already paid). The company delivers, assembles, removes and deep cleans items between customers. Fernish touts its sustainability credentials by guaranteeing that no furniture ends up in landfills; at the end of life, their items are donated to charities or shelters. A $900 bedframe at retail rents for $38 per month, while a living room collection of four pieces with a sticker price of $3,679 costs $149/month rental. There's a $99 minimum monthly charge and $99 moving fee if you move within your rental period.

We'll look again in more detail at subscriptions in Chapter 7.

Joymode

For any brands/retailers thinking that they're safe from the rental economy because they're not in the apparel or furniture sectors, there are startups jumping on the bandwagon across virtually every category. One example is Joymode (only in LA as of Winter 2019) which offers rentals of over 10,000 products from toys and electronics to vacuum cleaners and blenders. Starting at $29 a month for a minimum 3 months, customers can use the service to try a stream of products, from camping gear to home pasta makers. The stated mission is to "help you own less things", and Joymode targets items that people don't use frequently or may tire of quickly. Items are intended to be kept for a weekend or a maximum of 1 month before being swapped for the next items. Joymode doesn't allow you to purchase items, but it may be possible to extend your rental period if the item hasn't been reserved by another member.

Incumbents and Rentals

Faced with new competitors like Rent the Runway and Fernish, traditional retailers are scrambling to respond to consumers opting not to buy things. Banana Republic announced a rental service, Style Passport, initially for women's clothing at a $85 monthly price point for 3 items, while others such as American Eagle, Ann Taylor, Bloomingdales and Urban Outfitters have also launched rental offerings. As an example, the Urban Outfitters service, Nuuly, allows customers to choose and use 6 items from their Anthropologie, Free People and Urban Outfitters brands for $88/month.

We'll talk more about returns later in Chapter 8, but for now it's worth highlighting the changing shopper behavior that sees a significant percentage (20% in the UK, according to research firm Mintel[48]) of people engaging in a practice known as "wardrobing" ordering garments, wearing them, and then returning them to retailers as unwanted goods.

Incumbents could try to cope with both challenges by starting up a rental service. After all, they already deal with returns, some cleaning and repairs to resell garments without being paid, so it makes sense to consider if there's an opportunity to turn it into a paid service.

Power Shifts and the New Consumers

"We're much more research-led now in how we shop, and it's one of the biggest changes to consumer lifestyles. We know a lot more about both the product and the people who are selling it to us."

Tim Greenhalgh, Chairman and Chief Creative Officer, Fitch

As marketers, brands and retailers try to understand customers and macro trends, they need to fundamentally re-evaluate their role in the consumer economy. After decades of dominance where sellers have dictated terms to buyers, a common thread between all generations of shoppers is a new-found empowerment - the ability and the desire to research products that meet both their requirements and their values - seeing buyers take control. Changes to consumer behavior don't only impact brands and retailers. Adjacent and interdependent sectors such as advertising will be impacted too and will play an important role in how brands adapt. For example, leading Irish advertising agency, Boys + Girls, is working with its clients on themes such as Environmentally Conscious Buying and the switch to rental and second-hand as the concept and perception of ownership changes and so too, the resonance of advertising campaigns changes.

Access and The End of Information Asymmetry

"The power has very much shifted from those who make and sell products to the consumers who buy them. "

PWC

The old saying "Caveat Emptor" (Buyer Beware) came from the dominance of the seller in commercial transactions. A lack of knowledge on the part of the consumer and a lack of (access to) alternatives, usually left the customer at a disadvantage. Caveat Venditor (Seller Beware) is now perhaps a more suitable warning.

For a long time, retailers have held the upper hand over consumers, regardless of those sellers who professed the mantra that the customer is always right. Although business schools espouse the notion that the consumer is king, a lot of retail has operated on the basis of information asymmetry – relying on the consumer not having perfect knowledge in order to sell particular items or charge particular prices. Retailers' trusted position as the curators of goods and the controllers of information has been superseded by consumers who have access to global product, price and information, comparisons and reviews before, during and after their purchase.

Before online shopping, the order of choice was always the shop and then the product - if you wanted an appliance, you went to the appliance store and chose from what it offered. That is no longer the way of things - consumers are better informed, less compromising and have higher expectations that they can get the exact product they want, when they want it, at the lowest possible price. Today, a retailer's competition is not local but global: anyone that can ship the product to me.

The Super Consumer

The shift in the relationship between consumer and retailer is so marked that consumers report that they are now often better informed about products than a retailer selling to them. One survey found that 8 out of 10 shoppers believe they're more knowledgeable than retail store associates they are dealing with[49]. While it is easy for a consumer to deep-dive research on a product or category, store staff can be expected to struggle to have mastery level knowledge of every item in a store, unaided. We'll look at some of the technological solutions that retailers are turning to for improvements in Chapter 9.

Not only do consumers have more information, but they also have access to a wider range of products than ever before. As cheaper manufacturing has removed constraints on production, the resulting competitive congestion has begun to drive disequilibrium in supply and demand and add to the shift in power from sellers to consumers. In almost every sector, consumers can quickly find a next best alternative product, even if their preferred retailer has an exclusive arrangement with a single producer that would previously have limited choice.

Retailer Tactics

In Chapter 4, we'll examine some of the tools available to help shoppers shift the balance further in their favor, but it's useful to be aware of the kinds of tactics employed by retailers to pressure consumers into quick decisions. Many volumes written about the psychology of shopping and many physical stores today still rely on such practices. Online retailers too adopt a variety of techniques to reel in customers.

Many websites now sense if a customer is about to leave and pop up a discount offer to entice them to purchase. Many also offer consumers who have left un-purchased items in their basket a discount via a follow-up email if they complete the transaction in a given (short) time frame. Less transparent is the "only one left" banner which offers strong encouragement not to delay. The online shopper has no way of knowing if it's true. The move to augmented shopping, and beyond to delegated shopping, will continue to undermine retailers who rely on these approaches. As we empower our AI-agents to make purchases, they will be less susceptible to these kinds of sales "tactics".

Appealing to the New Consumers

"Increasingly, a brand is what people say about you — not what you say about yourself."

Neela Montgomery, CEO, Crate and Barrel

If this Chapter has made it sound particularly difficult to understand and address the preferences of different shoppers, I want to reassure you that it is possible to appeal successfully to wide ranges of consumers. By focusing on product range, customer experience, convenience and transparent brand values, brands and retailers can resonate with shoppers of all ages.

Though we often focus on the differences between age groups, the four most popular e-commerce sites have the same ranking among three key age demographics: in the US, the four most frequently shopped online retailers for Baby Boomers, Gen X, and Millennials are Amazon, Walmart, eBay, and Target. Discrepancies do not start until the fifth-place ranking, which is held by Kohl's for Baby Boomers, Costco for Gen X, and Best Buy for Millennials[50].

Brands and retailers should no longer define customers based on demographics alone. While age groups will continue to have some relevance, future-focused firms will offer a customer experience that is consistently relevant and convenient to audiences, human and digital. Instead of broad groups and overly simplistic life events, retailers need to be catering to people who operate along various continuums of rational and emotional considerations including:

- Sustainability vs Price or Convenience
- Research vs Impulse
- Ownership vs Renting
- Subscription vs Purchase
- Involvement vs Delegation
- Experience vs Acquisition

Behavioral marketing – which categorizes consumers based on their attitudes, motivations and interests – is gaining popularity as a more sophisticated means of customer segmentation. Digital marketing is moving towards segmenting people, not as representatives of an age or income group, but as individuals with highly specific interests and behaviors.

Market Research becomes Presearch

"In the insights industry, there is a real gap between what has been traditionally available and what we need today. The old methods that were invented before the digital era are not agile, precise, and predictive enough for our current needs."

Tim Warner, VP, Insights & Analytics, PepsiCo

The need to better understand changing customer preferences is changing the market research industry. Brands are desperate to look for early signals of emerging changes in behavior. Focus groups and surveys are now frequently too slow and lacking in scale in a connected world. So large consumer companies are turning to start-ups, such as UK-based Black Swan, that use AI to analyze consumer sentiment gleaned from sources such as social media, online forums and product review websites.

Big companies can no longer dictate consumer tastes as easily as they did in the past and they now have to adapt to trends that may be spotted first by more nimble competitors or D2C brands. In the US, large consumer goods companies have lost 2.4 percentage points of market share to smaller companies and private label products since 2013, according to Boston Consulting Group.

The possibilities now emerging for companies are as transformational as they are challenging. Businesses must rethink how they deliver value to the consumer, rebalance scale and mass production against personalization, and—more than ever—practice what they preach when they address marketing issues and work ethics. Brands must adopt a marketing approach that prioritizes individuals over cohorts, segments and personas - brands must implement a granular system to market to individuals (or their agents/proxies).

Retail is changing because the consumer has changed. New channels are popping up nonstop in physical and digital spheres. Consumers are now more informed than ever when it comes to the products retailers sell—and that's before they even set foot in a store. Retailers had the upper hand for decades but have now firmly lost it. A retailer who doesn't understand changing consumers will die.

Chapter 3: Contemporary Shopping

"In a way, the idea of the old bazaar has gone full circle: rather than visit somewhere where you can be surrounded by every merchant, you are now constantly visited (through your phone's location awareness and notifications – and, increasingly, domestic internet of things devices) by every merchant surrounding you"

Tom Goodwin[51]

Following on from the changes in consumer segments and macro trends discussed in Chapter 2, I want to spend this Chapter looking at recent technology-led developments and the topical debate that can't be avoided in any discussion about retail - the struggles of many well-known main street and physical retailers as shopping habits change. As we'll discuss, there have been many businesses that have not adjusted to the new reality of the last decade. Of course, the brands that went out of business did so for many different reasons - mismanagement, not embracing technology, economic factors beyond their control or not keeping up with changing consumer habits which meant that they fell behind the competition.

This Chapter explores how and where people shop, with a particular emphasis on how that's changed in recent 20 years - change that has signaled the beginning of the end of shopping as we know it. I will start by looking at the rise of e-commerce, and the impacts on physical retail. Then we'll move on to look at how this has changed how people approach shopping.

Although Millennials and Gen Z have grown up with connectivity and online shopping as normal, Baby Boomers and Gen X have also lived through significant changes in the retail landscape and remember a time before online shopping, global trade and big box retailers. But it is the emergence of online and latterly mobile shopping that has challenged brands and retailers the most, redefining how contemporary shoppers have come to view consumption.

What's Past is Prologue

The role of retailers has been the same for decades, if not centuries. Merchants have long been intermediaries between producers and end users. Retailers typically differentiated themselves on three things — assortment, service and price. Location was a key determinant in how important each of those was. The advent of technology has changed things irrevocably. Convenience is now perhaps the most important factor for many consumers - how quickly can a product be in their hands? Can they shop any time and through any channel that suits? Can someone/something else take care of it for them?

In her annual Internet Trends review, leading technology analyst Mary Meeker summarized the evolution of shopping over the last 100 years or so as follows:

Figure 10 Historic Evolution of Shopping. Source: KP Internet Trends 2018

To this summary, I would add a new pillar for the 2020s and beyond - delegated shopping and predictive retail (pretail). We'll explore these more in Chapter 7.

The Growth of Online

"Any retailer that ignores ecommerce does so at their peril. The days when online shopping was an up-and-coming challenger to the main street and the preserve of a number of savvy specialist retailers are well and truly over. E Commerce is and has to be at the heart of every retail business."

Almost is Not Good Enough, Andrew Jennings - Chapter 10

Online shopping is probably the biggest change in retail since, well, since retail itself became a thing. Shopping used to be quite simple, if limited, by today's standards. You went to your local store, department store or mall and bought whatever they had in your size closest to what you wanted. Sometimes, very helpful stores would ring other branches or offer to order in for you, at a significant delay. And you could only shop during the limited opening hours. Just 20 years ago, there was no such thing as online shopping - the only real alternative to going to a shop was choosing products from a catalog, phoning or mailing in your order and waiting for delivery, sometimes for weeks. But the last decade has seen a dramatic rise in online shopping, just as many smaller retailers had suffered an onslaught of competition from shopping clubs and out-of-town superstores.

When Humans Started Shopping Online

Early online shopping options were severely limited. Nowadays, it's hard to remember (impossible for most Millennials and all Gen Z) that at first there were few reputable online stores or marketplaces, most people didn't have fast internet connections and basic website technologies meant websites were dull, text-heavy pages, while secure payments options were virtually non-existent. Those early years of e-commerce were marked by an unsophisticated user experience. The UI of early e-commerce was slow; filling in details was cumbersome - the patented Amazon "One Click" buy it now button was a revolution in online shopping. The nascent sector relied on its inherent benefits of anytime, anywhere (provided you had a PC and an Internet connection) shopping to find its feet. It then expanded from books and CDs to more categories. Traditional retailers were forced to respond by building their own online stores, which only larger traders could do.

Skipping forward to today, it's hard to find anyone in the developed world who hasn't bought something online, and most people transact electronically on a regular basis from highly trusted, fast-loading, sophisticated-looking websites that wow us with personalization, beautiful photography, user reviews and simple, secure payments. And that's regardless of whether we're on a laptop, tablet or phone. When I say online shopping here, I mean navigating to a web site that sells products that are then delivered or available for collection. While that may sound obvious, it's an important distinction because (as we shall see later) online shopping is rapidly evolving to include other interfaces, platforms and channels, and no business can consider themselves as offering "online" purely by having a simple online store or online catalog.

As user comfort with the online shopping experience has grown, it now reaches into categories previously thought immune from online purchases due to a perception that physical contact with the goods was required before purchase; for example, Amazon is now the second largest apparel retailer in the US. Although Amazon or eBay may be the first to spring to mind when you think of online shopping, it's also worth remembering how many other products and services we buy digitally. The growth of services like Spotify and Netflix has made physical retailing of music and movies unsustainable, where once they were a staple of the main street, along with banks.

The reasons why people choose online are revealing about how consumer preferences have shifted, as are the reasons people choose specific channels:

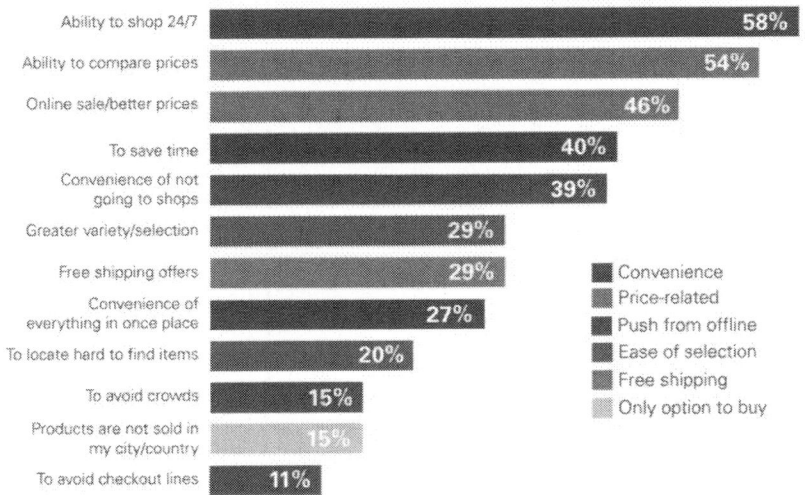

Figure 11 Reasons consumers shop online instead of in physical stores. Source: KPMG 2017

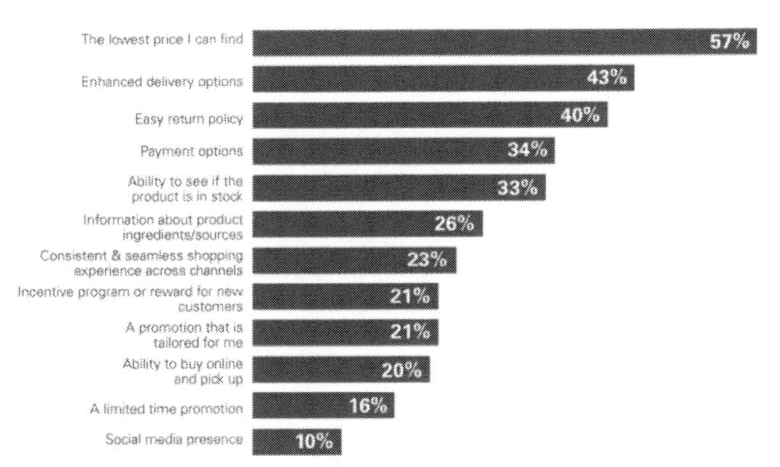

Figure 12 Factors influencing purchase channel. Source: KPMG 2017

Looking globally, different countries have shown differing rates of online shopping adoption for a variety of technical, geographic, demographic and cultural reasons. The UK for example, sees substantially more online shopping than other parts of Europe or the US[52]. In a 2019 survey, Episerver, found that 38% of UK consumers buy online at least once a week, compared to the US 26%, Benelux 22%, Australia 21%, Germany 20% and Sweden 20%. When averaged across sectors, online still accounts for less than 20% of retail value in most countries. China and South Korea lead in online retailing, with the UK leading in Europe.

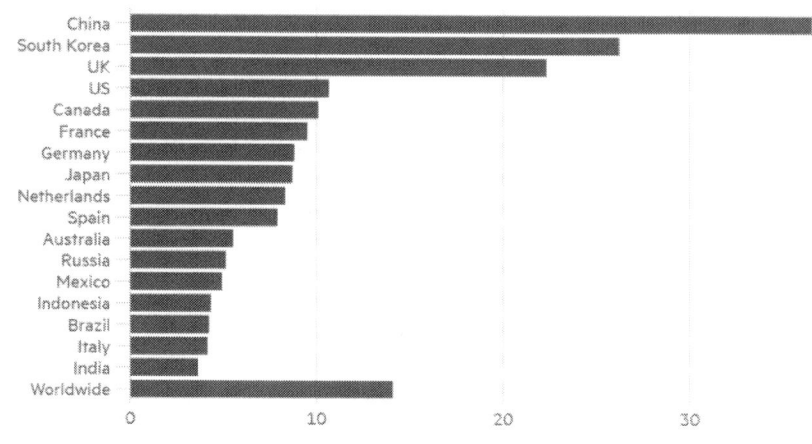

Figure 13 % of retail online across the globe. Source: eMarketer via FT

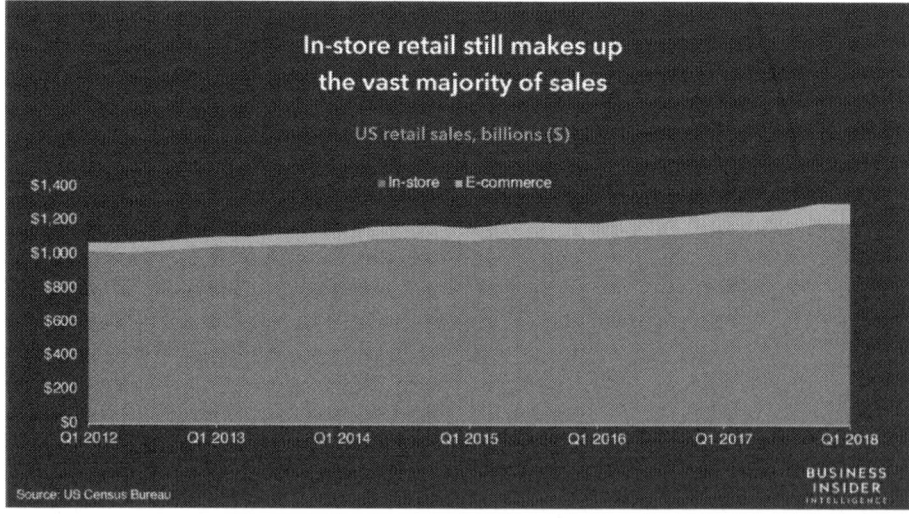

Figure 14 E-commerce share of US retail. Source: Business Insider

Of course, within the averages, there are significant variances across sectors - while some sectors have resisted the move to online, there are some where the vast majority of transactions have moved online. As e-commerce value now exceeds $400 billion, it continues to grow in double-digits each year with year on year growth in 2017 of nearly 16%.

E-commerce growth is continuing its inexorable march, but despite the warning signs, many traditional retailers have not yet responded with the required investment until it's too late. Looking at the graph below of the percentage of retail sales that are online, as analyst Ben Evans puts it[53]:

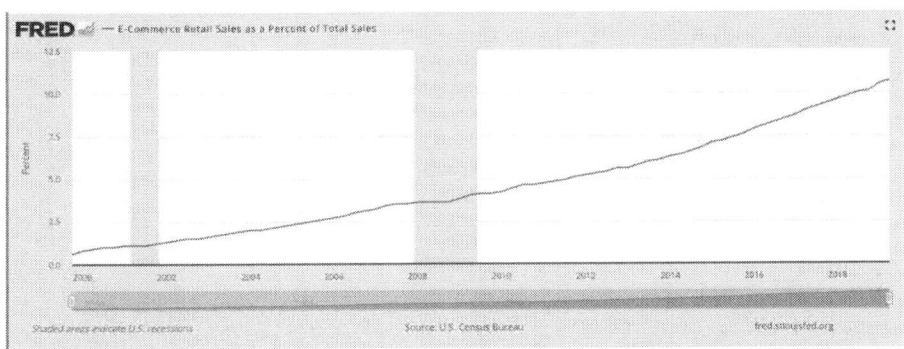

"I sometimes think this is a 'boiling the frog' chart: steady growth right from the beginning, and never any step change, but suddenly it gets too hot".

Basic Online Is Not Enough

As explained above, Online shopping began as a simple process - a searchable inventory of items, a product detail page (PDP) for each product with photos and specifications, a button to add to cart/basket and a checkout process that varied in simplicity from Amazon's One Click to tedious form filling. Now, retail sites need mobile optimization, social links, cross channel baskets, customer reviews, live chat and personalized recommendations with next day delivery to even be basically viable. These features, and more, are vital to support the increasingly complex purchase path of modern consumers.

Recent years have seen a democratization or at least proliferation of online technology. After an early period where only large players could afford access to ecommerce technology, now even sole traders can have access to sophisticated online sales tools. Some have turned to selling via marketplaces such as Amazon, eBay or Etsy, but those who want their own virtual storefronts have powerful options available; there's a choice of platforms on which to setup an online shop in minutes. These offer advanced features to ensure a speedy shopping service on a par with the leaders. Leading ecommerce platforms like Shopify, combined with advanced payment systems, enable merchants to combine offline and online experiences. Shopify's menu of features for retailers of all sizes includes even Virtual Reality and automated virtual assistants (bots) for customer service. The long tail of commerce is made up of small brands that can easily nurture a deep, direct, real-time relationship with customers using these technologies, without developing anything themselves or even requiring substantial expertise.

When Online Goes Wrong

"Shopping friction is the number one threat for your business today. There's $213 Billion of revenue lost from abandoned online shopping carts in a year"

Eva Press, North America Group Lead - CPG, Healthcare & Retail, Facebook

Not all online shopping is well implemented - just like physical, there are good and bad experiences. Not all retailers have grasped the importance of ensuring their online presence is fit for purpose and hassle-free for consumers. As consumers now expect wide range and competitive price as an absolute minimum, it's as important to ensure there are no barriers to service. For example, almost a third of customers will quit an online checkout if they are asked to create an account in order to complete a purchase.

According to research from Baymard.com, the following are the primary drivers of abandonment for online shoppers.

Extra costs too high (shipping, fees)	53%
Site required account creation	31%
Too long/complex checkout	23%
Total order cost not visible up front	20%
Didn't trust to input credit card	17%
Delivery was too slow	16%
Web site errors	15%
Returns policy unsatisfactory	10%
Insufficient payment methods	6%
Credit card declined	4%

Appealing to Customers

The contemporary shopper has been surveyed and analyzed extensively and there are plenty of resources defining best practice for online retailers. There is little excuse for brands and retailers that don't take the time to meet basic standards - failing to do so online will result in the same poor commercial performance as physical retailers who fail to ensure their store is well laid out.

As an example, here's one analysis of what matters to the modern consumer when shopping online:

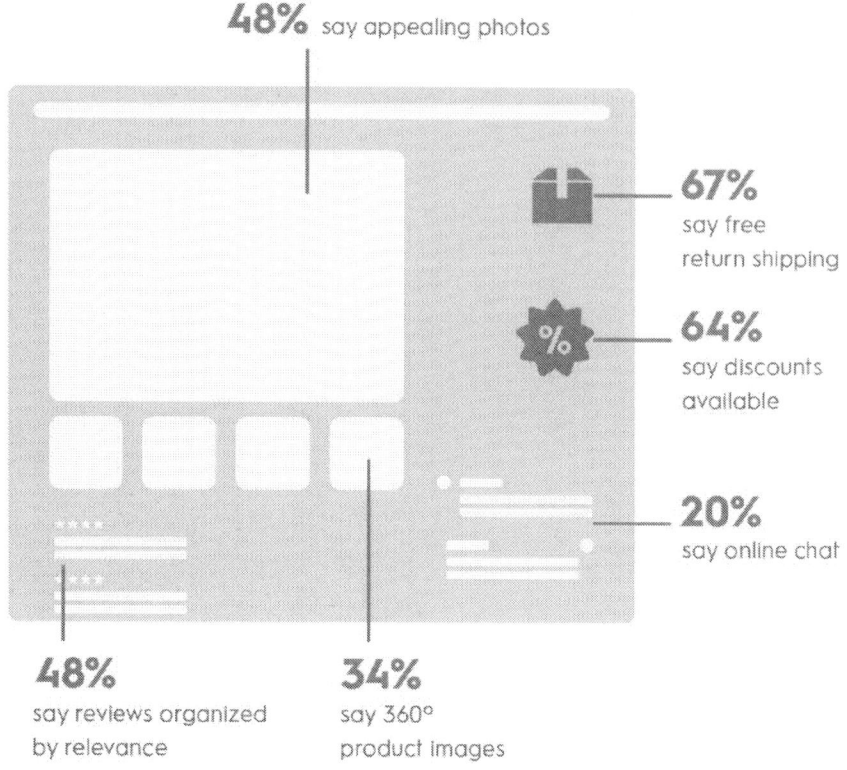

Figure 15 Contemporary Shopper Expectations Phononic's 2019 "Store of the Future" Report[54]

The Move to Mobile

Following hot on the heels of e-commerce has come m-commerce. Despite initial skepticism that people would shop from their smartphones instead of laptops, mobile shopping has now grown to undeniable proportions, exceeding desktop use. Shopify saw 66% of sales on mobile during Black Friday Cyber Monday (BFCM) 2018[55] - people browsing from desktop devices tend to spend longer on a site but statistics show that users typically move between devices as they consider their purchases.

With stats like these, it's safe to say that having your online store optimized for mobile is no longer an option, it's a necessity. Customers won't tolerate stores that aren't uniquely tailored to their devices. If you can't deliver an experience that's quick, convenient, and easy-to-use, don't expect your visitors to stick around.

As important as mobile has become, that is certainly not to disregard desktop - Other industry data still suggests that more conversions continue to happen on desktop in many industries with more complex sales. It's also common for users to move between devices as they research ahead of actual purchase, so continuing to pay a lot of attention to your desktop site makes a great deal of sense.

To App or not to App

There's an ongoing debate in the industry about how best to service mobile shoppers - with a mobile-optimized website, or with a dedicated app. While apps tend to offer enhanced experiences, they come at a significant development & maintenance cost, as well as requiring substantial effort to persuade people to download and keep the app installed. For companies that see a lot of business through Amazon or originating via Google searches (that link to their web site), an app may be an expensive distraction.

Apps vs mobile web is largely about the resources you have available for creating your user experience. We'll look in later Chapters at some examples of the effective use of apps, but for most retailers, a good mobile web experience with an effective, consumer focused operational infrastructure is preferable to a flashy but shallow app experience. I've seen countless retailers focusing on the front-end app experience without the systems and processes to back it up. There's no point in creating an amazing app, spending a fortune promoting it to drive downloads, only to frustrate customers with slow deliveries, out of stocks or restrictive return policies.

For those organizations that have the resources to invest into an app-enabled strategy, we are seeing increasing sophistication in shopping apps - that are now not merely transaction processors that mirror websites. Innovators are making the effort to include value-added services to justify the download and continued presence on phones and perhaps a slight flicker of hope compared to the user tapping Amazon (by far the most popular retail app across all generations) or Google and the sale getting away. If your app is there on the home screen - maybe, just maybe - the user will start their search with you.

App Experiences

Some brands and retailers have invested heavily in creating innovative app experiences to try to stand out from the crowd. For example, Amazon has added a live mode to its app that enables consumers to see how lipstick would look on them using the front camera on their phone, while Nike use advanced features in their app to recommend styles based on a scan of the user's foot. Nike Fit is a smartphone-based foot scanning solution that lets customers check their shoe size before they buy. When choosing a pair of shoes, customers are encouraged to use the app to scan their feet with their smartphone camera to get an accurate, personalized size recommendation. Given that shoes not fitting properly is one of the main reasons for online returns, the app aims to help both the brand and the customer.

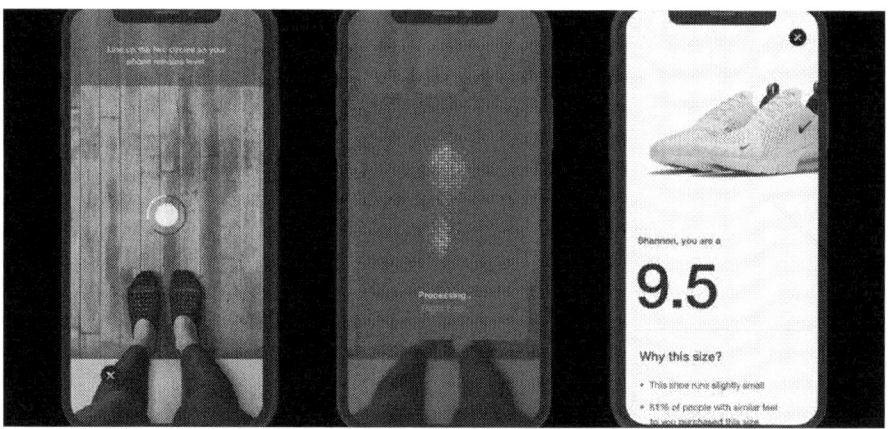

Figure 16 Nike foot scanner and shoe recommender. Source: Nike

In my experience, retailers have a negative and somewhat self-fulfilling attitude to apps. I had several C-level UK retailers tell me in 2017 that consumers "won't download retailer apps". They refused to accept that consumers would download an app that offered good functionality such as the ability to checkout and skip queues. They were right that consumers won't download poor apps - apps that simply replicated a mobile web site - taking up valuable space for no benefit. I can't help wondering, though, how many of the CEOs I spoke to were basing the assertion on their own preference rather than any firm data or understanding of consumer motivations.

In a slightly off-narrative retro move, some retailers are experimenting with text message (SMS) based commerce. There's no need to open an app or log-in or have an internet connection. As long as you have phone signal, you're good to go, and every phone type supports it. And there's no need for user education as everyone is familiar with how to send a message. Wellness drinks brand Dirty Lemon for example only takes orders via text – even if you go to its website. Once a customer has registered their details, they can simply text the company to order more drinks. Their payment details are linked to their account, so they don't even have to type them in each time.

The fact that our GPS-enabled smartphones go everywhere with us has opened a new market for location-enhanced buying experiences. For example, The Burger Laboratory in Seoul uses your location (with your permission) so it knows when you're nearing the store, and therefore, when to work on your burger so it's ultimately fresh and ready for when you arrive. If you stop, or detour, on your way to the store, it will pause the preparation until you start approaching the store again.

It's Still Early

Looking at these recent and current trends in online and mobile shopping, some may seem positively futuristic for certain sectors, but already somewhat stale in others. The one common trend is that virtually every sector is going to see a *further* increase in online shopping, especially on mobile. Even the most conservative estimates expect online sales to double in the next decade, in a stark warning to those brands and retailers still overly dependent on traditional physical stores. According to Google Insights, fully two thirds of people say they're looking to do more of their shopping online in the next year[56]. The advances in convenience that we'll explore in the coming Chapters mean that the current situation is far from the full extent of change, and rather than easing off, the pace of change will only accelerate.

The End of Physical Retail?

"Physical stores aren't going anywhere. E-commerce is going to be a part of everything but not the whole thing"

Jeff Bezos, CEO, Amazon[57]

As online continues to grow, what happens to physical retail? Looking at empty stores on main streets and headlines decrying the death of retail, you might think that people have already stopped shopping offline to a greater extent than the figures above indicate. And indeed, the distress many physical retailers are in is a very clear sign of change in how and where people shop in recent years. Before ever the emergence of online, physical retailing has previously been through several phases; Baby Boomers will have seen a lot of change and previous waves of closures as stores evolved through: Mom & Pop -> Main Street -> Dept Stores -> Mail Order -> Suburban Malls -> Big Box Specialists and Discounters. That list alone reminds us also that there isn't one "retail" - there are local stores, town main streets, city centers and out of town malls, each intended to serve different customer needs.

Most of the news commentary about the current predicament of physical retail focuses on store closings. However, a more instructive metric when discussing the challenges facing physical retail is to look at the net store openings. This table from CoreInsight shows how things have changed significantly in the last couple of years in the US. What it doesn't show is the type of stores - many new openings have been nail bars and vape shops rather than more established retail categories.

Year	Net Openings (Closings)
2012	2,395
2013	1,356
2014	1,013
2015	356
2016	1,367
2017	(2,847)
2018	(1,844)
2019	(4,691)

But while store closure numbers in recent years look dire (and are especially dire for those employees and neighborhoods impacted), there is some important context in the US retail sector - past decades have seen huge investment in building retail space and the inescapable conclusion is that in the USA, there are too many stores and a correction is inevitable - the US has 10 times more retail space per person than Germany.

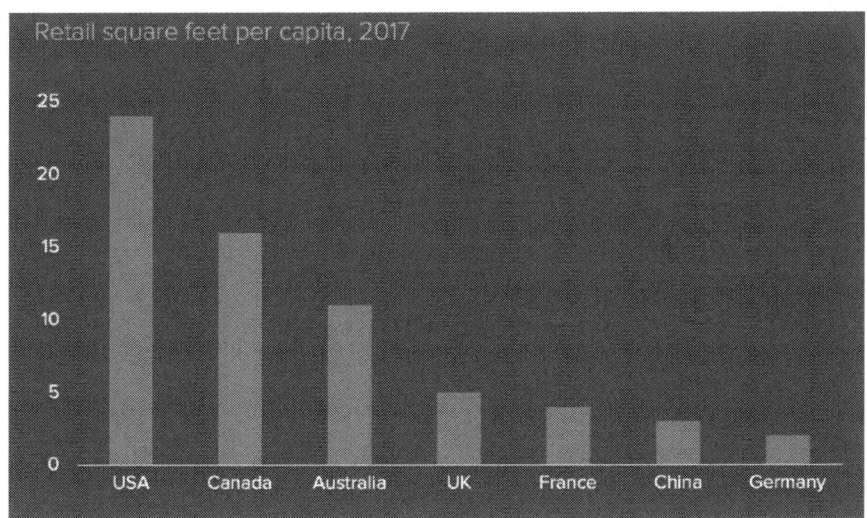

Figure 17 Relative Retail Space in major economies. Source: A16Z

Challenging Times

"Retail guys are going to go out of business. Retail chains are a fundamentally implausible economic structure if there's a viable alternative. You combine the fixed costs of real estate with inventory, and it puts every retailer in a highly leveraged position. It just doesn't make sense for all this stuff to sit on shelves"

Marc Andreessen[58]

Physical retailers have been hit by a combination of the 2008 financial crisis, competition from online shops and large supermarkets, belt-tightening by consumers and a feeling that developed societies have reached "peak stuff". And that is before considering the rising fixed costs facing most retailers. The rapidly changing consumer behaviors and preferences discussed in the last Chapter have been accompanied by a requirement to invest substantial sums in new technologies. Given that consumers now spend one in every five dollars online and many businesses are seeing 20% fewer sales on the shop floor as well as their fixed costs rising, it follows that profit margins will be squeezed in an industry long known for its slim margins. Looking to the UK for an example, main street footfall has decreased for four consecutive years[59]. Even if 2% doesn't sound much, just 1% could be enough to tip a store from profit to loss.

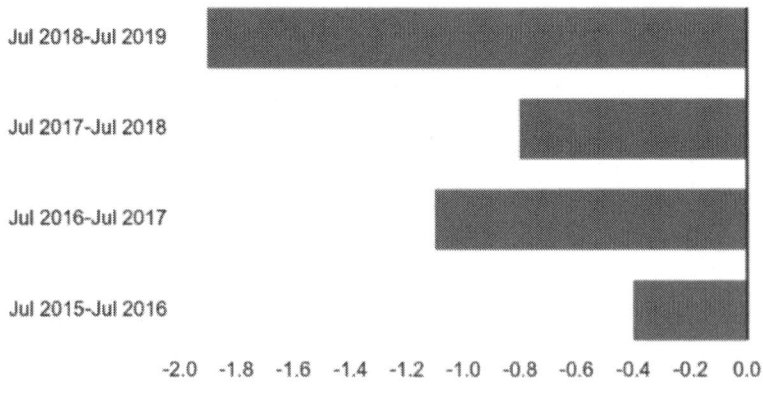

Figure 18 Falling Footfall in the UK 2015-2019. Source: Springboard

When humans stop visiting the main street or stop going to the mall, it forces dramatic change that financial models and town planning frameworks may not be ready to deal with. As stores fail, inflexible regulations may prohibit certain types of businesses taking them over, requiring onerous applications for change of use planning permission, leading to extended vacancies that further reduce footfall.

While it might be tempting for some who favor online shopping over main street retail to dismiss the woes of the main street, the dependence of major pension funds on retail rentals means you can't claim to be unaffected by closing shops just because your every need arrives next day in a smiling cardboard box. Town centers play an important social function and it's important to create vibrant spaces. However, as we'll discuss in Chapter 9, these may no longer be anchored on retail stores as we have known them.

Let's look now at some different sectors of retail and how they are faring.

Flagging Flagships

"I don't think you have a need for these massive stores. Shoppers are shopping completely differently. You don't need a full assortment. They have to become an experience, letting customers get to know who you are versus selling stuff."

Stacey Widlitz, President of SW Retail Advisors[60]

Although the reality of closures in small towns and main streets has hit local communities hard, the once glamorous shopping boulevards of the world haven't escaped the changing realities of retail. Formerly seen as a brand statement as much as a transaction site, even flagships stores in prestigious locations are not exempt from the changing realities of contemporary shopping. Gap, Tommy Hilfiger, Lord & Taylor and Polo Ralph Lauren have all closed their flagship stores on Manhattan's Fifth Avenue.

Those brands that are retaining a flagship presence are doubling down on making them deliver an even more strident brand message. Other retailers are reimagining the flagship concept instead of abandoning it altogether. Nike, for instance, opened a massive store on Fifth Avenue that doesn't have any cash registers.

It lets shoppers see details of items displayed on a mannequin by scanning the QR code and then having those items delivered to a fitting room or a designated pickup spot. Levi Strauss & Co.'s new flagship in Manhattan's Times Square features larger dressing rooms with call buttons and tailors who can add trims and patches to customers' jeans.

Doom on the Main Street

"The reality is we may need fewer main streets in the future. This opens opportunities to repurpose main street space, while [evolving] to meet consumer demand."

PWC

Across all large cities and small towns, the main street/main shopping district is of vital importance to the identity and vitality of the area. It is typically the focal point of the surrounding hinterland and a critical meeting point and local reference point. The closure of main street stalwarts is a very visible reminder of the scale of change currently underway. Aside from the human cost of staff left unemployed, it creates a self-perpetuating downward spiral - main streets become less attractive, stores close. Repeat.

Historically, town centers were much more heavily residential and it's a relatively recent phenomenon that they are seen as being for commercial premises only rather than places for people to live. While landlords and pension funds like the stability of 25 year, upward-only leases, which may have made sense in less turbulent retail times, this approach no longer makes sense in an environment where flexibility and even reinvention is required to compete and survive. But for many large and small retailers today, there simply isn't enough consumer spending to justify extensive main street presence based on current business models. Along with the rise of online, there's also been a big shift in how consumers prioritize where they spend their money. As discussed about the shift towards experiences over ownership, we're splashing out more on what we do and less on what we wear. Retail on the main street is getting a much smaller share of disposable income than it did a few decades ago - and that's before you consider the challenge of online.

Changing Malls

The growth of the mall (or shopping center as they are more commonly known in Europe), especially the out of town megamall, marked the last big shift in retailing before the advent of online shopping. Much to the chagrin of town centers, the rise of the automobile led to the creation of numerous sprawling malls on the outskirts of large urban areas. These retail destinations became icons for the growing middle class as shopping habits changed.

At their peak in the mid-1990s, the US was building 140 new shopping malls every year[61]. But malls were in trouble long before online in general and Amazon in particular was a force. As more people moved to cities, and interest in car ownership declined among younger generations, the over-supply of mall space was already an issue. The US recession of 2008 hastened the decline of weaker malls just as online shopping was finding its stride. While the top 10% of malls with large hinterlands and strong tenants have prospered as destinations even in the face of surging online sales, many mall owners have been forced to reconsider how they use their space - much like main streets need to, but widely refuse to.

Facing permanent structural change, some landlords have found alternative uses for some vacant shopping center sites, from storage spaces to hotels, while others like leading mall owner Simon Property Group (SPG) has added office space and gyms to fill gaps as well as announcing plans in 2018 to open at least five Marriott International hotels at its malls over the next few years. PREIT, which owns malls mostly located in the north-eastern US, is similarly planning to add as many as 7,000 homes and 3,000 hotel rooms in a dozen properties[62].

No More Department Stores?

"In 1985, US department stores took 14.5% of all retail spend. Last year they took 4.3%. The figure is still falling. The internet is often blamed for this. But the blunt truth is that US department stores just aren't very good retailers. In fact, most of them are abysmal"

Neil Saunders, CEO GlobalData[63]

If malls are a relatively new part of the retail landscape, department stores have been a staple of the sector for centuries. But they are far from immune to the changes sweeping the sector and in fact, according to many experts, Department Stores are among the most at risk formats. Department stores are no longer the cheapest, nor are they the most fashionable or the most convenient.

As humans stop shopping in department stores, more than 1,000 US department stores have shuttered over the past decade. The department store format, predicated on stocking broadly appealing goods, lacks the easy navigability of small stores or online sites, while offering none of the personalization or authenticity that resonates with contemporary consumers. Many of the more desirable brands are withdrawing from department stores in order to reclaim control of their appearance and going direct to consumers (more on that larger trend later).

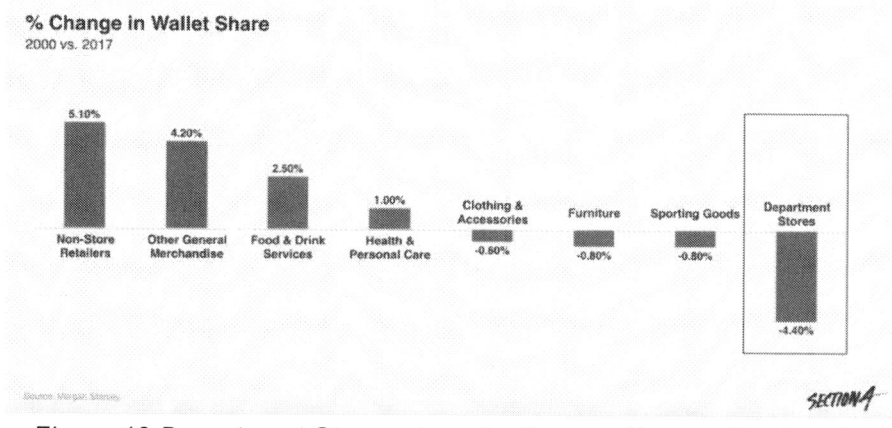

Figure 19 Department Stores struggle. Source: Morgan Stanley via Section4

Digging deeper into the recent struggles of department stores, it's noteworthy how many of them have become predominantly apparel stores as non-apparel categories that make up the other key departments, such as electronics or cosmetics, have seen customers migrate to specialists like Sephora or Best Buy where better range and service are available. And just as departments stores retrenched to apparel, there was a parallel shift in consumer taste to casual wear (as workplaces became less formal) and the growth in discounters. In 1987, the average consumer allocated 5.9% of their spending to apparel and services, but by 2017, that had halved to just 3.1%, according to a Deloitte.

Similar to the situation discussed above with malls, where the top 10% are thriving, some department stores with strong identities and customer service are facing better prospects - *"There will be survivors, I think Nordstrom is one of them, but the jury is out on who will be the others,"* says Author of Retail's Seismic Shift, Michael Dart[64]. Others are turning to partnerships and smaller footprint stores. For example, Kohls, one of the US's biggest department store chains with 1,100 stores, is leasing space to Planet Fitness to setup gyms in its premises. As well as garnering rental income, this also enables Kohls to reduce inventory and labor costs. Simultaneously, Kohls is stocking larger amounts of athletic wear to appeal to Planet Fitness patrons. This is alongside their partnership with Amazon to accept returns.

Life in Offline Yet?

If all the above sounds like grim times for physical retail, the harsh reality is that parts of the sector are facing existential challenges, but I believe that reimagining the role of physical retail will yield a sustainable future for many locations. Across all generations of shoppers, even the most digitally immersed, there remain reasons humans like shopping in stores.

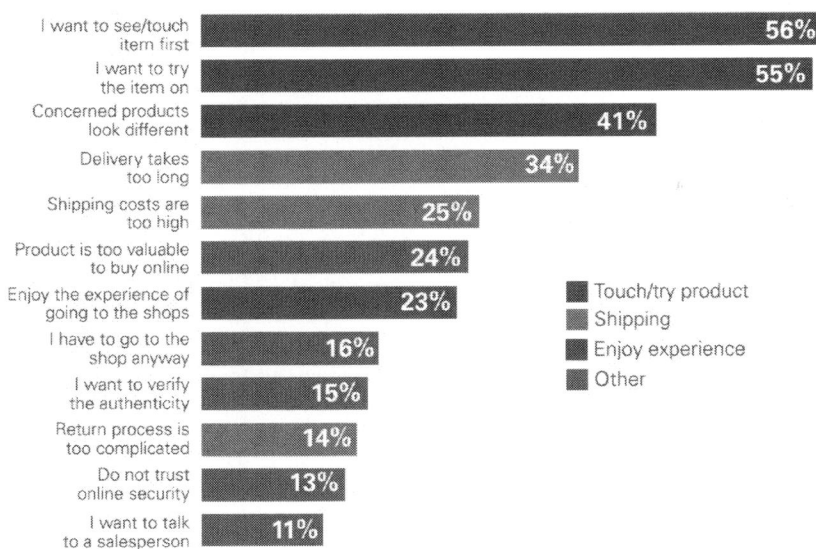

Figure 20 Reasons Consumers opt for in store over online. Source: KPMG, 2017

The ability to see, touch and feel products as well as take possession of items immediately consistently rank highest among the reasons consumers choose to purchase items in stores rather than online. The perception that it's easier to return goods to a store rather than packing and sending them back online is also a frequently cited factor. An efficient and/or engaging in-store shopping experience where shoppers can easily see, feel and try-out products — coupled with stellar inventory management to ensure the right products are in stock — can make or break physical retailers. The adoption of technologies to ensure a smoother and/or a more engaging customer experience will help physical retailers play to their strengths and build a position as part of a multi-channel relationship with consumers.

Changing the Channel

We'll talk more later about the store of the future and how physical retail might evolve, after we've examined the myriad technological and consumer behavior changes that lie ahead in the coming years. It's clear that business as usual is not an option for physical retail. In this section, we'll look at how shoppers have changed how they use and view retail stores, even if all retailers haven't caught up yet. The distinction between online and offline is becoming less defined - even if a customer transacts in store, there's every chance that they researched the product or stock level online in advance. But even when they're in-store, they may be online too seeking further product information, social endorsements or discounts.

Mobile Use In Stores

One change that's immediately obvious, if you look around when you're in a store, is that people are using their phones as part of their shopping experience. Since mobile phones gained internet access capabilities and barcode scanning apps, many traditional retailers have dreaded "showrooming" — when people pull out their phones in a store and start looking for a cheaper, or better product from a competitive retailer or marketplace once they've seen a product in real life. According to Google research[65], it's true that people are on their phones more than ever in stores. Nearly 60% of people use their phones as they shop in stores. But that's not necessarily bad news and a sign of a sale slipping away - customers in store may just be looking for additional product information, opinions from their friends, checking their bank balance or planning where they're going to eat when they've finished shopping. They may also be looking for coupons or offers from the store they're in.

I want to digress slightly for a moment to make a point about the unexpected impacts that technology can have and how unpredictable consumer behavior can be, catching out any brand or retailer at any time! I'm pretty sure that the product managers at Wrigley's didn't lose sleep the night in 2007 that the iPhone was announced (unless perhaps to wonder which model to buy). But they should have. This graph shows the dramatic impact on impulse purchase behavior in checkout queues as distracted shoppers ignore the high-margin items tempting them as they wait to pay.

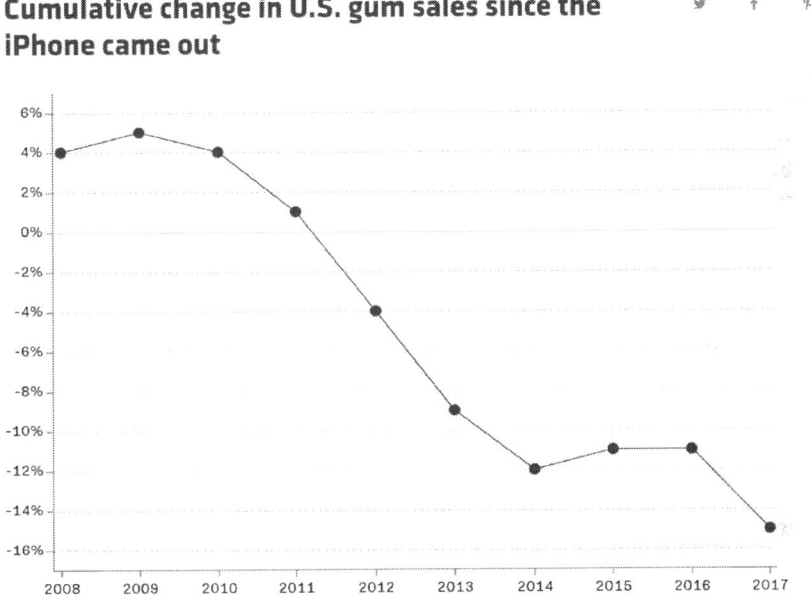

Figure 21 *Gum sales depended on shopper attention at point of sale. Source: Euromonitor via Recode*

The End of Online vs Offline

Before the Internet, going to the shops was a necessity, not a choice. Now that it's largely optional, the pressure on physical retail to offer something enticing or unique compared to online shopping is a vital point to consider when looking for differentiation. However, it is even more important to consider physical retail as a complement not a competitor to online - how they could combine to offer the best experience to consumers is often the better question than which one should "win". As we'll see, when channels work together, they combine to give the experience today's consumers want. That might sound simple but, in my own experience of running retail and from talking to retail leaders, many organizations still struggle to break down their internal silos to create a business that more closely mirrors consumers. Nearly all retailers still operate their online team separate from their traditional retail team. But as I keep saying anytime I present about retail, consumers don't think in channels!

Two Way Traffic

The modern consumer is likely to research their intended purchase extensively online. But their final decision point may be a visit to a store to see/touch the item in question. From there, they may choose to purchase the item in store, or they may go ahead and complete the order online. So online drives people to store and in reverse, stores drive people online. Or a consumer browsing in store may see something they like, but then wait until they are home later to research the item, check the reviews and order it for delivery. The relationship between physical retail and online retail has become a complex intertwined puzzle for brands.

Harvard Business Review[66] found in a large-scale study of 46,000 shoppers that only 7% were online-only shoppers and 20% were store-only shoppers. The remaining majority, or 73%, used multiple channels during their shopping journey. The study also noted that 60% of internet users start shopping on one device but continue or finish on a different one, and 82% of smartphone users say they consult their phones on purchases they're about to make in a store. Further emphasizing the importance of consistency across channels, conducting prior online research on the retailer's own site or sites of other retailers led to 13% greater in-store spending among omnichannel shoppers.

Retailers and analysts grappling with this have coined many terms to describe the phenomenon, the most common being "omnichannel." For me those buzzwords can be so overused that they start to lose meaning but whatever you call it, it's a vital concept. Whether you call it omnichannel, multichannel, unified or seamless shopping, delivering a good customer experience across a multitude of physical and digital channels is not easy. There's a saying in software circles that "you shouldn't ship your organization structure" - similarly, brands need to stop shipping their organization structure where online and stores compete with each other under different leadership, exacerbated by legacy incentive schemes and sales attribution.

Creating an enterprise adaptable for the future of shopping requires drastic changes to a company's organizational structure. At a minimum, physical stores and e-commerce operations require deep links if not full integration. Internal financial systems need to accurately reflect a customer's buying an item online and later returning it to a physical store. Ultimately, brands and retailers should integrate their e-commerce units into the rest of their commercial organizations, replacing channels that compete for sales from the same customer with a structure that puts the customer first across channels.

As consumers change their shopping journey, the more enlightened retailers will no longer distinguish between in-store versus online retail—a sale is a sale. The goal is to offer customers a consistent, relevant experience that provides the information they need and engages with them where and when they want. That means offering a similar experience in store, on mobile devices, and online.

Omnichannel - we're not there yet

"The omnichannel landscape demands that retailers focus on integrating all channels and touchpoints. It's more complicated than just offering click and collect"

Oliver Banks

Compared to what a consumer might expect, just stopping disconnects between channels or click and collect, doesn't make you an effective omnichannel retailer. It may be very difficult to reorient a business, break down long established and emotive bonus structures or attributions, but aligning operations across channels is essential. Consumers are impatient, connect with multiple devices and prefer to communicate on their channels (not yours). And when brands fail to meet their growing expectations, consumers show a propensity to quickly switch brands.

While operating effectively across channels may be the ambition, retailers need to ensure they don't settle for a mediocre experience across all rather than offering excellence. I'd advocate for offering excellent service in a carefully selected set of channels rather than trying to cover every conceivable option. For example, it's ok to decide to have a Facebook autoresponder pointing people to your online chat via web if you're not ready to staff up a social media team just yet. We'll come back to the topic of how retailers need to change to embrace omnichannel retail in Chapter 9.

When Humans Change Shopping

Brands and retailers, but especially marketers, obsess over the purchase journey - what is called the funnel in marketing textbooks - how do consumers arrive at that all-important point of handing over their payment? What are the steps along the way and what are the defining interactions? From the earliest stages of creating awareness, all the way to the purchase transaction and increasingly important post-purchase review, it now typically involves multiple channels and interactions. As we'll see later, people are changing where those interactions are taking place, and even automating them.

The New Funnel(s)/Shopping Journey

When trying to understand the typical purchase journey for customers, marketers have traditionally relied on a linear model. But the old assumptions that predate web and mobile technology are no longer applicable in a world of social media, peer reviews and algorithms. The path to purchase has become more of a cycle or even a web. Consumers move through and back and forth between the stages, influenced by a myriad of both offline and online factors at every stage.

There are multiple similar frameworks for codifying the consumer journey, dating back to the classic Awareness-Interest-Desire-Action (AIDA) model from 1925. A more up to date model to describe today's consumer is Awareness-Consideration-Conversion-Evaluation (ACCE).

- **Awareness** - discovery of a product and desire for the product
- **Consideration** - researching the product online or offline
- **Conversion** - deciding where and when to buy the product

- **Evaluation** - Post-purchase - reviewing, returning or recommending the product

Awareness/Discovery

Today's shoppers have a vast array of resources at their fingertips to help them discover, assess and buy products. They are constantly surrounded by direct paid media online and offline, as well as via peer recommendations. Even video games now feature paid placement as brands struggle to reach fragmented audiences. Cutting through the saturation to reach a target audience is getting harder, with many brands finding there is no longer any way to buy enough attention to succeed. Advertising budgets must be supplemented with a social media presence but also with careful attempts at management of "word of mouth" - trying to garner positive reviews of products from customers.

When shoppers are ready to search for a product, they turn to a search engine such as Google or go straight to Amazon – in fact, 56% of people are most likely to use Amazon for product search, 7% higher than Google. Social media has recently become a significant player in how consumers are influenced too - according to Royal Mail, 22% of UK consumers have purchased an item after seeing something on social media. Customers do still visit brand and retailer websites and over a quarter of shoppers still like to go into stores to find inspiration.

Already we're seeing a reduction in the human element of awareness - around one-third of Amazon's sales are based on its recommendation engine - algorithms that suggest products you might like based on your shopping history and the behavior of similar shoppers. Although we might not think of it as automated shopping, it's the first step in relinquishing shopping effort.

Consideration

I mentioned in the previous Chapter how all generations now typically learn more about the products that interest them than in the past. This is one of the most significant changes in shopping behaviors - in the days before the Internet, it was much harder for consumers to obtain details about a product, and they frequently relied on what their local retailer recommended, often unaware of any commercial incentives that might have been motivating the seller's apparently impartial advice. Replacing the curation of retailers are recommendation engines and replacing the tangibility of physical shopping are reviews. Along with social media, these are the new ways that people assess products for suitability, trusting these sources more than sales associates.

Consumers now independently research products before they purchase them - according to a UPS report[67], 90% of consumers research products before buying them online. While the amount of time a shopper devotes to research is typically proportionate to the expense involved, Millennials will go online to research a candy bar, checking its ingredients and the ethical credentials of the company, even for a $1 purchase.

As well as checking product details, consumers are weighing up information from reviews and recommendations. According to Pew Research[68], the vast majority of us — 82% — read customer ratings or reviews before buying something.

Conversion

When a consumer is finished researching product alternatives and is ready to purchase, they continue assessing offers. Even when they've found the product they want, and at a potentially acceptable price, the retailer isn't assured of securing the sale. Shoppers will now check factors like the returns policy (An inconvenient returns policy deters 80% of shoppers[69]) alongside the cost and speed of shipping, or the stock levels in nearby stores.

The decision to purchase is a function of price, urgency and experience. However, there are multiple dimensions to each of these and different people may care about different dimensions at different times or for different types of product. For example, people may be willing to pay a premium for more eco-friendly products, while some consumers may want to make an initial purchase in store but then switch to online repeat purchases.

Evaluation

The so-called purchase journey no longer ends with the purchase. Consumers who are in any way unhappy with the experience will likely express their displeasure either directly to the retailer in the form of a return or worse, publicly with a poor review. It's important that retailers solicit positive reviews from happy customers and move swiftly to remedy issues causing unhappy reviews.

In a US study from Brightpearl[70], 48% of online shoppers have left a negative review, with 8 in 10 likely to do so in the future. Interestingly, three-quarters of poor reviews related to post-purchase issues, such as deliveries and returns, not actual product concerns. The same study showed that more than half of all online consumers (55%) admit that a single unfavorable review of a brand or retailer halted an online purchase.

Direct to Consumer (D2C)

"A huge struggle is taking place between brands and retailers."

Warren Buffett, 2017[71]

As retailers contend with changing consumer attitudes and demands, along with the myriad technological advances, they are also finding growing challenges from another unexpected source - brands - the very brands they resell to customers. As if those in retail didn't have enough to contend with given the rise of online and of their rents, they now must look out for competition from their own suppliers!

The primary purpose of retailers has always been to curate goods and provide distribution for manufacturers, along with a trusted point of information for consumers. But disintermediation is a huge trend, as humans stop shopping in traditional retailer shops and instead opt to purchase goods directly from the manufacturer, bypassing the intermediary retailer - what's known as Direct to Consumer (D2C).

The technological and logistical realities of the modern world now mean that brands are no longer dependent on retailers in order to reach consumers. Many start-ups now eschew the traditional supply chain model for a direct to consumer model, while even the most established suppliers to the retail sector are weighing up the benefits of a direct to consumer approach.

The alternative to D2C - and the norm for many years now - is the traditional process of selling products via distributors, through individual stores, before the product finally lands in the hands of customers. It's a tried and tested method that works well for many businesses, but brands have long had a difficult relationship with those that purveyed their goods to end users. Now that there are credible alternatives, many are looking to reach consumers without intermediaries.

Removing the Retailer

The arrival of online shopping and its lower barriers to entry mean that companies with good products can now take orders from consumers directly online without setting up physical distribution channels - one unexpected consequence of the Internet and the ease of online selling is the emergence of a plethora of new direct to consumer brands. Entrepreneurs can bypass the traditional route to market where so much of their energies would have gone into "selling in to sellers", with countless attempts to reach the right trade buyers at large retailers. While a retailer does bring distribution to an audience of consumers, it also can be a distraction from a product focus, as well as a dilution of margin.

As we've seen, thanks to the power of the Internet for researching products, consumers frequently no longer need to rely on retailers for curation of goods - they can find what they are looking for, choosing from a larger range of products than any retailer can collect or present. Thanks to the reach of the Internet and the search and social media technologies built on it, brands can convey information about their products and services directly to consumers with a broader and cheaper reach than any mass media before online and with a consistency, accuracy and authenticity not available via a retailer.

The D2C model is not just a challenge to retailers; the new route to market is shaking up incumbent brands and manufacturers too, who previously relied on the barriers to entry created by distribution hurdles to safeguard their margins. Now major consumer brands such as Nike are joining start-ups and everyone in between, selling direct to reduce costs, improve customer experiences, and regain control over their brand. There's a growing number of businesses that operate entirely through D2C retail; for others, it's a starting platform from which to grow and prove demand before investing in a store network, either of their own or following the more traditional retail route. For yet others, D2C is a new way to interact with their customers and drive revenue alongside their more established sales channels.

Whilst D2C does have its own challenges, the potential financial benefits are certainly appealing. By cutting out the intermediary businesses can also cut out the related costs. In addition, D2C also brings new opportunities for creating personalized experiences and even personalized products. For start-ups, it removes the slow process of trying to identify, meet and convince buyers in each retailer to agree to trial a product before committing to a larger order. Now you can launch far faster and to a global audience - assuming they can find you.

Direct Relationships

Most brands still sell through retailers and will continue to do so; it is the obvious way to access a well-established distribution channel. However, selling through retailers makes it difficult to understand who actually buys your product. It also creates additional layers between the brand and consumer. Brands need to build closer ties with the consumer and maximize the number of touchpoints they have with their customers to gather more data. For example, Nike announced[72] a change in its distribution strategy, intending to terminate supply to smaller independent retailers to direct more sales through its own online channels and physical stores. The Nike SNKRS mobile app is now the exclusive channel for many new product launches. In the fiscal year 2018, over a quarter ($10.4 billion) of Nike's global sales were D2C.

Opening a line of communication directly between business and consumer also allows the organization to gain control (or regain control) of customer data and use that data to optimize and improve user experience at every stage in the process. What that also means is that selling direct helps to take command of the customer-business relationship - and right there is the fundamental reason why this business model is becoming so popular. For products that users won't stumble across in a major supermarket or a main street store window, staying at the top of consumers' minds might involve more creativity and a social media campaign. Consumers are far more likely to connect with a marketing message that appears on their smartphone screen, and has a button linking them to relevant content, than a generic ad displayed on a billboard or sign in a retailer's main street window.

D2C brands can also innovate due to their relationship with their customer - for example, as well as being a digital clothing store, the Bonobos app uses location data, user behavior and previous purchases to offer a virtual personal stylist, recommending a full outfit to wear each day based on climate, personal style and selected level of formality. This builds a connection between the user and the brand, entices users to look at the app every day, and suggests how new purchases can be styled, encouraging engagement, purchases and loyalty.

Some of the most interesting native D2C firms at the time of writing include:

D2C Brand	Segment
Warby Parker	Eye wear
Casper	Mattresses
Glossier	Beauty
Away	Luggage
Harry's	Male Grooming
Allbirds	Sustainable Shoes
Hubble	Contact Lenses
Quip	Toothbrushes
Everlane	Ethical Apparel

As some of these online D2C brands grow in popularity, many of them are opening physical stores, reinforcing the points made earlier about people still wanting to see and touch many types of goods, as well as giving the benefits of visibility in the real world to build awareness and trust in the brand. It's also a sign of the rising costs of acquiring customers online and the halo effect on online sales seen in areas near physical stores.

D2C is not only disrupting products. Thanks to the reach of technology and changes in regulation, start-ups are moving into some of the most change-resistant services sectors of the economy

– i.e. personal banking. After decades of inertia, consumers are being offered, and accepting, new financial services providers that have no physical presence. In stark contrast to the visible main street branch integrity of banks of old, all household names, new names like Monzo, Starling, Revolut and N26 are seeing huge consumer take-up - acquiring millions of customers in Europe without the overhead of a branch network[73]. This is an example of humans starting to shop for services that were considered safe from online competition - most people "shop" for a bank once and stick with it for life. There is a harsh lesson here, not only for the incumbent banks but for any sector that relies on inertia and fails to innovate.

When Humans Stop Shopping at Retailers

"traditional advantages of scale, big brands and mass marketing have been all but eroded"

Barclays[74]

This is not an easy reimagining of consumer spending. Retailers have no divine right to exist. The number of retailers we see today is a relatively new phenomenon, even if it's largely the only paradigm most of us have grown up with, making it seem perhaps immutable. It served a purpose when it was unthinkable for a manufacturer to deal with end customers directly. Shipping to a wholesaler has been far easier for brands than picking and packing individual items for consumers until recent advances in logistics. There are undoubtedly sectors where retailers do add value, but in others, physical showrooms run by a D2C brand will ensure the intended brand experience more authentically.

This is no small phenomenon - almost half of consumers (48%) now purchase from disruptor brands, according to the IAB's Disrupting Brand Preference report[75]. Eighty-four percent of these shoppers are under 54, and they are also more likely to have a household income of more than $75,000.

The Internet has revolutionized how brands reach consumers, eroding reliance on expensive television adverts and physical shops. Although often largely hidden when blame for retailers' troubles is assigned to "online shopping", the growth of D2C represents a subtly different issue. This is not about users preferring Amazon over their main street. This is about consumers being able to find the products they want directly from the manufacturer without need for an intermediary - be it a main street retailer or an online retailer like Amazon. Now, consumers expect retailers to add value (usually in the form of convenience) or get out of the way.

Private Labels

We've already touched on the massive shifts facing brands and their role in modern retail – for example, consumers looking for brands that align with their world view, not just their budgets, the willingness of consumers to switch from trusted incumbents to D2C upstarts if research and reviews show merit in the new product, as well as the tendency for some consumers to seek out healthier alternatives.

As loyalty to established brands fades, we are also seeing growth in private label products - not by any means a new concept - but growing in popularity as big brands lose their luster in the face of more skeptical customers. Spending on private label may now be seen as a sign of smart shopping rather than an embarrassing lack of ability to purchase "prestige" brands. Private labels also illustrate some of the difficult "frenemy" relationship between brands and retailers. Retailers see what consumers are buying, how much they are willing to pay and then source competing products and give them shelf prominence over big name brands that spend billions on advertising. As retailers see brands taking the D2C route, they recognize that in many cases it's getting harder to survive selling other peoples' stuff and so are taking ownership of the product creation themselves.

Big Business

Own brand labels are big business. At $39bn in 2018, Costco's "Kirkland" private label brings in more revenue per annum than Macy's and JC Penney's revenues combined and accounts for about 20% of Costco's revenue. In late 2019, Target introduced a new food brand, Good & Gather, to join their children's apparel brand, launched in 2016, that now sells more than $2 billion a year. US number 2 grocery retailer, Kroger, offers Simple Truth - the US largest natural and organic brand. If Kroger's brands were on the Fortune 500, it would rank number 138.

Big retailers are focusing on driving private label growth in a bid to exert control over value chain - Kroger sees customers that shop its own brands spend 25% more and is forming a partnership with Walgreens that will place a curated selection of Kroger's popular brands in select stores. Conversely, select Kroger stores will offer a range of Walgreens health and beauty lines, including Boots Alliance brands No7 and Soap & Glory.

When Humans Switch Shopping

These retailer brands continue to take market share from national brands. An IRI report shows that private brand sales across the food, drug, mass, dollar and club retail channels grew four times faster than national brands in 2018. Meanwhile, the national brands fighting back by trying to become more like retailers, as they test and deploy their own direct-to-consumer initiatives discussed above. Most well-known brands now operate their own branded e-commerce sites and many brands are testing new direct-to-consumer models, such as Gillette's subscription razor service. So far however, retailers are launching successful private brands more quickly than incumbent brands are developing customer acquisition skills.

For big brands and retailers, making assumptions about consumers and dismissing competition is dangerous. For companies that rely on inertia or brand loyalty, it can and likely will prove fatal to assume that humans will keep shopping in the way you expect, "just because they're used to it". There's a salutary example in the UK if you look at the entry of the German discount supermarkets, Lidl and Aldi. When they arrived in the UK, the incumbents weren't concerned; *"We welcome the advent of Aldi and others to come,"* said Tesco managing director David Malpas[76]. *"We can live quite happily in our part of the market and they can live in theirs."* A few years later, nearly two-thirds of UK households now visit an Aldi or Lidl branch at least once every 12 weeks, according to the research firm Kantar Worldpanel, with their combined market share over 14% of the $230bn annual UK grocery market[77]. Aldi, for example, takes private label to extremes: more than 90% of the products it sells are private labels, and the big brands are often sold at substantial discounts to traditional retailers.

Amazon Own Brands

Amazon has come in for quite a lot of criticism for its use of private label products to grow its own sales, even though it's a standard retail tactic and has been for decades. However, the concerns lie in

Amazon's ability to promote its own brands even when consumers are clearly looking for a big brand item, as well as its exclusive access to comprehensive data about what consumers are buying.

In mid-2018[78], Amazon had over 70 private label brands covering mainly apparel, homeware and electronics. Having come in for criticism, Amazon responded that *"Private label products are a common retail practice, and Amazon's private label products are only about 1% of our total sales. This is far less than other retailers, many of whom have private label products that represent 25% or more of their sales"*

Figure 22 A selection of Amazon Own Brands. Source: Amazon.com

"It'll Never Work Online"

"Is Netflix a threat? It's a little bit like, is the Albanian army going to take over the world? I don't think so."

Time Warner CEO, Jeff Bewkes, 2010

We're now at the stage where it's far harder to think of things that aren't sold online than ones that are. We saw earlier how online has grown rapidly in the last decade, yet many leading traditional retailers argued away the online threat, stating that their business couldn't possibly work online - "people would never want to order <insert their product name here> online", so while the rest of the world crumbled around them, they would be fine. This widespread refusal to accept change has left many retailers scrambling to survive, as we discover that online purchasing suits customers for almost all sectors.

It turns out customers care more about price, quality, customer service and convenience rather than harboring some irrational loyalty to a physical location which may or may not have the stock they want, and where they may or may not encounter helpful staff, after struggling their way through traffic, finding expensive parking and investing hours of time into the attempted acquisition of a product. If anyone doubts the pace of change and the willingness of consumers to amend even their most entrenched shopping habits, the above examples should serve as a reminder that it's unwise to dismiss the power of convenience.

The prevailing wisdom was that categories involving specialist measuring or highly personal decisions were likely to remain immune from the rise of online shopping. Yet from categories such as Spectacles (Warby Parker) to Beauty (Glossier, Sephora), Shoes (Nike) and even Mattresses (Casper), the rise of online is hard to ignore, as is the deployment of technology into physical shopping experiences. Virtually no sector is immune from the influence of online. Perhaps some high-end retailers will escape but even those have been enthusiastic embracers of change and investments. Let's look at a few sectors to see where humans have stopped shopping solely in traditional channels.

Beauty

"We have a direct relationship with every single person who buys something from us, unlike all of the incumbent companies that have been built through retail channels. We've never existed through retail channels. We don't have plans to exist through retail channels. The reason being we think that through using technology, we can do three things very differently, than what all beauty companies have done in the past. One is channel. The second is discovery, and the third is listening at scale."

Emily Weiss, CEO, Glossier[79]

The beauty & cosmetics area was one where it was widely assumed consumers would continue to prefer an in-store experience. But the traditional bastion of cosmetic sales, the department store, has been eroded on multiple fronts - online and specialist stores. Social media has bolstered the success of specialty stores and cultivated a number of billion-dollar upstart beauty brands that are going head-to-head with well-established players like Estee Lauder. Leading US beauty specialist stores Sephora & Ulta are among the most innovative physical retailers[80]. They are keenly aware of Amazon's growing share of the sector and its partnership with celebrities such as Lady GaGa brand Haus Laboratories, as well as the launch of its own private label brand, Find[81]. The innovation in this highly contested space is likely to continue - the coveted Millennial and Gen Z cohorts are open to digital tools to help discover, try virtually, purchase and share beauty products[82]. Beauty is second only to gaming as the most viewed topic on YouTube but has seen only about 10% of sales move online so far[83]. And increased consumer interest in transparency and sustainability has seen the launch of own-brand ranges such as Sephora's "Clean".

Apparel

The apparel sector will come up for discussion frequently in this book. We're all used to buying clothes and the sector's continued status quo, save for the vagaries of the actual fashions, seemed assured. Yet apparel is a sector in trouble. Spending on clothes is in decline, the apparel sector accounted for the largest number of store closings in recent years and it faces sustained pressure from new shopping behaviors, workplace policy changes to more casual workwear, questions about its environmental impact, as well as alternative business models such as those from The RealReal and Stitch Fix.

People aren't shopping for clothes the way they used to - apparel commands just half the share of household spend it did in 1977. Consumers in the US now spend more of their budgets on technology than on clothing and footwear. Despite reservations about how suitable it is for sight-unseen purchasing, online shopping now represents about one-third of all apparel sales and according to Digital Commerce 360.com, 38.1% of apparel retailers in the Top 1000 have zero or one store[84].

Homeware

The fastest growing segment in e-retailing in 2018 was home goods, exhibiting 23.7% year on year growth, led by Amazon who sold $16.2 billion, equaling the combined web sales of home goods by the next four largest competitors (Wayfair, Walmart, Qurate Retail and Williams-Sonoma). Almost 10% of IKEA's sales are online. UK online furniture retailer, Made.com, has seen sales rise in recent years as consumers embrace shopping for even large items online - according to their CEO, "Furniture online is where fashion was five years ago."[85]

Interior Design

When people stop doing things in ways we're used to, they can also start doing things they weren't previously able to do. Technology will enable people to access goods and services that they couldn't before; services that were previously prohibitively expensive can be democratized by technology. For example, Interior design is one of the sectors now available online. Thanks to new 3D rendering technologies, the once elite world of interior design has become more affordable and more accessible. There are now multiple services offering decor advice and curation without as much as a single physical home visit.

In the US, services such as Havenly, Modsy or Decorist will offer advice on a room by room basis, complete with iterations once you fill in a style questionnaire and supply measurements and photos of your room. Some charge per room, while others rely on the affiliate commissions from furnishings purchased via the service. In the UK, services like Homewings offer free initial consultations and consolidated deliveries of all your chosen furnishings.

Homes

While you can already actually order a small prefabricated home from Amazon, it's conceivable that one day you'll be able to purchase a full-sized home online. Already, the majority of modern house-hunting takes place online rather than via estate agent/realtor catalogs or windows.

Figure 23 Allwood Claudia | 209 SQF Cabin Kit for $8700 (with free shipping) from Amazon.com

Realogy, the largest residential real estate brokerage company in the US is partnering with Amazon so that Amazon shoppers interested in a home are matched with a Realogy agent. Once the buyer closes on the home, Amazon connects them with services and experts in the area via the Amazon Home Services and provides a range of smart home products like the Amazon-owned Ring smart doorbells, alarms, lighting and cameras. In a move that may see more of the house buying process move online, a partnership between start up Notarize[86] that enables people to get documents notarized online, and Guaranteed Rate, one of the largest retail mortgage lenders in the U.S. allows customers to close real estate transactions and execute mortgages online.

Automobiles

In most US States, it's illegal to buy a car directly from a manufacturer - you must buy a car only from an authorized dealer. However, this model is being challenged as humans want to stop buying cars in this way and be allowed to buy them online. Led by Tesla, legal challenges are being mounted against this constraining system and it's likely we'll see the US follow other jurisdictions where it's possible to configure, order and buy a car entirely online. Just 1% of used cars and 0.7% of new cars were sold online in the US in 2018.

Several young companies are attempting to put the dealership online. Companies like Carvana, Shift, Vroom and Joydrive are putting the entire car buying process online, allowing customers to buy, trade-in and even test drive vehicles without talking to a salesperson. A giant vending machine might seem an unlikely way to pick up your car, but Carvana has built an 8-storey building that can store 27 vehicles. Carvana customers can browse a range of more than 15,000 vehicles online, then finance, purchase, trade in, and schedule as-soon-as-next-day Vending Machine pickup or home delivery.

Figure 24 A Carvana Vending Machine

Aimed squarely at a generation that grew up with smartphones and can't imagine needing to haggle with dealers, new electric car brand Polestar (a sister company to Volvo) has launched a Polestar Explore app where you can read about the Polestar 2, configure it, pre-order it and eventually buy or subscribe to it without having to visit a website or show up at a retail location.

Research shows that few people look forward to the traditional process of buying a car, and many dread the dealer interaction - 42 per cent of would-be buyers do not end up getting a car because of the pain of the process and 33 per cent would trade-in far more quickly if the experience was smoother[87].

In an effort to make the showroom more relevant to the contemporary consumer, Cadillac has introduced a feature where customers can schedule a one-way video call (you can see them but they can't see you) with a sales associate at a dealer and get a one-to-one guide around the car(s) of their choice, asking questions as they go.

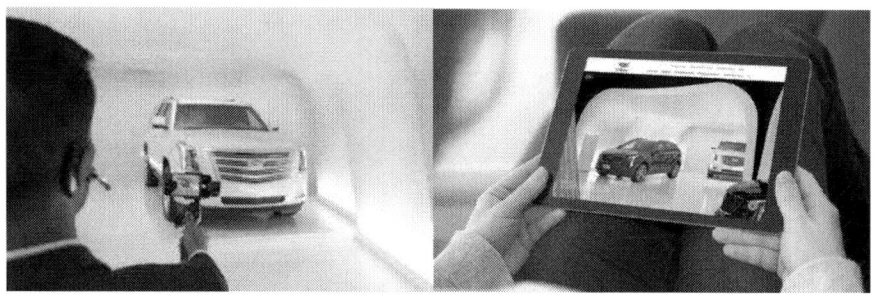

Figure 25 A Cadillac Agent (L) guides a customer (R) using the Cadillac Live video sales tool. Source: Cadillac

Pharmacy

The final example for this section on how shopping is changing involves Pharmaceutical products, perhaps more valuable to consumers than any other category after subsistence food and clothing. For many people, they have no choice but to purchase medicines which are frequently extremely expensive and only available through very controlled (and not always convenient) distribution. While over the counter and personal healthcare products are easy to sell online (as done by Amazon, Walmart, Walgreens, CVS, etc.), prescription medicines are not so easy, due to regulatory requirements and complex billing relationships with insurers and other players in the healthcare sector, where cash pay accounts for only 8% of the US drug market.

Services such as GoodRx Care, Hims, Hers, Nurx, Ro among others, offer customers an online medical service to get a doctor consultation, treatment, prescriptions and lab tests, but the interesting new entrant into this space is Amazon with its near $1 billion acquisition of PillPack, a service that creates personalized packages of prescription medicines and delivers them to customers in easy to use containers. It's hardly a coincidence that Amazon has added medication reminder functionality to its voice assistant, Alexa.

A special mention - Amazon

You can't credibly discuss the recent past, the present or the future of retail without devoting significant amounts of time to Amazon and the impact the now trillion-dollar company has had on shopping behaviors and the perception of retail. Most traditional retailers are obsessed with Amazon - a 2017 Reuters analysis found that nearly 700 U.S. companies mentioned the retail giant in their quarterly filings in the first half of the year alone. And while it's good to be aware of what Amazon is doing, how it's innovating and how it may impact the market, it's also important to remember that for all the coverage, Amazon accounts for just 4% of total US retail, though some estimates put their share of online spending at up to 50%.

The numbers relating to Amazon and consumers are sobering for any other retailer. When consumers are ready to buy a specific product, nearly three-quarters of them (74%), are going straight to Amazon to search - Amazon has overtaken Google as the key search engine for products. Fifty-eight percent of Amazon Prime members shop online at least once a week, while a whopping 9 out of 10 online shoppers visit Amazon at least once a month[88]. A comScore study of Holiday shopping in 2017 showed Americans spent 22.6 billion minutes on Amazon during December, substantially more than the combined total spent on the rest of the top 10 e-commerce retailers (16.6 billion minutes[89]). Nearly two thirds of Americans have bought something on Amazon[90].

And it's not just in the US; almost 90% of UK shoppers use Amazon and over 40% have access to its Prime subscription service; most Amazon.co.uk shoppers visit the online retailer at least once a month and just under a fifth once a week[91].

The formerly online-only retailer now occupies 20.1 million sq. ft. of bricks-and-mortar space, mostly in North America, after buying Whole Foods, the upmarket grocer, in 2017. Amazon opened its first branded shop, a bookstore in Seattle, in 2015. It now has 18 book shops in an estate that also includes 25 Amazon Go till-free stores from Seattle to New York and 18 planned Amazon 4-Star stores by the end of 2020.

Drawing heavily on both traditional retail practices such as private label, and investing heavily in myriad business models and advanced technologies to define the future shopping experience

(Dash, Alexa, Prime Air, Subscribe & Save, Scout & Amazon Go are among many that we'll talk about in later Chapters), Amazon is a formidable competitor and a consumer favorite. As we'll see throughout this book, Amazon is trying out a bewildering array of solutions to see what sticks. Drones, Robots, Dash, Key (Home, Garage & Car), Lockers, Anticipatory Shipping, Pantry, Voice and Go - as well as Air, Flex, FBA, Top-up, on top of Prime, Kindle, Video, Fire, Private Brands.

There are many entire books that look at Amazon and yet fail to explore all of its tentacles, so though we will make frequent reference to Amazon, this book will not seek to review every single Amazon initiative, but will discuss the most impactful ones, as well as a selection of the more speculative ideas that illustrate the scale of ambition and the willingness to experiment as it leads the drive to stop humans from shopping, or at least shopping anywhere else.

Another Revolution

"There's no doubt that retail is going through a huge period of disruption and technology is at the heart of the change. The old borders have gone, geographical borders are not what they were and the boundaries between online and offline are reducing every day. The winners are those who are thinking big, innovating fast, acting like disruptors and behaving agnostically across channels to make it easier for the customer and, ultimately, giving us consumers what we want."

Finlay Clark – Industry Head Retail, Google UK

Clearly, change is nothing new in retail. Over the decades, there have been several massive changes in retail, then as now, allied to the socio-economic and technological changes of the times. We've been through previous shifts from mom & pop stores/local stores to malls to discounters and more recently online. But while previous developments added choice and cost reductions, the more recent focus has been on convenience. The emphasis on speed will accelerate, and humans will largely opt out of certain types of buying.

In their attempts to better meet consumer expectations, retailers who want to survive will need to understand and embrace the changing ways people shop - even if that requires large-scale, on-going changes.

The culmination of the demographic and behavior changes we've talked about in this and the previous Chapter is the emergence of a hyper-informed, demanding and discerning consumer, regardless of generation. Today's shoppers are loyal only to their expectations of extreme convenience, accountable brands and transparent value.

Nobody in retail is immune from change. Unless you're offering something dependent on physical presence such as a nail bar or a hair salon, don't assume that shoppers won't be willing to buy online. And even if you're in that service business, make sure you've an online booking service or online interaction with your customers via CRM. Even offline businesses need to be online. And as we've seen, many online businesses can benefit from an offline presence or even just an interface for returns. There's no such thing as a purely online or purely offline business anymore. And that's a lot of change before we even consider the new ways to shop and selling to non-humans.

Consumer purchase behaviors are undergoing a titanic shift. Consumers are more informed, connected and empowered than ever and they know they have options as alternatives are only a click away. As far back as 2012, Econsultancy advised merchants "to make the purchase journey as short as possible." Today, that principle is even more foundational: fewer clicks, fewer screens, fewer fields, fewer taps, clicks, and swipes all add up to one thing: more customers. In the next Chapter, we'll look at how physical stores are also adapting to be ever faster.

The latest trends in retail are driven by a combination of an evolving technological landscape and the shifting preferences of consumers. By embracing these trends and preparing for them, retailers can look to the future as another positive opportunity to grow. Unfortunately, too many retailers are sluggish in adopting the retail strategies and supporting technologies to meet and accommodate consumers' wants. They fail to understand that these strategies and technologies are not fads, will eventually have to be adopted if they expect to compete, and that every day that passes without adoption contributes to lost sales and customer churn. Meeting consumers where they search, communicate, evaluate and buy, accommodating their communication and purchase preferences, and using data to foster and grow customer relationships – all these are must-do for retailers.

The changes we've seen in the last decade or so are just the beginning. We'll spend the rest of this book looking ahead to the even greater changes coming soon. Brands and retailers all need to change to meet the needs of the new shopper. Stores in main streets, malls and shopping centers need to reassess their function, provide a different experience, and see digital tools as providing a complementary service. Today's highly connected shopper doesn't think in terms of physical, online or mobile. They simply want to shop with their preferred store or brand how and when they want and enjoy the best experience possible when they do. Which means that retailers and brands must break from the siloed approach that assigned different teams and strategies to each of its channels and instead take an integrated view of its customers, operations and stores.

Clearly, today's shopper is very different than those of just a few years ago, whatever age group they belong too. While some traditional behaviors persist, what consumers are looking for, what's important to them and how they view shopping are all changing. Let's continue by examining how stores are attempting to make the shopping experience easier.

Chapter 4: Faster Stores

"We've seen how technology can make online shopping more efficient, with lower prices, more selection and increased convenience. We are about to see the same thing happen to offline shopping".

Hal Varian, Chief Economist, Google

The successive revolutions in retail over the last 50 years or so have made it easier to consume than at any point in human history. The move from "mom and pop" local stores to department stores, from department stores to malls, from malls to big box outlets, from big box to online has seen choice and product availability explode. Yet despite the change in store size, location and range, the in-store layout has remained relatively unchanged - shelves of items, fixed till positions and some form of physical payment mechanism, such as cash or a card.

We've talked in the previous Chapters about the impact of online shopping but the first set of technologies to look at as we consider the continuing evolution of shopping is how what can be called "traditional shopping" is changing. For years, the only real visible "technology" in retail tended to be the cash register. Now though, there are myriad technological approaches to easing the shopping process and most focus on increasing the speed of the shopping journey for customers.

As we've said, there are still a lot of positives about going to a store; seeing the item you want in real life and taking it away with you right then and there. But a number of things can slow down this process, referred to in the technology industry as "friction". Eliminating these delays, inconveniences and queues could make shopping a faster, more enjoyable and more efficient process for both the retailer and the consumer. The automation of shopping and creation of micro-conveniences - even when you didn't realize there was friction - is a key focus for retailers seeking to make stores a better experience.

Throughput

Many people still like physical stores and want to see familiar retailers remain on the main street and in the mall, but for such stores to be competitive in an age of online retail, as a minimum they need to operate more efficiently than ever before. Leaving aside political and public policy issues such as main street taxation, pedestrianization and expensive on-street parking, stores need to reduce their operating expenses and increase their operational efficiency, before we talk about improving or dramatically enhancing customer experience, a topic we'll return to in Chapter 9. Especially in sectors that require relatively little customer interaction, stores need to be able to serve more people more quickly without increasing costs, and preferably decreasing them. For stores not pursuing "experiential retail" - where the aim is to engage the customer - getting as many customers served in as little time as possible is a key aim.

Adding technology to existing processes is now a natural evolution in most industries seeking productivity improvements. New developments mean manual processes can be speeded up and even allow for agency to be transferred - what previously required a store employee can now be delegated to a machine or directly to the customer. Such changes can yield significant savings for the retailer as customers take on tasks such as scanning items for checkout. Another approach is to use technology to eliminate rather than speed up an existing process, thereby creating more dramatic overall speed improvements.

Intending shoppers go through a number of stages as they shop. Starting with a decision to enter a particular store, they then discover or locate items of interest, possibly seek some additional information, make a purchase decision, checkout and pay. Technology is being applied to each step of this journey with a mixture of solutions powering retail change that is visible and invisible (to shoppers). As we'll see in this Chapter, some solutions are predicated on the consumer supplying the technology themselves (a smartphone) while others are retailer-owned and operated.

Speed Shopping

Shopping is increasingly about speed. Unless looking for big ticket items or browsing for inspiration, people are spending less time in shops, expecting to find their target item (usually thoroughly researched online before purchase) and exit as swiftly as possible, often choosing physical shopping over online purely for the instant gratification or to avoid delivery hassles. According to surveys, the least popular aspect of physical shopping is waiting to pay - 75% of consumer's number one physical store complaint is waiting in line[92].

Figure 26 Speed is Important to Customers[93]

In this section, we'll examine 3 broad categories that are seeing major innovation and investment from leading retailers, all with the common theme of speed.

- Faster selection of items
- Faster ways to checkout & pay
- Faster ways to operate stores

Displaying Your Wares/Window Shopping

Before we even enter a store, technology is frequently being deployed to bombard us with higher quality messages; messages that are more relevant, contextual and up to date. Just as cheaper flat screens have permeated our homes and our hands, so too have display technology improvements taken up residence in many shops. With many printed posters in windows being replaced by large displays, stores now have much more eye-catching graphic communication opportunities.

Since the 18th century, retailers have relied on windows to offer consumers an enticing glimpse of what's on offer inside. The storefront area/window is one of a retailer's key interaction points for consumers. It's expensive space to rent, expensive to dress and slow to update at scale. Traditional window displays required extensive printing, sticking to windows, and timely set-up and teardown procedures - often at the mercy of mall owners for access. Window space was also typically very rigid, operating on monthly update cycle determined by a central marketing team in head office. I recall the low-tech days in retail when the best you could do in terms of localization was to send stores a double-sided poster and hope that they would be dynamic enough to change it around to suit local preferences. Despite the operational challenges of display poster management and attractively merchandising, window space remains valuable to retailers - it's an effective touchpoint for customers - highly visible and quite measurable.

As the cost of display technologies decreases, retailers are rushing to make their window space more dynamic. Now, a centrally controlled screen can be used to catch passers-by by showing full motion video with captivating messages. The messages can be changed dynamically based on time of day, weather, local stock levels or even who is looking at it. Got a lunchtime special? Then promote it only at lunchtime. Promote what you have in stock now, not what you had expected to be in stock when the poster was printed. Avoid a situation where you've printed a poster and sent it to stores for their windows only for the product launch to be delayed and leave you with empty window poster slots. While futuristic film Minority Report showed displays that adapted to customers based on recognition, before we get there (and we will), retailers are using dynamic displays to make their windows work harder and be more relevant based on other factors. Digital displays allow for variations that printed material simply doesn't.

Windows that Watch

"We track how many people are taking their photographs and sharing them back out. We also have methods in place to track how many people are passing by the windows, stopping and engaging."

Frank Berman, Chief Marketing Officer, Bloomingdale's[94]

The levels of data capture, analysis and dynamism for window displays now mirror the emphasis of a website landing page. The simplest solution is monitoring photos uploaded to social networking sites from the store location as an indicator of engagement, while the more sophisticated windows use sensors to track the number of passers-by, as well as any dwell time in front of displays. Japanese technology giant Fujitsu has demonstrated line of sight/gaze tracking that can then customize displays based on what consumers are looking at - so if a consumer is looking at a window, and paying particular attention to a specific item, the display can react with more detail about that item.

Figure 27 A Full Window Digital Display

Moving Inside

If fancy displays are designed to entice us into the store, once we're inside, the majority of effort is going into making the store more informative, more interactive and more helpful. As window-displays get larger, brighter and more responsive, it is the potential of additional displays within the store that are rapidly attracting retailer interest. Carrying the display screen theme inside, large displays are providing interactive store guides to assist with price display, promotional merchandising and wayfinding.

According to Premier Mounts, a company that develops digital signs for restaurants and other businesses, the average rise in annual sales attributed to digital menu boards at quick-service restaurants is 3% to 5% and somewhere between 30% to 40% of large, nationwide chains are now implementing digital menu boards[95]. McDonalds spent over $300m to acquire an AI company, Dynamic Yield, to power its digital drive-thru menu displays. Thanks to the technology, a different menu can be presented to each customer, factoring in considerations like the weather (more hot drinks on the menu in cold weather), stock levels in each restaurant and current order preparation times.

Back in 2015, Tesco created 2-dimensional stores in high traffic locations, like subways in Korea, by using displays with QR codes that people could scan to buy and have delivery timed for just after they arrive home after work.

Figure 28 A shoppable subway station display wall in South Korea

Shelf Displays

While online shopping has what's known as endless aisles which can display as many items as users are willing to scroll or search through, even the largest physical stores have a finite amount of shelf space and need to make the most out of available square footage. With developments in technology, attention is turning to the edge of shelves - a small space but very directly in the customers' eye line.

If you've visited a Best Buy store in the US since early 2019, you may have noticed that in many locations, they've rolled out miniature e-ink displays with pricing and product information replacing the traditional printed cards. Equipping shelves with dynamic price displays is initially expensive, (Best Buy spent $30m to outfit 150 stores) but offers several benefits to the retailer, along with the potential for full payback of the capital cost in less than a couple of years through operational savings. (E-Ink displays require very little power but can only display text rather than high resolution color images or video content.)

Figure 29 A Best Buy store in Manhattan with individual shelf edge price/information displays

Faster Prices

While most shoppers probably prefer cheaper prices, retailers are often more concerned about accurate and stable prices. There are often times when a retailer might be willing/able to reduce the price but is hesitant to do so due to the operational overhead of updating the price on the shelves. This may not be a problem for the owner of a corner shop, but for a chain or multiple with thousands of SKUs across hundreds or thousands of locations, printing and applying updated price tickets is a non-trivial concern. The logistics of deciding and then executing a price change leads many retailers to operate on a weekly or even monthly cycle of price changes and store collateral refreshes. This places them at a distinct disadvantage compared to online operations where prices can be changed instantly, or indeed varied dynamically for different visitors. The current cumbersome process typically looks like this:

- A pricing or propositions team in the retailer's HQ sets the retail price, based on various factors such as the wholesale cost, available promotional subsidies and sales targets.
- The pricing is approved internally, and tickets are sent to a printer
- The printed price tickets are sorted and sent to all store branches
- At the assigned time, store staff manually go around the store removing the old price and positioning the new price ticket for affected items
- A store manager or retail compliance resource typically checks the store to ensure that updated pricing and collateral is correctly displayed, usually sending photos of key displays to HQ for validation
- Prices are then usually fixed until the next cycle unless a major change is required for competitive reasons

As you can see, managing the display of prices in traditional stores is a slow and costly operating expense for retailers who would dearly wish to deploy their staff more effectively than on replacing pricing cards. Especially at sale time, where widespread updates are required, stores will often have to pay for extra staff shifts to display all the updated prices - ironically adding to their costs to sell the goods at lower prices. This places physical retail at a distinct disadvantage compared to online, where most sites use algorithms to monitor competitor pricing and can update based on the results of these algorithms as often as required - frequently multiple times per day. Such variability also allows for testing of price elasticity with small cohorts. Reacting to changes in supply and demand, competitor changes, promotions or even experimenting with price elasticity, web sites have almost infinite flexibility with pricing display. As long as retailers continue to run actual physical print jobs to change their prices in-store, online retailers will always have a significant pricing arbitrage opportunity.

While the advent of barcodes at least removed the need for retailers to label each individual item - though cumbersome, shelf-level pricing is a big advance from manual pricing guns and stickers on each individual item - printing prices at the shelf edge that matches the price to be paid at the till is a rigid one-size-fits-all approach. Now, in some physical Amazon stores, you need to scan the item barcode with your Amazon app to see the price - it's a different price if you're a Prime subscriber or not. This approach not only allows Amazon to offer special prices, but also provides a wealth of detailed insights - they can tell which items are being picked up, by whom and what the conversion rate is. In most jurisdictions, there are strong consumer protection laws that require stores to display correct pricing, with a risk of penalties for failure to do so. That makes auditable displays attractive to store owners.

If e-ink shelf edge price displays represent a first step into the future world of enhanced consumer information interactions in physical stores, the second step may see the installation of more advanced solutions. While the move to dynamic displays may provide long term benefits for retailers, it's of little benefit to consumers. Improved pricing may encourage some additional impulse purchases, but today's consumers are already extremely likely to price-compare online and simply challenge the retailer to match the best price available or lose the sale.

Although the initial goal for shelf edge price displays may be to improve customer communication and to reduce operational overhead, another key area of interest to retailers is that of dynamic pricing. While the benefits of timely price updates are interesting, displays also open the possibility of dynamic prices - prices that respond to people or events, not just updates from the pricing team. Department store owner John Wanamaker is credited[96] with popularizing price tags in the late 1890s and since then, consumers have been used to standard pricing rather than haggling in most stores.

In food retail, in-store dynamic pricing and other strategies have the added possibility of reducing food waste - retailers can respond easily to a product being near its expiry date and offer it at a discount, given that many consumers won't be willing to pay full price for it.

Beyond Prices - Faster Information

Consumers' knowledge and interest in more information is a topic we'll return to regularly throughout this book. While most consumers now enter a store armed with more knowledge than ever before, they are also eager for up-to-the-minute information about the products in front of them. As we'll see later, they frequently turn to their mobile to search for information, reviews and price comparisons, but shelf-edge displays offer retailers the opportunity to present timely information about products without having to ensure either a trained associate is nearby or that a printed card is available.

Figure 30 Kroger Self Edge Displays showing pricing and promotion information

Leading US retailer Kroger and Microsoft have developed a digital shelving system that can communicate everything from prices and promotions to nutritional and dietary information. Beyond the shelf edges, they are also experimenting with cameras to estimate the demographics of shoppers. This enables them to see if particular messages or prices resonate better with older or younger shoppers or if different genders respond differently.

I can imagine a future iteration of these technologies that would see the shelf edge display respond to what it can perceive - if it detects a consumer hesitating, it could flash up additional information. Or perhaps it could offer competitor brands the chance to display a counteroffer via real time bidding. Imagine if a shelf noticed you were choosing between products and could offer a brand the chance to give you a special deal!

Guided Shopping

One of the slowest elements of a shopping trip may be finding the items you know you want among the thousands of SKUs on display. Although supermarkets tend to lay out items in fairly logical groups, you may still struggle to find your favored item among the huge range of similar products. Regular shoppers may get used to where to look for their recurring purchases but often give up trying to find new items or infrequently purchased items, leading to lost potential sales. But it's not generally economical for stores to have sufficiently trained knowledgeable staff in every aisle to answer customers' questions. It's especially frustrating for retailers who have sourced the desired items to miss out on a sale just because a consumer can't locate it, just as it's frustrating for consumers unable to find what they want, even when they're pretty sure it's in stock.

In a Seattle suburb, not far from Microsoft's sprawling headquarters, you can visit one of the most advanced supermarkets in the world. Serving as a testbed for a variety of technology-based ideas for improving retail, the Kroger store in Bella Botega is one of only two places so far that you can see these technologies in operation. The first impression of this store is that it is like any other supermarket. The shopping experience is at first generally similar to the vast majority of large grocery stores. However, as you move along each aisle, you may start to notice the key enabling technology in this store - the shelf edges are in fact color displays - small screens that run the entire length of each shelf on each aisle. These displays show the price tags for each item, and also allow for video content to catch your attention, highlight special deals or promote new products.

Although full color displays with dynamic pricing can be very eye-catching, the Microsoft and Kroger teams have taken things a step further, building on the availability of these displays to offer what they call Guided Shopping - an innovative way to shop that guides you around the store. Several supermarket apps already offer to organize your shopping list into the appropriate order for a particular store layout to speed your journey through the store and avoid backtracking, but without detailed location tracking, they can't ensure you don't bypass the location of the items you're looking for.

But the Microsoft/Kroger Guided Shopping solution leverages the dynamic displays to show you around the store, item by item from your list. To start, you input your shopping list into their app, either manually or based on a shopping profile you've built up with them from traditional shopping. Then, as you enter the store, you open the app and it assigns an icon to you. When I tried it, I was a 'Carrot'. Then as I walked around the store, the screen display beneath each product I wanted flashed a carrot. Once I scanned the item and added it to my cart, the display returned to the static price information and I moved to the next item, with the app telling me the aisle and location, confirmed again with the flashing carrot motif.

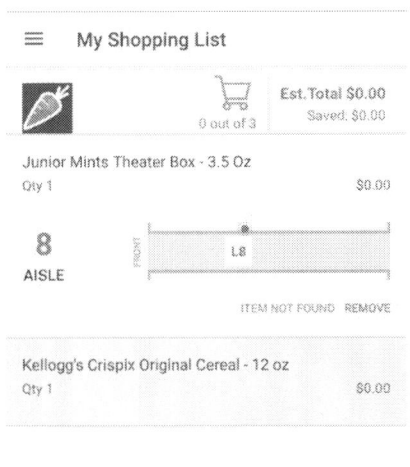

Figure 31 Kroger app showing my Avatar (Carrot) & next item location

Figure 32 Shelf display alternates between my avatar (carrot) and price information (R)

The Kroger app then offers you the chance to pay in the app for your scanned purchases and simply leave the store without queuing at any checkout.

Other ways to way find things

While the Kroger/Microsoft solution is very flexible, it is also currently very costly to deploy. Wayfinding in-store will likely see a variety of solutions being tested in the coming years, to better guide shoppers in a hurry to locate their items. As far back as 2016, Macy's partnered with IBM for a trial experience known as "Macy's On Call" where customers could input questions in natural language regarding things like where specific products, departments, and brands are located, to what services and facilities can be found in a particular store. In Europe, giant electronics retailer MediaMarkt has added test navigation features to its app, based on signaling installed in the ceiling lights to enable the app to locate the customer precisely.

Automating Physical Retail

Automating in retail isn't particularly new. Vending machines are a common sight (especially in cities like Tokyo where they seem to be on every street) for products from soda and chocolate to the Best Buy vending machines, common in US airports, to extend reach to even the remote piers. Incidentally, you will often see new retail approaches being trialed in airports as they are great venues for testing things - secure environments, a typically comparatively affluent demographic and a relatively technology-oriented population sample.

As we discuss these latest moves towards automation, you'll notice a variation in the rate of change across different retail sectors. Some sectors are easier to automate than others, and some parts of the shopping process are easier to automate. Some of the solutions shown in this Chapter are focused on improving narrow parts of the process, while others attempt to remove multiple points of friction, from the moment you enter a store until you leave clutching your purchase. The urgency of change is also in many cases related to the level of incursion from online shopping into a particular segment - shops feeling the pressure the most from online are the ones being forced into evaluating improvements to the shopping experience. In this section, I'll focus on the changes specifically geared towards helping the customer to shop more easily and faster. For retailers focused more on competing based on deeper customer experiences rather than on speed, we'll return to that topic in Chapter 9 - when it's not about experience it's about value and speed.

Avoiding Abandonment

Speed matters to retailers, not just impatient consumers - speedier transactions will reduce their costs, not just avoid lost sales due to abandonment. I had a conversation a few years back with the MD of a leading UK clothes retailer who told me they were seeing abandonment rates of 34% if there was a queue of more than 3 people at the till. While he couldn't tell me what proportion of those potential sales were completed later, either in store or online, it's clear that a horrifying proportion of sales is being lost due to a poor experience in shops, especially involving queues. And you can't blame Amazon for queues in stores being so long as to be off-putting. However, speedy transactions are thankfully more commonly the norm due to barcode scanning and more cashless payments. This reduces the number of till operators required, freeing up staff to spend more time advising customers or restocking shelves.

Although stores thrive on footfall and high conversion rates, and often seek to generate a sense of "buzz", having a busy store can also be a negative. Aside from abandonment issues, tests have shown that customers purchase less when stores are busy, feeling pressured by the crowds and keen to get out.

Of course, there are going to be peaks and troughs of footfall and, anyway, dealing with a surge of customers is, on balance, a problem that most store managers would like to have. One Head of a chain of retail stores I know told me of a boss who would call her when they walked past one of the stores and saw a queue. "Why don't you have enough staff on?", they would challenge her. On the days there weren't queues, the boss called and asked why there were so many staff standing around, and then rang the Head of Marketing, and asked why the campaigns weren't driving more footfall into stores. Retail is not an easy business!

While some purchases require an interaction between sales assistant and customer, many do not, with the only requirement being the payment and perhaps bagging of the item(s). Reducing checkout queues is typically a matter of opening more till points and optimizing the individual transaction time; another approach is to transfer the transactional element as much as possible to the customer, not store staff.

Self Service

One of the most visible changes to many stores in recent years has been the growth of self-checkout facilities. It is now possible, in many grocery and convenience stores in particular, to pick the items you want, bring them to a scanning machine, scan each item, bag and pay for them, all without interacting with a single member of store staff.

By shifting the effort to the customer, a store can typically reduce the number of staff on duty, perhaps replacing several checkout staff with a single operator overseeing several self-checkout machines and responding to their intermittent inability to process items successfully. The world's largest supplier of these machines, NCR, advertises that each of its self-checkout lanes, which cost around $30,000 per unit, typically pays for itself in twelve to eighteen months.

In the world of physical retail, there's been a huge trend in recent years to install self-checkouts in supermarkets. Although touted as speeding up shopping for consumers by reducing dependence on staffed checkout points, there are many who believe it's inspired even more by cost cutting than by a desire for speed. In truth, it's probably a mixture of perceived speed reductions, genuine speed improvements in some situations and staff cost reductions. Self-serve checkouts first became common in the 1990s. There are now well over 250,000 in operation worldwide. According to US retailer Target, approximately one-third of shoppers proactively choose self-checkout, even if a human-staffed point is available without a queue. Though frequently frustrating to use due to failures to scan and weigh items correctly, the cost benefits for operators of automated solutions are compelling - at airport check-in, for instance, the cost to process a passenger through an electronic terminal (14 cents[97]) is a fraction of what it costs the airline with a staffed desk ($3). And although some reports note a tendency for otherwise trustworthy shoppers to sometimes steal items, other investigations show that people spend more when they don't feel they and their purchases are being judged by a human cashier - a

McDonald's analysis[98] found that people ordering at kiosks spend an average of 30% more than counter-orders.

Kiosks Don't Judge

It's not only checkout self-service that is becoming popular. McDonalds is perhaps the most visible rollout of self-ordering technology. It offers global consistency of experience - I've walked into McDonald's as far apart as Seattle, Stockholm, Seoul and Singapore to see the same interface - without any language barriers.

The kiosks offer dynamic menu control, simply hiding items that are out of stock or unavailable. Automating the order taking process makes it easy to manage the sales process - especially the upsell and cross-sell. Instead of the traditional approach of training store staff and having update briefings for them on priority items, the kiosk can, with 100% compliance, offer guests the preferred optional extras. The addition of kiosks has also allowed McDonalds to offer "table delivery service", which makes for a more satisfactory experience than standing waiting for your food, blocking the ordering point for other customers.

Although the McDonalds implementations are thus far relatively straight-forward tech, other examples have seen the application of more advanced features such as sentiment detection to judge a consumer's mood and potential reaction to an additional offer. The use of such cameras to assess a consumer is a topic we'll return to in a later Chapter.

In terms of speed, an experienced human cashier will outpace a self-checkout, but in reality, it's usually a race between a cashier and multiple self-checkouts, so the overall throughput will be higher. There's also the phenomenon known as "wait warping" - the idea that giving the shopper something to do and/or think about gives the illusion that things are moving faster than they are. Some shoppers would rather feel occupied by scanning their own goods rather than wait for a faster staff member to scan items for them.

Better Scanning

Barcodes were first used in retail in 1974; the first product ever scanned at a checkout was a pack of Wrigley's Juicy Fruit chewing gum. Proving that innovation doesn't always require expensive technology, German discount supermarket Aldi print 4 barcodes on their own-brand items, one on each side of an item to make it easier to scan rather than having checkout operators hunt for a barcode - a simple low tech solution to faster checkouts.

The proliferation in recent years of self-serve checkouts is not universally popular but, like all technology, they are likely to improve. The cost savings are too attractive for retailers, even at the risk of some mild user dissatisfaction. We can soon expect even the self-serve checkout machines to boast new features, using technologies such as computer vision. In order to speed their operation and accuracy, the machines will soon have AI-enabled visual recognition technology to address pain points such as produce selection. The new versions will use cameras and Machine Learning to identify and suggest for example "1 Granny Smith Apple", rather than expecting the consumer to select Fruit->Apple->Type->Quantity. This will also benefit retailers in reducing barcode swapping scams and intentional item mis-selection.

As noted above, long wait time at checkout is the number one customer complaint in stores. From a merchant's point of view, if they add up the transaction times for a whole store over a long period, slow processing of customers is expensive. So, shaving even small amounts off transaction times is attractive to reduce queues.

Modern Shoplifting

If retailers are worried that humans may stop shopping, you can be sure they'd very much welcome it if humans would stop shoplifting! Although it's hard to get exact figures on customer abuse of self-checkouts and scanning solutions, some anonymous surveys of customers have suggested that nearly 1 in 5 customers have stolen items[99].

Less Checkouts

If you analyze the flow of shoppers who walk around a store, select the items and then bring them to a designated location for processing/payment, it's obvious that there's potential for a delay-inducing bottleneck at the point of scanning. It also means that items can't be packed if they need to be scanned at a fixed location before you leave the store. Solutions to improve this range from scan-as-you-go, to having roaming staff who checkout customers and accept payment.

Roaming Staff

This is being tackled in a number of different ways, depending on the sector. Apple Stores have always eschewed the traditional idea of a fixed till point - they have always offered checkout by any staff member via their mobile device. Once you can find a free associate, the dreaded concept of a queue for checkout is no more! This concept has now spread to others, especially in stores where a customer is typically buying a small number of items. Mobile checkouts in the form of a store member who can scan and accept payment anywhere in the store via a mobile device, are being trialed in stores such as Walmart, Macy's and Best Buy. In Walmart's first trial of its 'Check Out With Me' service, over 1 million transactions were processed during the Holiday 2018 season[100].

Figure 33 A roving Walmart employee who can process payments via mobile device

Scan-As-You-Go

For sectors such as grocery, where the customer may be purchasing a large number of items or there are higher numbers of customers, solutions that enable the customer to scan items themselves as they pick them are an alternative to fixed self-checkout scanners near the point of exit. These typically come in two forms - dedicated scanning devices or self-scanning via an app on the customer's phone. Depending on the store, there is usually some form of check/oversight by a staff member at the exit.

Dedicated Scanners

Before smartphones with cameras and apps capable of recognizing barcodes became common, some supermarkets had already begun to experiment with the provision of portable scanners for customers to scan items as they filled their shopping cart.

Dedicated scanners offer several advantages over app/phone-based scanners:

- They are optimized for scanning, using a laser rather than the camera to read the barcodes faster
- They are toughened and likely to survive a fall better than the customer's phone
- The retailer won't get any questions about compatibility where the app doesn't work on a customer's phone
- The consumer doesn't have to ensure their phone is charged sufficiently for a long shop (camera use is quite draining of a phone's battery)

App-based Scanning

Compared to dedicated scanners, asking customers to download an app and use their smartphone to scan has a number of advantages:

- Cheaper than buying a large number of scanners
- No need for a recharging bay for the dedicated scanners
- The phone apps can also process payments
- The phone app can provide additional product detail and offers

Continuing the theme of faster shopping, see below the Walmart in-store presentation of their latest scanning feature, where you can see the final check points for app users on exit.

Figure 34 The exit route for users of Walmart app at a Canadian store

Kroger's "Scan, Bag, Go" feature allows a shopper — either with their mobile or with a handheld — to scan products as they walk around the store, and then leave without waiting in line. It also gives them a running total of their spending was as they shop.

It's not just large supermarket stores that are adopting self-scanning solutions, with interest extending to smaller convenience formats such as 7Eleven. Starting at its concept store in Dallas and extending to selected New York stores, customers can use the 7Eleven app to scan an item's barcode and pay on their mobile. The phone is then placed on a reader situated near the exit which flashes and makes a noise to alert associates to the sale. One step that 7Eleven has taken to make its scan-and-go technology as frictionless as possible is personalizing the app experience. Customers who regularly buy the same items will be prompted with those products when opening the app, so they don't have to find the barcode and scan the product.

While there have been several initiatives recently that use a smartphone app to let customers self-checkout, apparel retailer

Stance[101] has tested a solution that doesn't need the app, as it offers a browser-based self-checkout option. Customers simply open a short URL on their smartphone and then scan the barcodes of the products they want to buy before paying. By removing the need to download an app, Stance has removed a barrier in the self-checkout process.

Better Scanning

Just as fixed self-checkout machines discussed above are changing to use computer vision to supplement or replace barcode scanning, there's a clear trend in app-based scanners to offer improved scanning technologies. Sam's Club, a subsidiary of Walmart is trialing an update to its app using computer vision to remove the need for barcode scanning. The new scanning technology will instead use computer vision and ML (machine learning) to recognize products without scanning the barcode, cutting the time it takes for the app to identify the product being purchased.

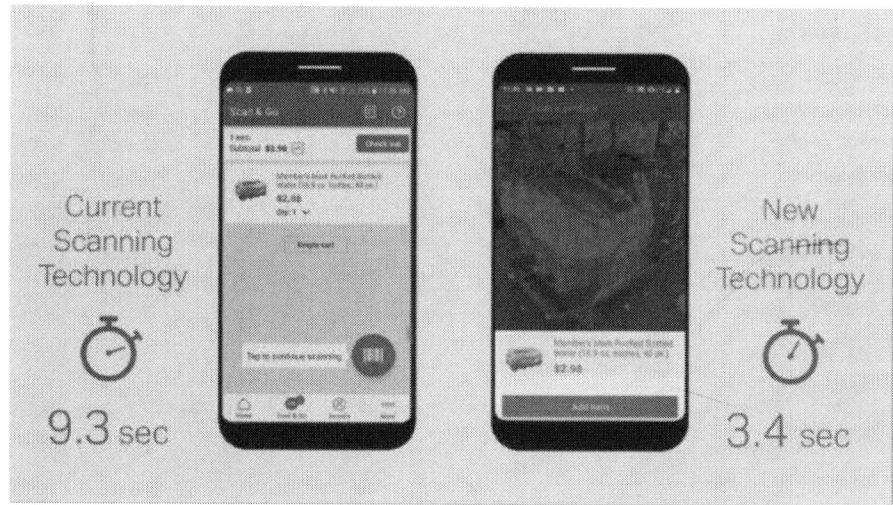

Figure 35 Sam's Club Scanning improvements

Customer Response

Self-service scanning checkouts are not universally popular with customers; their introduction is clearly a retailer-led rather than customer-driven development. But thinking back to Chapter 2 where we talked about differences in behaviors between groups, the enthusiasm for using self-scanning technologies varies greatly by age: three quarters of young people are interested in Scan & Go, with only 1 in 10 of those over 70 interested in the technology. This is due to older generations being used to a certain way of shopping and seeing no significant personal benefit in taking on what for years has been the work of store staff. It should serve as a cautionary reminder that stores need to cater for different tastes, and while they may choose to setup primarily for a certain type of customer, they can easily alienate a sizable demographic with overly insistent use of newer technologies.

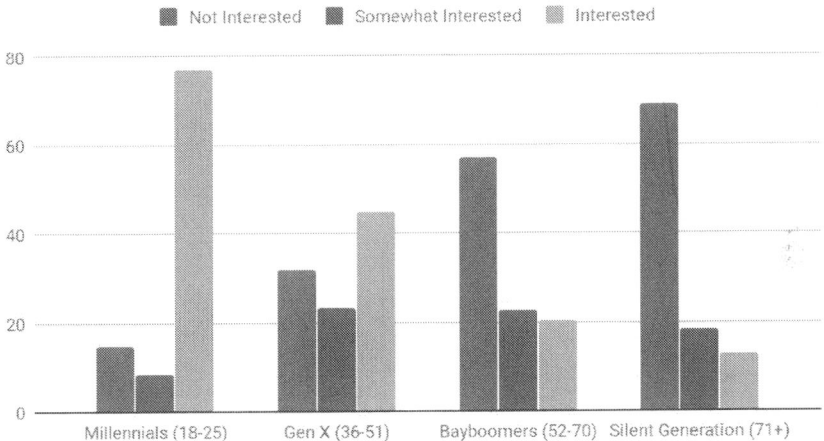

Figure 36 *Reported interest levels in Scan & Go technologies varies by demographics*[102]

According to Sainsbury's[103], in the 350 stores across the UK where its app-based scan and checkout feature is available, 15% of sales are now made through the app. When I tried using it, the requirement to sign up for their loyalty scheme (Nectar) before being able to use the app seemed an unfortunate barrier to usage. Shortly after opening a checkout-less, scan and go store in Holborn, London in April 2019, negative customer feedback saw the reintroduction of a small number of staffed checkouts to facilitate customers who didn't have the app.

No More Checkouts

Although moving the scanning from a central point to the point of item pickup is more efficient, scanning goods and then checking out as a final step, even when mobile, slows down the progress of the shopper as they move through the store selecting each item. The nirvana for both shopper and retailer would be to be able to walk into a store, pick up the items you want, leave and pay for them seamlessly. Although high tech solutions were mooted by IBM using RFID[104] technology as far back as 2006, it took until 2017 for this scenario to become even a limited reality.

If the elimination of checkouts and the associated queues is a physical retailer's fantasy, leading online retailer Amazon might not be the obvious source of a solution, but thanks to its application of technology to the problem, Amazon became the first to offer US customers a glimpse of one potential evolution of physical shopping.

Amazon Go

The next generation of shops may be radically different from what we're used to today. Taking self-serve to its ultimate conclusion, there has been a concerted effort to remove the entire process of checking out and even the need to self-scan.

The concept of a store without checkouts isn't as new as you might think. In 1937, an inventive grocer tried to create an automated store, called Keedoozle[105], that delivered customer orders via a conveyor belt system. Although he never managed to perfect the technology, recent advances have brought the idea back to the table.

In 2006, IBM showed a concept video[106] of someone picking up items and walking out of a store, apparently without paying for them. Using RFID technology, IBM imagined that such a store would be possible. The drawback of RFID is that the store would have had to add a tag to every item - and though inexpensive, it wouldn't be practical to add to every item in every store. Nothing much was heard from the technology sector on the idea for another 10 years.

"We asked ourselves: what if we could create a shopping experience with no lines and no checkout? Could we push the

boundaries of computer vision and machine learning to create a store where customers could simply take what they want and go? Our answer to those questions is Amazon Go and Just Walk Out Shopping."

Amazon.com

In December 2016, Amazon unveiled its concept store - Amazon Go[107]. A store without checkouts, you just grab the stuff you want and walk out, with the details of what you bought charged to your Amazon account as you leave. There are no cashiers, no lines, no fumbling for a credit card. You identify yourself to the system by scanning a QR code in your Amazon Go app as you enter the store. From then on, ML-powered cameras in the ceiling track your every move and note what you pick up (and if you put it back down). The initial store on the Amazon campus in Seattle is small at 1,800 square feet in size, stocking perishable grocery goods like bread, milk, and cheese, as well as pre-made snacks and fresh meals. In early 2020, Amazon opened its first larger format Go Grocery site at just over 10,000 sq. ft.

Figure 37 An Amazon Go Checkout-less store - entry gates (L) and the ceiling is watching (R)

Around the same time as Amazon unveiled Go, IBM was back with its Instant Checkout[108]. Although not as slick as the Amazon store, it is perhaps more practical for existing stores, requiring little in the way of retrofitting. IBM proudly claimed "it takes only five seconds for the instant checkout to complete a transaction for any number of items – unlike traditional self-checkouts and cashier checkouts that take longer the more items you buy, due to the need for scanning individual barcodes with instant checkout generally performing 15 times faster than a self-checkout, and seven times faster than a cashier."

In the U.S., the average convenience store visit lasts about three and a half minutes[109]—including the walk from car to store. It takes, on average, 71 seconds to select items, 42 seconds to wait in line, and 21 seconds to pay. The Amazon Go concept cuts out the 63 seconds of waiting and paying - personally, my record for a trip to an Amazon Go store is just 9 seconds! Alongside the customer benefits of not having to scan items or queue to pay, a system like this has other benefits for the store operator - it can, for example, relay real-time stock information to staff who can replenish items, avoiding stock outs.

While Amazon Go has attracted the most coverage, and around 25 stores had opened in the US by the end of 2019, there is a growing number of competitor solutions entering the space with similar solutions, aimed at helping incumbents compete with Amazon's new stores - examples include Grabango, Standard Cognition, Zippin, Sensei, Trigo and AiFi. It's unlikely that all of these will survive, and, in any event, I would anticipate either consolidations, or acquisition by larger retailers in the coming years.

Smart Carts

Another approach being put forward for faster shopping is to add technology to the trusty old shopping cart. Arguably easier than expecting customers to pick items while trying to scan them with a handheld scanner or with their phone, smart carts could allow for customers to use both hands to shop, while the cart contains the scanner, along with a screen to display a running total as well as promotions. Start-up Caper offers a cart with built-in barcode scanner and credit card swiper and it's finalizing the technology to scan items you drop in automatically thanks to three image recognition cameras and a weight sensor.

Figure 38 A prototype of a Smart Cart from Caper

When a customer exits the store, a green light on the shopping cart indicates that their order is complete, and they're charged. If something goes wrong, the light turns red, and a store employee is summoned. Caper and another start-up, Veeve, say it's much easier to add technology to the shopping cart than to an entire store.

Tech Too Far?

As is so often the case with new technologies, there has been some opposition to the advent of stores where the emphasis on convenience arguably has a human cost. Of course, no more checkouts means no more cashiers. According to the Bureau of Labor Statistics in the US there are 3.4 million people employed as cashiers[110]. Aside from the concern of people who miss the human interaction of a staffed checkout, the employment implications of a threat to what is traditionally a low-entry barrier occupation (i.e. doesn't require a degree) is a major potential downside to AI being deployed on a large scale in the retail sector.

There is a need for tech enthusiasts to manage any transition to automation realistically. As mentioned above, UK supermarket

Sainsbury's faced a backlash from customers when it converted one of its London convenience stores to a scan-and-shop only store, removing the option to pay manually. It has now had to restore a traditional till and two self-checkouts, alongside the app-based scan-and-shop process.

Aside from the concern about jobs, there have been other negative responses to Amazon Go and the march of automation, relating to the loss of social interaction. Though predictable for any new technology and unlikely to ultimately affect the rollout of similar solutions, it's worth remembering that new technologies will be criticized, sometimes resisted but usually improved by genuinely considering criticism, rather than just dismissing those raising objections as 'luddites'.

Waiting to Pay

People who lack experience of retailing might initially think that store owners and designers have always placed a high priority on providing quick and easy access to the goods customers want and therefore the emphasis on speed I'm talking about here shouldn't be seen as new. But while a quick journey in and out of the store may be what the customer always wants, that is not always the case for the retailer. For decades, retailers have engaged in the practice of "putting milk at the back", forcing consumers to walk through the store to get to popular and essential products, in the hopes that they would pick up other items on their way through. And although much of this Chapter is devoted to attempts to reduce the time customers spend in checkout lines, improving the speed of service can come with a downside for store owners - many place high margin, impulse purchase items along the queue path and see high attach rates as bored consumers make indiscriminate purchases as they hover.

Anecdotally, these purchases have dwindled in recent years as impatient line-waiters turn to their phone for amusement, rather than picking up the carefully positioned items, such as chewing-gum, as we saw in the previous Chapter. The financial impact of this is not to be underestimated: "The drudgery of unoccupied time also accounts in large measure for the popularity of impulse-buy items, which earn supermarkets about $5.5 billion annually". According to the New York Times[111], Americans spend some 37 billion hours per year waiting in line. However, as consumer expectations shift towards their own convenience, they are less willing to tolerate retailers who don't make shopping easy and hassle free.

Payments

Regardless of how quickly you can assemble the items you want to purchase and reach a point of checkout (as we've seen, hopefully without a queue), the length of time taken to complete the transaction is another important area of focus for improvement. It needs to be speedy but yet secure and retailers obviously want the lowest possible fees for processing payments.

Whether it's groceries or clothing, an important part of any transaction is, of course, the exchange of payment. After centuries of cash being the dominant mechanism for the transfer of value, the payments world has seen large amounts of innovation in recent years as retailers seek to make it easier and faster for us to buy things and financial institutions try to capture as much transaction value as they can.

Paying for things has gotten a lot more convenient over the years. From the rather imprecise mechanics of barter and the attendant problem of coincidence of wants, we moved to coins and notes with stored value, to credit/debit cards and mobile payments. Cash was relatively quick - though we've all seen the look of a cashier when tendering a note they consider too large for the transaction and then they have to calculate and gather the requisite change. Credit (and latterly Debit) cards are the globally accepted spiritual successor to the tabs once run by individual stores. 2016 saw card use finally overtake cash in the UK, with debit cards leading the way[112]. The popularity of contactless payments for small transactions has bolstered the switch from cash in recent years.

Faster Cards

If you ask anyone under the age of 30, they probably couldn't explain why some numbers on the front of a credit card are embossed and they'll likely never have endured the delay of a cashier filling in the details by hand and then handing over the multi-layer slip for them to sign, as was the process in the 1990s.

The ability to swipe a card through a POS terminal for the electronic transfer of the card details was a huge time saver compared to the manual transfer process. The introduction of chip and pin in 2004 was intended to reduce card fraud but for many people it was slower than swiping a card. Upgrades to the terminals can reduce the chip reading time from about 10 seconds to about 2 seconds, but that depends on merchants updating their terminals.

Contactless

Not long after chip and pin, the first contactless cards were issued. These allow for payments to be made simply by tapping the contactless payment method on a terminal. The contactless chip can be embedded in a debit/credit/transit card, a phone, a watch, a sticker or a key fob. In contrast to chip and pin transactions, contactless specifications require a contactless tap to execute in under 500 milliseconds. Ten years after the introduction of contactless to the UK, more than half of all transactions today - up to the £30 spending limit - are made using the 'touch and go' technology.

Phone Payments

In late 2014, Apple announced the launch of Apple Pay with the iPhone 6 - contactless payments built into the iPhone. Google followed with Android Pay (now rebranded as Google Pay) less than a year later and it's now common for most mid and upper tier Android handsets to include the technology (NFC) required.

Not all phone-based payments are contactless. In China for example, the dominant form of payment involves scanning a QR code with either the WeChat or Alipay apps. The importance of mobile Chinese payments providers is further illustrated by the acceptance of Alipay at over 7,000 US Walgreens stores[113].

Developing markets are also embracing the convenience of digital payments. In Kenya and Tanzania, M-Pesa is an SMS-based system for storing and transferring money. Although credit card payments are popular with consumers in many countries and offer fast payments in stores, there are many countries where credit cards and even bank accounts are less common. In these countries, mobile payments are even more popular. For example, credit card penetration remains at 10% or less in Thailand, Indonesia and Vietnam, while mobile payments are used by 47% to 67% of the population in those countries, according to data from the World Bank, Nomura and Japan's economy ministry.

Some retailers have developed their own payment and loyalty

platforms to increase customer lock-in. Among them is Starbucks, whose order and pay app represents over 12% of transactions, while its total holding from customers via Starbucks Cards (physical and virtual) is over $1.6bn according to their 2018 annual report. It's also interesting to see another of the world's most valuable companies, Apple, introduce the Apple Card (a credit card backed by Goldman Sachs) with rewards to entice consumers to stay within the Apple ecosystem.

Barclaycard Dine and Dash

Over one-third of diners in restaurants find waiting for the bill the most frustrating part of eating out, and one solution is to enable them to pay for their meal when they're finished, without waiting for the bill to arrive, then for the server to go get the card machine, then return to take payment. A small device from Barclaycard on each table is being trialed as a solution to this. The diners use an app to check in to their table and later to make their payment. The device color alerts restaurant staff that payment has been made.

Figure 39 Dine and Dash tabletop terminal from Barclaycard

Biometric Payments

Looking to the future beyond phone payments, there is likely to be an increase in biometric payment options aimed at increasing both security and convenience. The iPhone X popularized facial recognition as a form of identification, replacing the fingerprint. However, already in 2017, 700 KFC stores in China introduced Alipay's "Smile to Pay" facial recognition technology to authenticate payments. After consumer negativity that the camera wasn't always flattering, Alipay have added the option of "beauty filters" to present the customer with a more agreeable image as their face is validated.

Similarly, WeChat has introduced a new payment device for offline payments. The point-of-sale (POS) machine features a 10-inch screen capable of displaying promotional messages to the consumer, while a second screen displays customer information to the till operator. Given the controversy over facial recognition technology - which has been banned in some US jurisdictions - this technology may not become widespread outside China.

Figure 40 A WeChat Facial Recognition Payment device

Aside from facial recognition, UK company Fingopay has trialed a system based on scanning the unique vein pattern in a shoppers finger, while at time of writing, Amazon is reported to be working on hand scanning technology for payment authentication, that would enable people to pay with a scan of their hand, avoiding the need to take out a card or phone to pay[114].

Fast, Invisible & Future

Perhaps the most notable thing about payments is how much effort goes into making them invisible. Just as you now get out of an Uber or Lyft without the old process of fumbling with cash to pay for a taxi, many payments, even outside seamless in-app transactions have been reduced to the tap of a phone or card with no physical exchange and no concept of change being given back. With biometrics, just a quick glance at a camera can be enough to confirm a payment. Mercedes Benz has a system where the car can pay directly for parking or fuel[115]. I have a coffee mug that has a contactless payment chip in the base - we are going to see payments embedded more seamlessly and, in more devices, so humans spend less time thinking about payments.

As it gets easier and faster and less involved to spend money, there is a very real danger in such a world that we will spend more money than we intend to. Researchers coined a name for this: It's called the credit card premium[116]. In short, when you don't have cash, you spend more money. It makes perfect sense — parting with a crisp $20 bill is a little more painful than a thoughtless swipe of a card, even if you tacked on a few more items to raise your total to $25 that wouldn't have been possible with the cash option. The majority of consumers behave in this way, and businesses are foaming at the pocketbook to get in line. We are clearly in the middle of the culture of convenience at any (reasonable) cost.

Pay Later

Picking up on the generational differences we discussed in Chapter 2, the importance of available payment options varies across cohorts. Studies have shown that the younger generations are more credit averse than older generations, who quickly adapted to the novelty of credit cards. YouGov found that people of all ages make similar use of debit cards and PayPal accounts, but Millennials are significantly less likely to own a credit card than Gen X – at 51% against 71%.

In order to maintain their appeal to these crucial younger shoppers, retailers are rolling out buy now, pay later solutions with interest-free instalments via providers like Klarna, Laybuy and Afterpay. Among the big names adding these options are H&M, JD Sports and Boohoo.com.

Using Cash Online

Online giants Uber (via Walmart) and Amazon (via Western Union) both offer a mechanism to top up your online balance via cash or pay for purchases in selected stores, blurring the lines between online and offline but also enabling online payments via cash. Amazon Paycode is a feature that lets you complete a purchase online and then go to a physical location (Western Union, Safeway and others) and pay via cash within 48 hours to have your order shipped. The feature was available at launch in 20 countries, with more expected to follow.

Figure 41 Amazon accept cash for online payments via Western Union locations

Speed - Saving Time or Money?

If you look carefully at the trends appearing across retail, it's hard not to conclude that automation is invading retail at an accelerating pace. From finding products to paying for them, the shopping and payments processes (outside of luxury items) are significantly faster than ever before.

Moving along the continuum of solutions, retailers can look at automating existing experiences and then replacing them entirely. Although presented in the name of efficiency, it's clear that cost reductions are appealing to retailers as much as efforts to improve customer experience. This is especially so as operating costs for physical retail (at lot of which are staff costs) are coming under pressure from online. The starting point is the emphasis in recent years on speeding up shopping. Or is it an emphasis on reducing labor costs? It probably depends on which side of the transaction you're on. The truth is likely to be somewhere in the middle. But self-scanning for example takes a task that retail staff have typically done and transfers the effort, the former service, back to the consumer. And with this transfer comes cost savings for retailers, despite the increased risk of dishonesty. Although an experienced checkout operator will process more items per minute than typical customers, by having control of the process, we feel more empowered and time passes more quickly as we're involved and occupied, rather than standing waiting for someone else to serve us.

After Faster Shops

So, based on the trials taking place now, you can expect to see far more automation in stores - changes designed to reduce costs and make physical shopping faster. Automation of tasks, such as cleaning and stock monitoring, that take staff away from customer service. Will these be enough to save physical retail? Will retailers really redeploy rather than replace human staff?

Next up, having considered how existing stores are getting faster, let's look at emerging new ways to shop that, frighteningly for many retailers, don't involve stores at all.

Chapter 5: New Ways to Shop: Channels

"Every touchpoint — from digital to TV, radio and social networks — will let shoppers complete immediate purchases on the spot."

Greg Yevich, co-founder, OperationROI

Just as we've seen the emphasis on speed and convenience in physical shopping, there are myriad innovations to create ever more opportunities for purchases outside stores. For most of the last decade, this has meant online shopping via web sites and apps, but as we'll see, there are more ways than ever to shop digitally, many of which require less time/attention/interaction than a website.

Customers are shopping in new ways, in new places, at new times. They are researching, buying, selling and renting across a variety of new platforms, using an array of new tools to maximize their time and money. Many of these changes mean less time spent shopping as we've known it. In this Chapter, we'll see some of the new ways to shop, with transactions occurring outside brand or retailer-controlled platforms, and as new sources of inspiration replace advertising and more traditional merchandizing and promotional tactics.

So Many Channels

Retail used to consist of a fairly limited number of channels. The biggest variation for the latter half of the 20th century was the size and location of the stores. From department stores, to out-of-town retail parks to malls, most retailers stuck exclusively to physical stores, while some traded via catalogs. Few operated across all channels. Then came the explosion of online shopping as we've discussed, and now all but the smallest stores have a website, even if it's a simple hosted solution with a platform such as Shopify or maybe just a presence on a marketplace such as eBay or Esty.

But there's no respite for retailers after the great move online - now virtually every major retailer has an app and significant presence on multiple social channels as new ways to shop online emerge; it seems like the audience is getting ever more fragmented and digital teams have to contend with an ever expanding array of potential channels. Customers expect to be able to buy from their preferred supplier through whatever platform they are on in the moment without having to leave their experience and go to a retailer site or app - those brands and retailers which aren't buyable at all times stand to lose out.

Though a constantly moving target, the next generation of shoppable technologies and platforms need ongoing awareness from, and consideration, by brands and retailers. The good news is that an organization well setup for online interactions via web or mobile is probably reasonably well positioned to consider emerging channels such as social commerce and new interfaces which we'll see in the next Chapter.

Augmented Online: What's Next

"All evidence points to the fact that we are heading into an online retail future that could make ecommerce as we know it today, look like a catalog of old".

Reengineering Retail - Doug Stephens, Chapter 7

As discussed in Chapter 3, given how disruptive web and mobile shopping have been to retail already, it may seem strange to some to find it being discussed again under new ways to shop. Although only really prevalent for less than 10 years, it seems like we've been talking about e-commerce for a long time. I want to take some time here to review where we're at with online shopping - because if you're still thinking of it as new, or less important than your retail stores, there's little point in even talking about other emerging channels. A customer-centric strategy that is digitally focused is the foundation of any modern retailer - without this bedrock, you won't be able to adopt any other new channels effectively and you risk falling further behind.

If you have an effective web site and mobile strategy, then pause only briefly to congratulate yourself and get ready for the next paradigm shift. Digital shopping is entering a new phase, with soaring consumer expectations, and several important new technologies enabling more compelling experiences. The only consoling news is that many of the operational changes made to support your website will help prepare you for the next wave of digital shopping channels. Real-time inventory management, better product imagery, more complete product metadata and other work that underpins a modern efficient, digital organization are prerequisites for what's to come.

Building on the Basics

It used to be that building a basic web site and optimizing as best you could for a good Google search ranking was enough to tick the box for a digital strategy. Now, retailers must wrestle with whether or not to develop an app, whether their products are "Instagrammable" or whether they need to work with "influencers". Is your inventory management ready for showrooming (customers using mobile while in store) and webrooming (people using online to research and purchasing in physical stores)? If not, it's unlikely to be ready to cope with orders coming via social channels, via voice assistants or via a camera search.

Let's start with how familiar online shopping via a website is changing, before diving into the emerging adjacent digital channels. Simple checkout, good search, multiple payment options, customer reviews, clear delivery information and clear returns policy are now absolute minimum requirements and failure on any of these basics will likely send away shoppers in their droves. And remember that online, the next supplier is only a click away if your web site is slow to load, confusing or in any way lacking.

AI & Personalization

Algorithms can now trawl through masses of consumer data and identify patterns or probabilities that a human wouldn't see or think to look for. This enables the creation of personalized recommendations at huge scale. For example, coffee giant Starbucks uses the data gathered from its loyalty program to create over 400,000 highly personalized email variants per week, instead of the previous approach of using just 30 variations of emailed offers[117]. The data is also used to assess the popularity of products, gain insights into how different locations are trading and plan staffing optimizations for anticipated customer flows. Being a successful retailer at scale now requires deep technological expertise and application.

Though not as visible as the changes to physical stores in the previous Chapter, tools such as AI are having a far more immediate impact on customers, as leading retailers invest in technology to power efficiencies in both physical and online operations.

In China, leading online retailer Alibaba has invested heavily in AI technologies to improve its websites and apps. From subtle improvements in search results to fully individually personalized shopfront pages and chatbots, artificial intelligence is now at the core of Alibaba's e-commerce operations at all stages of the customer journey. In 2018, during the 24 hour 11.11 Global Shopping Festival, Alibaba for the first time achieved personalization for all of its China retail marketplaces, from the Taobao and Tmall homepages to special promotions pages to product details pages - some 6.7 billion personalized shopping pages were generated by more than 230,000 merchants. The payoff: personalized landing pages had a 20% higher conversion rate compared with non-personalized pages, according to Alibaba[118].

In Europe, the largest online fashion retailer, Zalando, has added an AI-powered recommendations assistant to its site. Once a customer selects a piece of clothing, algorithms instantly suggest an entire outfit to complement the selected item. The Zalando assistant makes its suggestions based not only on the style, but also considers the shopper's past choices and budget from previous orders[119]. Built with input from the firm's human stylists, the online platform can scale to offer instant fashion advice to consumers with highly personalized curation and accuracy far in excess of basic "you may also like" recommendation engines.

Shopping Platforms

As the digital commerce market starts to mature, the quality and depth of the services on offer "off the shelf" are improving and it's questionable for all but the largest retailers as to whether the decreasing compromises of packaged solutions don't outweigh the cost and complexity of building your own. The advanced features developed by the leaders in the ecommerce space are quickly available via shopping platforms, or in cases like the service "Amazon Personalize", available from Amazon itself for use on third party sites.

With Amazon Personalize, you provide an activity stream from your application – clicks, page views, signups, purchases, and so forth – as well as an inventory of the items you want to recommend, such as articles, products, videos, or music. You can also choose to provide Amazon Personalize with additional demographic information from your users such as age, or geographic location. Amazon Personalize will process and examine the data, identify what is meaningful, select the right algorithms, and train and optimize a personalization model that is customized for your data. All data analyzed by Amazon Personalize is kept private and secure, and only used for your customized recommendations. You can serve personalized recommendations via a simple API call. You pay only for what you use, and there are no minimum fees or upfront commitments[120].

Social: Buying, Selling & Customer Care

"Social media shopping through sites such as Instagram and Facebook is a natural progression as brands continue to try and reach the digital-native modern customer. With the sheer amount of time that younger generations spend on social media, the move to social commerce is inevitable. It is clear the nature of the shopping experience is changing dramatically, with consumers wanting a seamless and consistent experience across channels. Social commerce is now one of those channels."

Kevin Murray, Managing Director, Greenlight Commerce[121]

Although retailers may expect customers to come to their digital properties (web sites and/or apps) as they would have previously visited physical stores, the growth of social media brings with it a new set of challenges for brands and retailers. Interacting with customers via social media sites is a clear example of the changes facing retailers and brands - new channels appearing rapidly, loss of control compared to having customers in your stores or on your website, new commercial models and further pressure on inventory and logistics capabilities. It also shows how quickly change can happen - despite brands and retailers investing heavily in building web sites and apps, consumers now learn about products via photos uploaded to Instagram, rather than via the official product photos so carefully arranged on a brand app or retailer's website product detail pages.

While concerns about Amazon and Google taking shoppers away from retail stores may garner the most media attention, it's not only these giants that are important for searching and shopping - social media sites can be a major entry point for inspiration, discovery and transactions. In the past, someone looking for shopping inspiration and advice might have asked a friend or traveled to their local store. More recently, they would have been likely to go online and search on Google or visit a brand or retailer website. Today however, they're turning to a variety of social media sites to discover - in fact, 90% of people say they discover new brands or products on YouTube[122].

Social media is not only about researching and selling products - it is often the first port of call for dissatisfied customers to complain or seek redress. The speed and scale of social media is a double-edged sword - while brands will want new product introductions to "go viral", the ability for social media to amplify negative comments requires swift interventions to manage unhappy customers.

Growth of Social

Money typically follows people and as users spend more time on social media, it's inevitable that companies will look for ways to directly monetize in that environment. Why leave your social media to go to Amazon to buy a product if you can buy it directly from within the social media app? This provides social media companies with a much-desired revenue stream aside from advertising. According to Mary Meeker's 2018 Internet Trends report, some 55% of online US adults have bought a product after discovering it on social media.

There is however quite a big difference in the use of social media to inspire purchases across age groups. This 2018 study from PWC Ireland[123] shows how important it is to younger generations compared to older shoppers.

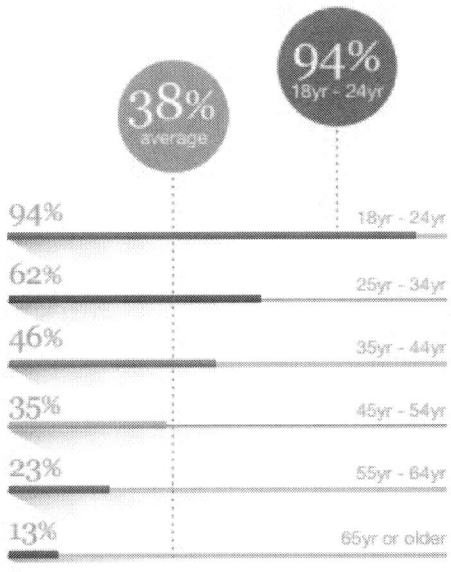

Figure 42 Social Media as an inspiration to purchase, by age group. Source: PWC

Going Where the Audience is

Discovering what consumers want, and when, is the key to a successful retail business. Understanding how to influence consumers into purchasing is a continual headache for brands and retailers. The process of finding out where people are, what they are doing and how they are consuming information has become dauntingly fractured.

Today's consumers are online, mobile, and social. And they expect their favorite brands to be so as well. We talked earlier about how retailers can interact with mobile users via a mobile web site and/or by creating a mobile app and working to grow the installation and use of the app. Whether a retailer chooses to focus on a mobile web and/or mobile app approach, either of those assumes that you can attract a consumer to your digital presence. Trouble is, people spend the majority of their time online on other platforms, and only visit retailer properties when they specifically intend to discover or purchase.

The amount of time that consumers spend on social media compared to the time they spend on the open web represents a huge shift. So, if you wish to engage your customers, you'll need to meet them where they communicate. Waiting for them to come to your communications channels is an open invitation for one of your more forward-thinking competitors to engage your customers while you sit on the sidelines, oblivious to the customer churn about to take place around you.

While some retailers will invest heavily in creating and promoting their own app to offer the best shopping experience, one of the strongest arguments against having your own app as a retailer is that you're better to try to sell to people where they are spending their time, rather than trying to lure them into your app. And where do people spend most of their online time? On platforms such as Instagram and Pinterest.

Listening

One of the best retailer trainers I ever worked with always emphasized the importance of listening to customers rather than rushing to sell to them. Even if a brand or retailer isn't yet actively creating and managing its presence on social media, you can be sure that consumers are talking about them, so it's important to be aware of, and able to manage, these discussions. Across all social media properties, it's vital to listen/observe before engaging. Each platform has its own norms, expectations and rules. Violating those customs for blatant self-serving interests will likely turn a retail revenue opportunity into a customer relations disaster.

Thankfully, there are plenty of tools now available to help brands find and manage opportunities for social selling, as well as identifying negative customer sentiment. Social listening tools can search platforms for mentions of company or product names (yours or your competitors) and bring them to the attention of the social media team to be routed to the appropriate sales, marketing or customer care staff. The prevailing advice of experts is that responses on social platforms should tend towards advice, information or help rather than high pressure sales.

To detect these buyer opportunities, firms need to deploy a social listening tool which automatically searches the social web for specific company and product keywords. These can identify buyer inquiries, and then capture, categorize, prioritize and route those buyers' online social questions and comments to inside sales for qualification and response. When responding, it's critical to recognize the reply should offer advice, information or help – and not be a sales pitch. There's a need to respect that it's a social forum, not your store - be accessible and inspiring, without being intrusive.

Selling on Social

The takeaway here for retailers? Those that want to reach Millennials and Gen Z had better make a commitment to social. Brands that are not active on social channels are viewed as less trustworthy. For example, Gen Z expects brands to showcase their personality online. If a retailer wants to connect and influence purchases, they need to be active and responsive on social. If a retailer isn't, their younger customers are. Many Gen Z apparel customers post pictures of items they are considering and then 46% make a purchase based on the feedback (social proof) to that post.

Looking briefly at what consumers are looking for from brands and retailers on social, the following list from Sprout Social provides an interesting insight into consumer thinking and expectations. As we've seen before, it's not just about pricing or products - consumers are looking for brand alignment and a 'tone of voice' that appeals to them as individuals.

Brand Actions that prompt Customers to purchase (2017)

- Being Responsive: 48%
- Offering Promotions: 46%
- Providing Educational Content: 42%
- Sharing Interesting Visuals: 38%
- Being Funny: 36%
- Providing Behind-the-Scenes Content: 27%

Faster Selling

Returning to the recurring theme of speed in contemporary trading, selling on social also changes the product release cadence required. In order to attract attention, appear relevant and claim a place at the top of dynamic feeds, brands need a constant stream of new products. For example, the traditional seasonal approach to fashion doesn't provide the regular new images common on

Instagram. It's pretty amazing to think that the appetite for new photos on Instagram is enough to upend decades of tradition, even among luxury brands who are now moving to shorter intervals between new product drops.

Social sites now account for about 10% of referral traffic to ecommerce sites, while nearly 1 in 3 Internet users have bought a product via a social site. While referrals are something web sites are very familiar with thanks to Google directing so much Internet traffic, the concept of purchases being made via social sites themselves is newer. Social shopping will continue to grow as new in-platform features transform the way people interact with brands and products. We'll discuss shortly how Instagram and Pinterest are pushing this agenda. Why are they interested in turning their social sites into shopping sites? Social networks are almost always free to the consumer end user, but yet incur sizable development and operating costs. In order to cover these costs, most social networks rely on selling targeted advertising to brands and retailers keen to reach their micro-segmented audiences. But direct advertising is not always welcome in a social media setting. Display adverts with loud calls to action may appear as intrusive. So commerce is another potential revenue channel that has social media platforms excited.

Instagram is the new Mall

"Instagram has become the window display for a new generation of savvy shoppers – and it's changing the way we consume style"

The Guardian[124]

Among the wide range of social media platforms in popular use at the time of writing (early 2020), Instagram has become a clear favorite for reaching consumers, with 71% of U.S. businesses already using Instagram. It's not hard to see why - of Instagram's 1 billion monthly active users, more than 500 million of them use the platform every day[125]. It's a mobile-first platform that's very visual, and offers a highly engaged, global, young audience attractive to many sectors - 88% of users are outside the U.S. 70% of Instagram users around the globe are under the age of 35. 80% of users follow at least one brand on Instagram, with 60% of these users saying they've discovered new products or services through the platform. At least 30% of Instagram users have purchased products they discovered on Instagram[126] and the site has progressively introduced shopping features to capture more value from the shopping discovery and intent it generates among its users. Facebook Head of Industry Karin Tracy says Instagram is now the number 1 source for discovering fashion and beauty products – 90 million people tap shopping tags every month[127].

Instagram has gained a reputation as a discovery channel for consumers, but it can also drive sales and advocacy for brands. Simply by being on Instagram, brands can make a positive impression on potential shoppers - Facebook claims[128] that people surveyed say that they perceive brands on Instagram as popular (78%), creative (77%), entertaining (76%) and relevant (74%). Of those surveyed, 87% said that they took action after seeing product information on Instagram, such as following a brand, visiting its website or making a purchase online.

Instagram has clearly seen the demand for improved commerce features and has steadily added several tools to make it easier for brands not only to promote their products but sell directly to consumers. These features include Business Profiles, Polls, shoppable Stickers, as well as improved analytics/insights about people that interact with their profile.

Instagram Checkout

Starting in March 2019, Instagram began adding its most advanced shopping feature yet - a direct, in-app checkout, so that people could purchase items from an Instagram post without leaving Instagram. This should capture more sales with less drop-off than when people leave Instagram to complete the checkout on a brand or retailer site (which may or may not feature a smooth checkout). Previously, while businesses could tag items in images as being for sale, the consumer had to be motivated enough to complete the purchase, having clicked through to the retailer site.

In order to use the checkout feature, the business posting on Instagram has to tag the items for sale in each post. Then, when consumers tap on those tags and see a product page, a "checkout on Instagram" button is displayed. Consumers can pay in three different ways: saving their payment information in the Instagram app (first time they shop), entering it during checkout each time, or paying with PayPal. Instagram has also added buyer protection and the ability for consumers to connect directly with brands as part of checkout. Instagram is working with partners like Shopify and BigCommerce to make it easier for merchants to integrate the checkout on Instagram feature with their existing e-commerce operations. Shipment and delivery notifications for purchases also appear inside Instagram, keeping users on the platform. Shortly after launching with major brands, Instagram expanded the checkout feature to influencers (more on this below), not just those businesses with commercial profiles.

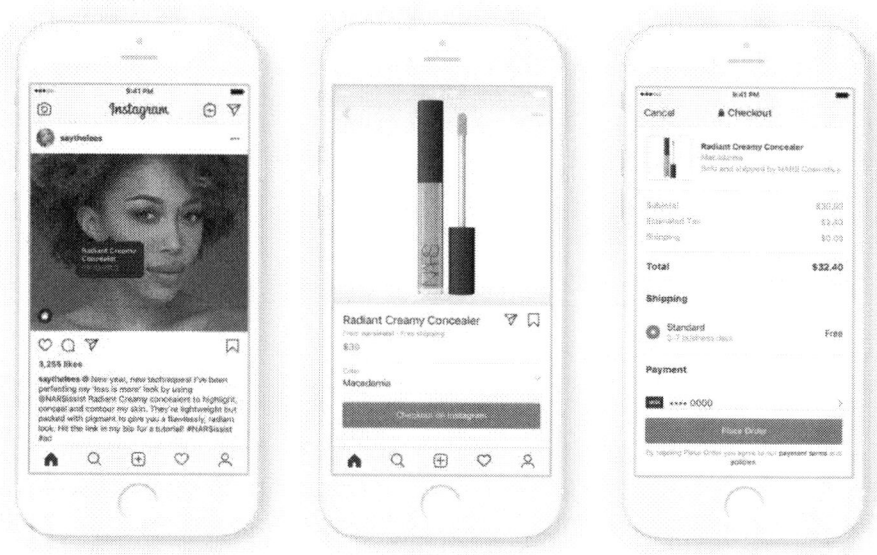

Figure 43 An Instagram Checkout Experience

While selling on Instagram gives brands direct access to a valuable cohort of shoppers, it does require relinquishing control of the customer. The primary relationship is between Instagram and its users, not between the brand and the consumer, except when things go wrong, the consumer will blame the brand more often than Instagram. The cut of the transaction that goes to Instagram makes the cost of doing business on Instagram potentially quite high. It's probably a step worth taking though for many brands whose users are on Instagram for hours per day - retailers need to be where their customers are and embedding shopping into their everyday activities is likely too lucrative an opportunity to miss.

Influencers

One of the defining factors of social selling is that brands and retailers aren't necessarily the primary curators in the way they have been. Influencers - people who curate products and post about them - exert tremendous impact on buyers. Influencers can tag specific products in their photos and their followers can purchase them directly without leaving Instagram.

While some influencers post about products purely based on a passion for their topic, many more are aware that their sway with consumers is valuable to brands. Agencies like SEEN Connects[129] and The Blogger Programme[130] advise companies on how to work with influencers and connect brands and relevant influencers. This begs the question for brands - are you ready for other people to sell your products for you? You may be used to managing professional retailers, but this huge new 'workforce' will expect some payback. However, influencers can bring your product to a vast audience instantly. This is about humans shopping from other humans more than from shops or brand websites.

Influencers hold tremendous sway over their followers and can command anything from $100 for a post, to thousands of dollars for a celebrity influencer endorsement. Eighty percent of teens say they now get their beauty tips from influencers, according to a survey of teen spending conducted by Piper Sandler[131], with 58% of those polled having made a purchase directly as a result of a social media post from an influencer they trust.

Pinterest

"When you see something on Pinterest you'd like to own you should be able to buy it, or something just like it, that matches your unique style. That's our vision for shopping with Pinterest."

Pinterest[132]

Pinterest described itself not as a social media company but as the "productivity tool for planning your dreams" when it filed to go public in 2018 and has become a firm favorite with consumers for collating items they like. According to Shopify, the highest average order value of social sales comes from Pinterest.

Pinterest may have only about one-third the size of user base of Instagram (a decidedly not insignificant 300million+ users) but the quality of their audience is of huge interest to sellers. Not only are Pinterest users collecting Pins of things that interest them, Pinterest reaches 83 percent of the highly desirable demographic of US women aged 25-54. These numbers are an indication of how much shopping is changing as people research, curate and then act on their interests via very non-traditional interactions with brands and retailers: 96% of users regularly research products on the channel, while 87% buy the items they see. 75% of saved Pins come from businesses as opposed to other consumers. A special type of Pin for businesses can share real-time availability, price information and descriptions with customers.

Particularly popular with customers in homeware, fashion and food, Pinterest claims that nearly half (47%) of people who engage with food content on Pinterest depend on digital shopping lists while they're in a store - a sign of how online and offline shopping are blurring.

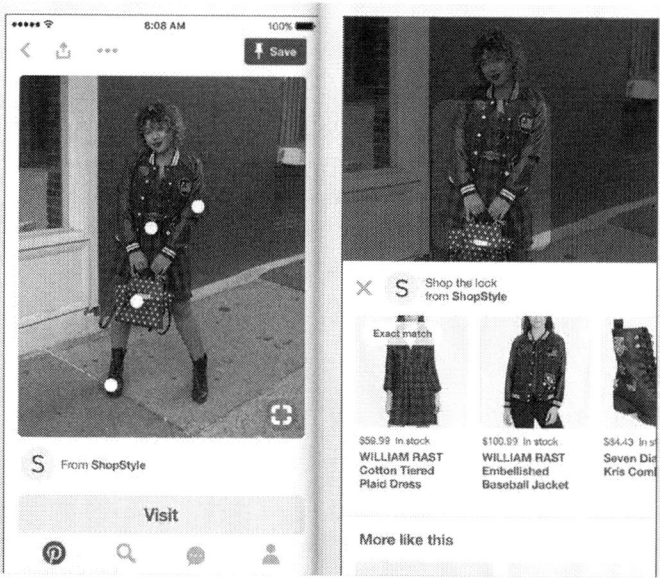

Figure 44 A Shop the Look Pin – Users tap the white dots to shop items. Source: Pinterest[133]

More Social Shopping

While Instagram and Pinterest are the current giants of social shopping, this may be a good point to bring together two key themes in this book - demographics and technology-driven new channels that are changing how people shop. Younger users are quickly discovering and adopting emerging shopping experiences on nascent platforms.

I'll bet that many top executives in retail haven't heard of apps like Dote, TikTok and Pinduoduo. Yet between them, these three apps boast over 800 million users, primarily in the coveted younger demographics. Amazon may still be the most popular shopping app across all generations, but additional apps that offer more social shopping features are rapidly gaining importance. Even teen favorite messaging and camera app, Snapchat, has expanded to include features to allow influencers create in-app stores to sell products with technology provided by Shopify. I'll look briefly at a few of the most popular apps in this section but remember that there are numerous more specialist apps for niche categories - for example sneaker marketplace app GOAT has over 12 million highly engaged users. And remember that examples quoted here may be already declining by the time you read this, to be replaced by new examples that didn't exist a few months ago.

Dote

Dote was founded to "build the ultimate shopping experience for Gen Z" and allows users to connect with and shop more than 150 brands. Its key feature is live-streamed Shopping Parties, an interactive live video feature where Influencers (known as Dote Creators), can broadcast to and chat with fans while browsing the app's 150 retail brands. The live nature of this social shopping is aimed at recreating the fun and discovery of going to the mall with friends, combining the convenience of shopping online with the social component of browsing with others. Shopping parties also include features such as giveaways and polls to drive engagement and viral sharing and typically last 15 minutes.

Figure 45 A Dote Shopping Party example showing the video of the host over the product information and audience live chat.

TikTok

TikTok was the third-most-installed app worldwide in the first quarter of 2019, meaning it deserves to be mentioned in the same breath as Facebook, YouTube and Instagram. It's a video-sharing app that allows users to upload videos of between 15- and 60-seconds duration. On average, TikTok users will spend nearly an hour a day on the app, and with over 50% of its users being aged under 24, it's the perfect platform to expose your brand to a young and engaged audience. TikTok has amassed over 180 million users in India and in late 2019, added the ability for posters to add a link to their website as part of their TikTok bio - the first early step into social commerce for the fast-growing platform.

For brands looking to engage on TikTok, it's important to note TikTok content differs entirely from other social media platforms. Unlike Instagram or Snapchat, TikTok is not a channel that demands perfection, Users want to see authenticity, comedy, imperfections and cool, engaging content. Just as with Instagram and Pinterest's move into e-commerce in their apps, TikTok introduced a feature called Hashtag Challenge Plus, that allows companies who run influencer campaigns on TikTok to directly sell products to the app's users. These sponsored hashtag challenges are Gen Z-friendly marketing campaigns where users are prompted to post videos of themselves using a product. TikTok has also experimented with full-screen ads, in-feed ads, AR lenses and stickers as ways for brands to reach customers. It is also significant that TikTok is one of the first Chinese-owned platforms to gain a substantial audience outside China, leading to regulatory questions.

Pinduoduo

Another interesting shift in selling behavior can be seen via Chinese app, Pinduoduo. Founded in late 2015, it offers discounts for shoppers who place group orders along with friends or family. Having gained around 200 million users, the platform offers wide range of products from daily groceries to home appliances. Users share Pinduoduo's product information on social networks such as WeChat and QQ and invite their contacts to form a shopping team to get a lower price for their purchase. Sellers offer discounts for these bulk orders, while Pinduoduo's model allows it to ship directly from the manufacturers, eliminating layers of distributors and retailers.

Getting Ready for Social Selling

As noted above, consumers have high expectations for their interactions with brands on social media. Retailers need to ensure that their support systems and back end operations are fit for the social media revolution – which means being able to respond to enquiries in near-real time, engage with consumers in the right "tone of voice", and fulfil orders as smoothly as any leading e-commerce site. It also means carefully choosing and resourcing the right social media platforms.

Plan to be poly-social

Unquestionably, to reach certain audiences, you need a presence on multiple platforms. The appropriate platforms will vary based on your product category and your target audience. Depending on your sector, it may be commercially sensible to de-prioritize or even ignore certain platforms altogether if they risk diverting resources from more suitable channels. But do ensure you make it a proactive considered decision and rather than miss out because of a lack of knowledge or understanding. And remember, when assessing any platform, to base your assessment not on your personal case but that of your audience. I've spoken to many senior retail executives who struggle with social media as they tend not to be personally familiar with newer platforms. Part of the issue with understanding social is that it covers such a wide range of platforms now, each serving its own micro-purpose. But when you think about it, this isn't dissimilar to physical retail - different store configurations in main streets or malls, areas in stores for promotions, for returns and service as opposed to sales - it's a clear parallel to say Twitter for customer service, Instagram as a shop window and YouTube as an advertising channel. Although it's very numbers-driven, social defies most traditional metrics - the number of directly attributable conversions is still relatively small, but a brand that isn't visible on social risks being invisible, or worse being excluded from conversations.

Creating a social media presence isn't something a retailer should undertake lightly, yet it's an essential part of any modern suite of sales and customer interaction channels. Though business may see it as a way to reach customers "on their own ground", the rules of engagement are different than they are in store. Retailers may find themselves surrounded by the very brands they are trying to sell, as well as influencers far more adept at social media than they are. Yet the size of the prize makes it hard to ignore. As we've just seen, there are plenty of rapidly emerging new alternatives to keep an eye on as well. Success in this new world requires new skills and cross-company cooperation from marketing and IT to logistics and PR.

Customer Care

Although brands and retailers might prefer that consumers perceived social media purely as an additional way to purchase goods, many people see such channels as a way to interact with as well as purchase from. If you are looking at social media from simply a click-to-purchase viewpoint, you may be missing out on a wealth of opportunities that social can bring to your business.

Social is now the number one preference for consumers seeking customer care. Much of this may be attributable to companies preferring these channels for a lower cost to serve than operating phone support, but it comes with high customer expectations - Sprout Social[134] found that 4 hours is the maximum people will wait for a response to their query (60% expect a reply within an hour), with 36% publicly shaming companies who fail to respond before then switching to a competitor.

The 2019 CMO survey[135] identified that social media spending currently accounts for between 11% and 12% of marketing budgets, with projected growth expected to bring that closer to 20% in the next five years. Clearly, many marketing professionals believe that social media is a vital way to reach consumers.

Social in Physical

Social platforms aren't only about online - there's a relationship between a brand's social media activities and those in physical retail. At the most basic level, a compelling social media presence will drive brand awareness and drive footfall to stores. Retail associates will tell you that a large number of customers coming into stores say things like "Where can I get that item I saw on your Instagram yesterday"? This makes the point that apparently different channels offline and online - and now social - are interrelated and must be coordinated to work together to appear seamless to consumers.

Some leading retailers are already using social media trending topics to promote in-store merchandise sales. For example, Nordstrom monitors which items on its Pinterest boards get the most pins and then highlights those items in stores with special tags. Nordstrom also analyses where its products are being shared on social networks and displays those products on in-store video screens.

Other Online Entry Points

Although not strictly social, I want to mention here also the growth in other online platforms that are not at first sight related to ecommerce but are additional sources of traffic with commercial intent. Take for example Google Maps. It is a starting point for consumers looking for retailers by location. The popular map app now includes recommendations to users for restaurants nearby that its algorithms think you'd like. For a business, it's important to ensure you rank highly on these kinds of recommendation engines. That requires careful monitoring of uploads/reviews related to your business, as well as frequent updates to your information such as menus and opening hours as these affect your rankings on Google Maps. Lots of positive reviews and photos of good food might see nearby users getting lots of recommendations to visit your restaurant and, given the ubiquity of Google Maps, this could be very valuable. Google Maps' move into commerce also now includes an order button, enabling users to go directly to place an order some restaurants.

Video Commerce in Social

"It has become increasingly clear that short video clips are the future of ecommerce. Think of them as compulsively watchable commercials—with a direct link to buy"

Connie Chan, A16Z[136]

If the first wave of online shopping consisted of static lists of items to buy, and the second was more dynamic lists curated for us by influencers and AI, the third wave of human-involved shopping may see the end of the primacy of lists, as video-led shopping becomes the preferred medium on social platforms. We've already discussed how sellers of all sizes can harness platforms such as TikTok, Instagram and Pinterest to reach large audiences directly with self-made videos, using just their smartphone.

According to A16Z partner Connie Chan, on Taobao (China's largest ecommerce platform) some 42 percent of product pages already include short videos with live streaming also growing quickly. From January to August 2018, the company generated more than $15 billion in sales through livestreams, up nearly 400 percent over the year before. Rural farmers in China are streaming direct from their fields to sell fresh produce to consumers, emphasizing authenticity and freshness and bypassing retailers. Sellers on these platforms such as Douyin (the Chinese market version of TikTok) and Kwai depend on producing entertaining videos rather than focusing on slick high-production-value commercials.

In the future, clothes shopping will be interactive. Instead of scrolling through static pictures or browsing by category, you can watch as a model tries on outfits in quick succession—every one of them purchasable. On Douyin, this is the status quo for fashion influencers, who might showcase five to 10 outfits in a single 15-second video. Shopping in this way is entertaining—more like watching a challenge than dutifully clicking through photos.

Further demonstrating the growing interest in the video selling space, Instagram owner, Facebook, acquired a video-shopping start-up named 'Packagd' in 2019 to help build a live shopping feature inside the company's Marketplace product, which will let users ask questions and make purchases while watching live video broadcasts.

Anywhere, Anytime Shopping

As well as discussing how humans will stop shopping in traditional ways, I want to highlight some of the new places they will be shopping. As we've seen, consumers have the ability to buy constantly at their fingertips via their smartphones and the access they give to brand, retailer and social shopping options. But I want to look briefly at some other examples of new physical shopping experiences, driven by technology, and some old ideas being rejuvenated. The emphasis here is on bringing the store ever closer to the consumer.

Uber/Cargo

If you thought you could escape shopping by jumping in an Uber and heading away from the Mall, you may be mistaken! Thanks to a start-up named Cargo, the next time you hail a ride, you may see a small box onboard with a QR code on it. Using the Cargo App, you can scan the code to purchase items from the box, which typically contains small items like gum, snacks and phone chargers. Uber riders receive 10% of their purchase value back in Uber Cash, which they can then use either on future trips or on other purchases made through the Cargo app while riding. Uber drivers also benefit, earning 25% of the value of items purchased from the Cargo Box in-car; they are provided with the boxes free of charge. Cargo sends drivers replacement stock as necessary, based on sales. Of course, Uber drivers also hope the provision of the service will lead to higher ratings from riders. Somewhat reminiscent of attempts by airlines to sell to you while you travel, the Cargo app also offers a selection of higher priced items for purchase and later delivery.

Figure 46 An In-car Cargo Box

Stockwell

Something of a glorified vending machine, Stockwell represents a reimagination of the concept with more variable product range and app-based payments. Intended to provide a managed 'store' in offices, apartment block or college dorm lobbies, shoppers open the cabinets via the app and pay for the items they remove (which is tracked by computer vision) using a stored credit card. The app provides real-time stock information, so you won't even have to walk to the machine to determine if your items are in stock.

Figure 47 A Stockwell "Smart Store"

Autonomous Mobile Stores

If those examples aren't futuristic enough when considering how sellers will get goods closer to consumers in the coming years/decades, there are several companies experimenting with self-driving vehicles that would enable a "store" to come to you, much as you might summon a taxi or order a delivery. Offering more variety than a delivery, you can browse the selection in the vehicle and personally select the items, with the seller hoping you'll be less able to resist the goods in person than you might when ordering on screen.

Figure 48 An Autonomous mobile shop prototype

Chapter 6: New Ways to Shop: Interfaces

As e-commerce evolves beyond retailer websites and apps to include social selling, even managing to keep up to speed with those developments will be inadequate for retailers and brands. Entirely new interfaces are emerging as consumers can now shop without lifting a finger, touching a device or even knowing the name of the product they want to purchase.

This is because how humans interact with computers is changing. New capabilities, powered by AI technologies, mean that computers can now see, hear and talk. Shopping is no longer defined by a consumer looking at a screen, clicking a product and completing a checkout. As we'll see in this Chapter, contemporary consumers can now choose to order items by typing in a command, sending a text, taking a photo or asking their phone or smart speaker to order.

Many of the new shopping interfaces require less human time interacting with a retailer or brand. Some of the new interfaces also exacerbate the trend of diminishing brand power by inserting a technology provider as a layer between brand/retailer and the consumer.

Challenges for Retailers

I was struck by a recent update (see image below) on the Domino's Pizza web site that shows the sheer breadth of options now available to reach consumers – a plethora of new interfaces it is experimenting with to ensure that a pizza ordering opportunity is never far away. I'm sure some will fall by the wayside, but the scope of Dominos' activities represents a daunting, yet impressive, commitment to experimentation and willingness to learn. It illustrates how much today's innovators are trying to be available to consumers at any time, anywhere, no matter what devices are to hand.

Figure 49 Domino's seeking to be available to consumers on every channel. Source: anyware.dominos.com

Visual Commerce

"We're going from computers with cameras that take photos, to computers with eyes that can see"

Ben Evans[137]

We've already talked about the impact that the rise of the smartphone has had on retail, due to mobile web and apps that enable shopping at the touch of the screen, and payments with a simple tap of the terminal in stores. While the browsing capabilities of these devices have been the most prominent shopping use case to date, the camera, with the computer vision it enables, is becoming important in a retail context as devices learn to see.

The smartphone camera is no longer just about taking great photos - it's now a key input method. Thanks to advances in computer vision, the camera can now identify objects in a photo (and therefore search for them), translate text if pointed at a sign, summon reviews of dishes if pointed at a menu. These capabilities are especially convenient for apparel, homeware and other highly visual items.

Use of the camera in mobile-powered shopping isn't particularly new - several apps have offered barcode scanning via the camera for years. eBay introduced its Red Laser app so you could find products in store and easily compare prices online. But shopping by pointing at a barcode or QR code requires retailers to undertake the tedious setup of QR codes that link to specific products, while the ugly codes can also look incongruous or intrusive on expensively-shot adverts. Recognizing a barcode is easy for a smartphone camera but now, thanks to advances in computer vision technologies, it's possible for a computer to see an actual image and understand what products are contained in the image - if not the exact item, then one that's similar. If the phone can identify items, it can find them via an online retailer and enable you to purchase without ever typing a word or product description. That's a huge change in how people shop - see it, scan it, shop it.

Image Search - A Picture's Worth a Thousand Words

"A lot of the future of search is going to be about pictures instead of keywords"

Ben Silbermann, CEO, Pinterest

According to research from Slyce.it[138], 74 percent of shoppers report that text-only search is insufficient for finding the products they want. Take for example if a consumer wants a new pair of jeans. A traditional search for "ladies blue jeans" might return thousands of results. However, if the consumer were to snap a photo of jeans they liked, a visual search could infer that the shopper was in fact after skinny jeans, with slight rips and a high waist. The visual aspect adds the less tangible variables of style that are harder to verbalize. Visual search is ideal for those "I know what I want, but I don't know how to say it" or "I don't know what I want, but I'll know it when I see it" moments that we've all felt while shopping.

Much of the previous Chapter about social shopping was about how items can be purchased once they are identified/tagged on a social platform and then made available for checkout either natively within the platform or via a link to the checkout process of a vendor. In this section, we'll look at the vast strides made in recent years aimed at enabling the purchase of untagged/unidentified items - if social platforms are growing places to discover content, there are still, of course, plenty of real world situations where you might see a product you're interested in purchasing without knowing its name or where to buy it.

Since the early days of e-commerce, online businesses have depended on the use of keywords. But if current trends are any indication, keywords may lose their central status in visual industries, such as fashion and home décor. Visual search or searching for items by uploading an image instead of typing a search query, enables you to search for things you can't easily describe. It can help in situations where you don't know the name of an item, or where you simply want to find "something like the thing in this photo". Visual Search means humans are less cognitively involved in shopping than before- "I want something like that" - less effort is involved than searching for an item by text, using unclear descriptive terms or search filters.

Visual search is made possible by recent advances in the field of computer vision, powered by Machine Learning (ML) technologies. Frequently referred to by the broader term "Artificial Intelligence" (AI), these capabilities rely on algorithms trained on millions of images to be able to recognize similar items as an alternative to text search, based on keywords, that has, thus far, been the staple of searching technology. Early feedback suggests that many US internet users would consider visual search a useful addition to regular text searches. In a RichRelevance[139] survey in 2018, 52% of users said they'd like to be shown similar products after taking a photo via a retailer's app, with only 18.5% saying they'd have no interest in such functionality.

Since launching Visual Search, Pinterest has seen its use grow to over 650 million searches per month. Interior design app Houzz has 'Visual Match' which allows users to upload a photo and search on its website catalog for similar products. Clothing retailer, Forever21 and its technology partner Donde Search recorded a 20–30% increase in conversion rates for the product categories when they deployed visual search[140].

Let's look at what Amazon, Google and Pinterest are doing to encourage people to shop using Visual Search:

Amazon StyleSnap

"We are highly innovative and customer-obsessed, and we will continue to create new experiences for customers to discover the products they want and love. We are incredibly excited about StyleSnap and how it enables our customers to shop visually for Fashion on Amazon"

Jeff Wilke, Consumer CEO, Amazon

It'll come as no surprise that a leader in this new space already is Amazon. Ever since their disastrous 2014 Fire Phone that offered "Firefly" visual detection, Amazon has continued its attempts to enable customers to shop using the camera. The more eagle-eyed users will have noticed that Amazon's shopping app already features two alternatives to typing in descriptions - camera and microphone search. We'll return to the microphone option later in this Chapter, but for now, let's look at the camera options.

In mid-2019, Amazon added a featured called StyleSnap to the shopping app. Its introduction was headlined on its web site as "StyleSnap will change the way you shop, forever"[141] which may be launch hyperbole but may also indicate that Amazon see significant potential in enabling this new approach to shopping.

StyleSnap allows users to upload a photo to Amazon who will then try to identify the items in the photo and offer them for sale – "all you need to do is take a photograph or screenshot of a look that you like". To get started, you click the camera icon in the upper right-hand corner of the Amazon App and select the "StyleSnap" option; then simply upload a photograph or screenshot of a fashion look that you like. StyleSnap will present you with recommendations for similar items on Amazon that match the look in the uploaded photo. When providing recommendations, StyleSnap considers a variety of factors such as brand, price range, and customer reviews.

Figure 50 Amazon App features StyleSnap to help shop for clothes from an image

Amazon has also partnered with Snapchat offering a new way to search for products on Amazon from within the Snapchat camera. Simply point your Snapchat camera at a physical product or barcode, and press and hold on the camera screen to get started. When the item or barcode is recognized, an Amazon card will appear on-screen, surfacing a link for that product or similar ones available on Amazon. Tap your selection to visit the Amazon App (if you have it installed on your phone) or Amazon.com, where you can complete your purchase or keep browsing.

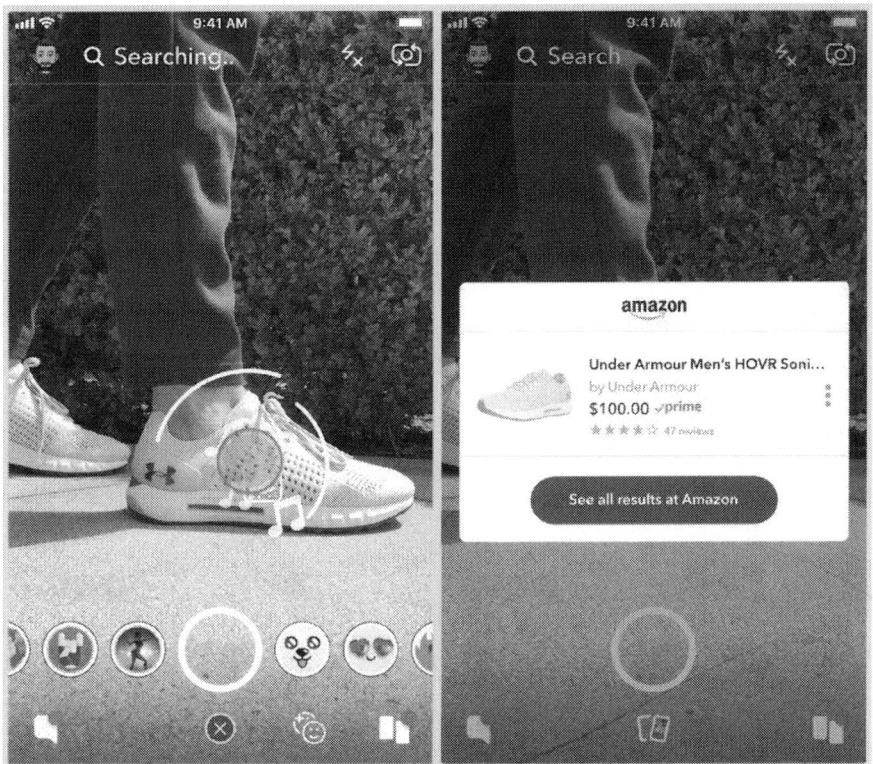

Figure 51 Favorite Teen App Snapchat partnership with Amazon to enable Visual Shopping

Switching sector to home furnishing, Amazon has also added a feature called Showroom to its website. It lets consumers place items into a virtual living room and see how well they complement each other. You can tweak the look of the flooring and walls (presumably to make it look a little more like your own living room) and swap in and out items from Amazon's catalog, including the sofa, chair, tables, lamp, rug and artwork. Naturally, Amazon's own Rivet and Stone & Beam brands are among the furniture options.

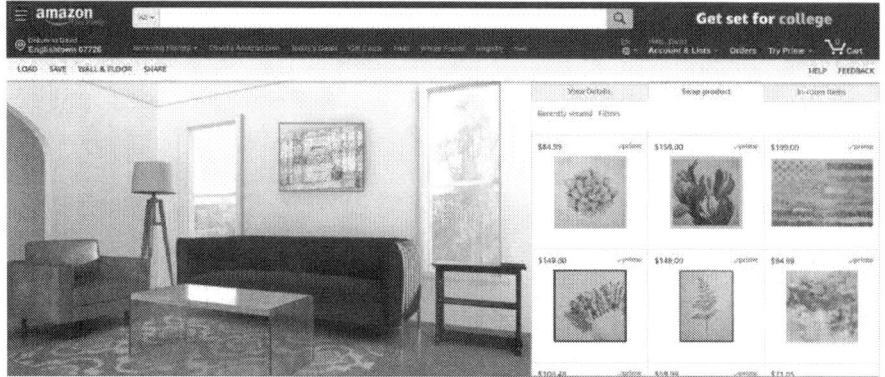

Figure 52 Amazon's website allows you to see different items of furniture in a virtual room

Amazon's interest in image-based shopping appears to be quite considerable with the filing of several patents in the space related to using a shopper's social media photographs to influence recommendations and creation of a virtual fitting room[142]. Finally on Amazon in this section, it also announced that the Amazon Echo Show smart display can identify images of household items held in front of its camera by asking "Hey Alexa, what am I holding?" Although initially aimed at helping people with visual impairment to identify items, it's not hard to imagine a use case of holding an empty carton in front of the Echo Show and asking it to order "another of these" before you throw it in the recycling bin. In fact, Amazon added barcode scanning abilities to some Echo Show models as I finished this Chapter.

Google Lens

With apps such as Google Lens, using its "Shopping Mode" you can point your camera at items and it will try to recognize them and link to websites that sell them. Or it can look at a handwritten shopping list and add the items to your shopping basket. In a retail setting, Google has partnered with Mars Food to enable its Uncle Bens products to display recipes, videos, ingredient lists, and nutritional advice on Google Lens when you point it at the product package. Assuming consumers are aware of this kind of functionality and find it useful, not providing it may disadvantage brands who don't optimize their products for a more visual shopper.

Pinterest

As a visual organization platform, it makes sense that Pinterest has invested heavily in developing its visual search capabilities. Pinterest introduced its first visual search tool, Lens, in 2017. It allowed users to point their phone at an object and see images of objects that Pinterest's algorithms think are similar to the one they're searching for. Pinterest revealed that tattoos, nails, and sunglasses are among the most popular items searched for using Lens. Other top searches by type include cats, wedding dresses, plants, quilts, brownies, and natural hair styles - fashion tops popular categories, followed by home decor, art, and food. To give you an idea of the scope of Pinterest Lens visual search capabilities, as at mid-2019, it could recognize more than 2.5 billion objects across home and fashion Pins.

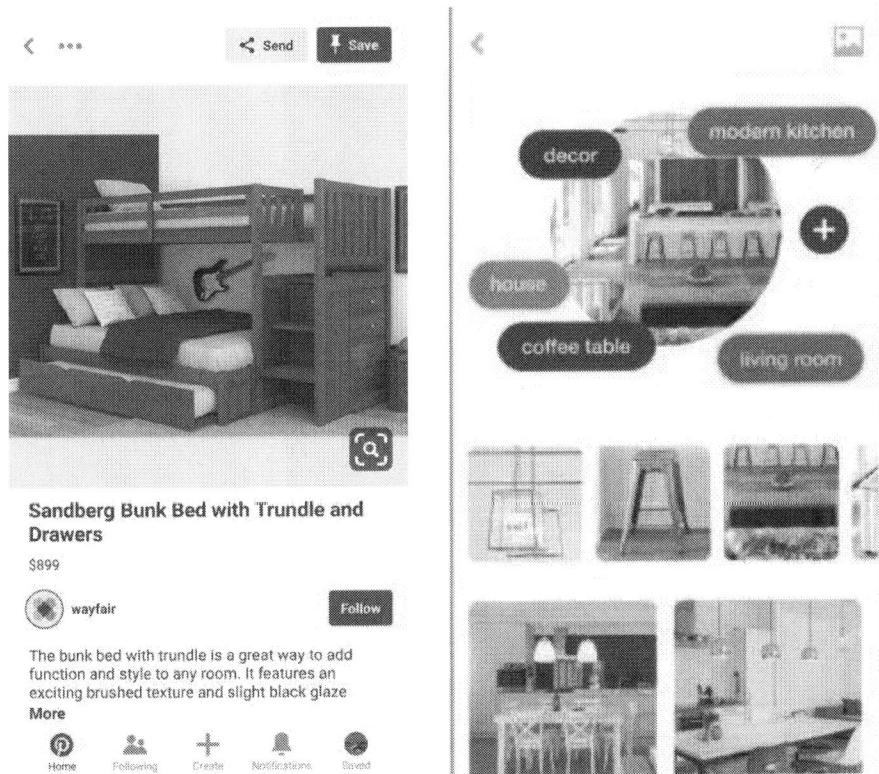

Figure 53 The prominent visual search link on a Pin (Left) and a Pinterest "Visual Guide" (Right)

Other Visual Search

As the trend towards visual search grows stronger, a number of retailers are adding visual search capabilities to their apps. In the UK, retailer Argos added Visual Search allowing customers to search for items based on taking a photo, uploading an existing image from their gallery or from the Argos Instagram feed. Marks and Spencers also added a visual search tool to its mobile website, conveniently making the feature available to people who don't have the M&S app downloaded.

Camera Commerce

As a non-scientific but pragmatic experiment, I tried both Google Lens and the Amazon visual search on a box of Lego. Both apps correctly identified it instantly and offered links to purchase it.

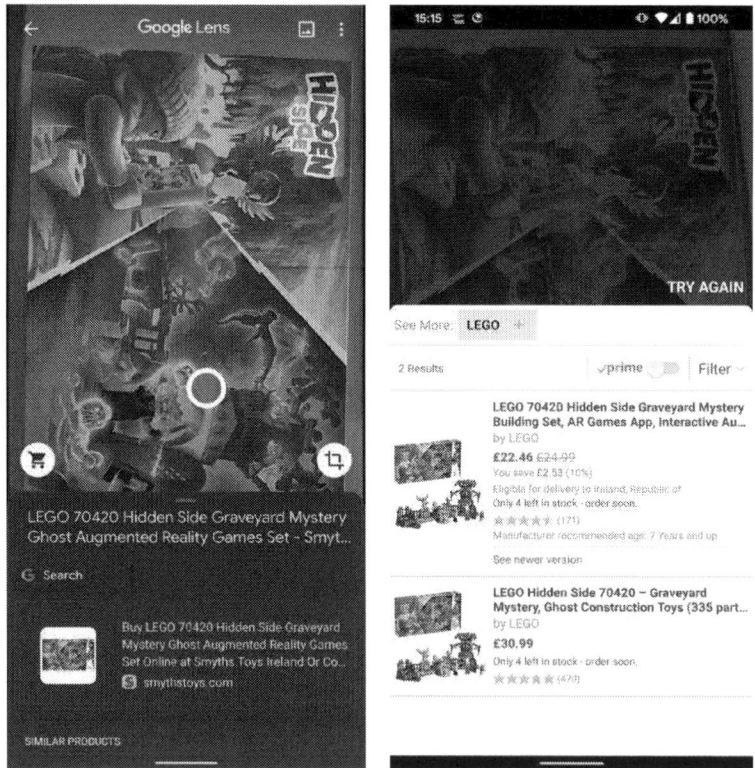

Figure 54 Google Lens (L) and Amazon (R) identify my Lego set and offer purchase options

When I searched for a branded battery, Google Lens offered a link to purchase it on Amazon. Amazon visual search did identify the battery correctly but offered its own brand substitute product and that of a competitor listed above identified brand, which was off the bottom of the screen.

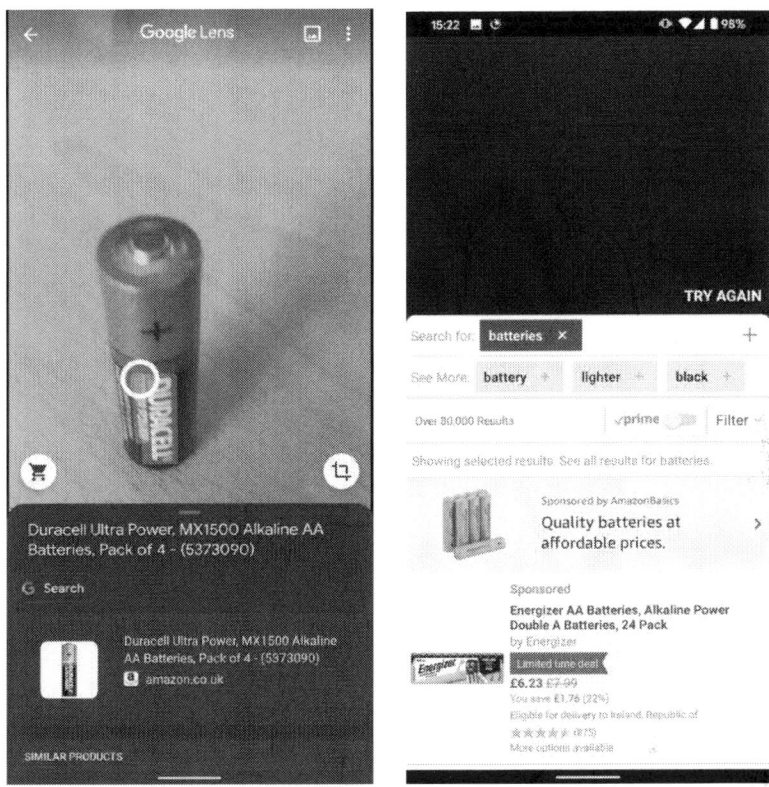

Figure 55 Google Lens (L) identifies the exact battery size and brand, while Amazon (R) offers alternative brands first, with the identified brand off the bottom of the screen

Smart Home Cameras

While smartphone cameras are the most common camera type these days, there are growing numbers of cameras being included in other products, especially smart home cameras. Most smart home cameras are for security purposes, but I have two cameras mounted in unusual places in my kitchen - on the edge of the waste bin and in the fridge. The camera that sits on the edge of the waste bin is there to scan the barcodes of items as I throw them out, with the companion app offering to reorder items automatically. The camera in the fridge means that I can see the contents of my fridge while I'm in the supermarket, removing that doubt of whether I actually need more of an item or not. Neither of these smart home products would have been possible without the reduction in the price of cameras and WiFi connectivity, driven by the smartphone supply chain.

Augmented Reality (AR)

Visual search technologies that can identify items in an image don't necessarily have to return links to shop for those products. More advanced solutions now enable software to overlay additional information over a live camera video feed, augmenting what the user sees - augmented reality.

AR is still an immature technology but is extremely appropriate in certain use cases and has been enthusiastically adopted by the beauty and homeware sectors, with some promising experiments in apparel. As you'll see below, this kind of technology is a significant threat to some of the remaining arguments justifying a visit to a store to see an item. Arguably, the ability to see an item superimposed in your own home is even more useful than seeing it in a store, where the scale isn't similar to your own home.

AR in Beauty

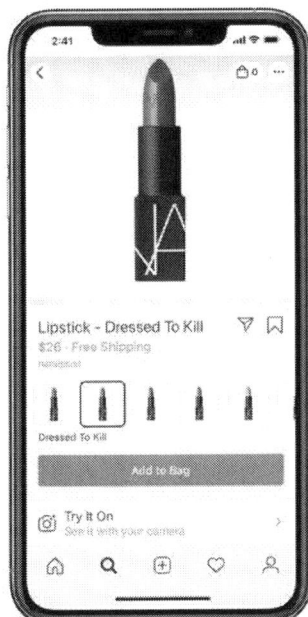 

Figure 56 Use your camera and AR technology to see how each lipstick shade looks on you. Source: Instagram

Instagram has adopted parent company Facebook's Spark AR platform to enable selected brands to offer customers virtual previews of how certain products would look on them. Early categories include cosmetics and eyewear. Users can purchase the products or share the augmented images with their friends. As we'll see later, Sephora has also turned to AR to make its experiences more interactive and engaging, while YouTube offers video previews with a split-screen view (see below). In early 2020, Pinterest also added an Augmented Reality feature enabling users to "try on" lipstick to see how it would look on them.

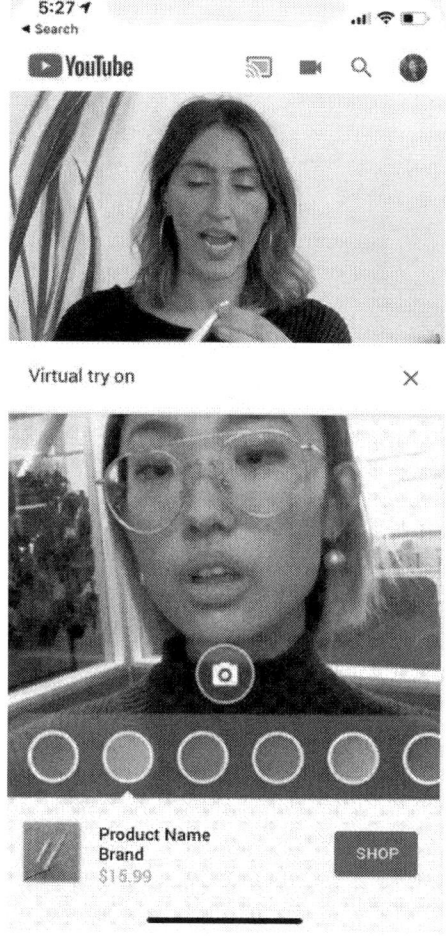

Figure 57 Watch an expert video on YouTube while trying on products via your camera before committing to purchase. Source: YouTube

AR in Homeware

Homeware is another category where AR can be particularly useful for consumers, alleviating some of the fears about purchasing items online. IKEA, Wayfair and Amazon are among the brands allowing you to see how an item would look in your home before purchase. View in Your Room lets me see how this pillow would look on my sofa:

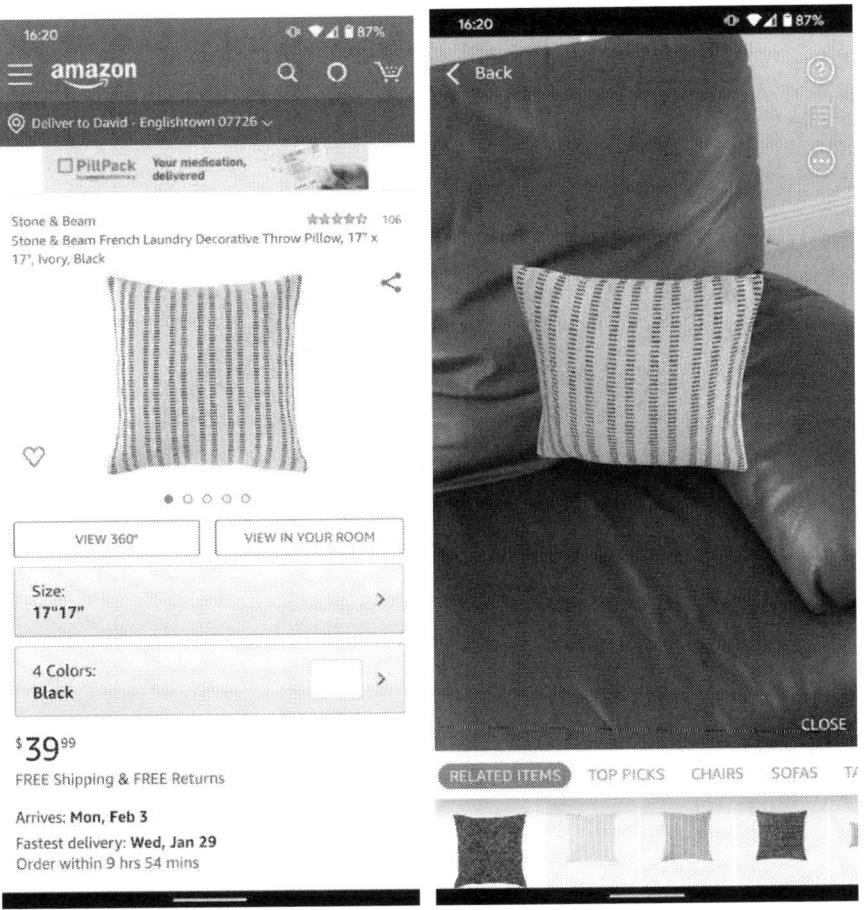

Figure 58 See a life-size representation of the item to "try" it on your home

AR in Apparel

Considering the challenges online retailers face from returns, especially in the apparel sector, anything that promises to reduce customer dissatisfaction is very welcome. Leading UK-based fashion retailer ASOS is trialing AR technology to show how clothes look on different shape models, attempting to help customers find clothes that better suit them. The initial trial has a sample of 800 dresses that can be viewed on 16 different models from size 4 to 18. The 'See My Fit' feature digitally maps the product onto models of varying heights and sizes based on the cut and fit of each individual garment. ASOS has also experimented with a Virtual Catwalk feature in its iOS app that lets you see models virtually in your own environment. Other apps such as Sizer and MTailor allow shoppers to use their smartphone camera to measure for the best fit.

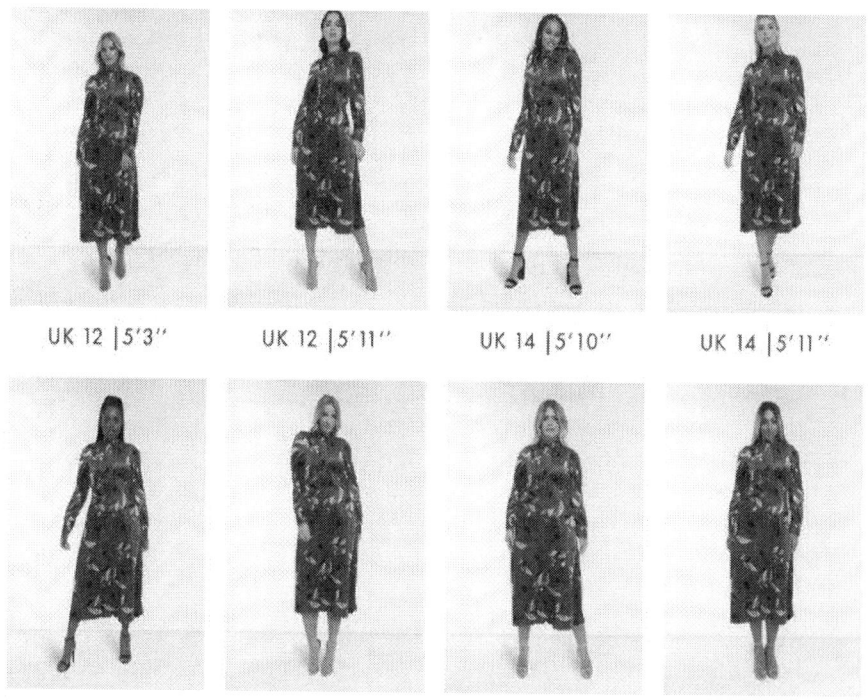

Figure 59 ASOS See My Fit AR feature. Source ASOS

AR capabilities on mobile can be slightly cumbersome to use as they require holding up your phone and looking at a relatively small screen. In the coming years, AR will be embedded in smart glasses (or even contact lenses), but for now, face-mounted products remain bulky and expensive and more suited to use in industrial applications. Microsoft Hololens, Magic Leap 1 and Google Glass Enterprise edition are ideal for situations where workers require complex visual information while keeping their hands free, though as we'll see later, some retailers will try using them to impress customers.

Snap to Sell

As we noted earlier, the rise of peer-to-peer marketplaces and second-hand selling are having a severe impact on traditional retailers as consumers resell goods among themselves, bypassing both brands and retailers. It's important to note here the importance of the humble smartphone camera in facilitating this change in shopping patterns. The ease of taking and uploading photos of items is what makes selling on these platforms attractive - a far cry from the early days of eBay where you had to take camera photos of items for listings, transfer them from the camera to a PC and then upload them to your listing. Selling is a whole lot more accessible now that just a decade ago. For example, popular Singapore app Carousell, boasts that it takes less than 30 seconds to upload your image and create a listing (for free) to sell an item. It also offers real-time messaging between buyers and sellers to enable instant negotiations. Once again, speed is to the fore.

Cameras Looking At Us

The use of computer vision technology in retail is not all one way - while it may be most obvious when consumers are pointing their cameras at something or asking a retailer's app to identify an item in a photo, there are plenty of examples of retailers pointing cameras at consumers. This too is changing the way humans shop, often without us being aware. As computers become able to "see", we'll notice them infiltrating numerous walks of life – there will be both an increase in the number of physical cameras watching us in more and more places, and an increase in what they are looking for as Machine Learning (ML) continues to improve their capabilities. Importantly, these developments will also mean that things we never thought of as computer vision issues will have technology applied to them.

Those humans that continue to shop in physical stores, will see a steady increase in the number of cameras being pointed at them - in some cases only if they are actively looking for the cameras, which will be subtly positioned. As we'll see in this section, some are for operational efficiency, while others are firmly aimed at improving the understanding of the consumer so that they can be better sold to.

It's also worth pointing out at this stage, that retail has been an early adopter of CCTV. On an average department store ceiling, there are typically several cameras feeding images back to a control room. There, a store detective or security team watch for suspicious behavior, particularly shoplifting. This has been normal now for many years, and most law-abiding customers barely notice the camera domes. But this approach is expensive to scale - it's labor intensive for humans to watch multiple screens, yet a large store requires multiple cameras to provide adequate coverage. But the new capabilities provided by improving Computer Vision change the game. With algorithms watching the camera feeds, there is no longer the chokepoint of what an operator can discern, usually limited to a single person at a time - algorithms can be trained to look for shoplifting at far greater scale than a human.

Despite the increased awareness of privacy in recent years, as I've explored retail concept stores around the world, I've seen that many of the implementations are *very* unobtrusive to consumers, perhaps to the point of being intentionally hidden. Let's look at how technology is being trained on consumers.

Footfall

Notwithstanding all the commentary and concern about online privacy, web site cookies and worries that online shopping sites are tracking you, when you walk into most retail premises on the main street, a sensor is used to count you. For years, stores have used this basic footfall measure (usually a crude infrared beam) to keep track of how many people come into their locations. It helps planning for staffing levels, working out sales conversion levels and other retailer KPIs. But as the sophistication of the technology available increases, these devices are being replaced with cameras that can do far more than simply count something as vague as "people".

One London company, Hoxton Analytics[143], offers a system using foot-level cameras to anonymously examine retail footfall (literally) by assessing footwear and using ML to figure out if they are male or female. By placing cameras at ground level throughout the store, you can anonymously track a person's journey through the store. A typical resulting report offers high level figures such as number of customers, gender, shoe size/brand, path through store, dwell time and conversion. Cameras on the floor level are unlikely to raise objections from consumers or lead to privacy concerns. While not exactly a scientifically robust survey, a few hundred shoppers that I have spoken to have few objections to floor level cameras tracking their movements in store anonymously. In a world becoming more concerned about privacy, it's seen as an innocuous intrusion.

Figure 60 An example of a discreet shoe-tracking camera

Sentiment Analysis

Automated sentiment analysis is now possible. A computer algorithm can be trained to determine sentiment from a photo of face. While it may brush too close to facial recognition for some, it is in fact purely about the system making a judgment as to a shopper's reaction to what they are seeing. Without a link to a recognition system, it is only capable of anonymously identifying a person as they walk around a store. Does shopper X look happy when they look at the mannequin and dwell for a few seconds, or do they curl their lip in dislike and hurry on by?

Figure 61 The results from my Google Vision API test shows this shopper is happy

French firm Quividi worked with leading mall owners Westfield to deploy cameras built into digital advertising billboards. Quividi systems can distinguish shoppers' gender with 90% precision, five categories of mood from "very happy" to "very unhappy" and customers' ages within a five-year bracket. To allay privacy concerns, the systems are trained to detect shoppers faces, but not to recognize them.

A Walgreens I visited in downtown Manhattan is one of several locations testing cooler cabinets with a (nearly invisible) camera in the door that can analyze customers' movements.

The All-Seeing Ceiling

On my first visit to a checkout-free Amazon Go store, I was pleasantly surprised at how little it felt like I was being watched. The high-tech cameras in the ceiling were pretty unobtrusive, painted black to blend in. I can't say the same for the new Walmart Intelligent Retail Laboratory in Long Island, just outside New York. Although Amazon Go is a finished concept that's now live in about

20 locations and the Walmart site is clearly a laboratory for testing ideas, it seems unthinkable that in an era of increased consumer awareness, there's going to be widespread acceptance of **40 cameras per aisle** watching over us.

Figure 62 An overhead row of cameras at Walmart Intelligent Retail Laboratory Store, Levittown, New York

When I visited the Walmart store, none of the shoppers seemed bothered by the overhead surveillance - most of us are too focused on shopping ever to look up. For Walmart, the cameras are intended not to watch the customers but the shelves (checking for stock-outs) and the aisles (looking for spills) so they can alert staff to situations needing attention more quickly. As long as consumers are reassured that facial recognition isn't being used, I suspect they won't object to cameras watching the store and products rather than them as individuals, but I do expect Walmart to refine the appearance of the cameras before using them more widely.

That raises a rather important question about the appearance of cameras - is there potentially a different consumer reaction when the cameras are clearly visible rather than integrated to the point of being non-obvious?

In a Kroger-group store in Redmond Washington, where they are also testing digital shelf-edge displays, if you look very closely at the end of each aisle, you might be able to see a camera watching shoppers (It's just under the Q logo)

Figure 63 A Kroger Store endcap with a camera to watch shoppers

Visual commerce and the use of cameras is a key trend changing how consumers shop. But as computers gain the power to see, they are also gaining the power to listen, meaning it's now possible to talk to computers and expect them to understand and answer us. This too will change how we shop.

Conversational Commerce

Many traditional retail transactions involve a conversation element. Customers frequently discuss requirements or product features with a sales assistant, clarifying details, querying returns policies and completing a transaction. How often does a retail exchange include phrases like – "Do you have this box in a different color? What can I get like this but under $200? Is there something that's stronger than this but no more expensive? Can I return it for free if I don't like it?"

This interaction is typically lacking in online shopping – websites tend to be a one-way conversation; consumers make a purchase decision based on price, their research, reading reviews and the product description provided on the site before reading up on policies and committing to buy. Yet, as online shopping has grown to encompass more complex transactions, and technology has improved, we're seeing a growing range of options that add conversational elements to online transactions, turning them into more tailored, precise and personalized interactive exchanges.

Talking (and Listening) to your Customers

Online businesses who want to be responsive to customers in ways that suit modern consumers, need to provide shoppers with interfaces to deal with queries in a timely manner, using the media preferred by the shopper. In many cases, this will be either a text or voice (phone call) interface.

Live Text Chat

Early websites and catalog firms offered telephone support for consumers, but such synchronous media may not suit consumers purchasing from their work PC or mobile on public transit. As the web evolved, email or an enquiry form were typical methods added for customers to submit questions. Then you waited, unsure if or when you would get a reply. It's a sure sign that a retailer doesn't understand the modern consumer when you submit a web form or an email and receive a response "Thank you for your query. We're experiencing a high volume of questions and expect to respond within 48 hours". While it may be a form of expectation management, anytime I see a firm quoting a 48-hour response time, my immediate take-away is that they don't care about me as a customer, so I look for alternatives.

Impatient consumers in search of rapid answers often turn to other channels such as Twitter for support, but savvy retailers can deploy chat solutions, that keep the conversation, and any potential controversy, out of the public eye.

As customers come to expect real-time answers, many online sellers have turned to chat based solutions. From a retailer or brand perspective, a live chat support agent can handle more customers at once than phone customer service representatives. A Telus study[144] noted that chat agents can handle up to six simultaneous customers, with "canned" responses available for the most common queries, suggested by AI.

Automated Answers

Having staff available to type answers to text chats received is a challenge - with the growth in popularity of texting, messaging and the huge cost of 24/7 contact centers for routine enquiries, it is not surprising that companies are investigating the use of automated text solutions to deal with the surging volumes of text queries coming into their businesses.

As technology improves, live chat support agents are being supplemented or even replaced with chatbots. Although chatbots started life primarily as a tool to answer only simple queries, they have taken on commercial roles as consumers get more comfortable conducting business via text messages. It is now possible to book a hotel room, retrieve your financial information, pay bills, get a medical diagnosis and much more via chat bots, with no human intervention on the part of the service provider.

According to the 2018 State of Chatbots report[145], 24-hour service was overwhelmingly (64%) the biggest benefit consumers perceived from chatbots. A surprisingly large number of people shop online in the evening - primetime for online shopping is between 8–9 pm, or even later when retail staff are typically not available. The problem is, that when customers are in the buying mood and the brand is not there to lend a hand, they'll decide to shop somewhere else.

Just as many of the questions store staff deal with each day are standard, predictable queries, online retailers and brands can expect consumers' queries to include non-challenging questions that can be easily answered. The consumers may have missed the information on the website, not be inclined to go looking for it, or simply want additional confirmation beyond what they've already seen. Simply product or operational (store opening hours, returns policies) questions are prime candidates to automate. Instead of having an expensive human resource answering these kinds of queries, automated text answering systems or bots are quite capable of parsing incoming text from the consumer, determining if it's a known answer, and replying appropriately.

Bots also reply with total patience and polite responses no matter the provocation. And with today's translation tools, it's easy to converse in different languages, cutting and pasting replies into a translation service (which admittedly may introduce some imprecision, but still can be very practical).

When you see the Live Chat window on a web site, you may no longer know immediately whether it's a human on the other end. It's more and more likely to be a bot, a simple form of "Artificial Intelligence" that can at least triage if not fully answer your query. As the capabilities of AI bots has improved, more companies are deploying them as a first-line customer support tool. With the ability to operate at large scale 24/7, they are an attractive alternative to high turnover call center staff and the attendant costs of retraining, scaling and 24-7 operations. Others have gone a step further to enabling full ordering and payment via messaging interface. A start-up called AdLingo[146] has created online display adverts that offer direct text conversations powered by AI, meaning customers don't even need to visit a retailer site but can get answers from an advert wherever it's displayed.

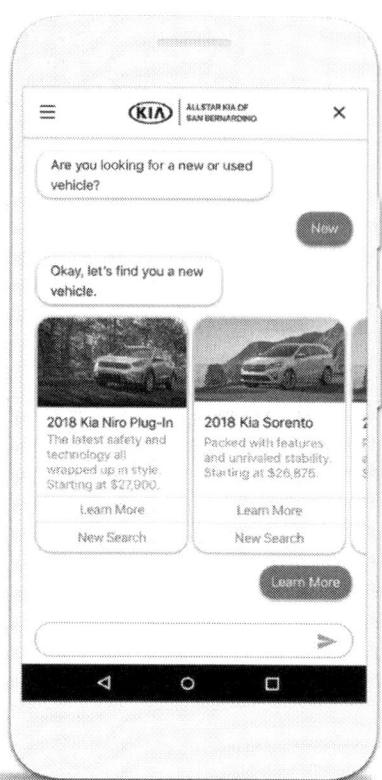

Figure 64 An intelligent ad - have a text conversation with an advert powered by AdLingo

Social Chat

We spoke earlier about meeting consumers where they are rather than always expecting them to come to your properties and this is true not only of social selling but also chat. Given that popular chat apps like Facebook Messenger and What's App have billions of users who have installed the apps to chat with their family and friends, it can make sense to use these same tools for business interactions. This gives shoppers a familiar interface and the in-app benefits of saved conversations and notifications, compared to the varying quality of chat interfaces provided by retailer apps and websites.

Leading messaging app, WhatsApp, has expanded the capabilities of its dedicated app for business owners with a "catalogs" feature that allows businesses to showcase and share their products with photos, prices and product descriptions, effectively creating a mobile storefront on WhatsApp. These catalog items can then be sent to customers in a WhatsApp chat message. The catalogs feature joins several others in WhatsApp designed with the needs of businesses in mind, including business profiles, quick replies for messages, chat labels and automated messages.

Business users can link to their Facebook or What's App messaging service from their app or website and make use of a management interface supplied by Facebook. Businesses with a Facebook profile can benefit from features such as Appointment scheduling via Messenger chats.

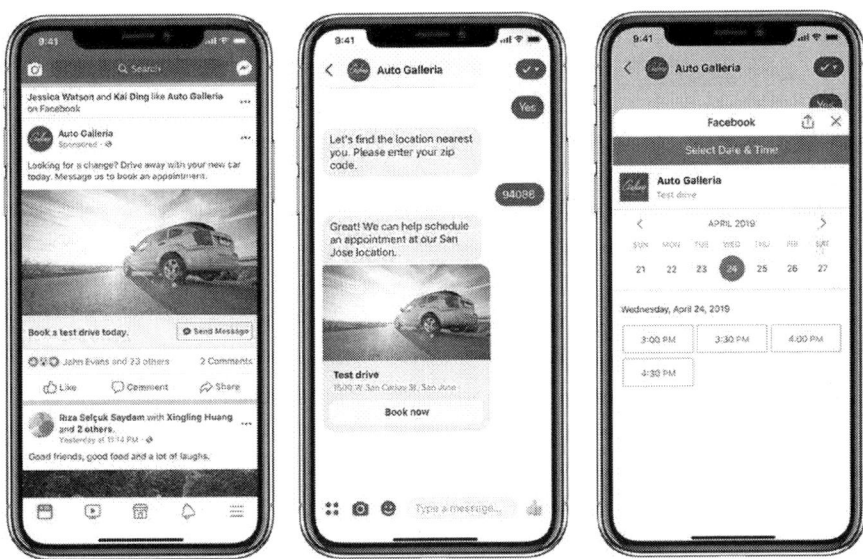

Figure 65 Facebook Messenger Bot Appointment Booking

Two supermarkets have recently deployed chatbots in trials - German discount supermarket Lldl created an automated chatbot to offer wine-buying assistance for shoppers via Facebook Messenger, while, in an interesting experiment in Mexico, Walmart allows customers to send grocery orders to its Superama supermarket via What's App, either as a text list or as a photo of a list. The order is then delivered as quickly as 90 minutes later with payment on delivery.

Apple has allowed businesses to leverage its popular iMessage platform for consumer interactions. In one example[147], basketball fans in Cleveland were able to order drinks for delivery to their seat using text messages to order - much faster than queueing to order and carrying drinks back to your seat!

Chat Platforms

Picking up on the earlier point that smaller businesses can access advanced technology, it's worth noting that leading e-commerce-as-a-service platform, Shopify, offers merchants an app (called Ping) to manage their customer conversations via any of Facebook Messenger, SMS, Apple Business Chat or Shopify's own chat messages. The integration with Shopify means customers can ask for package tracking updates, or just ask questions of a seller as well as completing purchases. Ping uses natural language processing, sentiment analysis, and other forms of AI to do things such as highlight conversations that may lead to big sales, alert a merchant if a customer is angry about their order, or flag conversations likely to lead to returns.

Even for non-technical organizations, it's getting easier to build custom chat solutions with services such as DialogFlow from Google or drift.com which provides a drag and drop interface to create a chatbot.

Group Chat

In a further development in this space and an illustration of how humans' approach to shopping is changing, there's an emerging practice in China of using Group Chats to build relationships with customers and sell to them. Analyst Connie Chan has written a detailed explanation[148], but in essence, it involves using private group chats that are limited to 500 members where companies can interact with customers in a trusted environment and provide tailored advice.

Leading brands such as Levi's, Sephora and Uniqlo have added AI chatbots to their apps to offer personalized styling tips to shoppers, opening another channel of communication to consumers to generate loyalty and additional sales. Starbucks, for example, introduced a text interface for orders.

A report from Juniper Research[149] analyzing the effect of artificial intelligence on the retail industry predicts a more than 10-fold increase in the number and value of chatbot based interactions in the next 4-5 years. The report also believes that chatbots will become a standard part of retail experience as their capabilities improve and both the customer benefit and cost savings become impossible to ignore.

The AI Answering Machine

Before there were websites or live text chat, people telephoned businesses when they had questions. And despite the convenience of text messaging, there are times when a simple phone call can still be the preferred option for a consumer. However, for businesses, answering phone calls is time consuming and can distract staff from other tasks, especially in small retailers.

With recent developments in voice recognition and voice synthesis technologies, it's now possible for automated systems to answer phone calls and field simple questions. With these systems, customers can speak naturally instead of following tedious prompts at the end of a long menu of options being slowly read out. Automated voice chat systems offer similar answering capabilities to the text chatbots described above. They simply add voice recognition to capture the customer request and then turn it into text for analysis and response generation. Finally, a synthesized voice reads the answer to the consumer.

It is estimated that in the US, small businesses receive 400 million calls from customers daily. Though these are an important, perhaps vital, sources of sales, answering them effectively is a big challenge. In fact, nearly half of small business calls go unanswered because staff are too busy[150]. Due to limited budgets or lack of technical knowledge, many small firms haven't invested in creating an online presence at the same rate as larger companies - less than two-thirds of small businesses have a website, leaving customers no alternative but to call for information or appointments. While some shoppers will persist and call back later, each missed call may represent a lost customer, or worse, a lost customer and a negative review.

Thanks to AI-powered solutions, SMBs now have access to the kind of scalable always-on phone answering technology previously only available to large companies. It's possible for a voice bot to answer and greet callers, provide basic business information, and direct customers to take online actions via text message. It also provides owners with transcripts of customer queries (which is a lot more actionable than a missed call notification) as well as insights into call volumes.

Imagine an example conversation between a small business customer (driving making a handsfree call) and an AI answering service (Meanwhile, the small business owner is serving customers, not answering basic queries):

> Business Voice Bot: "Hi, and welcome to Dave's - what can I help you with?"
> Customer: "What time are open until on Thursdays?"
> Business Voice Bot: "We're open until 8pm on Thursday"
> Customer: "What's your location?"
> Business Voice Bot: "We're at 123 Loreto Street"
> Customer "Thanks"
> Business Voice Bot: "Will I text you a Google Maps link?"
> Customer "Yes Please"

These kinds of automated services can ease access to information for consumers, while reducing the burden on businesses in providing answers. The consumer may not know (or care) that they were served by a bot instead of a human, as long as they got the information they required conveniently. We'll come back in the next Chapter to talk about how consumers can automate their side of the conversation in what may be the biggest change to shopping in decades.

Chat Challenges

While chat bots that work 24/7 and can handle thousands of calls without ever deviating from the company script are popular with businesses, consumers don't yet have a universally positive view of chatbots. While customers generally prefer chats to slower methods of interaction such as email, consumers are so-far more than twice as likely to be happy with a human chat interaction than a bot response[151].

A Usabilla report from 2018 estimated that 70% of consumers have already used chatbots, and that 54% would choose a chatbot over speaking to a human if it saved them 10 minutes. However, the report also found that a majority (55%) of those surveyed "preferred" to speak to human customer service agents. A Gartner study[152] predicted that by 2021, nearly 1 in 6 customer service interactions globally would be handled by AI. But it's not all good news for chatbots. Gartner also predicted that "40% of chatbot/virtual assistant applications launched in 2018 will have been abandoned by 2020 due to low-end solutions that deliver a poor user experience, create friction and don't deliver business benefit."

Automated chatbots (both phone and text) are improving rapidly and I believe we will see their continued development and deployment, especially in sectors with typically simpler interactions. The emergence of virtual assistants like Alexa and Google Assistant that we'll discuss in the next section could further complicate matters for the evolution of chatbots, as voice interfaces may play a larger role in direct sales. I expect to see continuing evolution of the chatbot technology, not just in getting better at understanding customer requests but also at analyzing consumer behavior for clues that they need help - e.g. a long dwell time on a sizing chart page or adding two sizes of an item to their basket - then the chatbot proactively interceding, just as a human store assistant might offer help to a customer seen spending a lot of time assessing their options.

Voice Commerce

"Echo has a way of sneaking into your routines. When Alexa reorders popcorn for you, or calls an Uber car for you, when your children start asking Alexa to add Popsicles to the grocery list, you start to want pretty much everything else in life to be Alexa-enabled, too."

New York Times[153]

Just as advances in machine learning have dramatically impacted the efficiency of computer vision, so too has the area of voice recognition improved exponentially in the last few years. This development has massive implications for our relationship with technology - providing an interface that is extremely natural for us.

Rapid Growth

Access to voice commerce relies on having microphones in close proximity to potential shoppers. Luckily, besides smartphones, only one other technology in history has been adopted by a quarter of Americans in just 2 years - AI-powered voice assistants in smart speakers. Their growth has been aided by their low price (less than

$50) but also clearly by consumer interest in voice interactions. As the growth of smartphones in many markets plateaus, Amazon, Google and others have been racing to take advantage of breakthrough improvements in speech recognition to enable smart speakers. Currently, they are predominantly used for music, smart home control or simple queries, but the companies are eager to monetize this new customer interface.

The most common voice systems in widespread use are Amazon's Alexa and Google Assistant. Each is available via phone and home speakers, though the smart speaker market is led by Amazon with its plethora of shapes and sizes (Flex, Dot, Echo, Echo Plus, Echo Studio, Show 5, Show 8, Show and Look), and Google who offer 5 sizes (Mini, Home, Home Max, Hub and Hub Max). And that's before you consider the support for both Alexa and Assistant via third party speakers and the more experimental form factors such as in-car Echo Auto, Echo Frames and even the Echo Loop (a smart ring). It took Amazon four years to populate the world with 100 million Alexa-powered devices. It took the company just one more year to more than double that number, with Alexa already integrated into more than 100,000 smart home products from over 9,500 brands[154].

It remains unclear how much use of smart speakers is incremental to consumer use of other technologies such as smartphones and tablets. If use of smart speakers starts to become substitutional, this may further concentrate power towards a smaller number of large technology organizations. In an Accenture/Harris Interactive survey of 21,000 people, 66% of respondents who owned a smart speaker said they used their phones less as a result.

Variety of uses

This change in how we interact with devices will take some time to become familiar. It requires user to adapt and to unlearn ingrained habits. Despite the advantages of voice over other forms of UI, the evidence suggests that early users are sticking to simple tasks so far. This is to be expected as people test the boundaries of what actually works, and as they get used to the previously impossible and implausible ability to talk to invisible digital assistants. But people will get used to it. Asking for a song is so much easier than searching in an app, knowing how to spell a song title, etc. I had honestly never realized that opening an app and typing the name of the song was a hassle. But compared to telling Alexa to play my music, it's a chore!

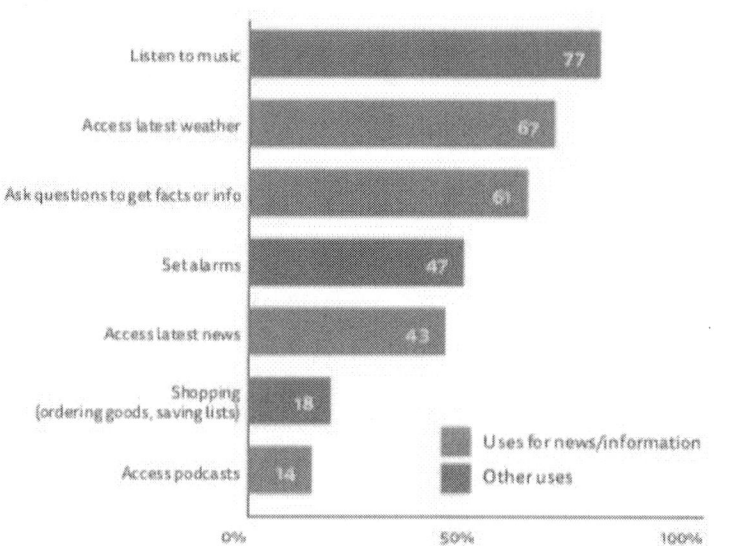

Figure 66 Shopping currently ranks towards the bottom of smart speaker usage

Ironically, the lack of a visual interface can sometimes slow us down. We're so used to seeing what a computer is doing or has found for us, we are slow to let go of control, lacking the trust to delegate to an unseen force. This challenge of designing for a new world of invisible agents acting on our behalf isn't easy - many people will have to unlearn their dependence on visual feedback and learn to trust - more on this in the next Chapter.

And as businesses react at different speeds, there is still no guarantee that your providers of choice have embraced the technology yet. You may be able to transfer money by voice with one bank but not another. The same was true at the start of the web - while now it's unthinkable for a business not to have a website, the same will be true in a few years for any company unable to conduct its business via voice. For businesses watching the emergence of this new channel of communication, it represents a challenge to decide how and when to engage with their customers. Even the managers of the UK Government web site[155], which gets about 3 million visits per day, are looking at developing voice support so that citizens can interact more naturally with the State's services.

Although some surveys have put the use of smart speakers for ordering things as low as 2% (which would still represent a substantial market of millions), others suggesting usage for shopping could be as high as 50%[156]. In a PWC report in 2018, 24% of people expressed a preference to shop via their online assistant vs online shopping. If voice-based shopping were to achieve anything approaching a quarter of online shopping, it would be a hugely significant new commercial channel.

Speak to Shop

Voice-based systems have a discoverability problem - it's hard for users to know what's available for them to say. It's noticeable that smart speakers with screens frequently prompt users visually with "Try saying X" to help educate users about their capabilities. In time, people will become more familiar with speaking to their assistants and will come to expect more from them.

Add to Shopping List

"We know when using voice technology, customers like to add items to their cart one at a time over a few days — not complete their shopping for the week all at once"

Tom Ward, Walmart's SVP of Digital Operations

Although technically it's not shopping, for many people the first step into the world of voice commerce may be adding an item to their shopping list. It can be very convenient when you discover a household item running low to direct Alexa or Assistant to add the item to your shopping list. Next time you're in the supermarket, check the list on your phone to see all the items you've added, arranged in a logical order, not the order you added them.

Google is using ML to make its shopping list solution more intelligent. Shoppers use voice to add products to their list, and then, behind the scenes, Google re-orders the items logically by category.

Faced with Amazon's growing ambitions in the grocery sector, traditional retailing giant Walmart has teamed with Google to test consumer interest in building their grocery lists by voice. By saying, "OK Google, talk to Walmart", they can add items to a list to complete the purchase later in the app or on the web. When a Walmart customer asks to order an item, the assistant will know to reorder the customer's preferred item based on their order history. The assistant will also inform the customer which item it's choosing and the price point. This feature means the customer doesn't have to speak the full name of an item when making a request. Instead, they could say just "milk" and the assistant would know they mean the "1 gallon of 1% Great Value organic milk" they ordered the last time.

Package Tracking

Another micro-convenience that voice introduces is access to parcel tracking. Alexa has an advantage of direct access to your Amazon orders, while Google has the advantage of being able to update you on any deliveries it can track by parsing your Gmail and extracting order details. A quick, spoken query of "Alexa, where's my stuff?" is greeted with a detailed reply "An order placed 18th October will be delivered 19th October". On the day of delivery, the Amazon Echo will glow to indicate a notification, while Echos with screens display that a package is due. These simple features make voice become part of the ordering experience - enquire at any time what's pending and en-route, then proactive notifications on the day of delivery, thus gently making you more comfortable with her (Alexa's) involvement in shipping and shopping.

It's not hard to see where the next steps could come, based on these simple entry points - the command to add an item to a shopping list could be responded to by an offer from Amazon or Google to complete the transaction for you and arrange for it to be delivered.

Send Me A Sample

As we move along the continuum of voice shopping, another feature is the ability to request samples. I recently saw an advert for a new flavor of drink. On the advert, was a logo saying the brand supported "Send me a Sample", a service that requires one-time sign-up to work. So, all I had to say was "Hey Google, send me a sample". "Sure, what sample would you like?". "Bailey's Almond". "I'll send you that now - look out for it in the mail in a few days". And sure enough, a few days later, the sample showed up in my letterbox. Brands are hoping that this level of convenience will spur more people to take action when they see a product of even passing interest, rather than the typical behavior of moving on to the next page without bothering to fill in a form, or navigate to a web site, or call a number. Brands such as Estée Lauder, Ferrero and Diageo are experimenting with this channel.

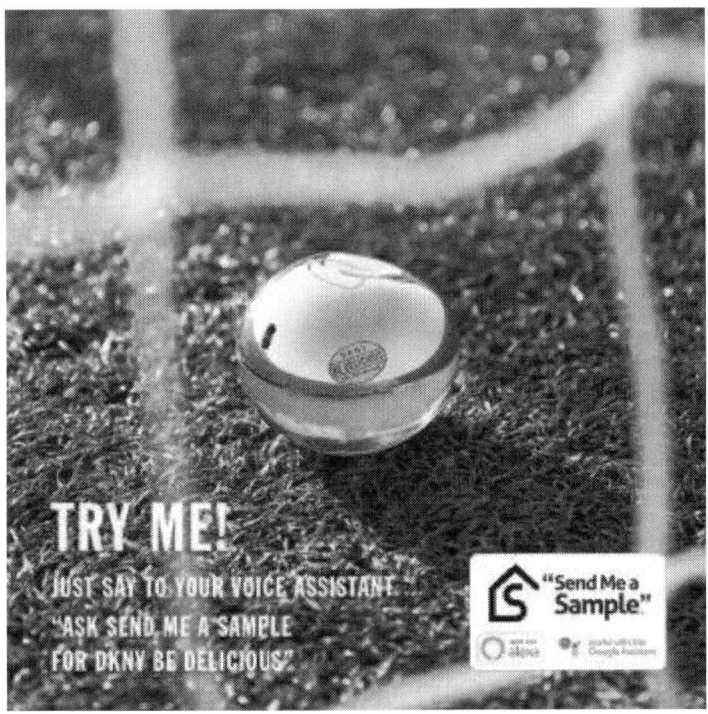

Figure 67 A print advert with voice activation via a sample request

Voice Ordering

Beyond lists and samples, Amazon's voice assistant Alexa is not just a source of answers, music and smart home control but also another sales channel. Google too is adding more retail partners to its voice shopping service too, as it seeks to capitalize on the convenience of voice shopping. So shopping can now be as simple as asking the little speaker in the living room to complete the purchase of whatever you want to be delivered the next day.

Simple Products

Alongside re-order commands where there's no real product selection, voice shopping will likely gradually gain some traction for small value, simple orders - slightly reminiscent of the early days of online shopping where customers got used to the practice with simple orders to build trust. Over the last decade, we've moved from ordering $10 books and CDs to now ordering $10,000 holidays and even new cars online.

A study from the PaySafe Group[157] found that more than half of consumers would use voice to pay for low value goods but were much more hesitant about making larger purchases via voice.

In a study by PWC in 2018[158], users were asked what they had purchased via voice and what they would be willing to consider in future:

Category	Have purchased via voice	Haven't yet but would consider in the future
Takeout Food	34%	35%
Groceries	31%	27%
Books	24%	23%
Home/Electronics	22%	26%
Transportation (Uber/Lyft)	21%	29%
Reservations (Restaurant)	16%	3%
Clothing	3%	22%

Dominos offers voice ordering for pizza once you've linked the Alexa skill to your Domino's account. Users can setup a standard order, which can then be ordered with a single phrase:
"Alexa, open Domino's and place my Easy Order." 7-Eleven has launched a voice-powered app that lets customers place delivery orders through their Amazon Echo or Google Home smart speakers.

However, while re-ordering your favorite pizza is easy, ordering other items can get more complex and worrying for brands. Take an example where I asked Alexa to order me 8 AA batteries. Sure enough, 8 batteries arrived the next day, but they were Amazon Basics brand. Had I been ordering visually I probably would have considered the Duracell or Energizer brands and then made a decision. But because I didn't specify "Alexa, order 8 Duracell AA batteries", she chose the Amazon preferred option.

More Complex Products

Other large retailers experimenting with voice interactions include online fashion retailer ASOS with the ability to ask Google Assistant to see a list of new arrivals and UK retailer Argos which has added the ability for consumers to check stock or reserve their order using voice via Google Assistant for pick up in store[159].

We will soon see more complex products and services made available via voice as both consumers and retailers get more comfortable with this new interface. As the technology matures and consumer confidence grows, voice will change how consumers interact not just with retailers but service providers of all kinds. Already, thanks to Hallmark, you can even ask Alexa to send a personalized greeting card!

In the UK, the National Health Service (NHS) allows queries via voice using an Alexa skill. This is currently just voice-based access to existing health information resources available via its website and app, but the improved accessibility of voice opens the content to a broader audience.

I've tried voice ordering several times and been impressed at the ease of use and growing levels of functionality available. One of the first orders I placed via voice was actually for a service rather than a good - as I gathered my belongings to go to a meeting, I asked Alexa to order me an Uber. That left my hands free to grab what I needed rather than looking at my phone. Another time, on a business trip to Seattle, I remembered that I had visited a nice restaurant near my hotel on my previous trip. As I walked down a street, I touched my earbud to summon the Google Assistant and instructed it to book a table for the restaurant for 7pm the next day. "Sure," it replied instantly, "I've confirmed the reservation with the restaurant and added it to your calendar". All this as I walked along without even having to look at my phone. But the most impressive real-world voice interaction I've had so far (as opposed to demos) was when my Google Assistant asked me if I wanted to check in for a flight the next day. When I answered yes, it asked a few questions regarding baggage and then presented me with my boarding pass.

Voice Banking

It's still early days for shopping via voice, yet companies are actively testing the boundaries of what consumers are comfortable with. Just as early e-commerce took time to gain trust, so too will voice. And there may be some types of interactions that won't fit well in the voice paradigm. Consider financial interactions – because already people are used to being able to pick up their phone, authenticate and see their account details, the next step of talking to your bank to get your balance may sound very convenient, but it introduces a whole new layer of privacy and security questions the banks have worked very hard to overcome for online banking and, more recently, for banking apps. For sensitive information available via voice, there are authentication considerations. Consumers will hardly be comfortable if anyone can walk into their house and ask the smart speaker for their financial details! Yet if you add a barrier such as requiring a PIN code to access information, that additional friction means it's just as easy to pick up your phone and access a banking app. Voice recognition, where the speaker can distinguish voices rather than just commands, may offer a solution.

In the US, TD Ameritrade introduced voice-activated stock trading via Amazon's Alexa and Google Home. They've also experimented with Apple Business Chat and Facebook Messenger to provide chat-based access. The largest volume of requests to Alexa has been for market updates and quotes. So far, voice queries account for less than 10 per cent of TD Ameritrade's client interactions.

UK bank Nat West is allowing customers to get bank balances via their Google Assistant; customers are required to say a partial voice PIN to confirm their identity to get the balance. Meanwhile in India, Amazon has enabled users to pay their utility and cable bills via an Alexa voice command.

In a further example of voice interfaces changing how consumers and businesses may interact, McDonald's has tested allowing job seekers to begin the application process using voice by saying "Alexa/OK Google, help me get a job at McDonald's". Alexa or Assistant will ask potential applicants for their name, their location and job area of interest, among other information. Then they'll get a text message with a link to continue their application on a phone or PC.

In September 2019, European budget airline, Easyjet became the first airline to build voice searches into its app[160] - instead of the 12 taps it typically takes to complete a search, customers can ask for flights between cities on particular days and see results instantly.

Exxon in the US has announced that by the end of 2020, some 11,500 of its stations will support using Amazon Pay via Alexa to pay for gas. Drivers can sit back into their car after filling up and ask Alexa to "pay for gas on pump 3" rather than having to take out their credit card. Of course, this coupled with existing pay-at-pump solutions, may reduce impulse purchases that many fuel stations depend upon.

Shopping without a screen - To See or Not to See

There remain some multi-step ordering processes that might seem hard to move to voice but as the technology powering voice recognition improves, 2019 has already seen Google expand its support for more complex bookings such as movie tickets and car rentals. Amazon has also demonstrated the ability to chain commands - e.g. taxi, meal reservation.

Additionally, Amazon aims to reduce friction in conversational devices and shopping interaction. Currently, when trying to book movie tickets, search for restaurants, and book a cab you need to open a separate skill for each of these tasks. The idea is to make these multi-turn conversations easier for the user. At its 2019 Re:Mars conference, Amazon announced Alexa Conversations, which enables a conversational thread across multiple skills, all in one coherent conversation. The "night out" conversation lets a user purchase movie tickets, make dinner reservations and request an Uber ride all in one conversation without having to wait and open additional skills to proceed.

On an Echo with a screen, you get something like the screen below. Otherwise, you get a verbal description and referred to the app for more details, though you can still complete the purchase purely orally.

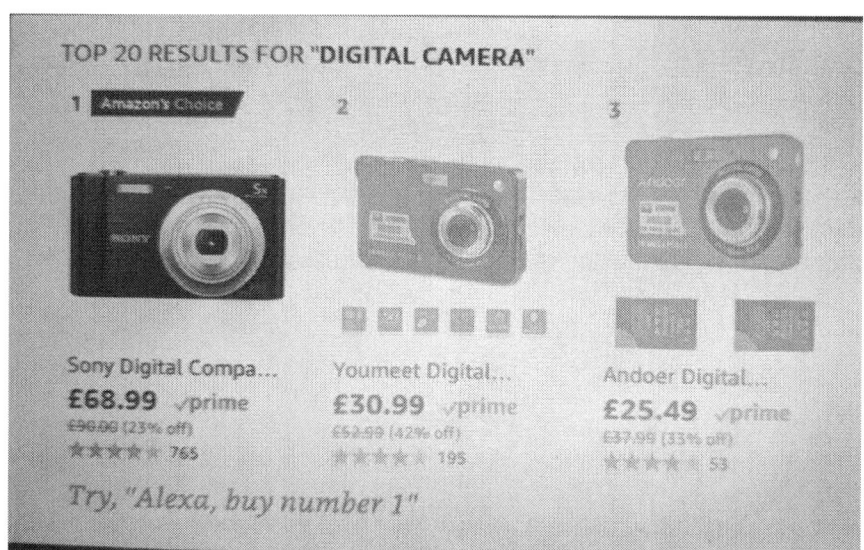

Figure 68 An Amazon Echo Show displays results for a voice query seeking a Digital Camera

Certain types of transactions that are very quick with a visual interface suddenly become less clear without a screen. However, as our assistants understand our preferences and we delegate to them, ordering can become quicker again. So, while trying to choose a seat via voice could be difficult, once my assistant knows that I'll always pick a window seat, it'll be able to carry out my instruction faster than I could achieve with an interface.

In just a few years, it's likely that you will spend as much, or more, time interacting with devices that have no screen as you do with devices that have screens, such as laptops and smartphones. While more expensive models (Amazon Show (5, 8 or 10 inch), Google Nest Hub and Hub Max) may include a screen, typically the more common models (Amazon Echo & Dot, Google Home & Nest Home Mini) don't have any visual display. Buying and selling without a screen represents a step change in the relationship between consumers and retailers/brands.

It's estimated that only 10-15% of smart speaker sales are of ones that include displays. Though Amazon and Google have both increased the range of display-equipped solutions, the low cost of their entry-level speakers and the perception from consumers that they can rely on their phones for screens many have held back the adoption of speaker devices with screens. In the interim, I expect to see the tentative growth of voice commerce support by a hybrid approach - where smart speakers with displays and smartphone screens will be used to clarify our intent in voice commands.

My first voice-only purchase was definitely unnerving. Though I'm the earliest of early adopters, I found this new method of shopping initially unnatural. In this case, I wanted to buy another Echo Dot smart speaker, so I was using Alexa to buy another Alexa device. "Alexa, order an Echo Dot," I commanded. She read out the product description and price and then asked me to confirm if I wanted to purchase, to which I answered "Yes".

I went straight to my email to see the order confirmation. There was the email from Amazon, just like a "normal" purchase. We're simply not used to buying by voice, but just like we got used to buying "it'll never work online" things, I expect we'll slowly adopt voice commerce too - initially from trusted brands like Amazon, safe in the knowledge that we can return things easily. For re-purchasing items especially, I can see voice ordering working well. For others, I think it'll take more getting used to. The growth of Assistant devices with screens will help - visual confirmation of what you're about to buy will remove a lot of the anxiety. Where you fall back to a visual interface on mobile, it pretty much defeats the purpose.

As we'll see later, returns are a huge issue for online retailers, and it remains to be seen if voice ordering will add to that. But it seems likely that Amazon will add the ability to initiate a return via Alexa too. Although easing returns is not always a good thing for a retailer, consumers love easy returns. I just asked my Echo if I could return an order and she helpfully suggested I visit Amazon.com/returns. But surely she should list orders I've made that are eligible for return and offer to start the return process for me? Shouldn't I be able to say "Alexa, I want to return the product that arrived today". She will of course know what it is, if it's eligible for free return and how best to send it back. "Ok David, I've printed a free return label on the printer in the home office - put this on an envelope and I've scheduled UPS will come to pick it up between 9 and 11am tomorrow because your calendar is free then...."

Voice Browsing

If smart speakers represent browserless shopping, there's also a role for voice shopping in our browser-dominated world. I anticipate a growth in voice-driven use of web sites - so instead of clicking and typing your way around a web site, imagine saying "Show me all the blue jackets in size medium that are in stock to ship". Although voice may not be suitable in all situations, for example in an open plan office, being able to navigate a site by voice would be significantly quicker than entering a search term and selecting multiple filters, as is common practice today.

A third-party developer called Voice2biz[161] has created a service to add voice to any Shopify-hosted e-commerce web site; it enables shoppers to make product queries and add items to their shopping cart via Alexa or Google Assistant.

Voice to Physical

As is the case with Social Media driving people to stores, we can also consider the role of voice in supporting store footfall. Google has introduced a voice feature to help consumers looking to make an in-store purchase with real time stock information in response to voice queries. For example: 'OK Google, where can I find a brown pair of men's Top-Siders, size 11, nearby?' The Assistant will answer with how many stores have the item and how far away they are. Participating retailers at launch include Saks Fifth Avenue, Bed Bath & Beyond, Home Depot, PetSmart and Sephora. The feature is powered by local inventory feeds sent by retailers that buy ads on Google.

Two Way Conversation

Currently, nearly all interactions with our voice assistants are initiated by humans - the assistants don't speak unless spoken to with their wake word. This is starting to change, however, as the technology develops - Alexa can now get our attention with a yellow flash of her spinning light. This frequently informs me when my Amazon items are due for delivery - after a soft ping to get my attention, I notice the light spinning yellow - "Alexa, What's my notification" is answered by "A delivery for David will arrive today". Useful.

But what about when she talks to us with suggestions? What if the notification light isn't a helpful update about a package I ordered, but a special offer on a product on my wish list? That is potentially interesting and valuable to me. But what if she started asking for reviews? We noted earlier the importance of reviews in the modern marketplace and Amazon often emails me reminders to leave reviews. Perhaps in the future I will chat with Alexa where she picks a good time to ask me "Did that product meet your expectations?". "No, I was disappointed with it". How useful would it be to brands if, upon detecting my displeasure, she could ask if it was ok to continue and investigate "Why not?". This could open an entirely new and almost real-time feedback to the product owner, curated by Amazon (at a cost). Thousands of reviews could be summarized by a sentiment-detection algorithm and passed back to the brand. There's a risk of irritation, but used sparingly, this could be very effective. I feel that many people would welcome to opportunity to have a conversation with a brand to give their feedback - essentially a focus group without having to attend. The Amazon Answers scheme already crowdsources feedback from customers via emails.

Any move away from screen-based commerce is a major concern for advertisers. Adverts injected into a voice transaction are likely to be perceived as highly intrusive and likely to meet with the same ad-blocking resistance that has become common in web browsing. As we move into a more voice-oriented world, many things will change. A less visual paradigm will particularly challenge our assumptions around, for example, advertising. While advertising can be somewhat intrusive in a visual world, it can usually be tolerated as we can (sometimes) ignore it on a web page and focus on the content we want. But in a narrow channel like voice, where there is only bandwidth for one message, we will not tolerate commercial intrusions and interruptions in our dialogs.

However, Spotify conducted some early experiments in mid-2019 with voice-enabled advertising with a limited set of Spotify Free users in the US. For users who had previously enabled the Spotify app to access their microphone (to enable voice-based search), adverts asked consumers to respond if they wanted more information - in the absence of a response, the next advert played, but if the user asked for more detail, additional information was played.

Voice Advertising

A frequent theme in the discussion of all the changes in the retail/consumer goods space is how they will impact not just the direct areas such as store closures, but also adjacent, highly dependent industries such as advertising. So it's not surprising to see (or hear) experiments from advertisers testing the viability of new interfaces such as voice for advertising purposes, especially as their traditional audiences get ever more fragmented and, in some cases, move away from screens where ads can be displayed.

Start-up Instreamatic allows people to talk at adverts they see and get an AI-driven voice response, just as you might talk to an Alexa device. Instead of an audio ad playing to a listener as a one-way communication (like every TV and radio ad before it), brands can now reach and engage with consumers by having voice-interactive conversations. The technology allows people to use their voice to set their advertising preferences, so a person can simply say "not interested" to tell a brand to stop targeting them with that product. Online music service Pandora has started testing these features.

Merchant Impacts

Not all of the developments in voice technology relating to retail are customer-facing. There are some examples of voice technology being used to improve business efficiency. For example, e-commerce platform Shopify has developed a solution where its merchants can manage their business with voice commands, asking (via Alexa) for trading updates.

Brands and retailers will need to keep a close eye (or should I say ear?) on the take up of voice commerce. If and when it becomes more popular, things like search engine optimization (SEO) – that you think you've just about grasped – will have to be re-imagined. Spoken queries means businesses need to be prepared to handle a massive variety of natural language queries, and even the colloquialisms unlikely to be entered in a search box but common in speech. Although well-labeled databases with good meta data should already be in place for e-commerce, they may require updates to handle voice queries - instead of relying on users ticking set filters, they may ask for "black or brown shoes, size 8, waterproof and not too formal".

In order to narrow the search criteria, the smart speaker or website will need to be able to respond by asking the consumer further details – "do you particularly want laced shoes or slip-on?" I also think that customers will expect voice interfaces to offer shortcuts - so instead of reading a long product description page, as is currently the case, they may ask specific questions to avoid the overload that is common today, when product detail pages provide very comprehensive specifications that are there for completeness but may actually be of little interest to many consumers. This means that merchants need to revisit their product listings to ensure they sound good when read out and aren't formatted just for on-screen display.

Ask and you shall receive

A major part of the new voice-led world is an Intelligent Agent (also known as Intelligent Assistant). Over time, all of us will have many, perhaps dozens of them, interacting with each other and acting on our behalf. These Intelligent Agents will be the "ghost in the machine" in voice first devices. They will be dispatched independently of the fundamental software and form a secondary layer that can fluidly connect between a spectrum of services and systems. They'll know the places we go, the people we interact with, our habits, our tastes and preferences, and more. Then they'll use this data to anticipate our needs.

We've seen successive big changes in how we interact with technology since the original punch cards, progressed to keyboards, then graphical user interface (GUI) and then touchscreens. But each requiring a proximate interaction with a device on your desk, lap or in your hand. It also created a barrier for those not familiar with the interface. But voice is a dramatic difference in terms of accessibility - my mother uses a computer only since she can talk to it.

The moment you ask an AI-assistant to complete a task, you're disintermediated - ask Alexa for a movie and she may choose to serve it to you via one service over another. Amazon may be paid for that. As a consumer, you may not care as long as you get the product you want at a price you're happy with. The supply chain doesn't matter to you. But it makes Amazon the middleman in a way it doesn't get to be when you simply open Netflix via a touch interface or a mouse click- if you command Alexa to open Netflix, Amazon now knows you're watching Netflix.

"By the way"

As I sat down to write some of this Chapter, I asked my Google Assistant to play some music; "Play some Dido" I instructed. "Sure, playing Dido from Spotify. By the way, she's performing in Dublin on December 1st." I was slightly startled by that response - did my smart speaker just try to subtly sell me concert tickets?

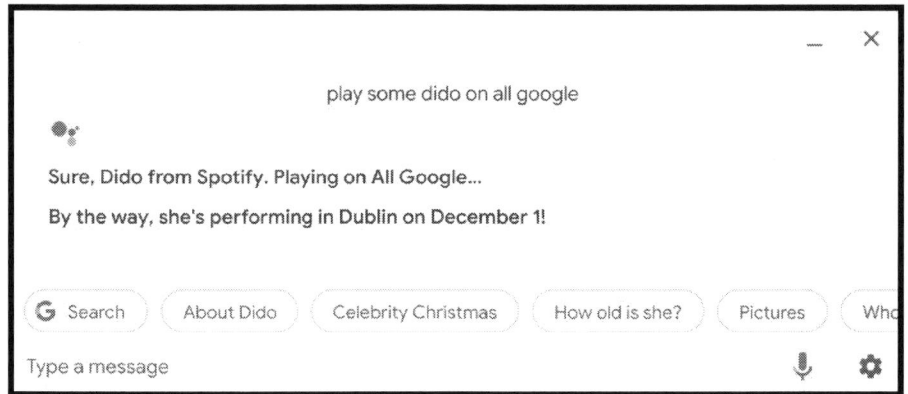

Figure 69 Google Assistant adds a "By the Way" to an answer

This is a kind of experience that we should get used to. Opportune, tailored, micro-selling moments will become commonplace. Adverts like this don't feel intrusive if they get the relevance right and can be dismissed with a "don't tell me about upcoming gigs". But what does it mean for how we shop if we have an omnipresent digital agent acting on our behalf, curating, looking to cater to our every whim, whether we know it or not? I immediately began to think of the retail implications of my Assistant's seemingly innocent little suffix, "by the way". This cuts out the need for mass advertising - target just the people who have listened to the artist or similar artists. Who owns that relationship? If I had answered, "Great, get me two tickets", what happens next and how does it differ from a traditional transaction?

Similarly, after answering my query to Alexa about how much Fitbit recorded for my sleep last night, she just said to me: "Because you use Fitbit, Amazon recommends you try another popular fitness skill called "5 minute plank workout" - do you want to try it"? This brings us on to the next major topic - where humans do less of the shopping as the machines take on a greater role.

Chapter 7: Removing The Humans

"Amazon wants you to stop shopping! Amazon doesn't want to deal with humans. It's all about APIs".

Wired[162]

One logical conclusion of efforts to speed up shopping and reduce friction is to eliminate friction altogether - by removing from the process the inefficient humans that add delays. In this Chapter, we'll examine how we've already started to distance ourselves from on-going purchase decisions and the potential to further automate our shopping decisions. Across all of the new platforms and new interfaces, the common thread is of course to make shopping easier - make it faster, more personal, less effort and through the gradual reduction of input to shopping, eventually eliminate our involvement in much of it.

Augmented Shopping

While most of this Chapter looks at the likely gradual reduction in effort we put into shopping, the first section will look at how those people that continue to shop themselves will be more efficient shoppers than before. Those that continue to shop will seek to improve their own efficiency. For cases where we're not ready to relinquish total control and involvement in shopping, and in cases where the shopper is motivated by the thrill of the hunt for a bargain, we will see an increase in what I term "augmented shopping" - cases where we use technology to assist us in achieving the optimum outcome in traditional shopping channels. In the future, few people will shop without some level of digital assistance.

When I mention augmented shopping, you might think I'm talking again about augmented reality (AR) but this time, I'm referring to tools that augment or enhance our ability to shop - make us more efficient, more economical. This includes apps to help us find bargains, redeem vouchers and compare products. These tools can help remove or reduce our failings and inefficiencies - building on the concept of empowering consumers by eliminating information asymmetry - not only about the product but also how best to acquire it.

Price Comparison

Recent years have seen the rise of price comparison sites, but they remain passive - consumers typically must be aware of the price comparison site, trust it, remember to use it and then be in a position to act on the advice rendered. This is frequently too much effort for a consumer and retailers continue to rely on information asymmetry to charge higher prices to at least some part of their customer base. Consider, for example, price match guarantees from some retailers. These are meant to reassure consumers that they are getting the best price but, in practice, retailers are rarely challenged to match a competitor price, relying on our inaction or perception that if they are willing to price match, then surely they aren't charging prices that are too high.

Already there are several plug-ins for web browsers that automatically check other web sites for comparative prices when we're browsing e-commerce sites. But we are seeing the rise of more proactive tools that will require less effort on the part of the consumer - building on the shifts we talked about earlier regarding information asymmetry, the advantage will shift further into the consumers hands. There have long been avid bargain hunters willing to go to great lengths to score a bargain, meticulously collecting coupons or scouring stores for bargains even if it involves some level of inconvenience, such as purchasing more of an item that you might ordinarily want but at a discount. But with technology, the information advantage is shifting in favor of the consumer - now capable of being in possession of near perfect information and with super-human awareness of bargains and deals.

This stage isn't so much about humans stopping shopping, but humans stopping shopping *on their own* - instead augmenting their shopping skills with digitally enhanced knowledge of shortcuts, time savers, money savers - any and all ways to get more out of our shopping. Shoppers will rely less on brands and retailers to inform and curate and look more to software for information to enhance their shopping experience. One aspect in this is how consumers can try to benefit from the multitude of discounts and loyalty schemes available.

Gifts, Discounts and Loyalty

Promotion coupons and codes are a valuable tool for retailers not only to woo shoppers, but also to track the effectiveness of various advertising channels. Loyalty schemes are popular with consumers, who feel they are getting something for nothing and being rewarded for their loyalty. They are also popular with retailers who carefully tweak their business case to ensure that the terms of the schemes are popular enough to appeal to consumers but still financially sound, retaining customers at a price that's more acceptable that the cost of acquiring new ones.

The economics of discounts offered by retailers often rely on psychological tricks and on assumptions regarding redemption levels. There are plenty of (in)famous examples of promotional schemes where the redemption rates exceeded expectations and rendered the exercise a loss maker, but far more examples of cases where loyalty points "expire" or require onerous conditions for use. Often, offer "deals" may appear to be good value and seem to constitute a reduction over previous pricing. However, upon closer examination, the promotions don't always offer consumers the best possible value.

The economics of loyalty schemes will be fundamentally altered as we move to more automated means of shopping - automated shoppers will be a lot more likely to use them than forgetful humans. Automated agents won't fall foul of retailer attempts to obscure and obfuscate offers and will claim any and all benefits, entitlements, lodging claims for refunds or discounts that we might not utilize.

There are already plenty of apps to help passive shoppers become more aware of offers - from apps like iBotta (which claims to have saved its users over $600m) and ebates, to services like Honey[163], that automatically applies coupons on popular sites as you shop, via a Chrome extension. Start-up DoNotPay.com has introduced a service where it will call company customer service on a consumer's behalf and then call the consumer when an agent is available, eliminating the time wasted waiting on hold, which is a major bugbear for consumers. It is also capable of identifying savings or unused subscriptions as part of its $3 per month subscription. A Canadian start-up, Drop[164], has created a loyalty app aimed at Gen Y (Millennials) that has gained over 3 million users. Using the Drop app to shop, consumers can automatically earn points to redeem at Amazon, Starbucks and others, while associating the customer's bank card means they can offer very personalized adverts based on your spending. Capital One Bank offers a service called Paribus that will automatically contact Amazon to request compensation if your guaranteed delivery is late.

While consumers may like these tools, retailer attitudes to them are not always positive. Just as PayPal paid a massive $4 billion to acquire Honey for example, Amazon warned customers that using the browser extension posed a security risk[165].

If you consider these apps as helpers or assistants, the next obvious step is to integrate them with other changes in how we approach shopping. By relying more on these tools, humans will further change how they shop.

Low Touch to No Touch Shopping

The shopping methods we discussed in the previous Chapters and the tools available to augment our shopping still involve some degree of human input, though they typically require less input than current shopping modes that require either a trip to a store, or an explicit intent to purchase via a purely commercially-driven website or app. The reduction of effort on the part of humans in discovery and transaction is well under way, not only in physical stores, as we saw in Chapter 4, but also in digital channels. This trend is in itself seismic for retailers. But the change is not stopping there. Now, I want to explore how humans are being taken out not only of physical stores, but also out of the shopping process itself.

Automating Purchase

If we move beyond the emphasis on automating tasks, improving efficiency and easing the burden of physical shopping, the next key topic to look at is the trend towards *lowering consumer involvement in decisions*, particularly on an on-going basis. This reduction in human input to shopping is a key trend for the next decade. Less involvement by humans is the first step towards their eventual secession from much shopping activity and that concept should terrify brands and retailers who are not adapting to survive in this emerging reality.

We saw in Chapter 4 the tendency to remove humans from various points in the retail sales and transaction processes, be it

McDonald's ordering kiosks, Starbucks Mobile app, self-checkouts, restaurants with pay at the table, or Amazon Go. But what if we look at removing humans from earlier in the chain?

In this section, we'll start with a look at the trend towards subscription models, as well as the new ways to shop that reduce the mental effort invested in, and the time spent shopping. Earlier, I noted the changes that technology has brought in shopper behavior during the research phase, as well as the shift away from ownership to access. The amount of time and on-going effort invested in many purchase decisions are decreasing rapidly, severely reducing the opportunities for retailer interventions.

Subscriptions

"Consumers receive things they need or want without having to make any decisions, and that creates more stable and predictable revenue streams for the businesses they patronize"

Utpal Dholakia, Marketing Professor, Rice University

I met the co-founder of Spotify in 2009 when he came to pitch their then-new concept to me. As someone running a business that sold millions of pounds worth of music track downloads per year, Spotify was a terrifying concept for me – he was proposing access to pretty much all of the music in the world for a monthly subscription. No more consumers choosing, paying for and downloading individual tracks - instead of owning individual tracks, consumers could rent access to all tracks. Fast forward just 10 years and the concept of music subscriptions is no longer new - it is the norm and I personally have been a Spotify user now for over a decade and have not bought a CD in that time, despite consuming more music than ever. The majority of the music industry now revolves around subscription streaming music services such as Spotify and Apple Music. While a small number of retro fans espouse the ownership benefits and sound quality of vinyl, less than 20% of music is now consumed via physical media. 80% of the $5.4bn retail music industry is now streaming[166]. Humans no longer shop for music - they subscribe to it.

Sign Me Up

You can now find a subscription for almost any category of product. The quest for convenience, and the attractiveness of the subscription model for suppliers, has led to established providers and start-ups looking to turn a number of formerly individual consumer decisions and transactions into recurring subscriptions.

Subscriptions aren't a new idea, but they are being applied to new areas. For decades, subscriptions were the province of periodicals, TV providers and utilities. Now, you can make a one-time purchase decision and rely on a brand or retailer to continue meeting your needs until you tell them to stop (assuming you remember to tell them). Fundamentally, subscriptions are scheduled repeat purchases but, compared to standard purchases, they are effectively invisible. Unless you check your credit card or bank statement, you won't see the monthly deduction, making it immeasurably less painful than actually repeating a transaction or even worse, handing over cash at a till. It's the ultimate example of what psychologists call "coupling"[167] - where there's a disconnect between when we consume and when we pay.

Subscriptions apply to both physical and digital goods. From Spotify and Netflix to Microsoft Office 365 Home, consumers sign up for recurring payments to get access to content and services in the same way as they do to receive physical goods, for example, from Razors (e.g. Dollar Shave Club) to Clothes (e.g. Stitch Fix) to Meal Kits (e.g. Blue Apron). According to McKinsey[168] research, some 50% of online shoppers have signed up for a subscription service in the past 12 months.

Entertainment services are now among the most common subscription offerings, with the speed and convenience streamed access to a vast library of content, offered by the likes of Netflix and Spotify appealing more to people than owning individual movies or CDs.

Similarly in corporate circles, many companies have moved from once-off purchases to using Software as a Service (SaaS) and choose to access Google Suite, Slack and other services on a recurring fee per employee basis - 84% of net new software is now being delivered as Software as a Service (SaaS)[169].

You can now outsource decision-making to numerous brands and trust them to deliver on your unique needs. That expectation has burrowed deep into the consumer psyche via a host of 'we do the thinking for you' subscription services: think razors, cars, music, food, and more. The subscription e-commerce market in the US has grown over 100% a year over the past 5 years according to McKinsey. For those consumers who have turned to subscription instead of shopping, the median number of subscriptions an active subscriber holds is two, but nearly 35 percent have three or more. Male shoppers are more likely than women to have three or more active subscriptions—42 percent versus 28 percent, respectively—suggesting that men particularly value automated purchasing and the ability to limit store trips.

When assessing subscriptions as a substitute for traditional shopping methods, recommendations, including word of mouth and positive online reviews, are key triggers for consumers to sign up. Unlike other shopping channels for non-commodity goods, consumers expect subscriptions to become more tailored over time as the provider gets to know them, and can then use data analytics to customize the content - for example to send more relevant products or make better recommendations for digital content.

When consumers are faced with a monthly subscription, the level of scrutiny in the decision-making process goes up. They enter into a new mental model where they process the question of whether it is worth it or not with greater scrutiny. There is both a positive and negative to this reality from the point of view of the provider. The negative is, it becomes a larger hurdle to get over for the consumer as they investigate the subscription's true worth more deeply. The positive is, that once they choose to subscribe, they become a much more engaged customer.

Crucially, subscriptions are most often a one-time decision - once it's made, there's no longer any shopping, just consumption. Already, many industries have been built on locking in customers either through defined mechanics such as subscriptions or frequently just the inertia of customers. Subscriptions were initially common for time-dependent things like monthly magazines or cell phone plan subscriptions, but recent trends towards cloud services rather than ownership for media (such as Music or Movies) have replaced ownership of DVDs/CDs for many people with subscriptions to services that offer access to far more content than anyone could typically own.

More recently, there has been an explosion in the number of subscription services for physical goods that weren't previously sold using a subscription model. As a business model, subscriptions are a hugely attractive method. Knowing that you have a steady revenue stream provides a level of certainty that accountants and investors love. The only potential downside is that it tends to lock the customer in at a particular price point with limited opportunity to increase the value of each sale. However, the lifetime value and the occasional cross or upsell makes that an easy choice for most businesses.

Subscriptions for Everything

Let's look at some of the newer areas for subscriptions that would previously have been a traditional purchase process. These will have a major impact on the retail sector if large numbers of people switch to this less involved method of shopping.

Automobiles

While it's long been common practice to lease a car rather than purchase it outright, there are now subscription packages where you can not only have the use of the car model you're leasing, but you can swap to another car for particular occasions - such as going on a road trip. For automakers and dealers, the notion of reduced involvement in what used to be one of the largest purchases made by a consumer, poses a massive threat. Now consumers are buying into the availability of mobility that meets their needs rather than purchasing or leasing a single car or truck model.

Furniture

Just as the music and movies industries have moved customers away from ownership of CDs and DVDs, there are now alternatives to owning large items such as furniture. Traditionally, consumers purchased furniture and frequently hauled it long distances when moving residence - the average American changes residences more than 11 times over the course of their life, according to the U.S. Census Bureau.

With the availability of subscriptions for home furnishings, consumers can now opt to change their furniture in line with their changing needs, tastes or location. Among the options in this space are Fernish (that we mentioned in Chapter 3) and Feather[170], which gives customers in New York City and some areas of California, the ability to rent furniture of all sorts, including Sofas, Beds, Tables and more from a catalog of its own designs as well as brands like Casper and West Elm. Customers can rent furniture either by piece or even opt for curated rooms - essentially opting out of the entire shopping process. From $19 a month membership plus a cost for each item you rent, Feather is aimed at Millennials or young professionals who rent their homes and move every couple of years. Feather offers the ability to rent quality furniture rather than the previous practice of buying cheap self-assembly furniture with each move. Delivery and assembly are included with the monthly membership fee and subscribers who particularly like the pieces they try can buy them outright.

As well as offering the convenience and flexibility consumers crave, Feather is also trying to align itself with the increased interest in environmental impacts highlighted in Chapter 2. Feather founder and CEO Jay Reno promotes the company as offering a fully circular system where used and unwanted items are returned to Feather, instead of ending up in a landfill. Interestingly, Feather sees its strength not only in its business model but also in its curation similar to that offered by a more traditional retailer - its range of furniture is varied, though not unlimited. "People actually don't want to have unlimited choice. They want to have a nice, curated selection of things to choose from a company they trust" according to Reno[171].

Clothing

If furniture subscriptions might help consumers delay a purchase decision that feels too permanent to handle, firms such as Rent the Runway (RTR) that we talked about in Chapter 2 might help shoppers stop making purchases that have gotten too easy. The dizzying variety offered by online shopping and the pressure to look great on social media create an intense incentive for people to continually expand their wardrobe, which can strain both budgets and the physical limits of one's closet. Rent the Runway opened in 2009 to rent special-occasion dresses, but in 2016, it launched a $159-a-month service that gives subscribers access to a rotating array of everyday clothing. Users can swap out for new pieces when they're done or keep things they like for an extra fee.

RTR now boasts over 11 million customers, suggesting that a significant market shift away from clothing ownership is indeed happening. In an interesting example of coopetition with the traditional apparel sales market, Rent the Runway and Nordstrom have collaborated to enable RTR returns via selected Nordstrom locations, building on RTR's use of WeWork locations for popup facilities, while, in an example of further expansion, RTR has announced it will work with West Elm to provide access to homewares.

Both Feather and Rent the Runway think they have identified places where the things people are supposed to own don't really line up with the ways they have to live their lives: many people rent their homes for a lot longer now, and the internet speeds up trend cycles and keeps permanent records of every outfit you've ever been photographed in. Owning things is great, but the constant pressure to shop and acquire—and especially to do so beyond one's means as a signal of success—is wasteful of both material resources and money. For some, buying flexibility and novelty without commitment or unnecessary waste might seem more appealing than owning stuff.

Kids Apparel

For parents, shopping for kids clothes can be time consuming, expensive and all-too-frequent as kids grow. Several companies have identified this as an area that would benefit particularly from subscription services: parents can now choose to have apparel or shoes delivered at regular intervals. For example, Nike has its Adventure Club service that sends new sneakers every month, two months, or quarter (60% of Nike's trial customers opted for the latter frequency), with a choice of style, from performance shoes for sport to casual everyday sneakers, and the ability to skip months and swap sneakers if they don't fit or their kid doesn't like them. And echoing the growing interest in sustainability, when the kids outgrow the sneakers, they send them back to Nike for donation or recycling. In the US, Target, Gap, Rent The Runway and Walmart also offer subscription boxes for kids clothes.

More Examples

Taking on the entrenched establishment of giants like Gillette and Schick, subscription services Dollar Shave Club (acquired by Unilever for $1 billion) and Harry's grew to a combined 14 million subscribers before Gillette responded with its own subscription offering. Uber is actively testing a monthly subscription pass that combines rides, Eats, bikes and scooters[172]. In this pilot phase, Uber is testing a few different iterations in San Francisco and Chicago, but each version includes a fixed discount on every ride, free Uber Eats delivery and free JUMP (bikes and scooters) rides. The pass costs $24.99 per month.

Other high profile examples of subscription solutions include Birchbox, which provides women with miniature portions of beauty products on a monthly basis for $15; American Eagle is offering an apparel rental service named "Style Drop" where subscribers pay $49.95 each month to take out three items at a time and JC Penney's Big and Tall subscription box. Mudjeans[173] allows consumers to rent 3 pairs of jeans and return them for recycling at the end of a year as well as swap them for new ones.

In the vast and growing area of video games, all of the major players (Microsoft Game Pass, Sony PlayStation Now, Apple Arcade+ and Google's Play Pass) offer subscription services with access to a curated, rotating library of games for a fixed monthly fee at significantly less cost than outright purchase of games.

As well as lifestyle, clothing and digital products, there's a number of other vendors trying the subscription model. Sonos has announced bundles of its speakers for rent, while Nespresso offers its machines virtually free if you subscribe to monthly coffee deliveries. Dell is launching a subscription model for its computers. Even Burger King has joined the subscription bandwagon, offering the BK Cafe subscription, in which you can pay $5 a month to get one small cup of coffee per day at its restaurants, so long as you download the Burger King App.

Amazon & Subscriptions

"With Prime, Amazon single-handedly — and permanently — raised the bar for convenience in online shopping. That, in turn, forever changed the types of products shoppers were willing to buy online. Need a last-minute gift or nearing the end of a pack of diapers? Amazon was now an alternative to the immediacy of brick-and-mortar stores".

Vox.com[174]

There's plenty to talk about regarding Amazon's involvement with subscriptions. It has seen subscriptions as a key part of the future of shopping since 2005, with the launch of Amazon Prime, and again in 2007 with the launch of Subscribe & Save, as well as its more recent focus on Kindle Unlimited, Ring Protect, Audible Membership and Subscription/Discovery Boxes.

Prime

You can't talk about the growth and importance of subscriptions to the future of shopping without mentioning Amazon Prime. *In the interests of full disclosure and transparency, I am an Amazon Prime subscriber and have been for 5 years now*. That doesn't make me in any way unusual. As of January 2020, there are over 150 million people globally who are Amazon Prime Subscribers. According to most estimates (Amazon doesn't release exact subscriber numbers), fully two-thirds of US online shoppers have either their own Prime subscription or access to a family member's.

When it was announced, many investors questioned the wisdom of the Prime Subscription (which was then $79 and offered unlimited 2-day shipping). But it wasn't really about the fee. While it provides a large upfront income, the tie-in it creates in the consumer's mind is the key competitive advantage. Once they've paid for Prime, consumers default to shopping on Amazon and quite literally stop shopping around - the commitment of the Prime Membership hooks the consumer who wants to "get their money's worth" so they stop checking other sites. In the meantime, Amazon learns more about them and markets directly to them in a terrific example of lock-in. The average Prime member in the United States spends $1,400 a year on Amazon, compared with $600 for non-members, and the gap is widening, according to Consumer Intelligence Research Partners. Author Doug Stephens[175] found that 96% of 2nd year prime subscribers renew for a 3rd, making it a phenomenally sticky proposition.

Prime membership grants access to an entire lifestyle of Amazon-powered seamless convenience - Prime has become the glue that holds together many of Amazon's other offers. For example, you can't shop via Alexa unless you're a Prime member, nor can you use Dash Replenishment Services (DRS) and Amazon Key. Amazon Day that we'll discuss in the next Chapter is also a Prime exclusive.

Subscribe & Save

Allows you to set up regular purchases of items you're likely to want on a recurring basis. So, for example, when I go to Amazon to purchase AA batteries, it offers me 5% off the standard price if I subscribe to receive another delivery in two months' time (which they say is the most common frequency for this item). If I subscribe to 5 products, the discount increases from 5% to 15%.

Subscribe & Save is available on thousands of staple items and offers consumers a degree of flexibility in for their shipments - any scheduled purchase can be skipped without cancelling the following delivery.

Subscription & Discovery Boxes

Building on the trend started by services like Birchbox or BarkBox, there's now a dedicated Amazon portal for subscriptions boxes - separate from the Subscribe & Save option described above that's intended for everyday replenishment rather than curated boxes. These boxes are meant to involve an element of surprise/discovery and so address one of the key criticisms of online shopping compared to physical retail - the lack of browsing and instore discovery serendipity.

Other Amazon Subscriptions

As well as Prime, Subscribe & Save and Subscription Boxes, Amazon offers Kindle and Audible subscriptions for ebook and audiobook content, and more recently bought PillPack which offers a personalized subscription service for prescription medications with monthly deliveries of individually packaged dosage packs grouped by time of day.

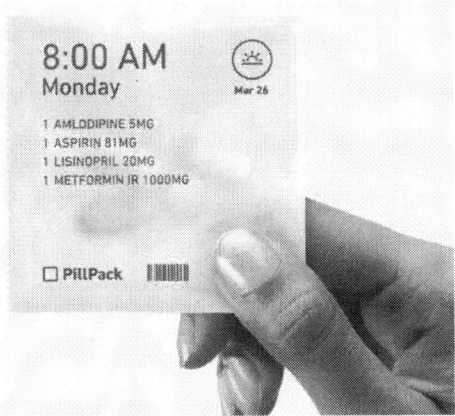

Figure 70 Amazon PillPack subscription prescription service

This move to stop shopping for prescribed medicines, which traditionally required a visit to a pharmacy and the attendant chance of additional purchases, is a major concern for physical store pharmacists. It also potentially gives Amazon access to a wealth of data to target adjacent services.

Retailer Reaction

As disruptive start-ups and Amazon familiarize consumers with subscription models, traditional retailers have moved at varying paces to adjust to this change in consumer shopping behaviors. This strong growth has attracted established consumer brand manufacturers and retailers to enter the subscription space, aware of the inertia factor once a customer is signed up to a service. Examples include, P&G (Gillette on Demand), Sephora (Play!), and Walmart (Beauty Box). The market has also seen significant M&A activity—in particular, Unilever's $1 billion acquisition of Dollar Shave Club (2016) and the $200 million-plus deal that the grocery chain Albertsons did for meal-kit company Plated.

The dominant popularity of Prime has led other retailers to scramble to assemble a competitive offer. Walmart, the largest retailer in the US, has responded with its "Delivery Unlimited" proposition offering $98 annual fixed fee for unlimited grocery deliveries, while Target acquisition Shipt also offers a $99 annual fee. CVS has introduced an annual membership subscription at $48 which offers free delivery on prescriptions.

Flexibility, Data and AI

The demands of the modern consumer can, at times, seem contradictory. Consumers want the convenience of not having to think about shopping for certain products, yet they want more flexibility than the blunt tool of a subscription that delivers the same amount of the same thing on the same day every month. But thanks to technology and logistical flexibility, modern subscriptions are not as rigid as before, enabling providers to tackle the convenience vs inflexibility conundrum. Subscriptions don't necessarily mean 'rigid' anymore. All of the recent start-ups based on subscriptions provide greater control over the cadence and composition of their deliveries, with their app putting power in the consumer's hand.

For example, clothing styling service Stitch Fix (more on them later) offers recurring timings but also lets its customers dictate when they want to receive clothing shipments and hopes that satisfaction with the service drives them to sign up for more frequent shipments. Under Armour's curated ArmourBox has 60- and 90-day options for customers who don't need new sports attire every month. Pet Food supplier Ollie changed their frequency options, but also their packaging - to facilitate larger, less frequent deliveries - in response to customer feedback.

An on-going challenge for many subscription service providers is managing product supply compared to actual consumer usage; consumers will be strongly motivated to cancel when deliveries pile up or there's a lack of flexibility in volumes to match their varying requirements for example, due to travel. In these situations, the nuisance of dealing with the supply/demand mismatch may lead consumers to perceive the convenience as lost. Subscriptions that sound convenient, if they aren't flexible, have the opposite effect to what was expected - the customer may feel that control of purchase decisions has been lost rather than managed.

Finding the right proposition for customers is a delicate balance - of course, if subscription services overcomplicate their parameters and negate the simplicity of the subscription model, this too will send customers back to the traditional shopping model. The key factor, which is readily available in the case of subscription services which have a direct customer relationship envied by traditional retail, is feedback. Subscription providers have ready access to customer insights as a basis to modify their existing subscription models. For example, Rent the Runway added a new, cheaper membership tier, which lends customers four items a month—from high-end brands, such as Tory Burch and DVF—for $89 per month alongside the unlimited items plan for $159 per month.

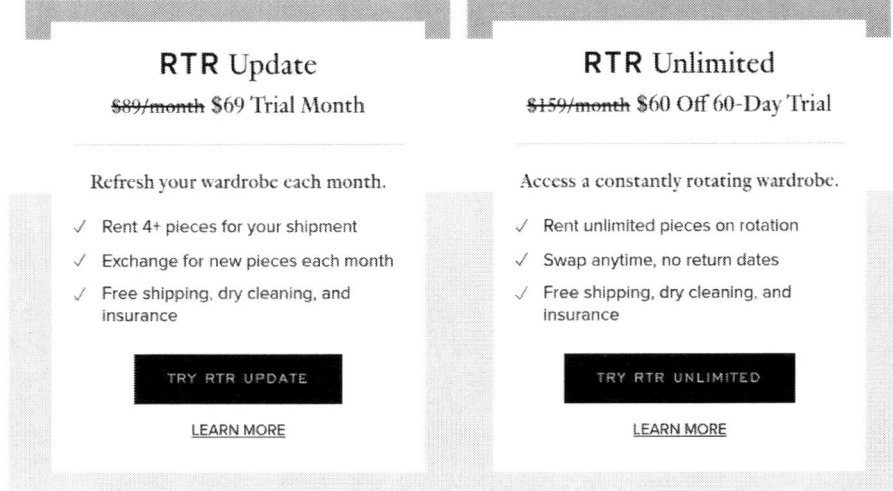

Figure 71 Example RTR plans, as at Sept 2019

In this area, there is help available for retailers - a B2B start-up named Recurly[176] uses machine learning to manage plans with a variety of billing models (e.g., fixed, seat-based, hybrid, and usage-based) and frequencies, and to extend to subscribers the ability to purchase single or multiple plans and combine them with one-time products or services. Recurly automatically prorates billing changes that result from subscriber upgrades, along with those arising from downgrades, refunds, or service credits.

When Humans Stop Subscribing

Subscriptions have very obvious benefits for sellers - once they've acquired customers, they can expect a substantial number of them, maybe even a majority, to continue to pay for the service, providing a predictable revenue stream. For consumers, subscriptions can also offer extreme convenience, as well as managed, predictable expenditure. But the increasing number of subscriptions now available may see consumers signing up for things they don't have time to consume or remaining subscribed to services or plans they don't need.

It All Adds Up - Subscription Fatigue

For quite a while, Netflix was the undisputed king of content subscriptions. Yes, Amazon Prime Video is also popular, but most people access that as part of Prime and don't think of it as a direct Netflix competitor. But suddenly, consumers are going to be offered Apple TV+, Disney+, Hulu, HBO Max and Peacock (NBC/Universal). As futurist Amy Webb[177] puts it, there are two crucial questions:

1. What's the consumer threshold for subscription spending?
2. Assuming most consumers don't have unlimited money, how will they prioritize what's available?

Monthly subscriptions are usually fairly small-sounding amounts. But if you sign up for something at $10 per month and then don't use it, you'll have wasted $120 in a year. If the sign-up option had asked for $120, there's every chance you wouldn't have signed up, but at $10 per month, it sounds much more reasonable. Subscription plans are generally fairly broad and carefully scoped to push consumers up to higher tiers - engineered to appeal to a wide audience while still delivering profit to the purveyor. That can make it hard for consumers to evaluate their ideal plan. Consumers tend to overestimate how much they'll use a service. The average American pays $237 a month for subscription services, according to a July 2018 report from West Monroe Partners[178]. Eighty-four percent of Americans also completely underestimate how much they spend every month, according to the report. Some providers do offer good value plans for multiple users – so, for example, Amazon Prime Subscribers can add family members who can also avail of free next day delivery. Services like Spotify and Apple Music offer family plans at a significant discount compared to purchasing multiple individual subscriptions.

Retention and Cancellation

The great convenience of subscriptions - that you sign up once and forget about it - is also a potential trap for unvigilant consumers. Although of great benefit for the companies who continue to collect the recurring revenue, consumers are often wasting money every month. But subscription services see churn of users as the months go by, even those with onerous cancellation policies. Even the best-performing services such as Netflix and Dollar Shave Club retain only ~50% of their customers for more than two years.

Churn is the biggest challenge for subscription providers. Churn, or the number of customers who cancel, is a key metric for subscription businesses. Given the typical high customer acquisition cost (CAC) for a new customer, it's vital that they stay long enough to generate a positive lifetime value (LTV) and provide enough data to enable meaningful personalization.

A McKinsey report on Subscriptions[179], found that nearly 40 percent of e-commerce subscribers have canceled their subscriptions. Many consumers who churn do so quickly; more than one-third of consumers who sign up for a subscription service cancel in less than three months, and over half cancel within six. The meal-kit category seems to have particularly high rates of cancellation within the first six months (60 to 70 percent and higher), probably reflecting consumers who overestimate their culinary abilities, even from meal kits.

Despite the high churn in many instances, the subscription e-commerce market is growing quickly. For consumers, subscription services, products or boxes offer a convenient, personalized, and often lower-cost way to buy what they want or need. Companies in the space must develop great experiences (as opposed to great subscriptions) to avoid high churn rates and to accelerate both growth and profitability. Subscriptions and the attendant flexibility can suit certain life stages, but for many, especially older generations, the precarity of the rental & subscription worlds are not appealing. The beauty for the seller is that it's a once-off transaction, and while many use obstructive tactics to make cancelling hard, there's a hope that without a visible proactive transaction, you'll just let it roll.

App Help

There are large numbers of apps (e.g. Truebill, Trim) dedicated to helping you manage your subscriptions. However, they typically require access to your bank details to scan your accounts for recurring transactions, which may dissuade some people from using them. Simpler options (e.g. Bobby) let you manually input subscriptions, allowing you to at least track the ones you remember to input. The growth of subscription tracking apps means service providers can't depend on inertia to the extent they may have in the past - yet another example of augmented shopping.

Even without app help, cancelling subscriptions is likely to get easier. The growth of this form of shopping has led to increased regulation in favor of consumers. For example, a 2018 California law, which requires businesses to provide a way to cancel subscriptions online, has outlawed the practice of requiring cancellation via phone even if you had signed up online.

Apple Inc., with its significant share of the market for digital subscriptions via its App Store, has responded to consumer concern about subscription creep and inadvertent signups. The company updated its guidelines for mobile developers to more clearly spell out what is and what is not allowed - it explicitly states that the monthly subscription price has to be clearly displayed. Messages about free trials have to say how long trials last and what will be charged when the trial ends. Both iOS and Android offer a single consolidated list of all subscriptions you've signed up for via their app stores, as well as single-button cancellation. As the subscriptions market matures and consumers become more aware of sharp practices from retailers, there's even a growing tendency for consumers to sign up initially with a short life or limited balance debit card to protect themselves from on-going charges.

Replenishment

"The answer is simple: for all standardized repeat purchases and non-tactile shopping trips, the Internet and home delivery will win. Recognizing this early is key for the survival of a retailer.

In the next 10 years, it is not inconceivable that people will receive 50 percent of grocery supplies through online ordering or predictive frictionless commerce".

Retail's Seismic Shift - Michael Dart & Robin Lewis

When it comes to groceries and household items, 85% of the items shoppers put in their carts are the same from week to week. What we think of as shopping is often just re-purchasing the same items, with little or no choice or decision phase.

"Same Again"

Although many people probably believe they aren't creatures of habit, the data shows we tend to purchase the same things repeatedly, largely sticking with the products we know. This raises the question about the efficiency of trekking to a store on a regular basis to repurchase the same things over and over again.

The concept of replenishment is somewhat similar to subscription, but often with the added element of a trigger other than time - we buy consumables as we need them rather than on a fixed schedule. For many of the items that we traditionally purchase repeatedly, there isn't a practical subscription offer available.

Retailers like nothing more than a captive customer and every visit to the supermarket is a chance for consumers to be swayed. Producers on the other hand want it to be easier for you to buy and harder for you to switch. Brands love the concept of replenishment - businesses depend on inertia and habit. Every time you enter a supermarket (at least once per week, often more), a brand runs the risk of losing you to a competitor who is better placed, better priced or better packaged. The advertising world exists to persuade you of the merits of one very similar product over another. Yet many are in fact commodities in pretty packaging and consumers might not notice a difference if the goods we in plain packaging - a fact emphasized by the popularity of private label products in many categories.

Once again, Amazon features heavily in discussions of replenishment. It has invested heavily in building solutions to make it easier for you to "Buy it again" or "Add to your Dash Buttons". Amazon wants you to stop shopping by making it a no-brainer to just "buy it again" instead of investing any effort into assessing alternative products.

Amazon Dash

"We've always said the best shopping experience for many items in your home is one that doesn't exist at all—there's no action to take—you don't even have to think about it. You know you won't run out of the essential items you count on most, so you can focus on other, more important things."

Daniel Rausch, VP of Amazon's Smart Home Division[180]

Such is its interest in promoting reordering, Amazon has an entire sub-brand for the task; Amazon Dash. Ranging from one-click buttons for items you want to reorder to a full logistics solution for automated ordering with API integrations, Dash is a perfect example of reducing human involvement in shopping.

Dash buttons and the Dash Wand

The Amazon Dash button (discontinued as a physical item in 2019) was first introduced to a skeptical audience on April Fool's Day in 2015. A physical, single purpose button that you stuck somewhere convenient in your house, pressing it saw a specified item delivered to your home the next day. It was very simple - essentially Amazon turning the Buy Now one-click button from their website into a physical item in your home. And of course, once it had gained that position, the chances were the consumer was locked into ordering that item and highly unlikely to switch brands or supplier. Order items that you needed to restock on a regular basis with the push of a button - you didn't even have to fire up your phone or laptop, open Amazon, search for the item and purchase it. It didn't feel *too* automated – you were still in control and had safeguards to prevent multiple orders - pressing the button again didn't work until any pending previous order had been delivered.

With individual buttons for each product and a non-replaceable battery that was going to expire, Dash buttons always felt like an interim or transitory solution, albeit one that gave Amazon's chosen brand partners unprecedented visibility and physical presence in consumers' homes. At its peak, the range of Dash buttons expanded to over 300 items before the concept was overtaken by the proliferation of smartphones and other smart home devices like smart speakers. Amazon discontinued the physical buttons in 2019, replacing them with virtual buttons on their web site and in the Amazon app but as Wired Magazine noted at the time: *"The physical buttons may be gone, but they were an experiment to help determine the future of shopping - a step towards interface-free and ultimately human-free shopping."*

While they made sense in certain scenarios - such as if you noticed the detergent running low as you fill up the washing machine - and the button was close at hand, the digital buttons have the advantage of being wherever your smartphone is (never far away for most people): You just open an app and press.

Building on the Dash branding introduced with the Dash Buttons, the next innovation from Amazon replenishment was the Dash Wand. The box of the Dash Wand describes it as "the quick and easy way to shop". It combines a basic barcode scanner with Alexa support in a small device you can magnetically attach to your refrigerator door. The idea is that you scan items in your kitchen to add them to your shopping list, or simply tell Alexa to add them to your list; then open the Amazon app and confirm your order. With its basic premise of scanning the barcodes on products you have in your home; it is of course all about re-ordering.

Auto Replenishment

If the thoughts of pressing a button (physical or virtual) or scanning a barcode is too much, then DRS might be for you. The genius of the Dash buttons was actually hidden in the technology behind them - the Dash Replenishment Service (DRS) - a service that any product owner can use to offer a replenishment service to their users at the push of a button (or some other defined trigger). The beauty of DRS is that it's usage driven. So, while Subscription can be based on likely usage, DRS is based on actual usage. All without the requirement for a company to create such a complex logistical platform itself.

Device manufacturers can integrate replenishment services that simply monitor usage and re-order automatically when consumables are running low, without even needing a button press. Examples include printers that can order toner or ink, devices that can order batteries, and water jugs that can order filters. Built using Dash technology, I have installed a WePlenish[181] connected coffee capsule holder that can automatically reorder my preferred coffee capsules from Amazon if it senses the level getting low.

Dash technologies are a great example of how even traditional non-tech companies can embrace technology without having to develop their own, as long as they are happy to cede some control to Amazon. It's in a detergent maker's interest to get their Dash button built in to your washing machine so that any time you see your supply running out, you'll just push the button rather than go to a supermarket where you may have a choice to change to a competitor. Consumers will pay a premium for the speedy, frictionless transaction. Although a mere button press, the DRS masks a lot of complexity - it places an order for an item and uses your stored payment and address details to complete the transaction. The time from pressing the button to receiving an email confirming your order can be less than 2 seconds.

As at January 2020, the Amazon website lists over 200 devices enabled with DRS. Some of Amazon's latest DRS experiments are adding new areas alongside the likes of toner for inkjet printers; a partnership with CPG company RB aims to automate the replenishment of several household products - Enfamil infant formula, Finish dishwasher tablets, MoveFree Vitamins and Air Wick Essential Mist diffuser refills.

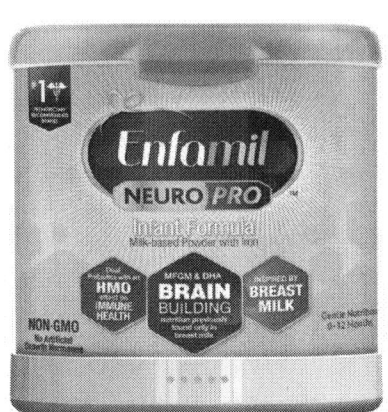

Figure 72 Smart containers with DRS to re-order as supplies run low announced at CES 2020. Source: Michelle Grant[182]

Dash Shelf

Announced quietly as a business-only product in late 2019 ahead of its 2020 launch, Amazon introduced a Dash Shelf in 3 different sizes that uses a built-in scale to determine the quantity of a selected item and senses, via weight, when the product is almost out of stock. Users can choose for the shelf to monitor stock of any supported product and reorder with savings of up to 15% on items from select partners, including Bic, Folgers, Keurig and 3M.

Figure 73 Amazon Dash Smart Shelf for Business. Source: Amazon.com

If this seems like an inconsequential product, consider the size of the global business supplies market and the impact on retailers that supply businesses if the management of restocking shifts to automated Amazon smart shelves.

Smart Home

While the Dash Shelf represents a service for business replenishment, my home microwave just reordered popcorn. It's intelligent enough to know that I just popped a bag and will soon need more - but it's saved me the trouble of adding popcorn to my shopping list or remembering to pick it up next time I'm at the supermarket. Thanks to DRS, the microwave can communicate my impending popcorn shortage directly to an Amazon warehouse to dispatch urgent snack supplies without any input from me. I know it's a decidedly first world snacking problem, but I've stopped shopping for popcorn, yet I never run out. It may seem like a small anecdote but imagine the impact as more and more microwaves start replenishing based on our usage. I and all the other consumers with connected microwaves (and before you ask, it's the number one selling microwave on Amazon.com), will no longer need our supermarket to stock popcorn.

In the future our connected homes will do all the low-level mundane reordering of household products, freeing up time to focus on more enjoyable tasks. Shoppers will no longer have to traipse down the supermarket aisles when they run out of bleach or toilet paper. They will spend less of their valuable time buying the essentials and I believe the impact on the physical store will be immense; retailers today should be rethinking store layout, trip drivers and the broader purpose of the store.

If popcorn seems a small example, then suppliers of other consumables must surely have taken note as Amazon announced an additional feature for Alexa to proactively let you know when you need to replace something (like a battery for your smart lock or security camera) and help you place the order. Alexa will send you a notification when it is time to reorder – or you can set up smart reordering to allow Alexa to automatically reorder the supplies before they run out. The new features will be available for you to replace batteries for smart locks, security sensors, smart lights and smart home cameras from August, Blink, Ring, Schlage, and Yale, air filters for Coway air purifiers, and more. The connection of Amazon's DRS and Alexa features shows the technological integration underpinning new ways to minimize or remove humans from shopping.

Alexa & DRS

In order to work with a wide range of devices and potential replenishment scenarios, Amazon is offering brands three different types of sensors to cater for various types of devices:

Consumable	Example
Stored in device	Batteries or printer ink
Device knows amount used	Detergent in Washing Machine
Device knows time used	Replacement head for toothbrush

By using these APIs, Alexa can help the customers manage their household supplies, by letting them know they're low or helping them to set up automatic re-orders in the Alexa app. If the customer chooses to set up smart re-ordering, that's when the Dash Replenishment Service will kick in. Unlike Amazon's "Subscribe & Save" shopping feature (which you'll recall is time-based), these smart home supply re-orders will only be placed when the consumable item is running low.

The benefit of this design is that it can help nudge smart home device users to place orders — with Amazon, the company hopes - just by having Alexa remind them. And it can also work even if the customer doesn't want to set up automatic re-ordering for some reason — perhaps because they shop for supplies locally or want to comparison shop online.

In addition to helping customers manage their household, the new feature will also enable smart home skill developers to establish recurring revenue streams associated with their devices. When a customer signs up for Dash Replenishment, Amazon pays out a one-time referral fee. And then as the re-orders come in, developers will earn a revenue share on all the orders placed — even if ordered manually following an Alexa notification. Of course, if the device maker is selling its own manufactured products, they'll earn even more. But this requires developers to become highly dependent on Amazon.

For a non-Amazon related example, consider the Bottomless Coffee company - they supply you with a miniature scale that tracks your coffee consumption based on the weight of the coffee to predict the right time to send you a fresh bag of coffee.

Figure 74 Bottomless Coffee supply their customers with a scale to track coffee consumption

Tying back to the discussion in the previous Chapter about conversational commerce and transactions via chat, the evolution of smart home commerce features may well lead to scenarios where you can "converse" with your domestic appliances to determine requirements. As mentioned, I already have a camera in my fridge (Smarter Fridgecam[183]) that can identify what's inside. The next step will be for me to be able to ask the fridge (via voice or text message) if I have enough milk, and it will reply "Yes, but at the current rate of consumption, you'll run out on Friday. Should I order more?" Or more depending on my preferences, if I don't have a subscription set up, I could ask my appliances to be more proactive - my washing machine could text me to let me know it's running low on detergent and will order more unless I cancel.

The Impact of Replenishment

When brands win a consumer's permission to automatically reorder items on their behalf, it has won customer loyalty of a level unprecedented in the history of retailing. Although they may have to offer an incentive to gain that loyalty - Amazon currently offers me 10% off my auto popcorn replenishment - the economics of being the automatic choice are compelling. Such features essentially lock the competition out of that consumer's wallet more-or-less indefinitely. This is a world in which brand-switching will be so much harder to effect; consumers will need stronger motivation than ever to change their default settings. Or they no longer be involved as they delegate their shopping. Digital assistants could put in place algorithms to decide what product to use for replenishment with a rule such as "if washing powder Brand X is X% cheaper or more than my normal brand, switch to it". We'll look at this in more detail in the next section.

Just for a moment, imagine a grocery store without replenishment items on the shelves. With significant challenges already from over provision of retail space, further large-scale changes in shopping behavior will be hard to accommodate. But the move to replenishment will drastically decrease the size of certain sectors of retail. If many people opt for automated replenishments, supermarkets can reduce their holding of bulky detergent and other household items. It is probably inherently inefficient to store brightly colored, expensively packaged items in an air conditioned and well-lit expensive space, when they could be shipped directly from a fulfilment center in anonymous plain and recyclable packaging. There's a large element of attention grabbing, brand vanity and merchandizing competition in today's packaging that could be completely eliminated, not to mention the impact on advertising for these product categories, which are typically among today's biggest spenders.

A significant proportion of the items we use on a daily, weekly or monthly basis will fade from our consciousness and be ordered for us by our technology. Our homes, autos, appliances, workplaces, pets and even our own bodies will begin to make many of these routine purchases for us. It's what I call the replenishment economy, a future state in which sensors, devices and robust analytics manage most of our daily, weekly and monthly product needs for us. And it will render today's marketing strategies for consumer packaged goods useless within a decade.

As AI technologies improve and homes become inexorably smarter, subscriptions will develop the smarts that they currently lack, such as automatic identification of holiday/travel dates and changes to our requirements for one-off events, such as parties, that they will be able to determine from our calendar.

Trust

Buying without Shopping changes the supplier/consumer dynamic. In order to earn consumer trust, businesses will have to work hard to become and stay relevant. Savvy businesses will have to ensure they've built in sufficient safeguards to avoid errors that will break the trust. If a consumer has signed up with your business to supply detergent, just a single instance of shipping an incorrect product could lead to the subscription being cancelled or the replenishment arrangement being ended.

Replenishment Negatives

Not everyone will welcome the advent of replenishment and subscriptions replacing retail and individual human shopping decisions. Some will argue that while you are at the store for fresh produce, why not pick up your own consumables? Consumer advocates in some jurisdictions were wary about Dash buttons and the associated lock-in and lack of transparency on pricing - to the point where they were deemed illegal in Germany.

There will also be contentious debates about the relative carbon footprint of individual journeys to the supermarket for consumables versus the emissions associated with deliveries. But ultimately, while I believe many people will mourn the loss of control, for many more replenishment for routine items will become at least partially automated, especially for certain sections of the population and at certain times of life.

The New Shoppers - Delegated Shopping

There are many reasons why people might choose not to do their own shopping, preferring to delegate the task to others. While some people enjoy shopping, many find it an unappealing chore. Even those who like it may find it hard to make time to shop, with other commitments squeezing the available attention that can be given to retail and procuring needs and wants.

Delegation of shopping to an agent was prohibitively expensive historically for the majority of people, but due to the rise of the "gig economy", there's a distinctive trend towards outsourcing of both purchasing and delivery tasks. So, while we may still make many of the purchasing decisions, the actual physical act of shopping is being delegated to another, often anonymous, human.

Gig Economy & Retail

The ubiquity of smartphones, connectivity and GPS has enabled the growth of countless services matching workers to tasks that would previously have been uneconomic to manage. The so-called Gig Economy; where workers agree to undertake tasks doled out via a smartphone app rather, than being employed on even a part-time basis, and which has already caused deep structural changes in the taxi, hospitality and delivery sectors - is rapidly encroaching on the retail world. Zero hours contracts attracted plenty of controversy as retailers tried to gain flexibility by lowering their fixed human costs, but nonetheless gig-economy-powered delivery services are rapidly expanding their scope to cover not just food delivery but also all forms of shopping.

Companies like Instacart rose to prominence by recruiting workers to fill online orders on behalf of grocery retailers who were unable to offer the service within their business. Now, more roles are surfacing that retailers and brands realize could be fulfilled by a fleet of non-staffers — people looking for one-off shifts to make a quick buck. Restocking shelves, for example, is something stores need done reliably all the time. So is loading and unloading inventory. A growing number of apps have launched over the last few years claiming to give workers more flexibility and companies more access to labor without incurring fixed overheads.

Instacart

Founded in 2012, Instacart is now valued at over $7 billion and has the capability to cover over 70% of US households, via its partnerships with over 300 grocery stores. Instacart customers can use the app to order groceries, for delivery or pickup, in less than an hour.

Instacart charges a delivery fee of $3.99 for orders in excess of $35, or an "Instacart Express" membership program for $9.99/month or an annual fee of $99, which includes unlimited free delivery on orders over $35. Instacart orders are picked and delivered by Instacart shoppers - gig economy workers who accept jobs via an app. They assemble the orders in the chosen supermarket(s) and deliver them to customers at the designated time slot. Instacart shoppers are examples of augmented shoppers - their routes through the stores are meticulously planned by advanced artificial intelligence-type solutions, and technology is deployed to make them supremely efficient shoppers.

By observing how shoppers have picked millions of customer orders through the Instacart app, they have built models that predict the sequences the fastest shoppers will follow. Instacart shoppers use this predicted fastest sequence to guide their route around the store. The deep learning model offers an increase in picking speed over humans of 50%.

For retailers, solutions such as Instacart can be an interesting alternative to building a dedicated e-commerce fulfilment platform - using on-demand workers to pick from existing human-centric stores instead of robot-powered dark warehouses. Offering services to consumers via Instacart does however empower Instacart with tremendous amounts of consumer data and may see consumers develop a greater loyalty to Instacart than a particular retailer.

Glovo

Spanish start-up, Glovo offers gig-economy shopping and delivery services via its app in selected cities in 20 countries globally. Offering a broader range of services than Instacart, 35,000 Glovers (as the workers are known) can deliver takeaway food, pharmacy goods, electronics, pet supplies, as well as groceries. With a claimed 5.5 million users[184], Glovo aims to be a delegated shopping experience across many verticals. Services such as Glovo can help local businesses compete with offerings such as Amazon Prime Now, which offers 1-hour delivery of a limited range of Amazon-fulfilled products in selected urban areas.

TaskRabbit

Consumers are turning to on-demand online services to find not only goods but also a range of services. Solutions such as TaskRabbit allow consumers to post a task, such as furniture assembly or wall-mounting a TV, evaluate potential workers to do the task and arrange for the completion of the task. Originally known as "RunMyErrand", such is the interest in this approach to delegation of activities that TaskRabbit was purchased by IKEA[185]. Summoning a curated "tasker" via an app represents a huge shift in how consumers are able to source resources to carry out services for them. With the ability to negotiate, compare reviews and pay via the app, platforms like these shift the balance of power not only from brands and retailers, but also service providers in numerous other sectors.

Delegating to AI

"Shoppers are outsourcing a whole host of retail experiences to algorithms, automation and smart devices: that means the automation of hunting, negotiating, purchasing, delivery arrangements and more."

Trendwatching[186]

"I estimate that a minimum of 25 percent of the consumer decisions we occupy ourselves with today will be entirely relegated to technology by 2025"

Reengineering Retail - Doug Stephens - Chapter 8

While apps like Instacart allow for the delegation of shopping, the decision makers and order pickers are still humans. This will no longer be the dominant mode of shopping by 2030. If services like those described in the previous section focus on delegating the physical shopping and delivery elements to other humans, this section focuses on the trend towards delegating the more cognitive elements of the shopping process to computers. This is a huge change.

In some areas, the speed and accuracy of automated shoppers are unbeatable - humans have already largely stopped shopping for stocks, with some 85% of transactions now being computerized with algorithms making the decisions. High-demand web sites such as those for event tickets work hard to deter ultra-efficient bots snapping up all the tickets for later resale. For those that choose to delegate the chore of shopping to a service such as Instacart thinking they are merely offloading to a human, they are unwittingly beginning to embrace automation too, because, as noted above, Instacart makes extensive use of Deep Learning to speed shopping[187] and Instacart uses human shoppers only because it's leveraging existing supermarkets in the absence of extensive automated picking and packing facilities. More on that in Chapter 8.

As technology becomes more capable, we're starting to see more examples of delegating day to day shopping to a non-human agent. For example, let's look at clothing service Stitch Fix, built to enable consumers to delegate their apparel shopping to algorithms.

Stitch Fix

"[Our customers] come to us because they don't want to go shopping. 5 years from now, people will say, 'Remember when we had to wander malls and find our own things? That's crazy!'"

Eric Colson, Chief Algorithm Officer, Stitch Fix[188]

It's not often a retailer uses AI to a greater extent than Amazon (though the service is hosted on AWS), but Stitch Fix may be among the most advanced users of AI in the consumer retail space. Stitch Fix is a company built from the ground up on algorithms. Its model wouldn't be possible without them. A more recent entrant than Amazon, it is algorithm-native - if Amazon is the Millennial of shopping, Stitch Fix is the Gen Z. Stitch Fix provides an interesting case study in emerging retail trends - let's look in some detail at its experience.

Stitch Fix is an online-only styling service that delivers a personalized shopping experience. You fill out your Style Profile and you are then sent a box containing a curated selection of clothing, shoes and accessories for you to try on at home. Simply keep the items you want and send back the rest in a prepaid envelope. Shipping and returns are free.

Stitch Fix employs a team of about 80 data analysts who develop algorithms to match inventory to customer preferences. Some 46% of clients provide their Pinterest profile as input for the stylist. Stitch Fix tracks what the person likes and doesn't like and uses those data points to inform the next batch of items the customer receives. Stitch Fix also uses algorithms not only to pick clothes for its customers but to actually design new pieces. If you're interested in more detail on how Stitch Fix uses algorithms throughout its business, the company has posted a detailed and very accessible animated overview at: https://algorithms-tour.stitchfix.com/

It now boasts revenue of over $1.5bn and over 3.2 million users who use the service to optimize their apparel shopping. It raises questions over the future role of stores and of retailers and may change the entire dynamics of apparel production and distribution. In its simplest form, it allows consumers to bypass the trek to store and replaces the possibility of an instore discovery with the expert recommendation of a personalized styling service, with delivery straight to the consumer. But it is the amount of data Stitch Fix collects and how they use it that will determine the evolution of the service and, perhaps, an entire sector of retail.

"If somebody is not receiving things that they love, they're going to stop [using Stitch Fix]. We live and die by our ability to personalize for people. That is our lifeblood."

Katrina Lake, CEO Stitch Fix[189]

The fact that over one-third of Amazon's sales are driven by the recommendation engines has long been a lighthouse statistic when discussing technology-enabled commerce. However, for Stitch Fix, 100% of their business is powered by recommendations - everything they sell is recommended to a consumer, rather than chosen by the consumer. It's hard to overstate the extent of this change in the world of shopping.

Brands, Intermediaries and Consumers

Stitch Fix poses an enormous challenge to clothing retailers. No physical store can scale the personalized recommendations, stock the tailored range of outfits or capture consumer feedback to the same extent. The data-fueled complexity of Stitch Fix's operations is hidden from the end consumer but, essentially, instead of a store buyer trying to predict what will sell to whoever walks in the door, Stitch Fix knows its customers, recommends clothes to them and gets direct feedback in a way a store can't.

For brands looking to reach consumers, Stitch Fix represents a new, highly targeted channel and an unusually two-way channel. Imagine that a clothing manufacturer could approach Stitch Fix and ask them to estimate demand for a new piece, right down to the split of sizes that would sell to the Stitch Fix customer base - all with an algorithmic confidence score. This is essentially enabling brands to get more direct access to customers, but with an assessment of what they'll want to buy, what the gaps are in their wardrobes and what the likely price elasticity is.

As each Stitch Fix customer is encouraged to give detailed, item-level feedback, brands can learn actionable feedback - that a particular item was unpopular due, for example, a lack of pockets or that the sleeves were tighter than expected on a certain size. The level of forecasting and feedback will make channels such as Stitch Fix very attractive to brands looking for direct market access and increased control over their brand, but at the risk of over dependence on the channel.

Stitch Fix not only changes the relationship between retailers and consumers but also further along the supply chain back to producers. Stitch Fix is replacing the role of the retailer, but with the added value of data which could ultimately lead to a service where producers can create clothes for a known market in order to reduce waste.

The growth of Stitch Fix has unsurprisingly gained the attention of other parties and Amazon has expanded its Prime Wardrobe service to include a Personal Shopper feature at $5 per month, with the ability to preview what gets shipped in your box (unlike Stitch Fix). Incumbent Nordstrom has introduced Trunk Club with the added benefit of alterations at Nordstrom stores.

When your Assistant is your AI-assistant

Services like Stitch Fix, although largely removing humans from the purchasing process, still rely on humans to initiate the process, either by requesting a 'Fix' of clothes or responding to a suggested complementary accessory. But it's not a large leap to imagine a more proactive role for AI in our shopping, perhaps even to the extent that AI will replace the need for us to make most of our current shopping decisions. As our confidence in the abilities of technology grows, and we come to trust it, I believe we will become more willing to delegate entire swathes of our shopping to technology, not simply pay another human to carry out our instructions as with the Instacart and Glovos of the world.

The AI-assistant shopping capabilities discussed in the previous Chapter are still very early products. Their capabilities will increase dramatically in the coming years and they will soon move from their primarily reactive responsive role into a proactive role, in many spheres. Although voice will be a primary way of interacting with this technology, it's important not to think of it as just a voice controlled technology - the AI "brains" making the purchase decisions on our behalf by predicting our needs will monitor us, speak to us, listen to us and transact on our behalf with myriad suppliers via APIs. This disruption of the shopping process, with the retreat of humans, will change shopping more than any other development in the next decade, with very big consequences for all players.

Already, Alexa can be setup to remind users when it's time to reorder items, watching your Amazon shopping habits to infer when you're due to reorder.

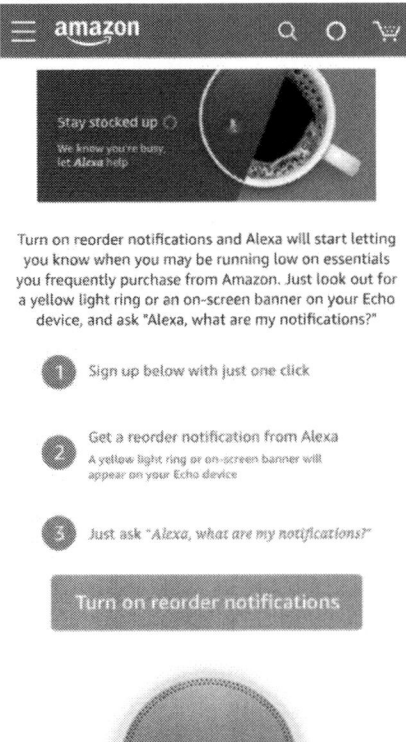

Figure 75 Setting up Alexa reorder notifications in the Amazon app

Would You Like Your Usual?

At its annual developer conference in 2018, Google demonstrated the Google Assistant capabilities with partners, Starbucks for example, that, based on your normal morning routine, your assistant preempts your likely imminent request to purchase coffee and offers to order your "usual". This convenience, removing the micro friction of ordering the coffee yourself explicitly may seem minor, but it's indicative of a trend that represents a huge change in retail. In the scenario of reordering my usual morning coffee each day, it removes any chance that one day I might choose a coffee shop other than my usual Starbucks. If my assistant takes care of my orders in this way, without me even having to ask for it, my involvement in shopping decisions will continue to decrease. Even if, one morning when the assistant asks, I might say "No, I don't want my usual, I fancy a change today", Starbucks and Google could easily form an alliance where the assistant responds by suggesting something else it predicts I'd like, or suggesting a loyalty save offer such as "Stick with Starbucks today and get a free Muffin".

Amazon presented a more complex vision for its AI assistant at an event in June 2019 introducing the 'Alexa Conversations' feature. This envisions a (near) future where your assistant can complete complex tasks that require interactions with multiple different service providers - so for example to arrange a night out, you could ask:

- You: What Time is the new Star Wars movie on this weekend
- AI: <Shows the times on screen from 3 local cinemas>
- You: Book me two tickets for the 8.05
- AI: Two tickets for the 8.05 on Saturday at <chosen cinema> will be $25 - will I book them?
- You: Yes
- AI: Done, you'll get an email confirmation. Will you be eating out near <chosen cinema>?
- You: I guess, is there a Chinese nearby?
- AI: Yes, there's China Palace near <chosen cinema>. They have a table for 2 at 6.30 - will I reserve it?
- You: Ok, cool.
- AI: It's forecast to rain on Saturday - will I book a ride to China Palace too?
- You: Sure
- AI: Booked. An Uber will pick you up at 6.10 to bring you to China Palace.

As mentioned in the previous Chapter about Conversational Commerce where we looked at a simple purchase of a product, this example illustrates how much more advanced the technology is becoming compared to the buying batteries example. In the above example, the AI has made several decisions, filtered several options and proactively offered additional services.

The increasing automation will happen first with willing partners, perhaps so gradual as to go unnoticed by consumers and competitor businesses alike. The announcement, in October 2019, that the Google Assistant could automate buying movie tickets is no doubt the first of many such advances - AMC and Fandango theaters in the US have worked with Google to facilitate faster booking of tickets where Assistant fills out the form and the user only has to confirm - a small improvement that saves a few seconds but history already tells us that users much prefer not having to fill out forms if it's possible to avoid that task.

Moving back to the Smart Home arena, Amazon's Alexa already offers a little-known feature called hunches where it detects smart home devices in an unusual state – so, for example, if you usually turn off the porch light but didn't, then your Echo can proactively suggest "Looks like you left the light on - want me to turn it off?". It's a small step from that to a commercially-laden hunch.

Pretail

"Anticipate Needs. Being quick is knowing what your customer wants before they want it."

Google[190]

While subscriptions and replenishment represent the automation of shopping for goods that we need on a recurring or frequent basis, such approaches comprise only a portion of our purchasing needs. Our voice assistants can respond to individual requests to purchase, and as we saw with the Amazon example in the previous section, can even offer proactive additional services.

As we move towards the logical conclusion of removing the humans, thus ensuring we automatically receive everything we know we need or plan to need, what about the things we don't know we need? What will discovery look like in this world? For our future needs, how much of the shopping process will be a result of explicit delegation where we task our AI-assistant, versus proactive/inferred by our AI-assistant?

Predicting is the Future

"Consumers would operate with the ever-present help of virtual digital assistants. These would not only anticipate our shopping needs but would also make intelligent recommendations to fulfill them. They would eventually even execute transactions on our behalf and manage shipping and delivery without much intervention on our part, save perhaps for final go-ahead approval."

Reengineering Retail - Doug Stephens- Chapter 9

There has been a shift away from products and services delivering convenience in isolation, and towards all-encompassing platforms geared to ensure everything is not just available, but ready – before, or just as, a need arises.

Telefonica Blog[191]

Assisting with our known, articulated consumer needs is only the first step for platforms such as Alexa and Google Assistant. Soon though, our digital assistants will become highly predictive about what we're likely to need or want and will progress towards a new level of convenience by not only removing the friction of procuring something, but even removing the friction of realizing we have an unfulfilled need or want. Everything you look at or buy online leaves a trail of data. Combine that fact with everything people like you buy, and ML can figure out, with remarkable accuracy, what you'll buy before you even realize it.

Telefonica has identified a series of emerging behaviors and grouped them under the banner of *'nowism'* – acting on needs only as they arise (which, over time, comes with using on demand services habitually), valuing time more than ever before and spending on services that can help save or protect it. So-called 'choice paralysis', arising from trawling and comparing endless options for everything one might need or want, has increased a desire for abdicating these time-consuming processes to someone or something else. In turn, with a desire to spend their time on things that are meaningful or enjoyable, rather than on searching, planning, and grappling with abundance, people will continue to seek out products and services that promise effortless decision making, immediate fulfilment, and improved relevance.

In the always-connected digital era with unlimited choice, price transparency, time poverty, channel blur and frenetic multitasking, we can't or won't wait for anything anymore. Instant gratification is the name of the game. You can go only so far with speeding things up before there's no more scope left to remove steps from the user interaction. The next logical advance is to remove all steps from the interaction by pre-empting the user, or at least offering solutions to the user rather than asking for inputs. Such is our demand for instant gratification that computers can no longer even wait for us to signal our intent - they must anticipate what we are likely to want.

This will come in one of two ways - predictions based on your past behavior or responses to your signaled intentions. So that could be a prediction that you might order a pizza because it's Saturday night, you're home, there's nothing in your calendar or correspondence suggesting any plan to go out, no indications that you've already eaten and a prior history of ordering pizzas on Saturday night. Or you could simply signal your desire to eat, a time, how hungry you are, any exclusions and a system could auction that intent to a variety of suppliers who would bid for your order - the opposite to how you currently search their offerings on a web site. Instead you'd post your desire to eat and they would respond with offers - this concept is explored in detail in the 2012 Book, The Intention Economy[192] and seems likely to be widely enabled by AI.

People Who Like This...

If this sounds like something more akin to science fiction than the reality of shopping, I can assure you it's not. In some ways, we're already a part of the way there. We've all seen web sites recommend additional products to us, based on what other similar shoppers have done. "Other shoppers also bought this" appeals to our sense of security in numbers, and likely our algorithmic agents will rely on this metric to some extent. This is the start of delegating the thought process, allowing influence/suggestion. We've always had some curation (every item on the shelves in a retailer was put there by a buyer) and even active bundling in stores, but this is different. It's personal. It's dynamic compared to a mannequin dressed to show a few items together. Thanks to Spotify's discovery algorithms and Netflix suggestions, many of us have already stopped choosing new music and new TV/movies. We're perhaps already less engaged and less independent in many of choices that we might think.

Amazon Samples

"Amazon is experimenting with the next phase in the evolution of online shopping — not shopping at all"

The Times[193]

In a short-lived experiment during 2019, Amazon enabled selected suppliers to use Amazon targeting data to select consumers to receive free trials of products the data indicates they may be interested in. Getting product into a prospective customers' hands is gold for brands - compared to the mass market of advertising, the cost of the sample is easily justified if you can get it to the right people. Brands who took part in the program paid $2 per sample, on top of the actual cost of each product.

This again is an example of the evolution that's happening before our eyes. Recall the "Send me a Sample" voice ordering I mentioned in Chapter 6? So that removes the friction step of getting a consumer to react to an advert by navigating to a web site to order a sample - replacing it with a simple voice command once their interest was piqued. With Amazon Samples, Amazon can profile their customer base to determine the warmest leads and charge advertisers for access to them. Amazon has unparalleled data on which to base the sample sending – it knows your search history, your purchase history but also the things you add to basket and deliberate on ...might a sample finally push you to move an item from basket to checkout? This level of hyper-targeting could finally address the age-old adage that half of advertising is wasted but advertisers don't know which half.

Whether consumers realize it or not, in the digital realm, predicting what we want to do next has already been used as a strategy to give us a faster experience. Netflix can proactively download the next episode in a series ready for you to watch offline as there's no cost for them to do so. Likewise, web browsers prefetch pages for links we're likely to click on so that it eliminates the load time by doing it in the background. But sending physical samples is a lot more costly than distributing a digital asset.

Before Amazon discontinued the scheme, Samples included items such as Maybelline mascara, Calvin Klein perfume and Kind bars, among other things. Schemes like Amazon Samples will continue in various guises as firms try to assess consumer appetite and the business models for these new technologies. Will consumers perhaps be irritated over something that could potentially be deemed as wasteful? Will they like the free samples or would they rather not be bothered with stuff they didn't order, even if it's probably relevant/interesting?

The End of Choosing or the End of Choice?

"When we allow complexity to be hidden and handled for us, we should at least notice what we are giving up."

Ellen Ullman, Life in Code

Eventually, inevitably, technology reaches the point where it can't respond to us fast enough to satisfy us - then the only way to be faster is to anticipate. As technology gains the ability to sense, predict and respond to our needs and is being integrated into our natural behaviors, becoming both more pervasive and less overt, present wherever we are and always accessible, does this signal a step change in our cognitive load? Will we stop making those small decisions we don't even realize we make today? And if we do, are we happy to let go? Shaving seconds off transactions/interactions that you would never have thought of as inconvenient may not seem important to you until that friction is removed and you realize its value and suddenly don't want to live without the advantage of it.

The shift towards shortcuts and prediction has begun. The first signs of daily or even hourly use of ML are here as our phone and its embedded assistant automate the ordering of your regular coffee. This removal of routine could be seen as an end to spontaneity (will you actually order a different coffee today?) but is balanced by convenience - both for you and for Starbucks.

The firms adding predictive AI will need to work out what's useful versus what's creepy. A proactive reminder that Mother's Day is coming might be useful if we've forgotten, but if we're in the wrong mood, we may feel it's intrusive, overly commercial, opportunistic and cynical upsell. Answering questions before we ask may be the holy grail for Google, but many people are likely to resist, at least initially, attempts at being too smart for our liking.

When Convenience Becomes Creepy

At what point does prediction become intrusive? If it's a logical extrapolation of previous behavior, I probably won't consider it invasive. So if I clearly have an interest in gadget purchases, it could make sense that when Google, Apple or Amazon release a new accessory, there's a strong likelihood that I'd be interested in purchasing it. But what if my AI-assistant detects that I might have a cold and offers to buy me a remedy? It's not shopping in the traditional sense if a sensor orders a cough bottle for me as soon as a sensor detects an elevated resting heart rate and breathing sound.

Thinking back to the cameras we talked about earlier, alongside actual shopping data collected about our retail habits, which provide fuel for ML models to turn into predictions, the emergence of Computer Vision technologies adds a further dimension. Any of the multitude of cameras that watch us, whether in our smartphones, our laptop's webcam or an Amazon Echo Show or Look, could potentially scan for opportunities to pitch more items to us. Merchants will have to be careful not to cross a line into privacy-invasion territory but it's quite easy to imagine a feasible future where an unsolicited email arrives offering us a new coat, in our size and preferred color, because the camera "noticed" that our current coat has signs of wear.

From Prediction to Prescription?

What if our AI assistant starts to advise us? Some will consider it nagging, but others will hand over the cognitive overload and come to view their assistant as a personal coach rather than a personal nag.

As our AI-assistants become more sophisticated and can include many additional sources of data, the role they could come to play in our lives is almost limitless. Consider if your AI-assistant recommends meals based not only on a diet plan you've agreed with it, but varies it based on your actual behavior and inputs from wearable sensors - imagine if you've had an indolent day and when it comes time for lunch, the AI-assistant chides you for not meeting your step goal and "refuses" to order the hamburger you might like for lunch and instead "advises" you to order the salad.

The UI of AI Shoppers

As our AI-assistants get to know us, they will constantly improve at choosing solutions or services to meet our needs. Yet, I believe there will still be a need to control their actions, whether to correct their mistakes or simply due to a reluctance to empower them too broadly, too soon. There is no consensus yet on what the shopping controls interface of the future will look like - how much control will we exert over our AI shopping agents? Will we be presented with tons of options and settings to maintain a sense of control but actually end up using only a tiny fraction of the settings presented to us (same as we do today on rich interfaces like PCs and even phones).

My expectation is that automated shopping user interfaces will gradually become less obvious, fading into the background as our AI-assistants get ever better at picking what we want and predicting what we need. The more we trust them, the less controls we'll need. Still, it's easy to imagine a progression - before AI shopping delegates are capable, they will need more guidance from us. So will we see fuzzy levels, where our agents have a degree of flexibility and we trust them to make a decision within widening parameters?

When it comes to product selection for replenishment, will your AI seamlessly switch for best value within your parameters? I'd expect early adopter consumers to have to fine-tune a suggested AI behavior profile, generated based on a scan of your shopping history, with a range of parameters to tweak - e.g. set sensitivity for certain factors. Eventually, I'd imagine you can have a conversation with your AI to train it to what you like - maybe give it an instruction – such as "if there's an offer of 10% or more off, buy it, or if the stock level on my size goes to less than 2, buy it". Savvy retailers will seek to game these developments - if they know that AI shoppers react to low stock warnings or certain levels of discounts, they will inevitably attempt to leverage these for their benefit.

Joining the Delegated Dots

As an example of a potential delegated shopping future, I want to outline what's currently an imaginary scenario to illustrate the kind of delegation we will see in the coming years. Although it may seem far-fetched, all of the components required to deliver this exist today but have not yet been joined together to offer a coherent, seamless, human-free flow. But it will happen, and it raises numerous questions, opportunities and threats for businesses.

Imagine a water pipe bursts in your home while you're at work. Disaster! Well no, thankfully you've installed a water sensor as part of your experiment with some smart home technology. The water sensor triggers a call to a local plumber. The local plumber isn't very technologically advanced and doesn't have an API to handle bookings. So, your Google Assistant uses "Duplex" technology to place a call with a synthesized voice making an appointment for a plumber to come. (currently Duplex is limited to Hair Appointments and Restaurant Reservations but booking a plumber is a very similar task). The Assistant shares your location and sends the plumber a one-time access code for your smart lock, valid only for the agreed arrival time. Your smart camera monitors the plumber's entry. When completed, the plumber is paid using your credit card on file with Google or via your insurer (who of course your assistant has checked with in parallel).

For now, the above scenario probably still needs some human intervention, for example to agree the price. But in the not too distant future, you'll be able to delegate power to your Assistant to say automatically authorize a payment of certain amounts in respect of certain tasks. Suppliers would know not to try and overcharge for fear of a bad review.

But one of the most significant questions in this kind of arrangement is, how does the assistant choose which plumber to call? This is the next generation of Search Engine Optimization (SEO). For humans, is this the end of choosing or the end of choice? Is it ok to remove spontaneity when the tasks are mundane?

In this case, urgency might trump price - getting the first available plumber is more important than the cheapest price. In other scenarios though, I might want my Assistant to choose the service provider based more on quality of reviews than anything else. But in less urgent situations, how will the non-human shopper make its decision. While early iterations will prompt for human intervention to confirm choices, I can envisage a rapid transition to more empowered AI decision-makers that will be somewhat opaque in how the choices are made - just as today's search results are opaque to most users but widely accepted due to their quality. As long as our AI assistants buy things or procure services that we're more or less happy with, it's unlikely we'll be upset and before long the prospect of making a decision of our own may seem quaint.

The New Consumers

What will delegating to an AI-assistant mean for retail? What happens when irrational, lazy and ill-informed humans aren't making the decisions anymore. I started this Chapter with the concept of augmented shopping and how tools could make us better shoppers. But even augmented human shoppers make bad decisions. We make bad decisions, for example, when encouraged by discounts. Discounts are usually about volume targets for the seller, not benefit to the buyer.

As Barry Schwarz describes in his book, The Paradox of Choice, if consumers have too much of a selection to choose from, they become frustrated and anxious and may even be turned off. AI-assistants will solve this - they can evaluate endless choices objectively and instantly against our preferences and priorities. AI-assistants are no longer about simple voice commands - they are also about awareness: our habits, our preferences, our location, our services; we connect them to our lives with APIs and our contacts. They are way deeper than the simple voice interface. Impressive as they are, what we have today are very much 1st generation products. They respond well to simple commands (and now even chained commands) and save time with routines (multiple actions triggered by a single command). But in terms of being proactive, they are just beginning.

Will AI-assistants change the Amazon habit? There may be times when Jet.com is cheaper if you're willing to wait a couple of days but today you just go with Amazon. Right now, you don't have perfect knowledge or perfect amounts of time. Thinking back to the importance of brands' values to consumers, in a world of delegated shopping and perfect/improved knowledge, your AI-assistant could warn you or avoid purchases from retailers or brands you don't approve of.

What will life be like if everyone can have a personal assistant totally attuned to their needs and focused only on predicting and satisfying their every whim? Over time, all of us will have many, perhaps dozens, interacting with each other and acting on our behalf. They will automatically deliver you the information you need to know, just as you need to know it. Rather than relying on a single input screen, or even a series of screens, we'll instead interact with computers with less friction. In our modern age of information, the average adult makes more than 20,000 decisions a day—some big, like whether or not to invest in the stock market, and some small, like whether to glance at your mobile phone when you see the screen light up. New AI-assistants promise to prioritize those decisions, delegate them on our behalf, and even to autonomously answer for us, depending on the circumstance. Much of this invisible decision-making will happen without our direct supervision or input.

Away from factories and offices, one of the most interesting questions of the AI acceleration will be the automation of life. Not only of physical tasks like household chores, but of our needs and wants. We've already talked about automated ordering but only in the context of replenishment. Soon there will be no more 'Life Admin' - not spending time paying bills, making mundane decisions. The next step will be for your AI-assistant to tackle the things you don't even realize are "friction" - usually get a taxi when you get off the train? Your Assistant will have it waiting for you in a perfectly choreographed routine. Instead of landing at an airport and firing up the Uber app to book a ride to a hotel where you wait to check in, future systems will work together to ensure that happens seamlessly, stepping straight into a waiting car and then going straight to the room that's expecting you, exactly as might happen for a person with a dedicated concierge or entourage of assistants.

How many more industries will need to adapt to humans delegating their more complex purchase decisions. Any business that doesn't have an accurate API linked directly into their inventory will be cut out of a growing market. For example, United Airlines has worked with Google to enable customers to check in using the Assistant - eventually an airline that doesn't offer the service will suffer as you can be sure that it will be deprioritized when I ask Google to book me a flight.

Don't Worry

Although it may seem to lack the personal touch a little, imagine if I'm having friends over for a dinner party in the not too distant future - "Alexa, suggest a menu for Saturday night's party" (don't worry, she knows who you invited and can check if they've turned vegan). What might be the hierarchy underlying her suggestion?

1. Guest preferences
2. Ingredient price
3. Ingredient availability at a local Amazon store
4. Dish preparation complexity
5. Carbon footprint of the meal

And meantime "Alexa, get me 3 quotes for home insurance" (don't worry, she knows all the parameters) and if it's less than last year's price, just go ahead". Or consider our future gifting - our AI will answer gift-givers questions, further limiting bad presents, but also limiting surprises: which would you prefer - the certainty of getting something you want or the surprise of getting something you didn't know you wanted but might actually not want?

Automating ACCE

Thinking back to the Awareness-Consideration-Conversion-Evaluation (ACCE) model discussed in Chapter 3, every stage needs to be reconsidered in the world of automated and delegated shopping.

Awareness - we human shoppers may no longer be aware of products - our AI-assistant will know what we need and find the product that most closely matches our needs and our criteria.

Consideration - our AI-assistant will instantly evaluate a product against our preferences and values. It can make informed, rational decisions with perfect information.

Conversion - once a decision is made, either fully autonomously, or with minimal intervention from a human to confirm a choice from an AI-curated shortlist, the AI-assistant will negotiate with the vendor to ensure timely delivery via a convenient and environmentally acceptable method.

Evaluation - assuming we don't show any dissatisfaction with goods our AI-assistant has procured, or we answer its query positively, our agent may rate the transaction positively on our behalf, posting a complimentary review on the vendor site. If we express displeasure or if the transaction doesn't go smoothly (e.g. a late delivery), our AI-assistant may blacklist the vendor for future orders and/or leave a negative review and/or seek compensation, all without our intervention.

Selling to Machines

"Rising numbers of consumers will feel comfortable outsourcing much of their retail to AIs and smart assistants, leaving those virtual entities to find the best products, prices and experiences. Time to start thinking now about what it means for you when you're selling to AIs as often as you are to humans."

Trendwatching.com[194]

Even if only a small portion of humans delegate their shopping decisions to their AI-assistants, the impact on retail, marketing and advertising will be massive. The fundamental concept of advertising is to inform and influence consumers, frequently appealing to their emotions as much as their rational side. Algorithms making purchase decisions are not going to be influenced by subliminal imagery or soothing music, instead focused on objectively meeting their human masters' needs. Algorithms will require proof of performance and verification of any claims; "new and improved" won't persuade an automated decision maker to pay a 10% premium over a product that its owner has rated as perfectly satisfactory. Retailers and brands must prepare for a time (soon), when alongside the predictable replenishment shopping, our AI assistants will be ready to take on non-linear purchase journeys that require comparison, choice and evaluation. Any retailer or brand who relies on impulse purchases will need a new strategy for dealing with AI that will be immune to temptations.

Recall my water leak scenario above and consider the questions about the commercial relationships involved compared to how a 'manual' situation would unfold today. How is the plumber chosen? Is it on the basis of proximity/availability, price, reputation? Will my AI ask my friends' AIs for recommendations? How is the price agreed?

Device as a Customer (DaaC)

"Retailers will market to smart homes, not just shoppers"

Dave Marcotte, Kantar Retail

Automated shoppers will consistently implement their owner's wishes and challenge retailers with a ruthlessness rarely seen from human shoppers. While human shoppers may relent on for example a desire to buy local artisan-sourced products in the face of a special offer from a mainstream brand, AI is less likely to change, and more likely to continue looking for the ideal product unless we tell it to compromise in the interests of speed. Our AI shoppers may also avoid unhealthy products, offering us the willpower we so frequently lack - a lack which currently benefits those making and selling sugary fare.

But this begs the question, how do retailers market to robots? How do you convince an AI that your brand of battery is better than a competitor's battery? How will retailers compete and make their product seem favorable to a device driven by preset business rules and without being influenced by any form of emotions? The rapidly rising discipline of behavioral economics will no longer be relevant in a world where robots and their algorithms go shopping. DaaC models will give rise to an entirely new model called Business-to-Thing (B2T) management[195]. D2C may no longer stand for direct to consumer but direct to computer.

I may have a perception that one brand is "better" than another, without evidence or even in the face of evidence to the contrary (which I may or may not be aware of). We've had decades of development of psychology around marketing - with all manner of approaches used to appeal to consumers. Take for example UK retailer John Lewis and its price-promise slogan of "Never Knowingly Undersold". This reassures consumers that they will get a fair price and many will shop without comparison checking. But an AI agent won't be swayed by a slogan and will instantly price compare globally. Psychology won't work on bots, but you can be sure that a micro-industry will spring up aimed at marketing to bots, just as there's an industry offering SEO services to "game" Google and Amazon searches.

Will Regulators Intervene?

As is so often the case in the modern world, policy and regulation is struggling to keep up with technological developments. We saw the example above of German regulator's intervention regarding Dash Buttons in physical form, but there has yet to be a concerted review of emerging retail solutions. If Amazon or Google develop their assistants to offer compellingly efficient shopping proxy services, is this anticompetitive? That will go to the heart of the debate - antitrust legislation was designed to protect consumers but wasn't conceived with the automated shopper in mind. It may be impossible to argue any consumer detriment if their agent always offers a good product at a good price, but it may technically be seen as anti-competitive behavior.

The ideal outcome, for a company such as Amazon, is to become your trusted single supplier for all your needs and wants. In return for your loyalty and trust, they will meet all your material requirements efficiently and, thanks to their market power, economically. For consumers, it could turn out quite well on a basic level. For brands, having an intermediary control access to consumers is more worrying - those unwilling to pay a "toll" might find themselves struggling to reach customers.

Will regulators seek to legislate to prevent consumers being tied in to automated replenishments from a single supplier? Could they prevent appliance makers from forming alliances with consumables suppliers that effectively default to locking out substitutes? Many will fear that in a Subscription/Replenishment scenario, it quickly becomes winner takes all. Others will argue that it's the ultimate consumer technology - your AI-assistant seamlessly switches for best value, saving the you not only money but also time.

Regulating AI-assistants?

It's quite easy to imagine scenarios where an AI-assistant is actually acting in the best interests of its creators rather than its users. There may be a tricky conflict of interest between an AI-assistant that caters to our whims with seeming impartiality and a commercially-motivated helper that can subtly manipulate us for profit. Should we consider regulation to control subliminal prompts from AI-assistants to make purchases? Just as we regulate advertising of some products to target groups (such as tobacco to children), should we prohibit Alexa from offering us a finance deal that we can barely afford? While search results on a screen are clearly labelled as adverts and we can evaluate them accordingly, if we ask Google for answers, or just to complete an action, will any payment flows behind the transaction be clear, and how concerning should that be?

The presence of smart speakers and other devices in our lives makes ever-more time and locations shoppable. While we are usually protected from commercial overtures in our own homes once we turn off the TV and close our browsers, it's entirely plausible that an AI-assistant manifested in a smart speaker could sense our mood and suggest a purchase at an "opportune" moment, where opportune means we are perhaps more vulnerable to suggestion than usual due to stress or some other circumstance. And AI will be able to gauge our mood through a variety of biometrics, including our voice, gait or expressions. And it will be able to preempt any objections we raise faster than the world's best salesperson. Thinking back to the voice example I gave earlier, where the Google Assistant prompted me that Dido was playing a concert, what if it had taken it further, checked my calendar and that of my friend, picked a suitable date, provisionally booked dinner and transport and offered me a wonderful night out paid for in 3 easy instalments, while in the background collecting commissions from the ticket seller, the restaurant, taxi firm and finance house? Perhaps I wouldn't mind and would enjoy the convenience of being able simply to say "Go Ahead". Or perhaps I would quickly suffer buyer's remorse and regret the expense or indulgence.

When Humans Stop Selling

It's not just about automated buying - there is also automated selling to consider. The core of retailing used to be curation - finding, stocking and selling the right goods to consumers. Many of these decisions were based on years of experience in buying, predicting the items that would resonate with customers.

Nowadays, many of the items offered to consumers aren't chosen by humans - they are chosen by algorithms trained to predict what we're most likely to buy. Amazon has replaced many of its buyers with algorithms[196], as machines proved to be more effective at deciding what to sell to humans. Software has now automated demand forecasting and negotiating prices with vendors.

The AI Generations

If AI-assistants creates new (non-human) shoppers, I wonder if there is an equivalent to cohorts/generations in AI shoppers? Will AIs act in similar ways and will marketers develop segments to target - so for example, will there be a cohort of AIs configured to be more responsive to price over say delivery time that discounters can target? If AIs are configured to observe our individual preferences, they are still likely to be categorized by marketers. In fact, it may make it easier for marketers to know what they are dealing with, as AI will be more predictable and consistent. For an AI that has been set to respect sustainability concerns above absolute best price, then marketers will know that if their product meets those sustainability thresholds, they can command a price premium.

Mass advertising will not disappear overnight, but its influence is certainly waning. Ads are shifting toward not just digitization but also personalization, powered by sophisticated algorithms and predictive models that analyze transaction data and digital-media trends (for example, what topics are hot on social networks).

We will focus in the next Chapter on the logistics and supply chain challenges and developments that underpin much of the change in retail. But regarding subscriptions and automated/delegated purchasing, it remains to be seen how the delivery experience will be managed. While I don't generally mind going to the courier company depot to pick up an item I'm excited to receive, having anticipated its arrival since purchase, I am not going to be very pleased to go in search of a package of some consumable that I didn't even know I needed, however pleased I might be not to run out of it. Perhaps this and the emphasis on reducing unnecessary packaging might encourage packaging that will fit through letterboxes.

Chapter 8: Demanding Delivery

"Fulfilment has become the new battleground of retail"

Neil Saunders, Managing Director, GlobalData

Many of the most impactful advances in retail-related technologies are not immediately obvious to consumers, yet they determine what products can be offered to who, where, when and at which price. The increased speed and automation of retail are only made possible by recent innovations in inventory, fulfilment and delivery services. It's now possible to have pretty much anything you can imagine delivered to your preferred location at record speed. Yet the complexity of getting an item to consumers in a timely manner is rarely appreciated by those placing the orders via their clicks, voice, cameras or AI-assistants.

In this Chapter, we'll look at the massive, largely invisible infrastructure powering today's retail services. We'll examine the extensive range of technologies being deployed with the aim of further reducing the time for deliveries - technologies also seeking the seemingly contradictory aims of simultaneously lowering both costs and environmental impacts. The steps from how a product is purchased to arrival at its final destination include not only its journey, but also its packaging - after we examine how your order makes its way to you, we'll look at how it's secured and presented and what that means to consumers and retailers.

Great Expectations

When I was growing up, there was a standard disclaimer on any mail order or catalog item - "please allow 28 days for delivery". That was the normal, near-universal timeline to receive your item if you didn't go to a store to purchase it. Faster postal and courier options were sometimes available, but the likes of FedEx and UPS were generally priced for business use and seldom seen in the suburbs.

In the early days of ecommerce, pioneering shoppers were effectively told when and where their packages would arrive and had to pay (sometimes substantial amounts) for the privilege of receiving them. Fast forward to today and the growth of online shopping, coupled with improvements at every step of the supply chain, means that 28 days has become less than 28 hours, with some sectors moving towards 28-minute delivery times as we'll see later. There are very few business sectors left where consumers will even consider waiting a month once they've decided to purchase. Some large ticket items may still come with that kind of lead time, but again, the move to rental models will challenge even the last holdouts of the 28-day era.

Speed & Flexibility

"The faster you ship, the more people buy"

RBC Capital Markets

Amazon is now capable of offering same-day and next-day delivery to 72% of the total U.S. population[197]. The vast delivery network enabling this speed is the result of significant investments totaling billions of dollars, building fulfilment centers. This has irreversibly raised consumer expectations and set the bar for competitors. And as we'll see, both Wing (sister company of Google) and Amazon itself are aiming for deliveries in less than 30 minutes in a race to faster delivery times than were imaginable. So that's as fast as things can get right? Well, at least until you consider the pretail we talked about in the previous Chapter.

Along with speed, consumers also expect retailers to offer a range of options for where an item will be delivered. It's no longer sufficient to offer delivery to a home or office address - customers expect to be able to choose from a selection of delivery and pick up locations that suit their busy lives.

Fast & Free

"Ten years ago, people thought two-day shipping seemed really fast; now we think two-hour shipping and one-hour shipping will be the standard."

Stephenie Landry, VP Amazon Prime Now

According to the research firm Rakuten Intelligence, between 2017 and 2019, the average time from purchase to delivery has declined from 5.2 days to 4.3 days. Amazon is faster still, at 3.2 days and that will fall further. Prime members can now expect 1-day delivery on millions of items. It doesn't stop there - PrimeNOW offers free *two-hour* delivery. Although it is only currently available to members with delivery addresses in specific postcodes/zip codes, it gives us a glimpse into what we can expect as the future norm.

A survey from Digitalcommerce360.com reported that among the 52 retailers tested, 25% offered free shipping on every order, with no minimum order size or other restrictions. Among the retailers that required a minimum purchase size for free shipping offers, the median threshold was $49.48. The report found retailers are good— but not perfect—at meeting their delivery promises. "The vast majority (86.5%) of the orders we placed arrived early or on time (30.8% were early and 55.8% were on time), based on the time frame provided by the retailer at the time of the order. In 5.8% of cases, the retailer provided no expected delivery date. Only 7.7% of the orders arrived later than the retailer promised".

The willingness of consumers to pay for delivery is generally quite low - the proliferation of free delivery options makes it harder for other vendors to justify an additional charge. A survey from analytics company GlobalData[198] showed that 42% of the UK's online clothing and footwear customers are not prepared to pay anything at all for delivery costs. Add to that, only 43% are willing to pay a maximum of £5 ($6.50), and just 15.3% are willing to pay over £5 to receive their orders.

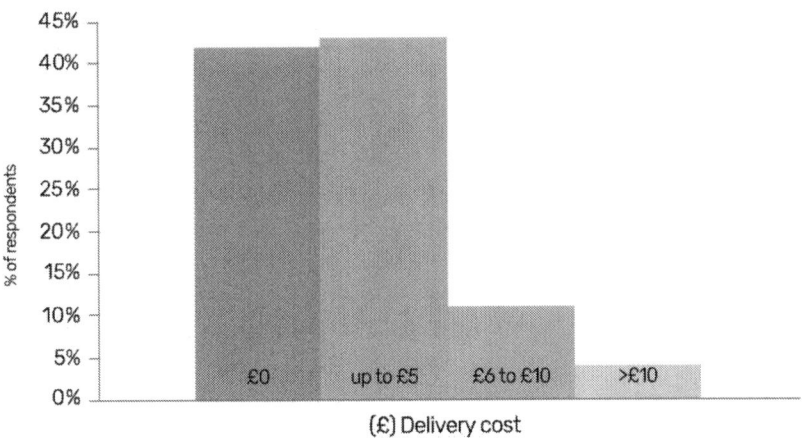

Figure 76 Maximum amount UK shoppers would pay for apparel delivery[199]

After Hours

"Late Night shopping" used to refer to city center stores opening until 9pm on Thursdays! Now though, people can and do shop anytime, anywhere. Consumer expectations don't just include fast delivery, they also expect to be able to order an item when it suits them, rather than meeting deadlines that would make the shipper's life easier - according to FedEx[200] CMO, Brie Carere, two thirds of online shoppers expect orders placed by 5 p.m. to qualify for next-day shipping, but many retailers have next-day shipping cut-offs before that time. However, with peak shopping times often 8-9pm, warehouses and carriers are working towards later and later cut off times with midnight now becoming the new normal. Some UK retailers have reported a surge in ultra-late-night shopping - 6% of transactions being between midnight and 06:00, with some seeing a 10% increase in customers shopping between 22:00 and 03:00[201].

To tackle this shifting behavior, FedEx has for example added an "Extra Hours" service, which offers next-day local delivery and two-day shipping to any address in the continental US for goods ordered online as late as 02:00. Rent The Runway was among its first customers. If there is some good news for logistics workers, it's likely that AI shoppers can be programmed to place replenishment orders at times that better suit suppliers, possibly even at times that are incentivized to help balance demand.

Decisive Delivery

Delivery speed has become a crucial aspect of the online shopping experience and a major decision factor for online shoppers. 53% of consumers have abandoned a purchase because of slow delivery times offered. To stay relevant in this environment, more retailers are responding to consumer demand - according to the Boston Retail Partners' 2017 Digital Commerce Survey, same-day delivery was offered by 51% of retailers.

Research shows consumers want a great shopping experience - not just easy selection and a good price, but all the way to delivery and beyond:

- 88% of consumers say the ability to track shipments in real-time is important to them.
- 79% of consumers would not purchase from a retailer again if the delivery was damaged.
- 75% of consumers agree that the professionalism of the delivery person is important.
- 70% of consumers agree that when the delivery person is dressed in uniform, it increases their trust.
- 69% of consumers would not purchase from a retailer again if their delivery was late.

Delivery time and cost are now substantial competitive levers. In the US, popular crafts marketplace Etsy.com prioritizes sellers who offer free shipping on orders over $35 in its search results, while Macy's has tested waiving its $8 fee for same day delivery on orders placed before noon, in order to bolster its sales.

Keeping Track

The consumer's interest doesn't end with rapid dispatch and a promise of fast delivery. They expect to be kept informed along the way. 88% of shoppers track their package once they are notified of its dispatch. Delivery firm Pitney Bowes[202] see that, on average, consumers check the tracking of their package 8 times for a typical delivery. And even here, new commerce channels are being used by consumers - you can check Amazon-dispatched items by asking Alexa "Where's my stuff?", while Google Assistant can tell you about any orders it can see from your Gmail. In the UK, the Royal Mail offers a service where you can say "Alexa Ask Royal Mail to track my item".

Amazon has also built detailed tracking into its shopping app giving an estimated time of arrival and as the courier nears the consumer's home, a live map showing where the courier is, how many deliveries they have before yours and an estimated time of arrival. Much like watching your Uber ride arrive, Prime deliveries also give consumers the ability to track a courier in real-time. Tracking has evolved from generic "on van for delivery since 06.41" that doesn't show an update until "delivered, 15.32" to a real-time report - "your driver is two deliveries away and will be at your address in approximately 20 minutes".

Retailer Pressure

Retailers understand that their customer base expects their goods to be shipped quickly with same-day and one-day shipping, so many are testing new technology and business models that can meet this new consumer preference, while exhibiting solid unit economics. Some retailers think that once a package leaves its warehouse, what happens next is out of their hands. Consumers don't agree. Many believe it's a retailer's responsibility to choose a delivery partner that represents their brand and customer service values.

Retailers who are concerned about the added cost of ultra-fast delivery should consider this: 1 in 2 U.S. consumers say same-day delivery would encourage them to shop online more often, and 74% say that, after receiving a same-day delivery, they would be more likely to purchase from that retailer again. And some consumers are still willing to pay for it — 47% say they have paid extra for faster delivery. That number is even higher for Millennials, with 54% saying they've paid extra. Finding new ways to cut fulfilment costs is vital to keep those site-switching shoppers coming back, as free deliveries and returns may boost sales, but they also erode margins, so a relationship with the consumer and consequent lifetime value become ever more critical.

Growing Volumes

"In New York City, 1.5 million packages are delivered daily to people's doorsteps—three times as many as in the beginning of the decade"

Center of Excellence for Sustainable Urban Freight Systems

As well as growing expectations for delivery, thanks to online shopping, subscription boxes and product returns, the total volume of packages wending their way to customers each day is growing rapidly and likely to increase as humans shop less but have more deliveries. Amazon Prime orders alone led to an astounding 5 billion shipments worldwide in 2017. Existing approaches to delivery are struggling to scale to meet demand and alongside the traditional carriers, Amazon itself and a array of new entrants are adding more delivery capacity, using a variety of approaches, as we'll discuss throughout this Chapter.

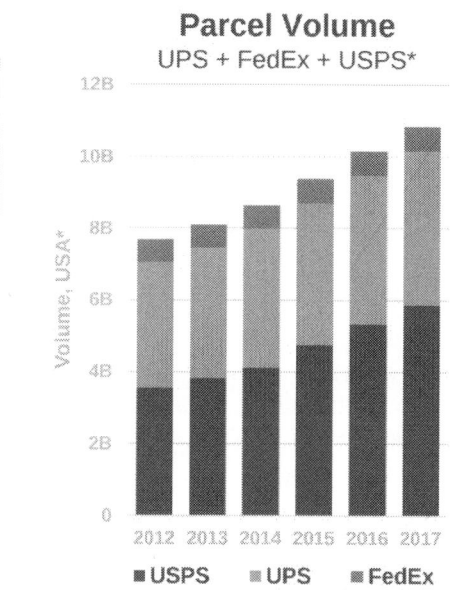

Figure 77 The growth of US Parcel volumes. Source: Kleiner Perkins 2018 Internet Trends

More Packages, Less Trips

According to figures quoted by KPMG[203] from the UK's National Travel survey, the number of shopping trips decreased from 332 per person per year in 2008 to 316 in 2016, a 7% decline. The equivalent US figures show an even greater decline of 13%.

The growing volumes of packages are causing headaches for cities across the world. Most urban areas aren't designed to accommodate the volume of packages, the number of competing delivery vans and the resulting congestion. Likewise, there's been a rising number of complaints of congestion in shopping market aisles designed for individual shoppers rather than professional shoppers trying to fulfil orders against the clock.

The growth in package volumes has led to significant growth in the delivery fleet - Amazon has grown its fleet of vans and trucks to over 30,000, whilst also recruiting private individuals to work delivering packages from their own vehicles through its Amazon Flex program. Other retailers have been enticing people to use their personal vehicles to deliver packages – e.g. Walmart's Spark Delivery. It seems likely that pressure will grow to find solutions to improve delivery efficiency such as shared local deliveries (where competing delivery services pool routes to avoid having 3 trucks covering the same route), or locker stations accessible to multiple companies (most are now proprietary).

Golden Era of Logistics?

Logistics, the commercial activity of transporting goods to customers, is already a $1.5 trillion market worldwide. The growth of online and the other new shopping methods discussed in this book will both fuel and be enabled by continued investment and innovation in logistics. Getting the item to the customer from the nearest warehouse is an area where there is no one-size-fits-all solution. Traditional parcel delivery services (Post Office and private operators such as DHL, UPS and FedEx) have seen huge growth but face demanding customers and start-up competitors, as well as the challenge of conveying everything from single item orders to groceries. The sheer variety of goods that can now be ordered is mind-boggling. Items that would once have been considered prohibitively difficult to manage are now routinely available in minutes, hours or at worst, days.

When Humans Stop Warehousing

Hiding behind many of the advances in retailing in the last decade or so are invisible but seismic changes in the supply chain. Just as we've seen humans become less involved in shopping, they are also becoming less involved in shipping and storing. Warehouses and fulfilment centers are now bastions of automation, replete with thousands of robot workers. Amazon now has more than 200,000 robotic vehicles it calls "drives" that are moving goods through its delivery-fulfilment centers around the U.S. That's double the number it had in 2018 and up from just 15,000 units in 2014.

Last Mile

Last mile is industry jargon for a key part of the logistics journey - the final part of a package itinerary - getting packages from where they are stored into consumers hands, or at least to their preferred location. With innovations we'll discuss in this section, from lockers to Amazon Day to Amazon Key for your home, garage or car, it's no longer just a porch or mailbox that is the packages' destination.

Last mile delivery is currently overwhelmingly completed by a person in a van. Even with the adoption of electric vans, these still represent a major contributor to urban emissions and congestion. As shorter fulfilment timetables are demanded by consumers, shippers have to find ways to move more products at a faster pace than ever. Improving last mile logistics is a key part of achieving this.

From Store to Door

In the food business, there's a phrase from 'Farm to Fork', to describe the various points in the chain from the origin of food to the final diner eating their meal. A similar description in the past was typically from 'Factory to Store'. Now it's likely to be from "Factory to Front Door or other designated location". As more products come directly to the consumer, without sitting on a shelf in a store waiting to be picked, the supply chain is changing rapidly to meet these new demands.

New Deliveries - Beyond the Doorstep

"For many customers, doorstep delivery works absolutely fine. But we do have customers who would like to have the option to deliver to an alternative location, perhaps because they're busy and can't be home. (Or) perhaps they live in a place where they don't have a doorstep."

Patrick Supanc, Worldwide Director, Amazon Delivery Technology

It used to be that the only delivery point was the doorstep/porch or letterbox at a house. Missed delivery notices were the scourge of both consumers and deliverers. As the volume of deliveries has exploded, technology has now provided a myriad of solutions and in the coming years, we will see missed deliveries become a thing of the past.

The Delivery Diversification

While we've discussed many of the innovations in speeding the shopping process, another key area of development is in the actual delivery of the goods to the consumer. As with other areas, it's all about choice - no one size solution fits all and retailers are trying new ways to make things ever more convenient.

Security company Yale isn't willing to give up on the doorstep just yet and has created a WiFi-enabled smart lockable delivery box. The box can be weighed down with sand or tethered securely to the porch, while owners can remotely grant access and get notifications of the box being opened via an app. Combined with a security camera, a box solution should be sufficient to deter opportunistic porch pirates even if it's not ultimately as secure as some of the other solutions we'll discuss.

Figure 78 Yale Smart Delivery Box

Alternatives to leaving items on a doorstep or porch are, most obviously, to divert the package to somewhere the recipient or someone who can accept the package on their behalf will be - perhaps their office address, or to a secure storage location such as a parcel locker or a retail store. More advanced solutions include smart locks that enable temporary access to the recipient's property.

Lockers

Lockers have proven to be a popular secure drop off point for deliveries to consumers not at home during the day but willing to stop by a local convenience store on their way home, where of course the store owner hopes they'll impulse-purchase something. Amazon operates a network of over 2,000 lockers (often located in convenience stores) and has announced plans to enable apartment block owners to locate a locker in their premises. As well as extending the locker delivery points to college campuses, Amazon has also been experimenting with temporary lockers at events such as Coachella, so revelers can still order urgent supplies. When a package is delivered to the locker, the customer gets a notification and can retrieve their item either by entering a code or scanning a barcode in the notification email.

Figure 79 Amazon Lockers in stores and in some private lobbies

Internationally, in France, Amazon.fr has placed over 1,000 lockers in supermarkets and smaller stores belong to the Casino Group, which is already a fulfilment partner for Amazon Prime Now express deliveries in major French cities. Amazon initially launched its "Counter" service in Europe, where customers can pick up items from participating Post Office and Newsagent stores - the packages are stored securely by the retailer, not in Amazon lockers, but is rolling the service out in the US with over 1,500 Rite Aid and GNC stores. Alongside Lockers and Counter, the final variant of Amazon pickup location are called Hub+. These are staffed locker facilities with an Amazon staff member who can process returns.

Key by Amazon

Innovations in retail don't take place in isolation, and parallel developments in areas such as smart homes technologies can also be harnessed for retailers' and consumers' benefit. For example, the proliferation of affordable high-resolution home security cameras and connected smart door locks mean it's feasible to remotely open a door and monitor activity.

Tying these technological building blocks together, Amazon has created the Amazon Key service. This works in one of two ways - you can fit a smart lock to your home's front door, as well as a camera, and the delivery person can unlock the door, placing the package in your hallway, under the watchful eye of your camera. Or, with select compatible car models, delivery people can place your package in your car as long as it's parked in an accessible location. And if access to your hallway or car feels too intrusive, Amazon Key can also be configured to work with smart garage door openers to leave packages in the garage. Frequent online shoppers might even equip their garages with a refrigerator to facilitate grocery deliveries.

Though still early, research has shown that consumers prefer the garage for unattended delivery access over unattended front door delivery by a 5 to 1 ratio. The final variant from Amazon Key is Key for Business, which is a system that allows building owners/staff manage deliveries, including hours and entry, by granting Amazon delivery staff a key fob compatible with most building access systems.

Walmart Inhome

If you're comfortable allowing designated trusted delivery people access your home but don't want the products just left inside the door as with Amazon Key, Walmart have trialed a service that literally puts your groceries into your fridge. Relying on body-worn cameras to give a complete view of the delivery person's path to your fridge, this service also requires a smart door lock.

Figure 80 A Walmart associate wears a bodycam to show the in-home delivery to the customer

In the UK, supermarket Waitrose has started to offer a similar scheme on a limited basis, known as "While You're Away". Customers who have a compatible Yale smart lock can participate, with delivery staff wearing a body cam that records video of them putting perishables in the refrigerator, while leaving other items on the kitchen counter or table as instructed. In a nice touch, Waitrose insists delivery staff don shoe protectors before entry, to ensure they don't dirty the house!

Offices

The growth in online shopping and the associated rise in packages has become a real problem for workplaces and apartments, with a daily deluge of deliveries requiring secure storage and distribution to individuals. Corporates and landlords are making changes to their buildings to accommodate the new reality of deliveries for staff and tenant by increasing the size of their mailrooms that had been shrinking. But many businesses are actively requesting their staff not to order for delivery to the office, despite the convenience for recipients and the certainty for the shippers of not having a missed domestic delivery attempt. As an indicator of how much of an issue it has become, office administration software firm Envoy that offers popular software for checking in visitors to corporate premises now offers an additional solution for package delivery management[204].

Anywhere!

If porch, locker, office, counter, hallway, garage or car delivery options don't suit, then this final type might be the solution - deliveries to anywhere! Thanks to the use of virtual location definitions, some firms are experimenting with offering delivery to locations with no physical marker. For example, retailer 7-Eleven has created 2,000 "hot spots" including New York's Central Park and Venice Beach in Los Angeles - customers need to download 7-Eleven's 7NOW app and select "Show 7NOW Pins" to find a hot spot near them. With a stated target of eventually having 200,000 hot spots, 7-Eleven uses Postmates couriers to fulfil the orders. Similarly, Dominos allows stores to create virtual delivery points that consumers can then choose. With an addressing scheme such as that offered by What3Words, which divides the entire globe into 3mx3m squares and gives each one a unique three-word name, it's feasible to identify any possible delivery location without having to use cumbersome GPS coordinates.

New Deliverers

If lockers, wi-fi enabled locks and remote access to cars aren't high-tech enough, there are plenty of further examples of cutting-edge technology being trialed to solve last mile challenges and cut delivery costs as shopping habits change. These include autonomous cars, sidewalk delivery robots and delivery drones.

These are technologies that are not yet widely available and still face many technical, regulatory and public acceptance hurdles. But their combination of potential cost savings, convenience and promised environmental benefits means that billions are being invested in developing them. So far, it's proving tough to beat the capabilities of a person who goes around making that last-mile delivery, but the labor savings that could be possible make automation compelling.

Autonomy - When Humans Stop Driving

While much of the mainstream media attention has been on the trials and tribulations of developing self-driving cars for passenger use, away from the spotlight, logistics professionals are interested in the technology for trucking and goods deliveries and this may be an area where we see initial deployments of autonomous robotic technology ahead of, for example, robotaxi services.

Sidewalk Robots

The next time you're walking down a sidewalk and think you spot a robot rolling in your direction, you might not be imagining things. Robots from leading provider Starship have travelled more than 200,000 miles in 20 countries, across 100 cities, in extensive trials of local delivery. These 6-wheeled autonomous robots travel at up to 4mph, have a capacity of up to 10kg and a range of approximately 2 miles, guided by 9 cameras, 8 ultrasonic detectors and a radar. Another provider, Kiwibot, is active on several US college campuses, which are more forgiving environments than public streets. When you place an order via the Kiwi app, one of the insulated bots picks up the order from the restaurant and brings it to your front door (or as close as it can reasonably get). You can even watch the last bit live from the robot's perspective as it rolls up to your address. When I spoke to a Kiwibot representative, he told me that their ambition is to offer delivery services at zero cost as the low operating cost of the robots could be covered with minimal sponsorship or branding - the bots acting as a mobile mini billboard.

Although startups Starship and Kiwibot have the largest fleets in operation, incumbent delivery firms are getting in on the action - Postmates has unveiled its Serve robot design, while FedEx is trialing a bot that can even climb steps to reach consumers' front doors. Amazon has also started testing its own small robot deliverer,

Scout[205]. Although late to the game compared to the start-ups, it's impossible to ignore Amazon's entry into the category. Scout joins a delivery fleet in a company which already has deep experience with robotics; perhaps more importantly, while others depend on deals with retailers and restaurants to fill their robots, Amazon obviously has a steady supply of packages to be delivered.

Figure 81 Postmates (Left) and FedEx (Right) prototype robot delivery vehicles

In an example of technology changing shopper behavior, Starship has surveyed customers and found a change in consumer attitudes - where previously shoppers "wouldn't have bothered" with small orders, they don't mind using robots for extremely small orders.

The response to sidewalk robots has been mixed - they've been outlawed in some jurisdictions but welcomed in others for trials. Most are currently human-escorted for training purposes but practical questions remain - what happens on narrow sidewalks when they encounter obstacles (human or otherwise)?

While most of the solutions on show to date are predicated on a seller dispatching the goods to the end user covering just the "last mile" with a robot, Amazon was granted a patent[206] regarding a different approach - the bot being dispatched by the buyer to pick up the item from a designated warehouse/fulfilment center or even delivery truck. However, given that the cheapest robot I've seen to date in this space costs over $3,000 (and some upwards of $15,000), I'm not sure there's a big market for consumers having their own pickup robot. But as the cost falls, you could see it becoming viable for say communities or places like industrial estates to have a shared robot available for use by some grouping of members.

Road Robots

For loads larger than would fit on a sidewalk or for bigger numbers of packages, you need larger vehicles. But perhaps you don't need the van sized vehicles that have dominated delivery services to date. Their current size and shape are not only to accommodate their cargo, but also to accommodate their human driver - if you remove that latter requirement, you can anticipate innovations in the design of the vehicles.

The Nuro R-2 is larger than the Starship Robot and travels on roads rather than sidewalks. At 25mph, it's not suitable for highways but is designed primarily for urban/residential areas. It is fully autonomous and can carry about 20 grocery bags (110kg/240lbs). US retailer Kroger has announced a pilot scheme to use the Nuro for grocery delivery in Texas, and Dominos has also launched a pilot with these vehicles. However, a previous pilot in 2017 between Dominos and Ford saw negative customer feedback from people used to pizza delivery to their door, being unwilling to go to the curbside to retrieve the pizza from their automated deliverer.

Figure 82 A Nuro R2 prototype road robot

Autonomous Cars and Trucks

While the smaller solutions we've just seen are custom-designed for delivery purposes, the bulk of autonomy industry attention is on removing the human driver from the types of vehicles we see today - cars, vans and trucks. In the retail space, Walmart has led the way with public trials of driverless solutions from Udelv, Waymo and Gatik. These are early trials and still require a safety driver in the vehicle but are a clear signal of interest from Walmart in understanding how driverless vehicles might fit into the future of shopping, whether it's ferrying people to and from stores, delivering groceries or moving goods between warehouses autonomously.

Start-up Einride began low-speed robo-deliveries between depots in Sweden in 2019. Its T-Pod trucks are significantly cheaper to build than a traditional truck and they can be remote controlled by humans from a command center. These are ideally suited to operating in fulfilment centers where there isn't public traffic and they can operate 24x7.

Figure 83 An Einride Autonomous Pod

The Last 50 Feet

Assuming that technologists and regulators can overcome the barriers to the safe deployment of autonomous technologies, where these solutions still seem to be lacking compared to human-staffed deliveries is in the final stretch to get the package to the recipients. Deliveries to the sidewalk are not what consumers are used to, and while the FedEx prototype can climb stairs, it can't ring the doorbell! Uber has demonstrated a drone that can land on a car roof - thus using a drone to get deliveries rapidly to a local human delivery driver who can finish the task more quickly. Ford and Agility Robotics have taken the issue of solving this problem seriously and have demonstrated a bipedal robot that can traverse the last few feet up to a door.

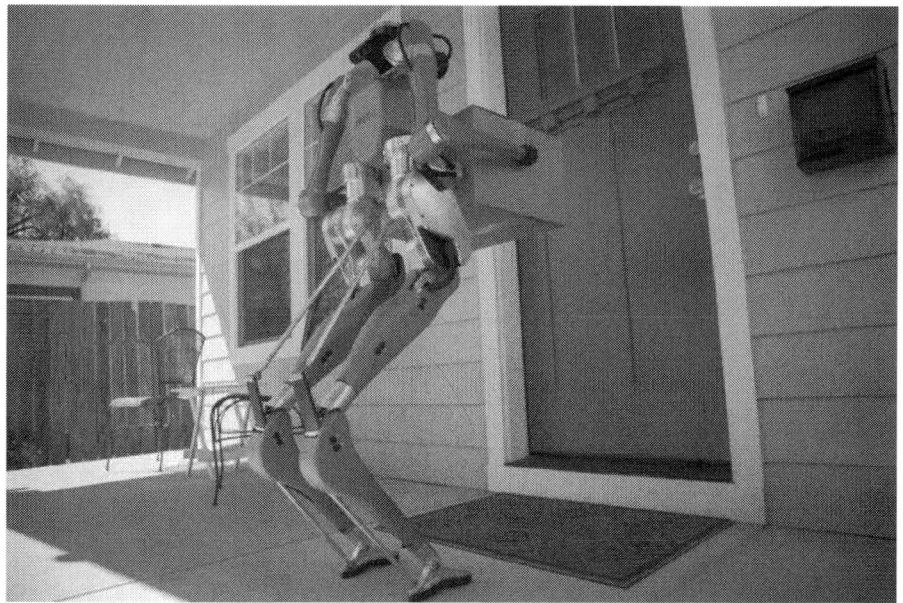

Figure 84 Ford/Agility BiPedal delivery Robot prototype

Drones

Several companies are looking above our streets and sidewalks for solutions to deliver packages faster and in a more environmentally friendly manner - lightweight aircraft that can carry small loads rapidly to customers without creating congestion.

Drone use in most countries is currently limited to what's known as visual line of sight (VLOS) operations - you can only operate a drone as long as the operator can see it. This rules out delivery use in most situations but that hasn't stopped 1 million users - consumers (88%) and businesses (12%) - registering drones with the US FAA. Both Alphabet and Amazon are at the forefront of developing drones capable of delivering packages, as well as working on the infrastructure that would be required for their widespread use, such as an air traffic control system.

While drones would offer very attractive economics to firms compared to staffed delivery vans, a number of practical issues remain before we'll see commonplace drone deliveries for packages:

- Where will drones land - if the recipient has a clear lawn or yard, it might be ok, but what about apartment blocks?

- Drones may have limited capabilities in anything other than excellent weather conditions

- Drones will likely have limited range and capacity, making them less attractive as substitutes for the costly practice of sending delivery vans to remote properties. (Although, 86% of Amazon deliveries meet the size and weight criteria to be delivered in this manner.)

- Will there be privacy objections from people who don't want drones (possibly equipped with cameras) flying near or over their property?

I'm sure that many of these challenges will be resolved, and drones will before long become another option for deliveries. And while delivery drones may seem to some to be a first world indulgence of the worst kind, people frequently make the mistake of assessing technology against their own needs or based on its initial use. Their use for blood deliveries in rural Africa by a firm called Zipline already shows a positive benefit, having completed over 45,000 deliveries, as at January 2020, in Rwanda and Ghana.

Figure 85 UPS (L) and Zipline (R) drones

In the US, delivery firm UPS has received FAA approval to begin testing its fleet of autonomous drones, starting with medical supplies on hospital campuses.

Figure 86 Amazon (L) and Wing (R) drones

In the retail delivery space, Amazon and Wing, a sister company of Google, have been at the forefront of testing. In describing its plans to the FAA when seeking approval, Amazon outlined its intent to conduct only flights of up to 15 nautical miles initially, during the day for items weighing 5 pounds or less (2.2kg). Flights would be in areas with low population density when the wind is less than 24 knots and flight paths would avoid sensitive government installations, hospitals, and places such as sports stadia.

Alphabet's Wing subsidiary is currently more advanced, having already run customer trials in Australia and Finland before extending to the US thanks to its clearance by the FAA. Items delivered in the trials include medicines, snacks and even piping hot coffee! The Wing aircraft don't land to deliver – it hovers and then gently lower the payload to the ground. Walmart, DHL and Uber are just some of the other big names who have announced their interest in drones for delivery.

While there are obvious privacy concerns with drones operating over private property, there are potentially additional business opportunities - for example, Amazon has filed a patent[207] regarding delivery drones checking roofs for damage.

I think it's worth pointing out the distinctions between potential applications of drones - I see the use of drones for emergency services as a very different thing than a delivery of a latte and worthy of a different regulatory framework. Developments such as drones and sidewalk robots, not to mention autonomous road vehicles will see protracted debates about regulation. Many will resist sharing our skies/pavements/roads with automated companions. Already, we've seen different jurisdictions react differently to emerging technologies from scooters, to e-bikes to self-driving trucks. But as a positive aspect, I expect in the meantime much emphasis on the environmental credentials of these newcomers over existing delivery fleets.

Although it will take years for national and/or international regulations to be agreed, expect to see innovators continue to push the boundaries and move their experiments to cities, States or countries with the most permissive legislative environments.

While drones can be used to speed up deliveries, and also to speed up activities such as scanning stock in a warehouse, flying robots have many other applications, almost all with an emphasis on speed. One of my personal favorites is the additional speed drones can bring to life-threatening situations. Ranging from use by firefighters to rapidly assess locations from an aerial view[208], to flying lifeguard drones that drop inflatable devices[209], to the delivery of a defibrillator to a cardiac patient[210] faster than any road-based ambulance can reach them, these are speed boosts that have very obvious benefits. Although some regulatory changes may be required, such uses should be possible in the very near term.

When Humans Stop Shopping, Picking or Delivering

However futuristic it may seem today, as you take a parcel from the UPS driver, ordered for you by your AI, in less than a decade, it's quite possible that many household purchases will move from their supplier to your home without a single human touch at any stage of the journey. Imagine your water jug orders a replacement filter for itself. The signal travels to the Amazon DRS, where it's relayed to a warehouse robotic picker which retrieves and packs it. From there, it's loaded by robot onto a drone that brings it to your home. Or, it's loaded onto a courier truck from which a robot approaches your door. Authorized by Amazon, your smart lock opens the hall door and the robot places the item just inside the door, watched by your in-home surveillance camera to provide you with peace of mind. No humans involved!

Click and Collect

Despite the incredible flexibility of delivery options now available, there's a growing trend among shoppers to order online and opt to pick up at a convenient time - knowing that the item has been set aside so, no hunting around the store, no out of stock when the customer gets there, no waiting around at home for a delivery, no granting of access to strangers and no making one's way to a pickup locker. This method is very attractive for retailers, assuming they have the inventory control systems in place, as they do not incur transport costs for individual packages to the consumer. Intra-store shipping is already commonplace, so facilitating pickup is often a small extension of that facility - in effect making it a public service where previously it was used to balance stock or in response to an in-store customer order. For items already held locally, it's ideal, but even where the item has to be shipped from another store or a fulfilment center, the chances are that a delivery to that store was already scheduled and therefore the individual customer item for collection doesn't incur a marginal cost.

Click and collect suits stores who have spent decades and millions of dollars creating a network of physical stores and ways to get products to them. And although they expected consumers to come in and search for items, now they are rapidly reconfiguring their stores to facilitate handing ordered items over to consumers. During a recent visit to Macy's flagship store in Herald Square, New York, I observed that the pickup counter was easily the busiest part of the store, and clearly in need of further staffing and expansion to reduce the queue. But I could also imagine the resistance from those in the business who would see it as the ecommerce team encroaching on "their" turf, literally.

Often referred to in the industry as Buy Online Pickup In Store (BOPIS), it is more commonly known to consumers as Click and Collect. In keeping with the popularity of fast and free shipping options, a National Retail Federation study found that free and fast were also the reasons that led people to opt for click and collect - 64% of consumers used it to avoid shipping costs, while 37% of shoppers saw it as a way to get their goods faster.

According to an Adobe analysis of the top 100 US online retailers, there was a 47% increase in online orders for instore pickup in 2018 over the prior year, while Coresight Research[211] shows a 56% increase in the number of grocery shoppers using click and collect, growing from 30M to 46M from 2018 to 2019. Some 40 percent of Best Buy's and more than 50 percent of WalMart's online sales already are picked up in stores.

Slightly over half (53.5%) of top US retailers offer BOPIS, and it's unthinkable that more sellers won't adapt their stores and systems to facilitate more collections. Just over 30% of Lowes and Target customers make an additional in-store purchase when collecting their online orders. While there are overheads in storing and managing online orders, the additional footfall is generally welcomed by struggling main street stores.

Click and collect isn't all upside for retailers though. The hassle, direct cost and opportunity cost of customers who click and *don't* collect needs to be managed. There may be various reasons why a customer doesn't show up to collect their purchases, but those that don't still expect a full refund. Although preferable to returns that might not be in resaleable condition, items that have been set aside for a customer who doesn't collect them may have missed out on other sales opportunities had the stock been available. A UK survey in 2019[212] found that shoppers had failed to collect over £200m of orders. Will this anti-social behavior eventually attract penalties? What if retailers charged a small restocking fee rather than offering full refunds? I suspect retailers keen to encourage people into stores will continue to absorb these costs and continue to see it as preferable to shipped returns - where there's two-way freight and delays with potentially devaluation of items.

To survive, even innovative retailers will need to constantly refine their solutions. Take clothing giant Zara for example - one-third of its global online sales are now picked up in the store[213], but that has created long lines in stores in some cities and waits for attendants to retrieve packages. To speed up the process, Zara said earlier this year it would roll out a robot-run version of click and collect, automating the service so that the collection points in brick-and-mortar stores will allow shoppers who have ordered items online to scan or enter a code; a robot will search for the customer's package, and then deliver it quickly to a drop box. Other retailers are struggling with the impact of online returns being made via stores which drives up footfall but not revenues - this is a problem in malls where rent is partially determined by footfall.

Curb Pickup

While click and collect typically refers to customers going to a store, locating the pickup counter and waiting for a staff member to retrieve their package, it is perhaps not surprising that stores are looking at offering pickup facilities aimed at drivers rather than pedestrian shoppers, given the popularity of drive-thru in the US. For some types of products, especially groceries, having them carried out to your car makes a lot of sense. Curbside pickup appeals to shoppers who want to grab their stuff and go without waiting in checkout lines or searching aisles for items. Picking up orders from stores can also be faster and more convenient than scheduling and waiting for home delivery.

For example, Target offers its Drive-Up service—when a Target employee walks out of the store and delivers the online order to the shopper's car in a designated area—in roughly 1,000 stores where parking is available. Target reported that it made nearly 2 million parking lot deliveries in 2018.

Figure 87 A Target Drive up pickup bay

"These options offer speed, convenience and reliability and as a result, they are quickly becoming the preferred fulfilment choices for our guests."

Target CEO Brian Cornell

Target has spent billions modernizing its stores and infrastructure to cope with changing shopping patterns. As well as opening new, smaller stores in city centers, it has expanded its options to offer same day in-store pickup or curbside drive-up and even same day delivery (via its acquisition of start-up Shipt). The availability of a range of same day options, has resonated with consumers who had not previously considered Target - about 20% of customers placing a same-day order in the second quarter were placing an order with Target for the first time.

As we saw earlier, Amazon's focus is on delivery (Prime, Scout Robots) and customer collection services (Lockers, Key, Hub and Counter) but it is also experimenting with Amazon Fresh Pickup locations in Seattle, requiring as little as 15 minutes advance notice to have your order ready before you drive to the location, pull into a parking space, and watch as your groceries are loaded directly into your car by an Amazon staff member.

Walmart offers pickup facilities at around 3,000 of its nearly 5,000 US stores. Walmart's expansion into grocery pickup has shown positive signs for the giant retailer. According to a report from Cowen and Company[214], between 11% and 13% of Walmart customers use curbside service, and by next year it will account for one third of Walmart's online sales. According to customer data from market intelligence firm Numerator, Walmart's grocery pickup baskets are much larger than in-store shoppers' baskets. The average spend per trip for grocery pickup is $124.86 while in-store is $49.70.

The data also show that consumers prefer Walmart's pickup service to in-store shopping. Thirty-nine percent of Walmart's grocery pickup shoppers want a quick in-and-out trip and 45% think grocery shopping is a chore. In addition, 76% found they save time shopping online.

In a slightly different approach to Amazon's Fresh Pickup, Walmart is also testing a kiosk in Oklahoma City that allows you pick up your online groceries at any time. Instead of parking and waiting for a staff member to bring out your food, you enter a pickup code and the kiosk automatically fetches the order for you to load it into your car.

In a trial that may signal a viable path for some vacant stores that could not survive as traditional, fully-staffed locations for the public shopping, Walmart has converted a former grocery store in Lincolnwood, Illinois into a pick-up only center. There is no public access to the building - all orders are brought out by staff to customers and placed into their cars. During the trial period, there's a minimum $30 order value, 3-hour order to pickup-ready time, and a $5 fee for the pickup service. With the repurposing of more retail space to facilitate customer pickup, it may be a future scenario to send your autonomous car to pick up your groceries for you.

The Dark Side of Delivery

"Nobody is looking at the environmental footprint of being consumers with all of this convenience"

Beth Davis-Sramek, Professor of Logistics, Auburn University[215]

The huge increase in the movement of parcels and the ever-increasing expectations of customers for fast and free or nearly free delivery has put huge pressure on logistics providers. Increasing consumer demand for instant delivery is driving industry players to sacrifice some efficiency in order to enhance convenience for customers. For example, the push for fast delivery can lead to increased use of air freight and multiple trips by half-empty trucks instead of waiting for a fuller load.

In Chapter 2, we talked about the growing awareness of sustainability issues among shoppers. While much of the focus so far has been on the environmental impact of fast fashion and plastics, the logistics sector is also relevant. There will be immense pressure on the industry from consumers, directly and via their AI-assistants, to somehow reconcile convenience with reduced environmental impact.

This environmental impact takes two main forms: increased CO_2 emissions from more delivery trips being made and extra waste from more cardboard or packaging being used. Since 2016, the transportation sector has been the largest producer of carbon dioxide emissions, overtaking power generation. The move to direct residential deliveries (from warehouse-to-retailer distribution) has also changed the packaging industry. The need to individually protect items for delivery to consumers instead of bulk orders to a retailer has meant considerable additional packaging demand.

Delivery Emissions

The shift away from efficient large-scale deliveries to retail stores towards expedited individual shipping to domestic addresses has dramatically increased the amount of delivery trips. The changes in shopping behavior we've already discussed have also increased emissions - consumers visiting stores to look at items and then ordering them for delivery doubles the trips involved in a single purchase, and that's before we consider the impact of returns which we'll come back to in the next section.

Sustainability improvement is now a major focus for all big carriers of packages. Expect to see UPS, FedEx, USPS and others rapidly expand the use of zero emissions vehicles in their fleets. From cargo-bikes and sidewalk robots to drones, any new delivery method will be judged as much on its environmental credentials as its contribution to faster deliveries. We may also see difficult debates ahead as delivery methods such as drones that boast strong zero emissions benefits[216] may face public opposition on noise or privacy grounds. And of course, trucks will remain necessary for larger items and may still be conventionally powered for years to come.

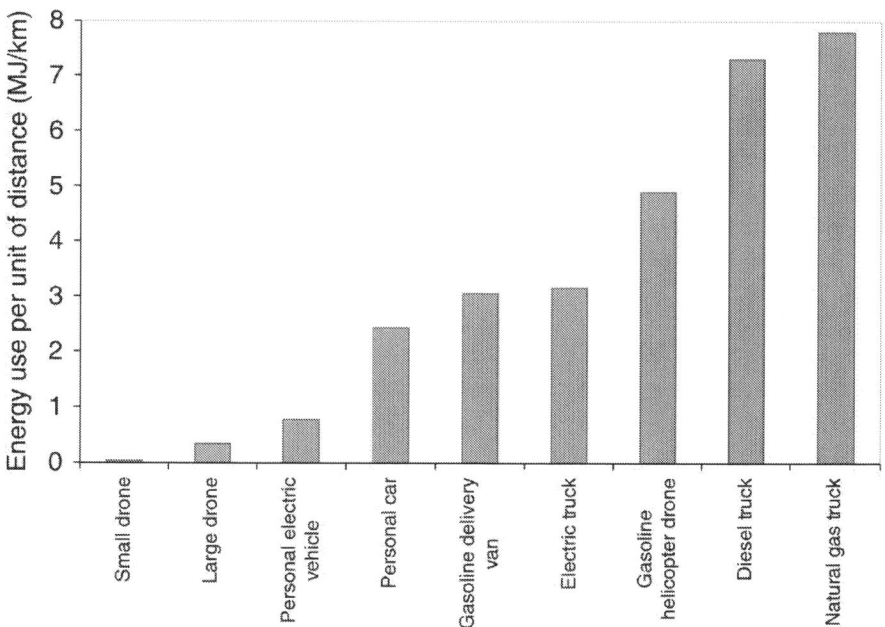

Figure 88 Relative energy use of delivery vehicles Source: Nature[217]

The Packaging Paradox

More frequent deliveries have led to increased demand for cardboard. The question of what happens to packaging materials after delivery is important. Consumers find it time consuming to break packaging down and can find it difficult to identify which materials are recyclable. According to the US Environmental Protection Agency (EPA), containers and packaging accounted for 30% of total solid waste generated in the last year. There is a clear opportunity to improve the recycling rate with cardboard, and the case for change is compelling, as recycled cardboard can be used to make new paper products - and 24% less energy is required than when making cardboard from raw materials. A greater focus on recycling cardboard packaging materials would unlock the dual benefits of minimizing landfill and reducing the resources used to produce cardboard.

I mentioned earlier the notion that a move to a more subscription/replenishment model could be an opportunity to reduce packaging complexity. The growing importance of branding over the last 50 years, as well as the sheer variety of goods for sale has given rise to a progressive growth in the sophistication of packaging.

But in a world of online shopping or click and collect, the need for distinctive packaging is vastly diminished. If you're no longer vying for eyeballs and to stand out on the store shelves, packaging can be far more subdued - it simply needs sufficient branding to reassure the online purchaser that the good is in fact genuine. An algorithm isn't going to be impressed by a colorful package but may be swayed by a package that is compact to ship or receives positive reputational reviews for being easy to open or environmentally considerate. Retail packaging is often deliberately oversized. Whether to gain attention on busy shelves or simply to deter shoplifting (small packages are easier to steal and conceal), packaging isn't generally designed for easy packing and shipping - what looks good on shelves doesn't necessarily mix well in a delivery box.

In China, Cainiao, Alibaba's logistics affiliate, uses ML technology to predict the size of boxes required to efficiently pack orders consisting of items of various sizes and weights. The company said its solution reduces the use of packing materials by more than 10 percent - significant across 42 million deliveries per day.

Although packaging may no longer be seen by the customer prior to purchase, many brands still see packaging as an important part of the customer experience and promotional strategy. The phenomenon of "Unboxing" Videos puts pressure on brands to make packaging highly appealing so that the chances of the video being shared increase. According to Google in 2017, the amount of time people have spent watching unboxing videos on their phones is the equivalent of watching the holiday classic "Love Actually" more than 20 million times[218].

Consolidate and Slow Down?

"The time in transit has a direct relationship to the environmental impact. I don't think the average consumer understands the environmental impact of having something tomorrow vs. two days from now. The more time you give me, the more efficient I can be."

Patrick Browne, Director of Global Sustainability, UPS[219]

Defaulting to express delivery for everything, even items where there is no urgency, has become the norm. This is another area where delegation to AI-assistants could prove very useful. For sellers trying to smooth peaks, they could instantaneously negotiate with your agent for a slightly delayed delivery in exchange for a discount - your AI will know if that's acceptable. But the improved forecasting made possible by your usage monitoring should render that moot anyway.

It's also worth remembering that speedy delivery done well doesn't have to be negative - the items eligible for same-day delivery are typically common orders, like diapers and detergent, that can be pre-positioned efficiently close to where consumers are most likely to order them. That cuts down on transporting things by air, which emits dramatically more carbon than ground transportation.

Amazon Day

As the dominant player in the e-commerce space and with unparalleled influence over consumer behavior, I want to look briefly now at Amazon's stance on environmental issues. Although the company has faced criticism for its environmental impact, including from within its own workforce, its stated ambition is to power its operations using 100% renewable energy and to reach 50% of all Amazon shipments having net zero carbon by 2030. In a high profile move to demonstrate its green credentials, in mid-2019, Amazon placed the largest order of electric delivery vehicles ever, at 100,000 vans. However, with a growing fleet of over 50 freighter planes, the emissions further up the supply chain will also need further attention.

I mentioned earlier the benefits of consolidated deliveries instead of a stream of individual packages to one consumer or address. Although Amazon Prime members have long had the option to downgrade from 1- or 2-day shipping to "no-rush" shipping, the incentive of a $1 voucher was far from compelling. However, with the introduction of the "Amazon Day" initiative, Prime members can pick a day of the week to take delivery of their recent orders. The boxes arrive together on the selected Amazon Day in fewer outer boxes, although consumers can still select individual items for express delivery if required. Similarly, Target revealed that it is testing a program where e-commerce orders are eligible to have multiple packages consolidated into a larger shipment with consumers rewarded with a discount.

Conscientious Consumers

I believe we will see a significant shift in shipping preferences in the coming years as consumers become further aware of the environmental impact of their delivery choices and opt for either slower shipping or better planning of orders to reduce the associated emissions and impact. Whether facilitated by initiatives like Amazon Day, or the repositioning of slower shipping options as "Green Shipping" or simply changing defaults from free and fast to slower and discounted, brands and retailers should be proactive about capitalizing on the consumer goodwill that is available. Perhaps Amazon will introduce "Prime Green", which defaults to slower shipping of items in highly distinctive colored packaging that gives its subscribers a virtue signal on their porch.

Alongside the environmental impacts, it's also important to consider the human impacts of the changes being driven by the demands of cheap, fast deliveries. There are frequent reports of huge pressure on delivery workers, as well as companies who use customer tips to make up basic wages. Just as with consumers who punish firms whose ethics they disagree with, companies will see demands for proof that logistics workers are being treated fairly.

Comparing the environmental impact of traditional store shopping with that of online shopping is tricky, In the coming years, we will likely see multiple conflicting reports on the relative merits of a trip to the store, versus online shopping for delivery, as various vested interests seek an angle or a headline. It's a complex area and it is very difficult to come to a single, simple definitive answer. In some cases, it may be more efficient to go to the store in an ICE car where you were planning to complete multiple errands anyway. In other cases, an online order with a slower delivery option that comes via an electric vehicle may be the environmentally sound option. Factor in returns and the total carbon footprint of the transaction may change significantly. The outcomes of reports in some cases will depend on how far back up the supply chain you want to go, and how granular the details are, which variables are taken into account and so on - all reports will come with caveats and wide-ranging assumptions. For example, some of the commentary I've seen regarding how pickups from physical stores involve less emissions fail to consider the emissions of all the store staff who drive individually to work each day, while some suggesting that online deliveries are more efficient, overlook the impact of warehousing and data centers.

Rather than simply debate, many brands, retailers and consumers will look for efficiencies that reduce environmental impacts without totally removing conveniences that have become expected. A study by consultancy Bain & Company[220] found that by doubling the average number of items purchased per ecommerce transaction and avoiding split shipments, retailers can reduce average per-item emissions by 30 per cent. Leading online retailers are already offering customers greener-seeming options: Walmart is incentivizing customers to order items that are available from a single fulfilment center by waiving delivery fees. Since early 2019, online marketplace Etsy offsets the carbon emissions from items bought and sold via its platform.

Both stores and online retail will be challenged by consumers to take decisive action to reduce their impact, regardless of the relative impacts of one over the other. The total environmental impacts of all shopping must be reduced - consumers need to return less items, retailers and brands need to improve packaging and carriers must optimize deliveries using zero emissions vehicles and efficient, rather than absolutely fast, deliveries. Automation and AI-assistants will play a large role in reducing the impacts of shopping as they can focus on efficiency with far greater purpose than humans. Predictive retail must focus on reducing the overhead of human inefficiencies while still maintaining, or even improving, the perceived level of convenience.

Logistics

"Our customers are consistently telling us one of the big drivers of that improved customer experience year-over-year is inventory availability both online and in stores"

Corie Barry, Best Buy CFO

Nowadays, to offer all the shopping options available to consumers, much of retail is actually about logistics. How do retailers keep up with the infrastructural demands of meeting customers' expectations? Brands and retailers now need to be expert in how to store, pick and pack goods, not just in determining what goods to sell. In the race to keep up with Amazon, the largest retailers are spending billions to extend and automate their fast fulfilment capabilities. For everyone else, there is a range of choices to assess as they strain to keep up.

Warehouses & Fulfilment

"To survive in the post-Amazon era, the way companies have been storing and delivering physical goods to their final destination will need to change profoundly in the next decade".

Simon Wu, Cathay Innovation

Getting any one of millions of products to customers in any location in less than a day may be a monumental challenge but doing so in a cost-effective way is even harder. Add in the requirement to do so in an environmentally sustainable way and it starts to look even more daunting. Amazon was famously unprofitable for many years, ploughing all of its earnings into building the infrastructure to support its growth. Billions of dollars were invested in creating a logistics and fulfilment capability second to none.

Amazon now has 110 fulfilment centers[221] in the US. At a time when main street retail space is in retreat, e-commerce shipping and distribution warehouses are growing fast with 243 million square feet of industrial real estate erected in the US in 2017[222]. While, converting struggling malls into sought-after warehouse capacity may seem straight-forward, industrial space is typically lower value than retail space, so investors won't like to see the value of their assets being downgraded. Of course, some value may be preferable to none. There may also be zoning or other regulatory obstacles, and local cities may also object as warehouse space replacing shopping malls yields no sales taxes.

Warehouse space is big business - in 2019, Blackstone[223], the world's biggest private equity investor, spent $18.7 billion in the world's largest private property deal to secure nearly 180million sq. ft. of warehouse space. The growth in warehouse demand, especially near major urban centers, is leading to increased costs, which is making it harder for smaller operators to compete. Despite the challenges that main street retailers face from outdated rates regimes, online firms are facing rising costs too. According to Real-estate consulting firm CBRE Group[224], rents for U.S. warehouses of between 70,000 and 120,000 square feet rose by more than 33.7% over the past five years, to an average of $6.67 per square foot.

As online retailers seek more storage and fulfilment capacity closer to large urban centers, they are turning to new warehouse designs - with multi-story designs emerging, despite the increased costs associated with building ramps for trucks and elevators for forklifts to access multiple floors. Amazon signed a lease for the first three-story warehouse in Seattle, where Home Depot will also lease capacity.

A new model has also popped up to rent the unused corners in warehouses, like an Airbnb for spare capacity to store and ship inventory. Start-ups such as Flexe, Flowspace and CubeWork offer short-term rentals that are flexible on the amount of space and location — helpful for a retailer that doesn't want to commit to leasing a whole building.

Future Warehouses

Though not as glamorous as experiential retail, warehouses are the lifeblood of modern retail. Increasingly bastions of high-tech automation, they are capable of storing and dispatching mind-boggling numbers of products, or Stock Keeping Units (SKUs) in the jargon.

Warehouses typically look very dull from the outside - slab-sided buildings with no distinguishing features beyond a lack of windows and multiple docking bays for large trucks. Inside though, they are frequently extremely high-tech enclaves of robots and powerful algorithms managing the flow of goods in and out.

New warehouse projects aren't like most existing warehouses, the majority of which were built years ago. CBRE reports[225] that only 4% of today's available logistics and warehouse inventory was built after 2008, indicating that most space being used today was built prior to the e-commerce boom, and is not equipped for the needs of today having been built for humans rather than the now pervasive robots. Automated Storage and Retrieval Systems (ASRS) are featured prominently in many distribution and fulfilment center projects. The robotics-driven technology can safely retrieve merchandise placed at heights of more than 120 feet. Amazon has over 200,000 robots in its facilities, with some capable of lifting 3,000 lbs. (1,400kg) racks of items.

For some variety from all the Amazon-based examples in this book, let's also talk about Ocado in this section. The UK-based firm is the world's largest online-only grocer and recently became a supplier to Kroger, the second-biggest food retailer in the US. A modern Ocado fulfilment center is home to over 1,000 robots, which fetch food items from crates, delivering them to workers at a rate of 3 items per minute for packing. Operating 23 hours a day, 7 days a week, each robot is capable of carrying 340kg; has a forward-facing laser and camera which detect obstacles, such as fallen items, as they travel at up to 9 mph (14 kph). The time to complete a typical 50-item order is now just a few minutes.

Figure 89 Ocado warehouse robots travel across boxes of products

Over time, Ocado plans to streamline the ordering process as far as it possibly can. CTO Paul Clarke suggests that the company could acquire consumption data from your smart fridge, listen to what recipes you're talking about via a smart assistant like Amazon's Alexa, and even mine your calendar for data so it knows you'll be cooking for friends next weekend. Ultimately, he says, it would like for *"the right groceries to turn up, at the right time, as if by magic, without you even having to ask for them."* Supposedly, therefore, if customers can stomach the loss of privacy, Ocado offers something valuable in return. *"We can free people up so that they have more time to experiment and experience the delight of food."*[226] Once the orders are ready to leave the warehouse, the influence of technology still isn't finished. Ocado's delivery planning and routing algorithms[227] assess 4 million moves per second to determine the optimal route for each van.

As well as examples of automation from Amazon and Ocado, human involvement in the complex supply chain that feeds retail and online sellers is reducing in other sectors too. Fast Retailing, the world's second largest fashion retailer and owner of Uniqlo, has partnered with Japanese robotics start-up Mujin to deploy robots capable of folding clothes. Although a simple task for humans, folding clothes requires a level of dexterity that has long evaded robots, but the new robots can complete the task flawlessly 24 hours a day, without the need for breaks. In China, local e-commerce giant JD.com recently unveiled a big new Shanghai fulfilment center that can organize, pack and ship 200,000 orders a day. It employs four people — all of whom service the robots[228].

Organizationally, these changes are another huge upheaval on top of all the customer facing challenges discussed earlier. Boston Retail Partners' 2018 Customer Experience/Unified Commerce Survey found that only 5% of retailers have achieved "shop anywhere/ship anywhere" unified commerce, while 53% reported some amount of omnichannel integration. Though largely hidden from the customer, establishing and operating the right supply chain is vital to deliver the customer-facing omnichannel experience demanded by contemporary consumers. Walmart has merged its distribution, e-commerce-fulfilment, reverse logistics, inbound and outbound transportation, and automation strategy functions.

Where to Warehouse?

Traditional retailers are scrambling to leverage their existing assets close to customers to gain an advantage for rapid deliveries - large areas of their stores are being converted into fulfillment centers. Target in particular has focused on store-based fulfilment.

Store Fulfilment

"In Q1 2019, Target managed to fulfill four of every five online orders from its stores, a volume means stores are effectively doing the work of 14 fulfillment centers."

John Mulligan, COO, Target

Not all fulfilment is done from warehouses or fulfilment centers. For traditional retailers, their store network, recently seen as their Achilles heel in an online-world, is vital in competing against pure-play online retailers. Thanks to their locations close to population centers compared to large out of town warehouses, stores can be key to faster deliveries. In the US, Target has seen a dramatic increase in fulfilment from its stores, growing from 50% of orders in 2017 to 80% in 2019, giving it a 40% cost saving.

Many retailers are now looking at installing micro-fulfillment centers (MFC) that combine the efficiency and accuracy of large-warehouse sorting with the close-to-the-customer appeal of store picking.

But a warehouse that depends on robots come with strict (and costly) construction requirements. Some purpose-built facilities are now required to have super-flat floors (known as FM1) enabling precise robot operation to within millimeter tolerances.

Outsourced Fulfilment

For smaller retailers, who can't afford to invest in their own fulfilment capabilities but still need to compete with larger suppliers, an option is to outsource. Shopify, the leading e-commerce platform that already enables sellers to operate complex online shops, has signaled its intent to expand the services it offers its merchants with the $450m acquisition of a warehouse automation technology company for its Fulfilment Network Service. Meanwhile, eBay has announced its intention to offer Managed Delivery, an end-to-end fulfillment offering for eBay sellers. The company will store seller merchandise in third-party warehouses, allowing for faster fulfillment, while giving sellers the option to provide free shipping with a turnaround time of two or three days. Startups like Huboo also aim to solve the fulfillment challenge that most online stores face, especially smaller ones. The service promises to store your stock, and then "pick, pack and deliver it" automatically as customer orders are placed. The idea is that by outsourcing fulfillment, online shops can focus on the parts of the business where most value is added, such as customer service and choosing which products to develop and/or sell.

Anticipatory Shipping

When I talked about pretail (predictive retail) in the previous Chapter, I was referring to a future where items would be delivered to us before we even realized we need them. While this may seem a little futuristic, Amazon has already been thinking for many years about moving goods closer to potential purchasers. In August 2012

Amazon filed a patent (granted December 2013) for what it termed "anticipatory shipping". This involves *shipping the package to the destination geographical area without completely specifying the delivery address at the time of shipment, and while the package is in transit, completely specifying the delivery address for the package. In some embodiments, speculative shipping of a package may occur in anticipation of a customer ordering items in that package, but before such an order has actually occurred* - in other words shipping an item Amazon thinks you might order in your general direction and then adding the final details of your address once you confirm your order. The patent application (which of course may never be implemented) also covers the concept of making speculatively-shipped items available to other consumers based on proximity at a discount, instead of incurring return shipping costs. This patent, if implemented, represents using the parcel carrier network as an extended and more local warehouse.

Reverse Logistics

Having spent so long discussing all the pressures for high speed delivery and the companies vying to control the last mile with all manner of robots, it's time to turn the discussion to the costly section of logistics known in the industry as reverse logistics, and known to consumers as returns.

Even if a retailer has jumped all the hurdles of selecting the right products for sale to their target consumer, attracting the audience, competing on price and delivery to get the product to the consumer, they may fall at the final hurdle - how to handle the large percentage of online purchases that are returned. It's not uncommon to see return rates of 30 percent or more for merchandise that's bought online. Clothing returns can be above 40 percent. So, a profitable transaction can turn into a loss making nightmare, and even worse into a negative experience for consumers that yields a damaging negative review.

When Humans Start Returning

Returns can be for myriad reasons - the item may be somehow different than the consumer inferred from the online photographs, it may be faulty, or the shopper may simply have changed their mind. Many consumers buy clothes with the explicit goal of returning them; for instance, they buy several sizes of the same product to see which one fits in a practice known as *bracketing*. Some consumers also admit to wearing an outfit only to pose for a social media photo before returning it.

Consumers want returns to be hassle free - they want to be able to return the unwanted item by post or by returning to a convenient store or drop-off point. Retailers too, want returns to be quick, although their desire to speed returns is not just an altruistic customer-pleasing imperative. Getting goods back, processed and ready for sale again can be crucial in securing the best price for it - with some goods ageing rapidly, you don't want to have to discount it because it's past its desirability peak due to your slow processing of a return. That's assuming the goods are returned in condition for resale - returns that can't be resold may head to outlet sales.

Return Mechanics

In their attempts to ease returns, many businesses have tried novel solutions to save the customer the trip to the post office to return. RetailX research[229] found in 2018 that 62% of multichannel retailers in the Top 500 retailers allow ecommerce orders to be returned to their stores. This figure was up from 43% in mid-2017, while 21% of support returning ecommerce orders via a drop-off at a third-party location.

The mechanisms available for returns are familiar from our discussion of the growing delivery options earlier in this Chapter. Consumers can opt not only for BORIS (Buy Online Return In Store) for multichannel retailers, but also return to lockers and specified drop-off partners for online retailers. Nearly 60% of Americans prefer returning purchases to a physical store rather than mailing in their product, according to a UPS study, and 70% of online shoppers made an additional purchase when returning an item to a store.

Walmart intends to accept returns at the front of its stores instead of expecting returners to go to the customer service desk, usually buried at the rear of the store. Walgreens has partnered with FedEx to accept online returns in thousands of Walgreens nationwide. Consumers can even print return shipping labels in store if they don't have home printing facilities. Kohl's has also expanded its partnership with Amazon, which allows customers to bring their returns (packaged or unpackaged) to 1,150 Kohl's stores across the US. Amazon itself is now accepting returns of purchases made online in some of its Amazon Go stores; Amazon also accepts returns in its 19 Amazon Books locations, three Amazon 4-star stores and Amazon Hub Locker locations.

In the UK, shoppers can return John Lewis purchases to the Waitrose driver delivering their groceries (the two companies share an owner), making for a handy drop-off for consumers and a cheaper return channel for John Lewis.

By now, many companies have built in free returns shipping to the cost of products. And consumers have come to expect to be able to return products easily, at no cost or risk to themselves. So, a brand that rescinds free shipping is likely to put itself at a competitive disadvantage. Brands themselves, in other words, are unlikely to help bring about the change needed to reduce the environmental footprint of returns.

How and where consumers return goods is important to retailers. Returns made in stores are cheaper for retailers to process. According to AlixPartners[230], the returns process costs retailers $3 per package when customers return them to a store. But when a customer mails the package back, retailers spend up to $6 per return. For retailers that outsource the cumbersome process of reverse logistics, it's even pricier — it costs $8 per return when returned to a third-party processor and takes longer before the item is available for resale.

Policy & Abuse

An online store's return policy can be a decisive factor for people when choosing where to shop online - 8 in 10 check the return policy before committing to a purchase - if they don't like either the returns policy or the return mechanics available, they may move on to a competitor site. The minimum required level of free, fast delivery *and* free returns is a very big ask from the customer but is becoming an expectation.

While retailers are working hard to adapt to new shopping behaviors, they are also working hard to prevent any new forms of "shrinkage" or increased costs. With worrying numbers of shoppers wardrobing (i.e. wearing an item once and then returning it as unused), many online sites are considering their options to reduce the volume and cost of non-genuine returns. UK-based online fashion retailer ASOS has admitted checking people's social media accounts where its security teams had spotted a repeated and suspicious pattern with returns. If this were to become standard practice for retailers, for example, to check that people weren't wearing items they claimed weren't delivered, this would be a potential use case for a kind of reverse visual commerce - the retailer using computer vision to check images to identify possible returns abuse.

Perhaps less controversial than looking at social media, some online retailers are experimenting with tags to make it harder for people to wear an item once and return it as new.

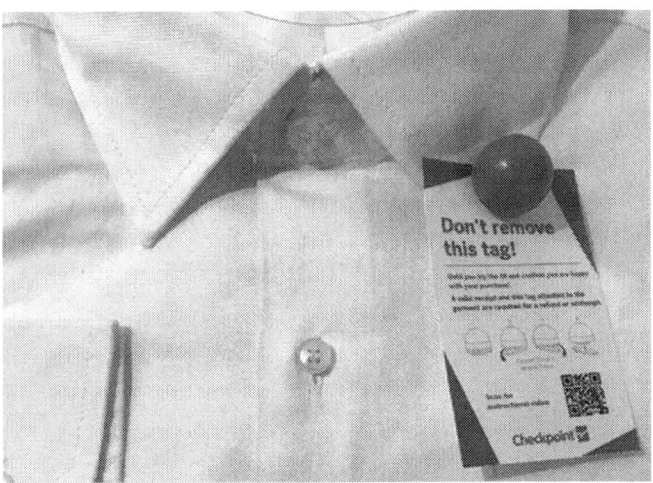

Figure 90 Some brands are experimenting with methods to reduce disingenuous returns

Bad PR

Supply chain and logistics operations are not visible to the consumer when they work, but when they fail, it can have serious commercial consequences. According to the Pitney Bowes Global Ecommerce Study[231], 90% of online shoppers in the US will take an action that can hurt a retailer's brand in response to a bad post-purchase experience. Their reactions range from sharing their frustrations on social media to never purchasing from the offending site again. Among Millennials, 30% will go public about their poor experience, complaining in an online review or social media post, potentially affecting the buying decisions of their entire social networks.

The importance of the post-purchase experience to consumers was further validated by retailers. According to the study, successful high-growth retailers (25% or greater YoY revenue growth) place a greater emphasis on the post-purchase consumer experience than their slower-growth competitors. This includes providing services like free returns and day-definite guaranteed delivery. 54% of high-growth retailers offer 2-3-day free shipping, while 60% of low-growth retailers (10% or less YoY revenue growth) offer 4-7-day free shipping. High-growth retailers also tend to meet or exceed consumer demands for accurate, real-time tracking, free and fast shipping, easy returns with pre-printed labels, prompt refunds and even attractive branded packaging.

For brands and retailers keen to avoid negative experiences caused by shipping, there are tools available such as lateshipment.com that tracks all packages sent, and uses AI to predict potential delays, which can then be proactively notified to customers, potentially mitigating the negative experience.

AI and Returns

As we conclude this section on returns, I want to look at the impact of technology on this particular aspect of shopper behavior and the associated pain for brands and retailers. As humans stop shopping or shop with additional technological aids, can returns be reduced? I expect that the early years of delegated shopping will see an increase in returns - as we get used to the idea of handing over agency to our AI-assistants. As they learn, the returns rate should go down, potentially significantly as they become better than us at knowing what we like and make fewer mistakes.

However, retailers keen to reduce returns are already looking to AI for help. Indian e-commerce giant Flipkart and start-ups such as Supply.ai have been researching the use of algorithms to make a real-time assessment of your level of return risk. Based on the items you've browsed, behavior from similar shoppers and other factors such as the number of items in your basket, an algorithm can decide to increase shipping charges to deter try-before-you-buy shoppers or even offer an incentive discount if you make the purchase non-returnable.

Chapter 9: What does the Future have in Store(s)

"If you dislike change, you're going to dislike irrelevance even more".

Gen Shinseki

The shifts in shoppers, shopping, stores and delivery that we've discussed so far will result in seismic changes to the entire retail and consumer goods experience. A recurring question in debates on the future of retail is what will all these changes mean for physical stores - what will happen the very high-profile retail space that is so much a part of our cities, towns and streets? In a world where humans have largely stopped visiting stores to shop for many things, what role will stores of the future play? How will they fit into the changed experience? How can existing stores, retailers and brands change to stay relevant?

Stores clearly need to evolve to maintain humans' interest in physical shopping so that they choose to go to a main street or mall (over shopping online or delegation to an agent) often enough to justify the costs of running a store. Stores need to compete with the new channels we saw in Chapters 5 and 6, and go beyond simply speeding up the experience as we saw in Chapter 4. The biggest change is likely one of perception - retailers need to change their own perception about their purpose - few will be able to survive if they continue to see their purpose merely as selling items. However, retailers face a daunting challenge in terms of understanding which new retail strategies offer the best chance of success - it's a multifaceted challenge because there is no one size fits all solution.

Today's store owners, already contending with evolving customer preferences, aging IT infrastructure poorly suited to adapt to modern demands, as well as competition not only from Amazon but also from manufacturers going D2C, now face an additional challenge—meeting customer expectations, across generations, in the same store. And generations have differing expectations for what they want in a store experience. For example, Gen Z is the first truly "digital native" generation - they know what they're looking for, they've often researched a purchase before they enter the store and, when they do need help, they expect the store associate to know more than they do. They also want an associate that isn't pushing products that aren't relevant. That means store associates' skills and tools need to change - they need to be sufficiently trained and equipped to handle any situation that arises, whether that's recommending complementary products or, if something is out of stock, shipping it to the customer's home from a warehouse or even a nearby store. It also means that associates need to be incentivized and remunerated differently.

As sales volumes continue to ebb away from stores and sales per square foot decline, the response of most retailers is almost automatic: cut labor, reduce costs, sacrifice service. But that only exacerbates the problem. With even less service to differentiate the stores, customers focus on price and convenience, which strengthens the advantages of online retailers. If traditional retailers hope to survive, they must turn the one big feature that Internet retailers lack—stores that offer the human touch—from a liability into an asset.

Consumer Engagement Spaces

"As consumers become increasingly technologically entrenched, they'll crave far more and better physical retail experiences. And so brick-and-mortar spaces will offer retailers and brands the opportunity to draw the consumer into the brand story, deliver a remarkable and immersive brand and product experience, and ultimately galvanize their relationship with consumers. A relationship that can then live across multiple buying channels"

Doug Stephens, Retail Prophet.com

The basic physical retail experience in many stores hasn't changed much in decades. Typically, you go to a store, search out the item(s) you're looking for, take it to a till, pay and leave. If you're in need of assistance, you track down a store associate and ask a question. Despite the inefficiencies, it works well in many situations. However, as people get used to the convenience and precision of online searching and shopping, physical shopping can seem haphazard, except when we're intentionally just browsing.

In Chapter 4 we looked at how some retailers have experimented with speeding up traditional shopping. In this section, we'll look at more changes that may find their way into our main streets and malls as technology focuses not just on speed but on overall improvements and the stores themselves start to change in response to all of the trends we've seen.

The store of the future may not necessarily be the endpoint for a transaction, but more a part of the pre- and post-purchase journey or part of the total relationship between brand and consumer. It seems unavoidable that the shift to more convenient channels for many purchases and replenishments will continue to expose the over-building of retail space in many countries. Of course, retail isn't going to go quietly into the night, and, despite widespread closures and layoffs, the sector remains a highly visible and, in most cases, defining part of our urban landscape.

Physical shopping has plenty of drawbacks - getting to the store may not be easy, there's no guarantee it'll have what you want (or that you can find it if it does) and there may be a queue for fitting rooms or just to pay. Then you may well discover that another store had it cheaper than you paid for it. Yet physical shopping also has much in its favor. There's nothing quite like touching a product before you buy it - people do still like to see actual products. There's always the chance of a serendipitous discovery of something you'd no intention of buying. There is the opportunity (in some stores) of a conversation with a knowledgeable associate who can help you make an informed personal purchase decision. And there's the instant gratification of leaving the store clutching your purchase. Shopping can also be a social experience and often mixes with coffee or having a meal. Physical retail isn't going to disappear. Closures and consolidations will continue but the concept will persevere and survive, though probably much changed.

Many transactions will gradually become fully automated, but humans will continue to visit stores for some purchases. However, what greets them will mostly be very different from the physical retail experience of today.

The Store of the Future

"Protect the magic and modernise the rest"

Stuart Machin, Managing Director, Food, M&S

I expect to see two main categories of retail stores in the future - those that try to continue with the appearance of traditional approach - i.e. little apparent technology (albeit exploiting non-customer facing technology to improve operations) and those that go all-in on being a part of an omnichannel or experiential customer proposition. Very few retailers will survive without increasing their dependence on technology, though its visibility to consumers will vary greatly. Some will emphasize the technology, while others will focus on the human touch. Retailers of the future will thus compete primarily on one of two things - operational excellence or enhanced customer experience, each of which will be driven by the appropriate use of technologies. An essential part of this transition will be the organizational changes required to transition from the ingrained view of stores and the processes that perpetuate them. But no amount of technology will make up for retailers who fail to improve their basic operations and fail to focus on delivering what the consumer wants - whether that's value, convenience, transparency or more likely, all of these.

The store's role has changed, and so must the store itself. Stores are no longer just a selling space, they're also required to be the warehouse, billboard, catalog, fitting room - but not necessarily fulfilment point - for consumers. Making this happen will require a great deal of technology, a great deal of change (physical and human) as well as difficult financial upheaval, involving both store owners and landlords.

According to A.T. Kearney's 2019 Consumer Retail Technology Survey, three-quarters of shoppers are familiar with new retail technology but only about one-third of them are experiencing it on a regular basis in the stores they frequent. Seventy-two percent of respondents said technology that reduced checkout time was most valuable to them, while 61% of respondents said technology that reduced the time spent navigating the store was most valuable.

Technology for Operations

Although not obvious to consumers, running an efficient retail store, especially at scale, is difficult. Away from the more eye-catching innovations of in store displays, checkoutless technologies and consumer apps, successful retailers are investing in solutions to improve the efficiency of their operations. Improvements to staff communications/training, scheduling and stock management may make the difference between profitability and closure.

Stock Management

It may seem superfluous to point out that you can't sell customers goods that aren't on the store shelves, but every day, millions of dollars in sales are lost when stores fail to move goods from the stockroom to the shelves in a timely manner, disappointing shoppers, frustrating suppliers and unnecessarily costing stores profits.

Shopping in Walmart's most advanced prototype store in Long Island, New York doesn't immediately feel very different from a traditional supermarket. And that's by design. Its key features aren't very obvious or unsettling for consumers. Consumers rarely stop to think about the fact that everything was in stock and the technology that made that possible. The Walmart approach of ceiling mounted cameras and high-tech shelf sensors is expensive and requires store retrofitting but does remain effectively out of the consumers view. We'll see below the alternative of using robots.

Another major area of focus for future retailers will be the use of technology to improve the efficiency of labor utilization. We'll look later at the clienteling tools that stores will deploy to ensure staff have access to timely information about products, stock and customers, but retailers will start to look to technology to optimize staffing levels, monitor staff performance automatically and provide a level of intelligence to each store with forecasts of local weather and other factors that might impact store footfall and therefore the required staff level. There will also be an uptake of staff shift scheduling solutions to take the drudgery out of rota creation, with staff able to swap shifts or request extra shifts via a simple app.

Robots in Stores

Customers who venture into physical stores in the future are increasingly likely to encounter robots. Some experiments with customer-facing robots (such as Softbank's Pepper and Lowebot) haven't proven popular. Although many people are used to automation at checkouts, there are now several firms using robots up and down the aisles to automate routine tasks. This poses significant employment questions concerning the elimination of jobs, but from an operational point of view, robots are reaching the point where they can perform tasks such as cleaning and stock checking with viable accuracy and cost benefits compared to humans.

Returning to the topic of stock management and shelf optimization, solutions from Simbe or Bossa Nova robots can scan shelves and report missing items, incorrect prices or layout errors (planogram compliance is a big topic in retail management). For example, Bossa Nova devices can analyze what's on the shelves with computer vision. The robots drive autonomously through store aisles figuring and not only evaluate which items are in stock, but also help locate misplaced items. In just two minutes, one robot can image 25 meters (80 feet) of aisle. This enables stores to have an up-to-the-minute picture of stock. Retailers may have to reassure the more privacy-paranoid customers that robots aren't using facial recognition and are watching only the shelves, not them.

Figure 91 A Bossa Nova autonomous robot checks the shelves

Walmart is also deploying hundreds of machines to scrub the floors of its stores. An associate riding a cleaning machine might take 2 hours per day. Walmart has ordered more than 1,500 semi-autonomous cleaners, deploying them to nearly half its stores.

Experiential Retail

"Stage Retail Experiences or be Commoditized. Most retail is just painfully boring. In fact, the majority of store chains, malls and shopping centers have become beacons of boredom, monuments to mediocrity and havens of ho hum."

Doug Stephens, The Retail Prophet

A potential customer entering a physical store is an exciting prospect for a brand or retailer. The fact that they have chosen to spend some of their time looking at your merchandise represents a golden opportunity to influence and maybe even close a sale. At a minimum, regardless of whether there is an immediate sale or not, the interaction will likely determine the future of your relationship, if any, with that customer.

To earn their place in the modern shopping journey, stores need to be enticing for customers, exploiting the benefits of a real-life interaction. Stores must be repositioned as genuine destinations - it can no longer be just about stacking products on shelves and hoping customers will find and buy what they want - that is accomplished more easily, for most products, online. When humans do go shopping, retailers need to up their game.

Consumers are frequently choosing to spend their money on experiences rather than material goods. To keep up, retailers are trying to sell their customers both. In response to findings that all generations from Millennials (73%) to Boomers (46%) are more likely to visit a shopping center if it also offers leisure or entertainment experiences, more U.S. malls than ever before are devoting spaces for experiential offerings such as yoga or cycling studios - the number has more than doubled in the last 10 years from about 6,000 in 2008 to over 14,000[232]. In an era where the majority of purchasing decisions are based on wants rather than needs - most developed countries shoppers' basic needs have already been met – emotions, derived from values, play an important role. For products not purchased via replenishment, emotional connections and entertaining experiences may offer a way to gain the attention of consumers.

Before retailers move towards some of the more expensive experiential experiments that we'll discuss, I urge all retailers to ensure they have first created a solid engagement platform for their customers. It's amazing the number of retailers who don't make it easier for consumers to shop, by providing the information that they already know consumers value. As a result of online experiences, in-store shoppers now expect to get detailed product information in the store, read ratings and reviews, get help physically finding products, get access to the best price, and be able to skip the cashier line on the way out.

Experiences

In China, JD.Com is the second largest e-commerce business, behind Alibaba. JD owns 10% of Chinese supermarket chain Yonghui Superstores and has a major partnership with Walmart. JD has launched a new grocery store concept called 7FRESH. When shopping for produce in 7FRESH, you can use your mobile phone to scan a barcode on a pear, for example, and see detailed product information (farm of origin, sugar content, customer reviews, etc.) on a screen above the produce section. Alibaba has a similar digital grocery store concept called Hema. At both Hema and 7FRESH, you must have the retailer's smartphone app installed to even get into the store, because you're going to use that app to scan your own purchases and complete the transaction without ever getting in a checkout line.

Sephora

In stark contrast to the beauty displays in department stores of old, Sephora stores devote significant portions of their floor space to things other than shelves of cosmetics. Instead, you'll find stools facing tables of iPads. Here, consumers can learn about various products and try various looks with technology-enhanced sales tools as part of Sephora's Teach, Inspire, Play (TIP) program. In a radical departure for store metrics, a customer conversion isn't the only focus - the intent is to create a positive customer interaction and experience that leads to brand engagement, sales, loyalty and advocacy.

Lululemon

Popular athleisure apparel brand Lululemon is expanding its physical footprint with the opening of megastores, featuring yoga and HIIT (high-intensity interval training) studios, locker rooms, and seating areas that serve coffee, smoothies and healthy snacks. One-third of Lululemon's Mall of America site (6,000 sq. ft) is dedicated to the experiential areas, which even feature a separate entrance from the retail area. Customers using the studios can try new Lululemon clothing in classes before purchase.

Interactive Displays

I mentioned in Chapter 4 how screens are starting to permeate stores. Although most consumers now research on their own screens before they enter a store and carry their own screen with them, more screens throughout stores will appear in the future. The next generation of displays add interactivity - digitally augmenting the physical items in store. Relatively simple and inexpensive compared to other solutions, they can combine the ability to interact with a product with the web-like abilities to offer detailed product information, reviews and even ask questions, without having to find a store associate.

As one of the key advantages of stores over online is the ability for consumers to see, touch and feel a product, expect to see more retailers try interactive displays and solutions like those from Perch, which uses sensors to react as consumers pick up specific items. Not only can they offer context-specific information on nearby displays, but brands and retailers can collect web-level data in a physical environment. Such technologies even allow retailers to A/B test merchandising and make real time changes. High-end retailer Rebecca Minkoff saw a significant sales lift with interactive touchscreens that let shoppers choose products to be sent to their dressing rooms. The dressing room mirror/screen also enabled them to view those same items styled with different colors, sizes and looks.

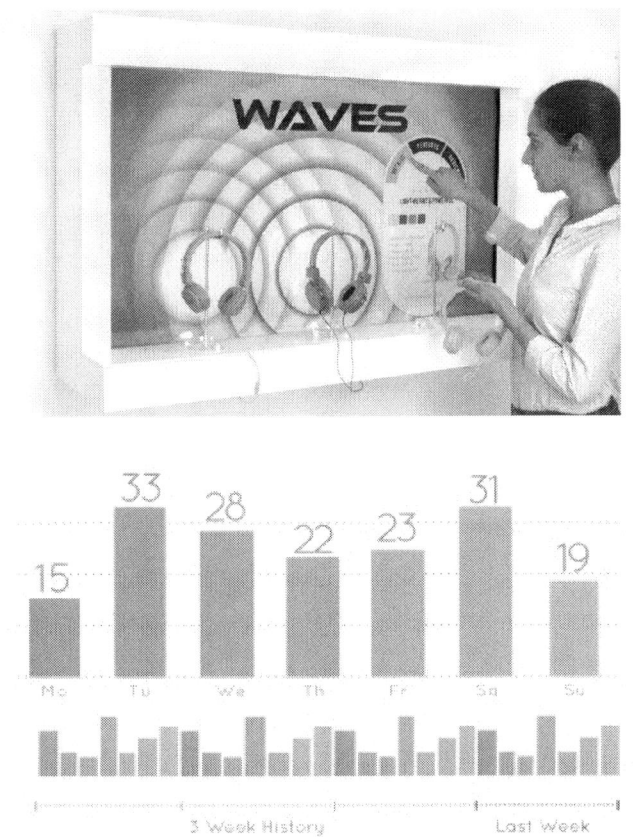

Figure 92 An interactive display unit from Perch (top) and an example of customer engagement tracking (bottom). Source: Perch

Virtual Reality (VR) and Augmented Reality (AR)

Some in the retail industry believe that the key to retaining consumer interest in physical retail lies in creating memorable experiences with advanced technology that consumers won't have access to outside the retail environment. Among the most commonly touted solutions are Virtual Reality and Augmented Reality. Virtual reality headsets enable the creation of immersive graphical experiences, while Augmented reality headsets show digital items overlaid in the real world.

Cost, hygiene, usability and even operational challenges including battery life make VR headsets a niche. They can provide totally compelling experiences but are hard to scale. I've observed retailers offering VR experiences, but they have been marred by queues and the awkwardness of putting on a headset in the middle of a public space. Although standalone headsets make it more practical than ones that require a tether to a high-power PC, that's still not ideal in most retail environments. Brands such as the North Face, Lexus and Volvo have experimented with VR apps and, while I do expect we will see shopping solutions that leverage VR, they will likely be aimed at the early adopter home VR user before in-store use.

Where VR may have a short-term use is in improving retail in areas like training or testing merchandising layouts as in the experiment shown below conducted by Kelloggs and Accenture[233]. Walmart also uses VR simulations to test associates for management aptitude.

Figure 93 Kelloggs and Accenture VR recreation of a supermarket shelf for training

As you might expect from a natively online company, furniture retailer Wayfair's first physical store is designed to maximize the physical interaction with the customer. In its first store in Massachusetts, Wayfair uses VR headsets to guide customers, as well as AR technology on iPads in an attempt to create a shopping experience that melds the best of online and offline shopping.

However, AR headsets remain expensive and unwieldy. Undoubtedly as the technology improves, they could become part of an enhanced shopping experience, but I think any widespread benefit to retailers remains years away. AR does make sense for high-end furniture, such as Natuzzi, who use Microsoft Hololens headsets to help customers envisage entire rooms.

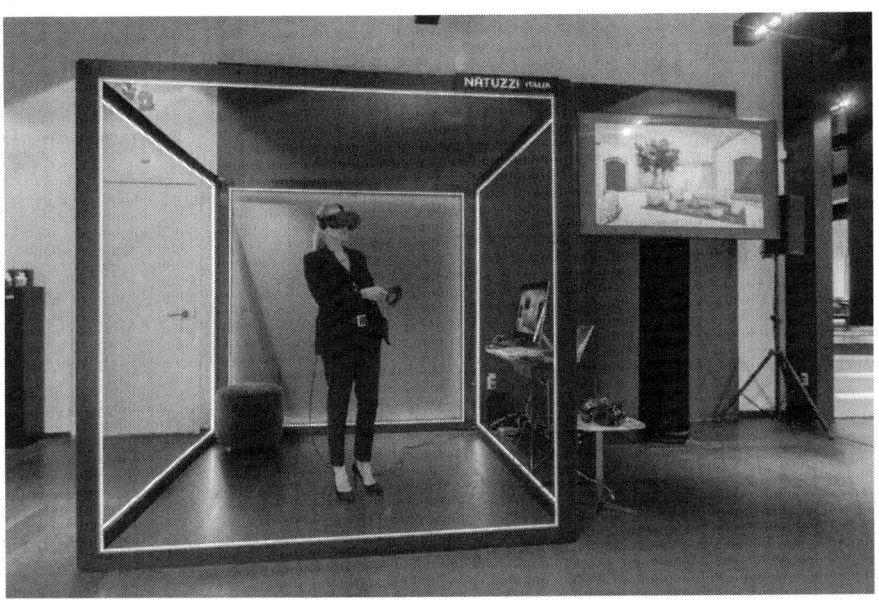

Figure 94 A Natuzzi AR experiment in association with Microsoft

What might prove more useful in the short term could be selected phone-based AR experiences. These are already in use in a number of popular apps, and the major mobile operating system providers (Apple and Google) are developing their AR platforms (ARKit and ARCore respectively).

As we saw in Chapter 6, examples of AR experiences in apps are already popular in some sectors - retailers in homeware, apparel and beauty categories are already benefiting from adding AR experiences to their apps. Although these are more typically used in a home setting than in a physical store, the ability for consumers to "see" products in their own environment can reduce returns as consumers make better choices after visualizing in their own environment.

For in-store use, navigation information which may be useful in larger stores, as well as overlay of additional information can bring products to life. Home Depot, IKEA, Lowe's, Pottery Barn, Amazon, Wayfair, Target and Houzz are among the homeware brands using AR, while Sephora and YouTube have pioneered its use in the beauty space. Houzz reports that mobile users who engage AR are 11 times more likely to purchase and spend 2.7 times longer in the app. In early 2019 in London, Snapchat and Lego collaborated to set up a popup store with no products - it contained only Snapcodes, that when scanned with Snapchat enabled access to an AR shopping experience. Sephora installed an intelligent digital mirror in its flagship store in Madrid to deliver hyper-personalized experiences and product recommendations to shoppers. Shoppers able to scan QR codes on the mirror to buy the items online or locate them in the store. In another example, Spanish fashion retailer Zara piloted a scheme where customers can point the Zara app at shop windows and see the models brought to life in short videos. Any of the looks in the videos can be ordered directly on screen.

A Dose of Reality

"Many analysts have spent an enormous amount of energy on the idea that retail needs to become more experiential. A 2019 prediction is that a great retail experience will be as much about not disappointing, confusing, or interrupting shoppers as it is about delighting them."

Kantar

Technology can help retailers across a number of challenges, with vendors promising buzz-word laden benefits such as maximizing customer service, anticipating customer needs, business efficiency, and more. But it can also distract from the basics and burn huge amounts of money.

For all the techno-excitement about virtual reality or augmented reality, the bottom line remains the pressing reality for most retailers. While consultants and solution vendors talk about the need for stores to create more "experiences" to stay relevant, there is often little practical advice on how to cost, scale or actually do this. Realistically, many consumer product categories don't lend themselves to experiences, or the margin they carry doesn't. I've read many books from retail experts who dramatically proclaim that experiential shopping is the *only* salvation for physical retail. While there are categories of retail that will be enhanced by experiential approaches, there are also many that don't need it. I'm in favor of implementing useful new technologies but not lose the benefits of physical stores with overwhelming application of technology. When assessing the opportunities for improved retail experiences, it's important to remember the goal isn't to build an app, nor is the goal to "use" VR/AR. The goal instead must be to create an experience that will attract customers - paying customers - to your brand.

Many of the solutions that will help physical retailers survive and even thrive are going to be invisible to customers, except in the guise of improved service. I would caution anyone who thinks they can paper over fundamental inadequacies with a fancy experience - consumers will see through the technology if their core needs aren't being met. I get a sense of desperation in many of the retail books I've read - clinging to the hope of experiential as salvation. I don't share that optimism. I think people will see through it to the end game of a product sale, however slickly it's presented as an experience. I also don't believe that the vast majority of supply chains in any form can afford experiential selling that may only suit luxury goods.

The Price of Appmission

As discussed in Chapter 3, retailers have a 'complex' relationship with apps. Apps that are merely poorly designed catalogs that offer no added value are of course not welcome on peoples' phones and don't deserve to be there. For those retailers which don't have sufficient justification for their own app, they must make sure to offer an omnichannel experience via a mobile optimized experience and a presence on the appropriate social channels. For others though, the power of an app is necessary to deliver the best possible experience; for some flagship experiences, you need an app. You can't get into an Amazon Go Store, for example, without the Amazon Go app.

It is critical that apps are designed with ease of use - nobody downloads an app then reads the instructions - technology needs to be intuitive so instructions aren't required. Here are some examples of stores that require the app, and others that look to simply enhance the in-store experience for those that have the app.

Nike (App Required)

"It's a digital experience, brought to life in a physical space"

Mark Parke, CEO, Nike

If you visit Nike's flagship store on Fifth Avenue in New York, you need the Nike app to checkout as there are no cash registers to queue at. NikePlus members can reserve items on their phones and ask to hold them for pickup in an in-store locker. Instead of asking employees if products are available, Nike app users scan codes on sneakers and clothes, and the items are sent directly to a fitting room. Customers can use the app to scan and pay for their purchases without the need to wait in line at the checkout. They can also use it to scan the QR code on any mannequin to see full details in the app of the outfit it is wearing. Scanning a product barcode will bring up more info on the product, including if it's in-stock in the store. There's also an array of other useful concierge services and rewards available.

Amazon GH Lab (App Required)

As if its own bookstores, 4-star stores and checkout-free Go stores weren't enough experiments for Amazon in physical retail, it could also be found at the largest mall in the US, the Mall of America in 2018. There, in a popup collaboration with Good Housekeeping Magazine, it set up a concept store. Shoppers armed with the Amazon app could scan codes (called Amazon SmileCodes) beside each of the carefully curated items to add them to their virtual shopping bag. Customers did not take anything home with them from the store - all fulfilment was via Amazon delivery. The requirement to use the Amazon app wasn't a significant barrier given its popularity and prominent position on most peoples' phones.

H&M

H&M updated their app to add more in-store features, having previously seen the app as a tool primarily for users to browse their wares from anywhere but the stores. However, the latest version now offers an in-store mode to locate items. It also offers a sustainability tool to surface information about specific factories and locations used by the company's supply chain as well as sourcing methods and traits of various fabrics.

Dollar General

Away from the world of flagships stores, discount chain Dollar General has added BOPIS and an in-store cart calculator to its app - the latter feature gives customers a running total of their cart including taxes and any coupons/discounts before they head to checkout. In some stores, the mobile app also lets customers scan and pay for items in stores using their phones, skipping the checkout line, but at the time of writing, it's available in less than 500 of the chain's 15,000 stores. In an appreciation of customer needs, Dollar General has paid particular attention to minimizing the size of their app for patrons who may have limited memory on their devices.

Online, Mobile and the Future Store

Taking the development of store experiences as well as customer and logistics systems to its logical conclusion, you can imagine a near future shopping experience transpiring like this: A customer starts browsing at home or work, looking for a new outfit for an event. Having shortlisted a few items, the customer checks the opening hours of their nearest store and receives confirmation that the items they just looked at are in stock in their size. A store assistant assembles the items and has them waiting in a changing room, along with some suggested items based on the customer's previous purchases.

In the nearer term, we will see retailers harnessing AI solutions to offer consumers much more contextually relevant information - for example, while customers in many cases can already scan item barcodes in stores for information, they are typically presented with the same web page they might see from anywhere. However, when a retailer knows the customer is in a particular store when scanning, they should present personalized information including other relevant items in that store the customer should try with the scanned item.

Non-tech Experiences

"We don't have tech in our showrooms and it's intentional, and it's because she [the customer] is inundated by it. Our stores are a place where she can come talk to a person. To feel familiar I'm not going to put a nine-foot screen in there, I want her to feel like she's at home trying on clothes with her best friend."

Caroline Brown, Director of Experiential Design, MM.LaFleur[234]

Of course, not all experiences revolve around technology, and, in fact, consumers who choose to visit physical stores instead of shopping online may particularly appreciate retailers who focus on analog experiences that emphasize human and sensory experiences with authenticity or human interaction, over technology. Although you might expect a digitally native brand like MM.LaFleur (which describes itself as a wardrobe solution for professional women) to go high-tech when opening physical stores, they have instead opted for no-tech. For retailers who place less emphasis on an in-store sale, they can focus more on brand education using the space traditionally reserved for speculative inventory for customer engagement instead.

Building on consumer interest in sustainability, UK supermarket Marks and Spencer has installed in-store vertical farming units to let customers experience fresh herbs grown in store using a high-tech growing chamber from provider Infarm. Each in-store farm unit uses 95 percent less water and 75 percent less fertilizer than traditional soil-based agriculture and is capable of producing the equivalent output of 400 square meters of farmland. This is an example of innovation that appeals to customers without involving intrusive technology.

Figure 95 An indoor farm in an M&S Supermarket

Customers want service, not science fiction

"There are so many retailers chasing and leaping aboard bandwagons today. Not nearly enough are genuinely innovating - and many aren't even getting the basics right."

Neil Saunders, CEO GlobalData[235]

The best retail boss I ever worked for once told me there were only three things that really matter in retail: People, Detail and Focus. There's two parts to People - knowing the people you are selling to, and investing in the people who sell for you. Detail means attention to detail across your products & operations and Focus is a reminder that you can't be all things to all people - decide what you do and be exceptional at it.

Despite the important role it can and will play, the future is not all about technology. Good retail is still largely a matter of operations and execution. As marketing magazine, The Drum put it, "*Customers want service not sci-fi from main street retailers*"[236]. Its study found that 81% of UK shoppers felt that personal touch had disappeared from retail customer service and almost a third (32%) blamed an over-reliance on technology for this decline. Half of those polled thought that companies use technology to save money, rather than improve customer experience.

As customers grow more comfortable with omnichannel shopping, they grow less tolerant of disappointing in-store experiences. When main street retailers blame online vendors for their struggles, they tend to overlook their own contributory negligence: stores where sales associates are hard to find or unhelpful; frequent stockouts, long checkout lines; returns desks hidden at the back of the store or in the basement. 75% of Millennial and 53% of Gen X shoppers have left a store without purchasing an item and instead bought the item online due to out of stocks[237]. While it's impractical for stores to keep a stock of everything, it's positive to see Walmart store associates have an app that allows customers to order and pay for items (including with cash) to be shipped while inside a physical store. Although the consumer could have left and ordered the item from the store's website, so the sale isn't lost, the simple act of empowering the store associate to process the transaction can make the consumer feel like they got extra customer service.

No More Paper Receipts?

As far as many people are concerned, the addition of technology throughout the sales process will neither be easy nor welcomed by all. Not all new technologies are obviously clearly better than the status quo. While they bring advantages in terms of cost or convenience, they may also bring challenges such as worker displacement, social exclusion, privacy invasion or negative environmental consequences.

Take digital receipts as an example. On one hand, they are less messy than paper receipts, don't waste paper, are searchable/archivable (persistent) and never require till rolls to be replaced. But on the other hand, for some people, they raise privacy concerns. How can you be sure that the store issuing the digital receipt won't use the digital interaction to store the customers' details for future use (such as unsolicited marketing communications) or store them insecurely?

Surveys show that consumers still prefer physical paper receipts more than 3 to 1 when shopping in stores. Yet according to a Green America report[238], receipt use consumes more than 3 million trees and 9 billion gallons of water, and generating receipts produces more than 4 billion pounds of carbon dioxide.

Future Formats

"We believe stores will become smaller. They will become much more a blend of picking up stuff you've ordered online and returning products you didn't like. They will be much more service orientated, with less display, and then you're going to have flagship [stores] where brands can really showcase what they can offer."

Achim Berg, McKinsey

We're seeing significant changes in size, location, fulfilment capabilities, and staffing when it comes to brick-and-mortar stores. Success metrics are changing, as are assessments of purpose and overall value. Retail stores may not be in the same physical locations as they traditionally have been. If footfall to malls and main streets is falling, retailers need to consider if they also should find places that better fit into their customers' lives.

Those humans that continue to go shopping in physical stores in the coming years, will encounter a much wider variety of stores than at present. There will be a mixture of stores that look like today's but rely on technology to track customers, stores that don't have any items for immediate purchase, stores that exist primarily to take back items purchased online and stores replete with incredible technology to lure in customers. Formats are changing - department stores are declining in popularity as consumers opt to shop in specialty stores that are easier to navigate or in boutique stores that increase the chances of a serendipitous discovery.

We will continue to see changes on main streets and in malls. Though not the same singular shopping destinations of the past, they remain high footfall and important social places. Stores will continue to open as chains prosper that operate efficiently, appeal to modern customers and straddle the offline and online worlds seamlessly. Some will try new formats, new partnerships and new experiences. New online and D2C brands will be joining the main street, but changes and significant investments will come also from established retailers like Nordstrom, IKEA, Walmart and Target, all trying to increase their relevance.

Let's look at some of the changes in physical store formats:

Size Matters

"Big stores are IKEA's foundations, but we need to shift our foundations because we've realized we need to move into the city centers. We know we want to move closer to the customer and give them more options"

Peter Jelkeby, Head of IKEA UK & Ireland[239]

For most of the last 50 years, retailers have been used to growing. Having moved from small stores to department stores to strip malls to out of town mega stores, the US in particular has more retail space per capita than anywhere in the world. But as shopping behaviors change and people use the endless aisles of the internet to browse product selections, the push for ever-expanding physical stores is no longer sustainable. Many retailers have lost focus and relevance for their consumers with the quest to fill the space with merchandise, that all too frequently ends up being heavily discounted.

As humans shop in new ways, retail space will have to adjust - bigger is no longer better as shoppers are better informed, less patient and in many cases no longer as willing to drive to out of town malls. For example, IKEA, renowned for the size of its stores in suburban locations has started experimenting with city center locations for smaller showrooms in London, Paris and in New York. The new IKEA store due to open in central Vienna in 2021 will have no car parking, and items too large to be carried will be delivered within 24 hours. There is no longer a one size fits all approach to stores. Retailers are adapting their retail estates to ensure they can service their customers when and where they want. Starbucks for example now has a range of store formats from a mobile-powered "pick-up only" format (in Penn Station, New York) to its giant Chicago store that spans 5 stories, alongside its burgeoning coffee delivery services in many countries. Just as Starbucks is experimenting with pick-up only, McDonalds has a trial takeaway-only store London with a new "grab-and-go" format with no seating area, compact self-order screens and a reduced menu.

Refurbishment

Although physical shopping offers clear tangibility benefits for shoppers, that doesn't mean shortcuts can be taken on creating an attractive environment for customers. One obvious distinction between newer specialty stores and incumbent retailers (especially department stores) is the decor and ambiance. Physical stores that want to attract customers will need to invest. Even if they choose to eschew advanced technology, at a minimum, stores must refurbish after years of neglect and underinvestment. Updating a store to be relevant and attractive to shoppers requires big investment, but this is existential - any retailer who thinks business as usual is ok will be gone.

Retailers, large and small, are trying to lure consumers away from their laptops and back to the shops, installing features that aim to make shopping less arduous, stressful and time-consuming. Some stores may arrange themselves more like web sites - Urban Outfitters, for example, switched from layouts with items distributed around the store to a more digital layout - all of the same items together, just as they would be on a web page.

Target & Walmart

"We think the differentiator is going to be what the in-store experience is like. The store isn't going away."

John Mulligan, COO, Target

In an ambitious - but ultimately successful example - Target embarked on a $7 billion capital investment plan in 2017 to refurbish its stores, open new smaller stores (one-third the size of standard Target stores) and create a logistics capability to support its online growth. It has now over 100 small-format stores located in major metropolitan areas, and 500 modernized stores, with the revamped stores delivering a 2%-4% increase in sales. Among the changes Target implemented were the use of mannequins to display apparel with a coherent "look" styled by visual merchandisers instead of just shelves and racks of clothes. The stores got upgraded lighting and lowered shelving units to improve visibility and reduce the sense of clutter.

Similarly, Walmart has embarked on an extensive and expensive refurbishment program to upgrade 1,000 of its stores, spending over $2 billion to remodel some 500 stores with improved lighting, wider aisles and self-checkout facilities[240].

Malls

"Over the past 10 years ... we have seen the heightened value and improvement of the best centers, and a substantial deterioration of everything else. What was good is even better, and what is not good has gotten much worse."

Bill Taubman, COO Taubman Centers[241]

The mall has been a mainstay of retail for over 50 years now, yet one in four U.S. malls is expected to close by 2022, according to a 2017 report by Credit Suisse. In the malls that are surviving and even thriving in the new world of retail, the emphasis has shifted from traditional shopping. From mini golf to gyms to beauty salons, much of the time a consumer spends at a mall no longer involves picking up goods as mall owners invest in leisure facilities in spaces previously occupied by stores. America's newest mega-mall in New Jersey is 55% entertainment and just 45% retail - with its star attractions being an indoor ski slope, ice rink, water park and a Nickelodeon theme park. Even with footfall driven by these leisure pursuits, the mall's 350 stores will still face challenges compared to their online competitors, due to local "blue laws" that don't allow shops to open on Sundays.

For malls that haven't adapted, vacancy rates are deteriorating to unsustainable levels. Those that depend on department stores as footfall-driving anchor tenants have been particularly badly hit as department stores lose customers to specialist stores and discounters. For some malls that can't survive, their fate is to be repurposed as distribution facilities as online sites seek additional warehouse space close to urban centers.

Reducing the Risk of Retail

For brands not ready or able to take on the very expensive and extended timeframe task of building a permanent physical store network to reach more consumers, there are more options than ever before to create a physical presence with less investment and knowledge of the intricacies of effective retail operations.

Pop-ups

One of the challenges of establishing a physical store is that main street and mall landlords typically require long leases, often multiyear without even a chance to review for often 5 years, and with upwards-only rent reviews. Prestigious street locations often command 20+ year commitments. This has made physical retail inherently unsuitable for start-ups or transient collections of goods. Yet cities around the world are grappling with a vacant storefront crisis, promoting a pragmatic rethink in some quarters.

The growing acceptance of pop-up temporary stores means businesses can now test their propositions in some high footfall locations. This appeals to younger generations who are used to and indeed expect turnover and change, not the staid unchanging main streets of old. It resonates with their changing tastes and the ephemeral ethos of these cohorts. UK start-up Appear Here is an online platform for businesses seeking short term store rentals and has attracted investment from US retail real estate giant and Mall owner Simon Property Group, while US-based firm Storefront offers over 10,000 pop-up properties globally. Akin to a pop-up mall or shopping center, Boxpark uses refitted metal shipping containers to rapidly create a shopping and dining space offering affordable and flexible leases for both large and small brands. This concept has been successful in up-and-coming areas of London such as Shoreditch, creating a retail space without building a strip mall.

Just as fast-fashion relies on using the Fear of Missing Out (FOMO) to entice customers to visit their store regularly, pop-up stores that rotate their tenants can bring a hint of dynamism to otherwise static streets and malls. Customers typically visit fast fashion stores 17 times per year in search of new items vs 4 for traditional department stores, so the lure of new products or experiences is undeniable. Temporary pop-up shops are going to be a permanent part of the new retail landscape.

A 2019 report[242] from retail estate services firm Cushman & Wakefield identified six subcategories of pop-up stores:

- Pop-in Stores - temporary shops in a department store or existing retail chain.

- Experiential pop-ups - stores are selling experiences, more than merchandise.

- Media/Entertainment pop-ups - pop-ups tied to television shows or movies.

- Hospitality pop-ups - partnerships between brands and hotels or restaurants.

- Event pop-ups - shops are tied to an event like a record launch or concert.

- Retail Marketplaces - permanent spaces with a rotating line-up of pop-up brands.

Partnerships

The pressures facing the retail sector have created unusual partnerships and I believe will continue to do so. Attempts to survive declining footfall and changes in shopping behaviors will lead to previously unthinkable or untried partnerships, as brands and retailers look to share the risks and costs, as well as potential benefit, from attracting more customers.

In a partnership announcement in late 2019, Target and Disney revealed a plan for 25 store-in-store small Disney stores in Target locations. Measuring just 750 sq. ft, which gives room for about 450 products, this opens up Target customers for impulse purchases of Disney merchandise without having to visit a Disney Store.

In the UK, apparel and food chain Marks and Spencers has even tried a partnership with Hi-fi, home cinema and TV specialist Richer Sounds as M&S looks for compatible concessions, while clothing retailer Next might have seemed an unlikely place to find your next smartphone from mobile operator O2. Expect to see more unusual partnerships as traditional category barriers breakdown.

Retail As A Service (RaaS)

For those not ready to set up their own pop-up store or take space in a partner's retail estate but who still want to get products in front of an audience, a solution like retail-as-a-service start-up B8ta might be suitable (Macys has invested in B8ta). Essentially, this is renting fully serviced space in a store where brands don't have to worry about any of the usual hassles of retail operations. B8ta offers brands space in their stores to showcase products, starting with just one product. In keeping with a modern shopping concept, each item on display has an interactive screen beside it that offers product details, but also captures data on what interests consumers. Brands can update the screen displays in all B8ta stores remotely to test how new information presentations or pricing changes resonate with shoppers. B8ta store staff complete sales for all brands on display in each store as there is no inventory accessible to customers - it's all kept in a storeroom so the shop floor is always tidy, unlike the frequently messy shelves of traditional stores. A similar concept in the UK, Situ[243] offers an "inspiration space to discover, learn, interact, meet, work, eat and drink", creating a shared store space in central London.

Figure 96 A typical B8ta store with interactive displays for each product

Online Goes Offline Too

Somewhat ironically, much of the future of physical stores actually lies in the hands of brands that began life online. As DTC companies grow, they typically find the need to establish some level of physical presence. Due to the rising costs of acquiring customers online, it may actually be cheaper to have a physical presence as a way of raising a brand's profile. This may take the form of one of the less risky methods above, a conventional display in traditional stores, or there may be sufficient funding to open a small number of starter stores. Setting up a physical presence allows online-only brands to reach a new audience, as well as form a tangible relationship with their online customers, which typically grows trust and loyalty.

Brands like Casper, the online mattress company, along with Warby Parker, the online glasses company now have more than 100 physical stores each. And of course, as we discussed in Chapter 8, stores can serve to reduce warehousing, fulfilment and delivery costs.

Outer

One D2C company is trying a different take on showrooms - it enlists its customers as its ambassadors (called hosts), getting them to open their homes (well, their yards) to potential shoppers. So, if you're interested in buying some Outer furniture, you can browse listings from Hosts, and then go to their homes by arrangement, seeing the products in actual day-to-day use in their yards.

The hosts are paid a fixed fee by Outer for showing the products but can opt to act as a "digital only showroom", offering just photos and not home visits. For some it's a step too far into the gig-economy but for prospective purchases, it's a chance to see a big-ticket purchase in an authentic use, not a traditional, staged showroom, and talk to real owners.

Stores that don't sell

I suggested above that the stores of the future will reduce the emphasis on sales to instead either form a part of the customer journey or a potential endpoint for a transaction. Conversion, once a key metric, will be of little importance to the retailer of the future; even though I might have left the retail space empty-handed, it can no longer be assumed my experience was negative or won't culminate in a digital purchase later.

However, some of the stores of the future will take this to the extreme and not have any merchandise for sale. US Department store giant Nordstrom has opened stores that don't sell. Dubbed Nordstrom Local, these small stores offer personal styling services and alterations, and serve primarily as a hub for picking up online orders and returns.

Primarily-online apparel retailer Bonobos was acquired by Walmart for over $300m in 2017. Their 20 stores ("guideshops") don't carry in-store inventory and act as product showrooms: they have items in every color, size, fit and fabric available to try on, but keep no product in stock for immediate purchase. In store, you try things on and pay for them, but you don't take anything with you - your purchases are sent to your home, as if you'd ordered online. The stores also accept returns, though with the chance to try clothes on, their return rates shouldn't be like their exclusively online peers. Waiting for delivery of products chosen in store is of course far less inconvenient now than it might have proven before the logistics innovations we discussed in Chapter 8. With deliveries in some cases being possible within hours, items selected in store for delivery could reach a customer's home before they do.

The Associate of the Future

As the role of physical retail in the purchase journey changes, the role of retail associates will also change. Automation will continue to replace humans for checkout and routine tasks such as inventory checks. In theory, that will free up staff to provide more customer advice and assistance, with clienteling apps (see below) enabling them to establish relationships with customers based on data about their preferences, behaviors and purchases. We've already seen how important retail is to the economy as a source of employment and how the drop in retail jobs is a serious concern. We may see more stores without staff in traditional roles, such as Amazon Go, or stores where robots greet or assist consumers, but even in the most digitized store, the need for the human touch will remain.

In physical stores, along with customers being able to touch the products, the sales associates are the key difference compared to online sales. However, they are often paid little more than the minimum wage and reliant on targets to earn commission, which means their advice may not always be impartial or in the customer's interests. Most retailers simply train their team to close out the register, stock shelves, and keep the floor clean. To thrive in the new world of retail, it is more important they teach their team how to identify a customer's needs and wants, match those needs to a selection of products, and show them the value in their options.

Sales associates need to be empowered to interact positively with customers. Reward schemes need to be designed mindful that a consumer may walk out without completing the sale but perfectly happy with the interaction and later completing the transaction online. In today's retail world, such a sale would typically be credited to the online team, with the store associate receiving no commission.

Apps for Associates

"Putting mobile devices in the hands of store associates is now a necessity to keep up with the customer who has a plethora of information available at her fingertips. Associate mobile devices enhance the shopping experience by accessing real-time inventory and customer data and offering the ability to service customers and process transactions anywhere in the store."

Perry Kramer, VP, Boston Retail Partners

There's a sign behind the counter of my local convenience store warning staff "No Mobiles", clearly aimed at ensuring the staff stay attentive to the customers and the store presentation. However, it many stores, you'll see management encouraging staff to use mobiles to better serve customers - so you're likely to see more technology in store associates' hands. In order to improve efficiency and enhance customer service, retailers are leveraging a range of apps to improve training, communications with store staff, shift scheduling and stock visibility as well as mobile checkout. Boston Retail Partners found in 2017 that 9 out of 10 retailers see a benefit in putting mobile solutions in the hands of store associates.

Large retail organizations, in particular, can struggle to ensure all of their staff have timely access to the information they need to provide the level of service to which their organization aspires. Consider Apple Retail, which has some 70,000 staff globally, across just over 500 stores. Without associate-level technology, briefing them accurately and ensuring compliance would be serious challenges. Apple retail staff begin their shift with an app called Hello, which briefs them on the most important "need to knows" of the day. A second app, Loop, functions as an internal social network where staff can share learnings with each other.

Customers like the human touch of physical retail, but expect the associates to have super-human knowledge. Clienteling solutions such as those from Redant offer the sales associates details for existing customers including contact preferences, preferred sizes, past purchases and personal tastes, as well as a summary of client activity online and recommendations for cross-sell opportunities, all in the palm of their hands.

We saw earlier how Cadillac is using technology for associates to offer virtual visits to car showrooms. Other apps such as Hero enable store associates to chat and even livestream video chat with customers who have questions, want to interact with an associate but can't make it to a physical store.

Data in Retail

When you visit a retailer's web site, thanks to cookies (or your login), it knows instantly if you've been there before. It knows what you've looked at before, what you've bought, what you've not bought. What you've returned. It knows what you've searched for, what you've added and then removed from your basket, as well as what your shipping preferences are. But when you walk into a store, you're unlikely to be similarly recognized, unless you're a very frequent visitor to a very small store. That doesn't have to be the case any longer.

While many reminisce about the good old days of retail when store staff had the luxury of knowing their customers personally, that's not a scenario in modern mass retail, where it's impractical with minimum-wage employees and variable shopping patterns. Online sites may lack a personal interaction, but they have mountains of data to help understand customers. Simply adding Google Analytics to your site will give you a wealth of data, for free, about where your customers are from and how their visits to your site unfold. You can see in the data what's popular, what's confusing and what's downright poor. Without such quantitative inputs in physical retail, it can be hard to know what's going on, especially in large chains.

There are, however, several technical advances to improve the quality of the information available to physical retailers. As we saw in Chapter 6, these range from the ingenious to the potentially intrusive. But they offer retailers potentially valuable insights into knowing their customers and, theoretically at least, using that to improve their service.

The Numbers Game

Retail has long been a numbers game. Retailers obsess over metrics like sales per square foot, time to turnover, like for like increase etc. A single percentage point can represent millions or billions, with consternation among markets when like for like sales are down by 0.5%. Rightly so, as margins in some sectors are just a couple of percent. That doesn't leave much room for discounts, loyalty schemes, unforeseen circumstances or unexpected levels of returns.

But in recent times the focus on the numbers has shifted to numbers of store closures, number of layoffs and number of once-invincible firms filing for Chapter 11 or CVA protection. In order to shift the conversation to more positive metrics, retailers need to re-evaluate how success gets measured. The numbers that retailers currently rely upon come from a simpler time, when tracking how humans shopped in stores was all that was required. In this new world of everywhere retailing, the standard metrics like sales per sq. foot, profit/loss by channel, traffic count and basket size are not the only metrics to consider.

In order to start talking about positive numbers once again, it's vital that the retail sector shift away from old metrics that are holding them back - it's time for a new set of more modern metrics. Retailers, in some cases, need to start thinking more like brands than relying on quick one-time sales. Metrics like Lifetime Value (LTV) are key indicators that start-ups and D2C brands reply on but they don't yet feature in the earnings reports of major retailers and incumbent brands. Likewise, modern retailers need to think more like online operators who obsess about customer-centric metrics. Retail merchants with physical spaces not only need a sense of their online metrics, but also in-store analytics - tracking, understanding and responding to detail regarding traffic, dwell times, and other shopper behaviors related to actual sales at the register, using tools like heat maps of shopper movements, which measure traffic over time in areas of your stores.

Privacy and Prediction

Although there is significant debate about online privacy, the modern shopper is under at least as much surveillance in a contemporary store as they are when online they can at least reject cookies or browse incognito. Retailers have myriad motivations to watch customers in stores. From simple security against shoplifting to tracking pathfinding through the store, to queue lengths and facilitating staff planning, retailers are now watching customers intently.

In order to provide the expected level of service at a personalized level at scale, retailers will need to focus much more intently on data collection and analytics. Future retail success will require the use of data analytics to recognize shopping patterns and demand trends, to better manage demand planning and customer relationships. The retailer of the future is much more data driven than before and looks beyond their existing weekly performance dashboards to predictive analytics - it's no longer enough to be reactive.

Most consumers imagine that large retailers have sophisticated modern inventory systems but would be amazed to learn how many are held together with simple spreadsheets, text messages, manual counting and paper forms. This is not going to be sustainable for much longer. For example, US apparel retailer, The Gap, is using AI to curate localized assortments at store level, building predictive demand models at style level. Art Peck, President and CEO of GAP, proclaimed at the ShopTalk 2019 conference that *"If you're not doing this 5 years from now, you won't be around."*

Consumers expect that retailers will make use of the data they hold. In a world where there's a growing wariness around data privacy, shoppers will at the very least expect that when corporations are in possession of data about them, the firms will make good use of it to make personalized offers. According to a 2018 Accenture Global survey, 91% of consumers prefer brands that provide personalized offers or recommendations, while 3 out of 4 consumers are willing to actively share personal data in exchange for personalized experiences. One example of this is US homeware store West Elm who have developed a "Pinterest Style Finder" to scan a customer's Pinterest boards to understand their personal style and create a list of recommended home décor and furniture items to match.

Local Inventory

"Physical stores serve an indispensable role during the consumer journey and should be enhanced through data-driven technology and personalized services in the digital economy."

Daniel Zhang, CEO, Alibaba

If e-commerce is putting pressure on physical retailers, especially smaller independent stores, perhaps another strand of digital technology can come to their rescue. One of the key reasons that people shop online is certainty - the stock indicators are generally accurate, and delivery options are fast and flexible. An emerging technology now promises to level the playing field for local stores, by creating a Real Time Local Inventory (RTLI) system that enables online shoppers to find out if their desired product is, in fact, available down the street rather than from some distant fulfilment center.

There was an award winning series of commercials in the 1980s from a UK telephone directory company, encouraging customers to call their local store to see if the item they wanted was in stock (search "JR Hartley" on YouTube if you're too young to have seen it). Though very old fashioned now in the days of a Google or Amazon search, the point still resonates for physical retailers vs online - the lack of certainty over stock can be a huge deterrent against local shopping. According to Google Insights[244], nearly half of all shoppers now say they confirm inventory before going to the store. Mobile queries for "Where to buy" + "near me" have grown by over 200% in the past two years.

Solutions like that offered by UK start-up NearSt, mean you can check if a local store has an item in stock without leaving home. Thanks to a partnership with Google, the price and inventory information is available from a simple product search. Improvements to the convenience of local shopping may be further encouraged by the now widely held desire among consumers to live more sustainably. Purchasing locally from stores may help reduce the emissions from package delivery and returns. The growing emphasis on local retail in partnership with online was further evident in Google's 2020 acquisition of Irish start-up Pointy, for $150m, which also helps local stores appear in search results.

When Retailers Stop Shopping

Most people shopping in retail stores spend very little time thinking about how the goods they are perusing actually got there, but of course there's a complex buying function that decides what products the retailer will buy to sell on to shoppers. In most cases, retailers are themselves shoppers. Just as with retail sales to end consumers, the buyers in retailers who deal with wholesalers and directly with brands, are employing technology to improve their performance. For example, German online retailer Otto uses an AI-powered stock management system that buys goods without human intervention. It has been trained by looking at 20 billion transactions and 200 variables such as previous sales and weather. It has reduced product returns by 2 million and surplus stock by 20%. Similarly, UK supermarket Morrisons has automated 99% of the 20 million daily replenishment decisions it makes with technology from Blue Yonder[245]. Even within Amazon, AI is replacing head office staff as well as warehouse personnel - Bloomberg[246] reports that purchasing managers are being replaced by algorithms.

The New Main street

"There is no point clinging to a sentimental vision of the past"

Bill Grimsey, 2013 UK High street Review

"An evolution of main streets is happening in front of our eyes. Shops whose products can be bought and delivered easily and cheaply online are being replaced. Rather than lament what has gone, we should try to enjoy what is to come. Main streets have the potential to become bigger social hubs than before, with theatres, bars, gyms, restaurants, local markets and new homes replacing the fascias of nationwide brands. But this evolution is going to take time and will need vision and determination from local authorities and landlords."

Graham Ruddick, Deputy Business Editor, The Times[247]

With all the changes in the composition and purpose of stores, how might main streets of the future look? Given that local councils largely control the makeup of main streets via planning laws, there will need to be collaboration between enterprises and planners to manage the evolution of our towns and cities. If traditional retailing can no longer be relied upon as the anchor for town centers, there is a need to look at the desired mix of residential, leisure, entertainment, education, cultural and commercial office space, that will exist alongside the stores of the future.

In many ways, the main street of the future will see stores reverting more to their original purpose - a storehouse for goods closer to the consumer than a manufacturer's warehouse. Those goods will be available for display and for dispatch, with both pickup and return services as a standard part of physical retail.

There are many elements of the current shopping paradigm that objectively make little sense given current technology but are clearly products of history - we're still living with a retailing infrastructure that predates contemporary technologies. Retailers hoping to have the right mix of styles and sizes in stock at the right time and at the right price for the right consumers to come along is a very speculative approach. Shipping items hopefully to retailers in expensive city center locations only to have consumers order them online is likewise inefficient. Given the cost of building and operating retail space, using it to store, display and transact in products such as detergent is far from optimum - storing it in inexpensive dark warehouses that supply it as customers need it makes better sense.

Planning Challenges and Planning for Challenges

I don't personally subscribe to the "death of the main street" narrative so commonly emblazoned in headlines as and when retailers go out of business. This over simplification tends to ignore the fact that online retailers go out of business too, new physical retailers are still opening new stores and there are alternative uses of retail space that may enhance urban life if we can see beyond an assumption that retail is the only or best use of all city center space. If rents and/or rates were lower, maybe we'd see more spacious shops and room for craft/pop-up shops. Or more town square type retail experiences such as that favored by Apple. I expect we'll see a main street of the future full of coffee shops, showrooms, workspaces, culture spaces and residential spaces, alongside retail stores that are a crucial part of an omnichannel experience.

Both city planning authorities and companies need to think carefully about what the new retail experience could become in the digital age, and about how to shape it for the good of the urban environment. They may need to let go of long held notions that long-term leases and upscale shops are preferable for shopping precincts. For smaller brands, pop-up stores may become much more normal, as might spaces that change use based on time of the day; for example, using flexible furniture to transform stores into social spaces in the evening, allowing smaller retailers to pay only partial rents. Larger brands will continue to invest in flagship stores, that offer experiences and statements of the brand, as much as sales.

The challenges facing physical retail are complex and expose inadequacies in planning regimes, pitting vested interests against fast-moving technological and consumer changes. There tend to be a lot of emotions attached to discussions where livelihoods are on the line, and much resistance to change, often accompanied by nostalgia and a sense of entitlement to continue the status quo. But rather than lament what has gone, we should try to plan what is to come. We're likely to see continued attrition and consolidation as smaller retailers that either can't or won't invest in improving the customer experience fail.

Just because something has been the same way for 2,000 years, 200 years or just 20 doesn't mean it's the ideal way forward. It may feel right as it's what we're used to, or it may be staunchly defended by those whose livelihoods depend on it, but objectively, its time may be over whether everyone likes it or not. So much commentary about the main street seems to expect it to remain unchanged, rather than accepting that it faces multiple forces that mean the status quo is unsustainable. Shops whose products can be bought and delivered easily and cheaply online are being replaced and will continue to be as people stop shopping on main streets for many product categories. And it's not only stores - other reasons to visit the main street are dwindling – for example, visits to bank branches banks replaced by online banking and apps.

Faced with the new realities of retail, executives have plenty of excuses up their sleeves – ranging from the weather to declining footfall and the rise of the internet – for falling sales but no one admits to lacking skills and vision. Amazon has been around since 1994 and the iPhone since 2007, so retail bosses have had plenty of time to react and adapt their businesses.

The Physical Fightback

What's a traditional retailer to do in this changing world? Well it seems that many have chosen to bury their heads and hope for the best, others complain about perceived injustices while others take radical steps to update their businesses. I expect that you'll see more moves from brands into what has been traditionally retailers' space, taking control of their message directly to consumers. But it's hard for brands - as anyone who has run retail will tell you - it's not as easy as you might think to find, train and retain high quality staff who will provide the customer experience desired by head office and brand guardians.

Regardless of location, and regardless of whether it's a small corner shop, a stoically retro store or a beacon of high-tech experiential demonstration, stores of the future will share the following minimum characteristics:

- A digital presence that complements, not competes
- Accept contactless payments
- BOPIS, BORIS
- In store order for delivery is available
- Staff not measured or incentivized on old conversion metrics

With those basic improvements in place, stores will have the platform to provide the interactions that modern consumers are looking for. They may still have to renegotiate rent, seek changes in rates, reduce the store size, form partnerships and refine their environmental credentials, but there is little evidence to suggest that consumers have any desire to see town and city centers devoid of retail and other services.

Main street Health

I mentioned in the partnerships section above about how Kohls is converting former retail space into gyms. This is illustrative of a trend that may play a large role in the future of shopping - people shopping not for goods, but for services and activities. That remains the clearest example of where physical retail retains an unassailable advantage over online. The largest growth categories in main streets in the last ten years has been nail bars and gyms. You can't realistically delegate shopping for such personal services to even the most intelligent AI-assistant - at most it can make an appointment for you, but the physical service delivery takes place in a physical store.

Alongside gyms, another health-related bright spot for physical retail into the future is healthcare services. As well as offering traditional medicine products, the main street is going to be home to a widening array of healthcare services. These are simple, practical footfall drivers that can also serve to relieve pressure on strained healthcare infrastructure by moving care, into the community rather than confining it to clinics or hospitals.

Walmart has opened a "Walmart Health center" in its Dallas, Georgia, store, offering services like dental, mental health counseling, X-rays and audiology. The clinic is in a separate building next door to a Walmart store to give a sense of privacy for patients. In the UK, the National Health Service (NHS) is working with pharmacies to offer free checks in stores covering blood pressure, cholesterol levels and mobile electrocardiograms (ECG) used to spot irregular heartbeats.

Omnichannel

"The way I see it, if you are a brick-and-mortar retailer, you either embrace a digital strategy to become omnichannel or do nothing and become irrelevant"

Jun-Shen Li, former SVP, Walmart global e-commerce supply chain

From stores to online, tele sales, mail order and indirect/3rd party, the concept of channels is a mainstay of retail thinking and organization structure - it's evolved from single channels to multi-channel to omni-channel and finally beyond channel thinking to a seamless experience. Regardless of how organizations structure their teams, consumers don't think in channels. They skip from an app on their phone to a website on their laptop to visiting a store to placing their order via Instagram. And they expect to be able to return it easily to the store, by post or even to a local drop-off point that suits them. They expect consistent information and responses at every turn but tailored to the device and platform they are on.

Retailers have to stop thinking in channels, whatever the historical operational challenges. These changes need difficult discussions and careful realignment of sensitive things like attribution and even remuneration. I've sat in meetings where people employed by the same company have argued against process changes that would increase overall sales at the cost to "their channel" - but their reaction is driven by the personal loss they stand to suffer when changes are made, based on outdated reward structures that are no longer fit for purpose.

"Over half of our store sales involve an online journey, and over a third of our online sales involve a store experience"

Erik Nordstrom

Consumers do not consider if the store associate helping them is getting the attribution for the sale that completed online but picked up in store. To a store associate who greets the customer, possibly answers questions and hands out the package, they have the opportunity cost of that time that could have been selling. However, the head of online sales most definitely thinks it counts against their P&L, while the head of retail believes the store has done the work and should count it as sale for their team. As former Apple SVP of Retail, Angela Ahrendts said: *"No matter how that customer comes in and buys, you have to look at it as one P&L. This is the issue, companies try and make these stores work on a standalone basis."*[248]

Closer integration between digital and offline is crucial for any large retailer. IKEA, for example, has adapted its app to support shoppers who are planning an in-store visit, helping them to make a shopping list and browse stock, rather than encouraging them to complete the sale online. In a truly omni-channel situation, old-world concepts such as attribution of sale to a channel may be nearly impossible. What if a consumer sees a product on social media via an influencer, then visits a store to see a product, but finds it out of stock, where they then use an instore kiosk to order it from another store for delivery to their preferred locker? Is that an online sale, or a store sale? The consumer doesn't know or care, but this seamlessness is not possible, for a variety of technical and human reasons, in the vast majority of retailers today.

The Store in Seamless Shopping

"You can't just look at the profitability of one store or the profitability of one app or the online business. You have to put it all together: one customer, one brand."

Angela Ahrendts, former SVP of Apple Retail

Most retailers and suppliers are underprepared to deliver truly multichannel commerce with a modern in-store experience. The end goal is to be channel-agnostic, to capitalize on the incremental sale and opportunity, as the lifetime value of the shopper becomes a more important success metric for both retailers and suppliers. Retailers need to keep a close eye on their retail estate to optimize their consumer reach and cost profile. Take Swedish apparel retailer H&M, which changed from its announced store opening plans in 2019 to open 130 stores instead of 175 - *"By continuing to integrate our physical and digital channels we are making the shopping experience inspiring, easy and convenient for customers wherever we meet them."* said H&M chief executive Karl-Johan Persson[249]. Burberry, on the other hand, is concentrating on its flagship stores and social media. It plans to refurbish more than 80 of its key stores and to close 38 secondary stores. Online, Burberry concentrated on growing consumer engagement via social media platforms including Instagram and WeChat.

Physical stores provide much of what consumers want in a retail transaction. But as emphasized, the customer journey is no longer solely built around in-store shopping. A wave of technologies has upended the old ways of retail, along with changing consumer habits. It's now all about merging ecommerce platforms with physical customer experiences. The digitization of brick and mortar is upon us. Proactive retailers are setting out to curate an omnichannel customer journey through automation, machine learning, and personalization at scale. They are deepening their understanding of customers and delivering real-time and evolving experiences for them.

Incrementalism

As I said at the start of this Chapter, there is no one size fits all solution. The only common thread is that every retailer needs to embrace change and innovation to some degree. For some, incremental improvements may be sufficient to survive, while others may have to reinvent themselves more dramatically to weather the twin onslaughts of consumer change and emerging technology-enhanced competitors.

Incrementalism often gets a bad reputation and is overlooked by those seeking "big bang" changes. But the relatively simple adoption of best practices such as click and collect may win retailers positive reviews from customers, or a partnership to accept parcels may bring additional footfall. For most retailers it may be better to start with the basics, then take small steps, before embarking on any more ambitious experiments.

The New Retail

"Retail has been rapidly shifting due to consumer, economic and community demands, and the increase in experience-based retail environments is a direct answer to today's modern consumer demands. The catch is, they also want this at their convenience and often with a socially good attachment linked to their spending decisions."

Nicole Leinbach Reyhle, Retail Minded and the Independent Retailer Conference[250]

The scale of the change facing retail is huge. Regardless of company size, every retailer must find a way to start leaning into store experience improvements and digital innovation. Historically, mobilizing an organization to develop and integrate breakthroughs that threaten the base business has been one of management's greatest challenges.

Stores are no longer simply about browsing and transaction - they can be pickup & returns points, support givers, brand awareness beacons - things that don't sit well with traditional retail economics and KPIs.

Hard to Change

It is difficult for main street retailers to simply reimagine their approach to brick-and-mortar retail, as most of them are locked into long store contracts that make a dramatic change very difficult. Unlike pure-play ecommerce brands that are opening up physical stores for the first time, they may not have the luxury of redesigning their entire shopping experience from scratch or tailoring it to work with ecommerce. Store closures for renovations may see a retailer slip from consumer consideration, while disruptive changes to the store may also see shoppers leave and never return.

Repeated challenges I've incurred when working with many clients include culture, organizational alignment, disparate applications, siloed data, unstructured data, data quality and budget. I've found many retailers recognize the technology barriers but seem to get blindsided by the culture and organizational alignment challenges. Retailers will need to make changes to their staff skillsets, employing data analysts and developers, or buying in services. For example, Target employs more than 3,000 software developers, having taken most of its core IT work in-house as it shifted focus and skills to grow online sales.

Skepticism

Most retailers I've met are skeptical of new technology. And while I'm frequently an advocate of using technology to improve processes, ask any retailer and they'll tell you they've been offered a bewildering array of technology options, all promised to be the silver bullet required to save retail. Much more has been promised than delivered over the years, as tech suppliers over-promise and retailers struggle to execute change effectively.

Alongside their techno-skepticism, most physical retailers don't have an investment mindset. That may sound like a sweeping generalization, and there are certainly exceptions, but there are longstanding (if not good) reasons. Retailers have been trained to be frugal and cautious, operating on margins thin enough to make other industries weep. Where they need a quick sales boost, the default tactic is usually to discount, not to invest. There's also the cost factor - rolling out virtually any technology at the scale of a major national retailer, with hundreds, thousands or even tens of thousands of outlets, is hugely expensive and time consuming. Finally, there's also the human factor - training retail staff to operate new technologies is an additional complication that can derail technology deployments.

While it is sensible to critically evaluate new technologies and the promises of techno-optimists, it is also dangerous to dismiss technology, even if it at first appears to be less than astounding. Recall that the first iPhone had no App Store and the first iterations of Alexa couldn't order products.

Getting the timing right is difficult and moving too soon can be just as costly as failing to react to a trend in time. I've sat on both sides of the table - as a Head of Retail for a chain of 70+ stores worried about my weekly numbers far more than even next year, and as a tech entrepreneur pitching a start-up idea to some of the largest retailers in the UK who seemed out of touch and short-sighted. Many of the technologies in this book are vastly complex and it may take many years for them to become widespread; some may be as much as a decade away from mainstream use. But in a world where retailers routinely signed 25-year leases, a decade isn't that long and 5 years is distressingly fast.

Product categories which shoppers once bought in stores, might be bought elsewhere now, and the nature of in-store sales and service has been permanently altered. At the same time, the integration of digital tools in physical stores is in its infancy. The confluence of these changes demands a baseline reinvention of store formats, their operation and their purpose. Today's stores are far from ready for the future of retail that awaits.

Chapter 10: Retail Futures

"I don't think retail is dead. Mediocre retail experiences are dead"

Neil Blumenthal, co-CEO Warby Parker, January 2017

It's clear by now that humans are no longer shopping the way they used to. They are changing the how, where and when of shopping. In some cases, they expect much more from their shopping experiences, while in other cases, they are opting out of shopping altogether, delegating it to technology. As this unfolds, our preconceptions around the roles of the participants, the allocation of space in our towns and cities, and the application of technology are all being challenged as the entire consumer supply chain tries to adjust to the needs, expectations and preferences of the contemporary and future consumer.

Commerce has been a central activity and economic driver for centuries, evolving through artisan, mass distribution, retail, main streets, catalogs, malls and out-of-town. From the ancient Greek marketplace (the Agora) and medieval travelling salespeople to classic department stores and today's specialist outlets, retail has changed form many times before but perhaps never as much now, as it seeks to serve a more convenience-oriented, environmentally-aware, and experience-craving shopper, who may not even be human. The combination of changing shoppers, changing shops and the emergence of automated consumers is rewriting the rules of retail in ways that will create winners and losers, as well as impacting how we live.

"The majority of retailers are stuck in survival mode - Playing catch-up in perpetuity is preventing retailers from seizing new opportunities"

BDO

According to a survey by accounting firm BDO[251] in late 2018, we've arrived at a situation where 54% of traditional retailers say their business is "just surviving". For a sector so vital to the economy, employing so many people and with such influence on the character of our towns and cities, this should be alarming.

Less Is More

As Gen Alpha (the cohort after Gen Z, born since 2010) reach their 30s around the year 2040, they will recall the start of the 21st century as a period of great inefficiency. They'll have largely forgotten the time when people devoted huge amounts of time to replenishing consumables with weekly trips to a supermarket or when we went to stores to discover they didn't have the item we wanted and couldn't seamlessly arrange for it to come to us. They'll shake their heads at the notion of searching for items rather than having an AI find ideal purchases, and they'll chide the older generations for their wasteful attitudes to reuse.

The path to this future will be rocky for many entrenched incumbents, painful for those whose livelihoods depend on the status quo and slower than many techno-optimists may predict. Yet is full of opportunities to reduce waste, revamp norms that have outlived their origins and contribute to a more convenient and sustainable future.

No More Generations

Marketers who believe they can rely on the old concepts of marketing to generations will rapidly lose customers to firms using AI to target individuals, not cohorts. The shopping generations will be replaced by individuals loosely grouped, based on behaviors and attitudes that owe less to their date of birth and more to their values and openness to technology. Many, if not most, of these shoppers will spend less time shopping.

Non-Shoppers

Brands and retailers will find themselves trying to appeal to a cohort of "non-shoppers" who eschew ownership in favor of timely access. These non-shoppers will subscribe to everything they don't need to own; from cars and furniture to music and appliances. Their consumables will arrive automatically as required, with the occasional, targeted sample of something new to try. Some people would doubtless find such an existence joyless, others would find it liberatingly free of consumption choices. And that's just one of the marketing challenges ahead. Another cohort will delegate their shopping to their AI-assistant, leaving brands and marketers with an even harder task - to satisfy an objective shopper, immune to many of their age-old tricks.

Convenience Wins

Unless engaging in shopping for leisure, consumers will spend less time shopping and favor the stores that have reduced friction to the minimum. Concepts like Amazon Go, that remove the need to queue, or stores that make it easier to find what you're looking for will put pressure on stores that fail to innovate. Retailers that don't offer fast, flexible and/or environmentally sensitive delivery options will perish. So too sectors that have relied in the last decade on inertia or consumer reluctance to shop for certain products online, will see that unless a physical presence is required, consumers are open to ordering virtually anything online, and then returning it if unhappy.

New Shopping

There are many new forms of shopping emerging, primarily in the digital realm. Consumers can now buy the items they see on social media, without the need to visit an actual "shopping site". Instead of searching by typing in a search box, computer vision can recognize items from photos or just by your pointing your camera at something. While the popularity of smart speakers means you can ask Alexa or your Google Assistant to purchase with just a voice command.

Consumers will continue to visit physical stores - probably with a greater emphasis on combining it with a leisure or social aspect – but not necessarily to complete a purchase.

Automated Shopping

Consumers will continue to turn to technology to make shopping more effective - giving them digital help finding the best products and best prices. For those people who truly want to stop shopping, they can delegate the task to another human (via myriad apps) or to an AI Assistant. The rise of services such as Stitch Fix will see curation and personalized recommendation available at infinite scale. Ever-smarter homes will seek to remove the drudgery of reordering and the battleground for consumers may move away from traditional advertising and retail channels, especially for CPG/FMCG.

Routine purchases of products that don't have much customer engagement will move to automated replenishment with subscription business models. The delivery cadence will be controlled by an AI within parameters set by the consumer and scheduled for maximum efficiency and minimum environmental impact. Even though some will prefer a "I may as well get it when I'm at the supermarket anyway" approach, others will appreciate making store trips only about more interesting purchases. This will change the shelf requirements in stores, as well as significantly affect the packaging and advertising sectors.

After Human Shoppers

"I think that consumers will become much more time-poor and they are going to rely much more on algorithms or AI to actually pre-empt their shopping needs, that will free up time for them to focus on shopping with the brands and products that really engage them. There will always be a place for consumers to go to shops, to experience things, but I think those things are going to be things that they care about."

Jon Copestake, Senior Consumer Goods Analyst, EY[252]

Humans will stop shopping - for certain categories, the days of humans placing orders are already numbered. For other categories, humans will stop shopping in the ways and channels we're used to, and that's an equally massive change. For yet more categories, humans will continue to shop, but will not do so without the benefit of technology to augment their decisions.

It's already evident that many consumers have stopped shopping in the traditional places, at the traditional times. They're bypassing the traditional methods of finding and paying for items. A small but growing number have stopped shopping and started renting. They're stopping buying and starting to sell (peer to peer), lend, share and swap. Next, they'll stop buying and start replenishing - shopping that isn't efficient, enjoyable or demonstrably better in some way than online shopping will be eliminated by automated solutions or delegation. Finally, they'll stop shopping and expect someone else to or *something* else to do it for them. This is the roller-coaster facing contemporary brands and retailers.

Behind the Scenes

In order to meet consumer expectations for product selection and expedited delivery, the usually invisible world of logistics has seen an explosion in investment, automation and innovation. From robots operating in fulfilment centers to drones being tested for rapid deliveries, there's a huge focus on the capabilities that enable much of contemporary shopping developments.

As well as the hidden developments in logistics, retailers are evaluating and deploying a range of technologies to enhance the operation of their stores, their ability to gather data about customers and to empower their associates to better meet the needs of customers.

Where they are persuaded of the need to invest, it can be tempting for retailers to focus on investing in front-end experiences (such as websites or mobile apps) which serve as the first point of contact with customers. Doing so without enhancing their back-end operations can lead to brand-damaging poor customer experiences when logistics fail to deliver on the flashy front-end promises.

Not having an API may soon be the equivalent of not having a web site or not being on Google/Amazon. For all the experiential stuff, if the consumer simply instructs their AI to find it and sort it, you need to be ready. It's emblematic of the challenges business faces to keep up. Even if you've got a website and a social strategy, a failure to implement an API could lose you bookings from the not insignificant cohort that have "moved on" from using websites and apps for interacting with businesses and instead rely on their AI-assistant.

Physical Stores

"The future is fewer, more impactful stores"

"Amazon", Knights & Berg, Chapter 1[253]

Around half of all US households are now reckoned to have signed up for Amazon's $119-a-year Prime service. According to estimates[254], these consumers then spend 10 percent less in physical stores. Figures[255] also show that, compared with a decade ago, Americans now spend 13 fewer hours a year travelling to stores or browsing the shelves.

These changing shopping patterns which have emerged rapidly over the last few years are posing a huge challenge for traditional retailers of all sizes and locations - from shopping malls to main streets to corner stores. Some stores will undoubtedly not survive, particularly ones whose product line doesn't require "experiential retail". There are those that will lament the loss of local stores, mourning the loss of the social interaction. But that's not the purpose of shops - and we shouldn't force that role upon them. The better question is whether we can maybe repurpose the space?

Varying Impacts

All of these changes come with consequences that nobody can escape. Even those who choose to opt out of technology augmented shopping will find their options diminishing. The shifts in behavior are already changing the character of towns, cities and malls the world over. Of course, one can't refer to all brands and all retail as a single entity. The changing behaviors will impact different sectors very differently but with one common certainty - nobody will escape the changes unscathed.

The New Retailer

"Even if you're on the right track, if you just sit there, you'll get run over."

Will Rogers

Retailers and brands need to do more to ensure it's easy to do business with them, for both human and digital customers. It's astounding how many companies still fail to get the basics right, but the retail future will expose them more cruelly than ever before. Those that don't offer transparency, or worse, those who act disingenuously, will find ethical consumers ever more willing to take their business elsewhere, even if it comes at a marginal cost. Humans will stop shopping with brands who don't value them, and they'll have ever-vigilant digital help to assess thoroughly who meets their multifaceted expectations.

As consumers change how, where and why they shop, as well as even ceding control of some of their household budgets to digital helpers, brands and retailers need to redouble their efforts to adapt to the new world. Even those that have identified and navigated the moves to online, mobile and social selling can't relax.

The new retailer has to be ready to meet their customers, human and digital, in any channel at any time. They need to communicate their values as transparently as their value and be flexible enough to meet changing expectations across a range of business models. And all done offering the right balance between personalization and privacy while fending off upstart rivals and simultaneously minimizing their environmental footprint and respecting their workers' rights.

Retailers will need to change both internally and externally - existing organization structures and processes aren't designed to operate with the required level of flexibility and efficiency. The metrics to be tracked by management and investors to quantify success also need to be reconsidered. All but the largest brands and retailers will need help from technology specialists and will be forced to forge partnerships or buy-in technology services.

New Roles

As the next wave of retail innovation takes hold, we need to reconsider even the vocabulary we use. The separation of roles within the supply chain will blur as brands sell D2C, retailers seek to form relationships with customers and consumers range from technology-augmented humans to artificial intelligence-powered agents. What we refer to as stores may no longer "store" items for sale but rather act as a showroom and a micro fulfilment center. How we perceive stores - their purpose, their funding and their staffing will all change. The compression of the traditional consumer business model means far less distinction between brand, wholesaler and retailer.

New Technology

If you say "e-commerce", does that adequately cover an AI system ordering an item for a drone to deliver? The changing generations and the technology they have access to are creating a whole host of opportunities for people to buy differently. Whether you agree that people will shop more, less or the same as they do now, the certainty is that the ways people shop will change and there'll be more technology involved with each passing year. The backdrop is not just changing technologies but changing consumer attitudes, driven largely by demographics.

While the first wave of online shopping made it easy for shoppers to buy the things they wanted without having to go to a store, this soon evolved to include rudimentary recommendations and suggestions. The next evolution will be to create recommendations and predictions based on far more personal data. For those who don't share their personal data, there will be a plethora of new augmented shopping services to super-charge our capabilities with super-human knowledge about markets; for example, you'll see curation and advice services that will recommend when is a good time to purchase a product or service based on historical pricing patterns, anticipated discounts or expected price increases. Already emerging in the travel and hospitality sector (where Google Flights will track a route price for you and alert you to increases), the next generation of services acting on consumers' behalf will consider complex factors such as delivery options, not just simple price comparisons.

New Economy

Of course, while technology is a key factor changing consumer behavior, brands and retailers have myriad other challenges to consider. New business models such as rental and second hand, the rise of subscription and the growth of delegation are all clamoring for attention and consideration at retail strategy meetings. Accenture[256] has highlighted four key business models:

- The Sharing Economy - where consumers rent instead of own
- The Personalization Economy - where consumers expect curated, personalized deliveries
- The Replenishment Economy - where smart devices automatically reorder products
- The Services Economy - where consumers want someone else to undertake tasks for them

The Automated Consumer

"Customers don't want to shop, they want things that help them live a better life to magically appear."

Dan Makoski, VP of Design, Walmart

We've grown used to dealing with companies through their automated interfaces: Self-checkout, IVR menus etc. But are they ready if we reciprocate? How many firms are equipped to cope with an automated agent operating on a consumer's behalf? So far, the majority of effort has gone - correctly - into creating web sites and mobile apps that provide excellent consumer experiences for human shoppers.

Dealing with AI-assistants will require brands and retailers to adapt their marketing and advertising messages to cater for two very distinct audiences - human and machine. The humans will continue to make irrational, emotional decisions and be subject to manipulation and influence. Their automated counterparts will expect machine-readable specifications on which to make rational decisions that align with their human owners' values.

If this seems far-fetched, there are already early elements of this scenario in place, but as with so much of the future, it's about piecing together the parts into a coherent system. I can already search on some sites for sustainable options, I can use a comparison service that tracks prices and alerts me to price drops and I can automate ordering on other sites. All we await is a service that brings these together into a holistic shopping assistant.

Change on the scale we're seeing in retail and consumer spending is bound to be highly contentious. It is upending long-held norms in very visible ways, reshaping our main streets, leading to layoffs and creating social and environmental challenges. Unlike many previous technologies, the impacts of recent changes may not seem like progress to everyone.

Advertising - When MadMen met Robots

Although the future of advertising is in itself worthy of an entire book, I want to devote just a small section to it here, to highlight the impacts on advertising of the shifts described in this book. As a sector almost totally intertwined with the consumer economy and having been through its own online revolution in recent years, with print and traditional media, such as TV, mirroring the pain of physical retailers, advertising is now facing further existential change. Inextricably linked with the welfare of brands and retailers, advertisers don't enjoy a good relationship with many modern consumers, who, wary of privacy invasion, are turning to ad-blockers and expecting their browser to protect their privacy (some 30% of Internet users regularly use ad-blockers and Apple has introduced a series of measures in its browser, Safari, to thwart unscrupulous advertisers trying to track customers).

While brand segmentation and global supply chains have given us huge variety, too much choice is not necessarily a good thing. Brands spend billions with advertisers to convince us of the need for numerous different brands of detergent. Yet the majority of detergents are fundamentally the same, with much of the differences being marginal, illusional or simply value signaling. Those that are genuinely different tend to reply on less mainstream promotion of a kind that favors authenticity, rather than mass media messaging. Consumers skeptical of advertisers are now empowered to research products thoroughly to ensure that the goods match the brand promise - few will take the word of the advertiser without corroboration via Google, social media or online reviews. And, in scenarios where replenishment and subscriptions lock in customers to certain goods, attempts to encourage switching may prove fruitless or hugely expensive.

As AI-assistants proliferate, advertising agencies will have to persuade their clients who expect mass media visibility that targeting non-human purchasers is not only possible but viable, even essential. Take, for example, text searches; about 70 percent of word searches done on Amazon are for generic goods. That means consumers are typing in "men's underwear" or "running shoes" rather than asking, specifically, for Calvin Klein or Nike. If an AI shopper isn't configured to weigh brand heavily over other factors, generic searches may become even more common. If the future is being a seamless, automated part of consumers' requirements, this will not sit easily with for brands (or their advertising agencies) who expect to be front of mind.

If AI-assistants are to be trusted, consumers will have to believe they are acting preferably in their best interests and at least in an objective/neutral manner. If a user feels that an advertiser has infiltrated their Alexa or Google Assistant and is offering biased advice, that could prove fatal. Users will expect some influence to have been exerted, but it must be subtle - just as they know that brands pay for placement in physical stores and associates may be incentivized to push certain products - to avoid intrusiveness. For example, a branded filter on Snapchat feels more like acceptable sponsorship and could create positive brand association (PBA) rather than Alexa annoyingly trying to sell you a product.

Advertisers, already concerned about the concentration of control in digital reach, will also have to look for ways to work more closely with the major platforms if they wish to try to promote their wares on new channels such as voice, which don't offer visual ad inventory. As discussed earlier, the weighting given by Amazon or Google to a particular response may include advertising payments. Perhaps transparency will rule the day and advertisers will be very clearly offering an incentive - if you ask your Google Assistant to order detergent, perhaps the reply will be "Do you want your usual brand, or save $1 if you want to try Tide? Reply: Usual, Try Tide or Tell me more about Tide".

One leading New York ad agency exec told me his CPG clients were terrified when considering the possible directions that future shopping could take. The disintermediation of voice platforms, the emergence of replenishment and the fragmentation of shopping channels are all worrying them as much as the climate change and transparency concerns of consumers.

Getting Ready

If that seems daunting, it is. One of the most common lines of thinking I come across in retail is the tendency to resist moving with the times as the focus on eking out a minor like-for-like growth. Just as so many incumbent retailers resisted moves to the internet, or improvements in delivery times, I've been struck in more recent conversations about the lack of awareness of emerging technologies, let alone any comprehensive evaluation of their applicability. It is admittedly very hard to keep up with the endless tsunami of new technologies, but any reasonably sized business can afford to assign some resources to this, or to buy in the expertise. One of my favorite images that I use all the time in talks about innovation is this one. It would be funny were it not so commonly true.

Figure 97 It's hard to make time for innovation

As noted earlier, I do understand skepticism and caution regarding the hyperbolic claims of IT solution vendors pushing "the next big thing". Although this book talks extensively about technology changes, I want to emphasize the importance of understanding not only the tech but also the human angles.

In many cases, technology solutions are quickly commodified and widely available for use without major technical understanding or integration effort. Those firms that win are not necessarily those first to invent or embrace a technology - it is those that do so for the benefit of the customer.

Policies & Regulation

Given that consumer spending is such a vital part of the economy, and indeed, society, there are significant amounts of consumer protection legislation in most countries. Reflecting the previous power dynamic discussed earlier, most of the legislation is aimed at ensuring consumers are treated fairly by the once powerful retailers. Many jurisdictions also legislate to protect workers in the retail sector and in some countries, most notably India[257], legislators are grappling with how to rein in the power of online platforms, perceived as a threat to established retailers.

The simple fact is that much of the legal framework governing commerce is not fit for purpose in a world of omnichannel sales, automated agents and gig workers. For example, outdated statutes that limit trading hours – which may have been designed to protect retail staff but are a blunt instrument that predate online shopping. Such protections should be regulated under employment legislation, not banning Sunday trading for physical retailers already struggling to compete with the always-on nature of other channels.

There is reluctance to address issues such as business rates and commercial zoning in city centers – but expectations need to change - main streets may no longer be a dominant source of rates revenue and huge rental incomes and those who depend on the status quo will resist changes that disadvantage them. Whether at Federal, National, State or local levels, those who control commerce policies need to reconsider how to regulate the future realities. Do consumer protections such as distance selling regulations apply to automated orders the same as human-placed orders? Are automated stores subject to opening hours restrictions or is an Amazon Go store not more like a giant vending machine than a traditional convenience store? For example, vestigial laws such as US requirements that cars be sold via a dealer instead of direct from a manufacturer are madness in the modern age and must be updated.

The New Norm?

Generally, when discussing emerging technologies, we tend to overestimate the effect of a technology in the short run and underestimate the effect in the long run - this is known as Amara's Law[258]. For example, just 10 years ago, an assertion that 4 billion people would have a computer in their pocket with more power than a supercomputer and access to millions of apps would have seemed ludicrous. But it's only taken 10 years for the smartphone to reach this prevalence and now it seems perfectly normal.

Once a technology is launched, it is no longer considered "future" even though it would have seemed (and been) utterly impossible a few years ago - one generation's future is the next's norm.

Very significant uptake of some new technologies may take 10 years and thus be imperceptible on a day to day basis. But I think few people would describe online shopping or mobile as new anymore yet look at all the big-name companies who failed to respond. The arrival of new technology can sometimes happen gradually, then suddenly. Many workers will be unaware of the threat to their position until the exponential progress of technology creeps up and overtakes them. Even for those who see automation as a remote prospect, there's a strong chance that AI may already be determining their shift, route or activities.

But as technology embeds itself deeper into our lives, it is worth noting that technological developments are becoming more complex as the quick wins are largely achieved. What we now talk of as the future requires growing levels of investment, access to larger data sets and bigger changes in consumer behavior and acceptance.

It's important to remember that individuals, communities and societies will embrace the future at very different rates, which will cause tensions. Much of the existing consumer economy is facing fundamental, even existential, changes. On the surface, computers that predict our whims and cater to them may seem a good thing. But at what price will such speedy convenience come and with what wider consequences?

In the last decade or so, billions if not trillions of dollars have been invested in all manner of technologies, gadgets and infrastructure to make our personal lives more convenient. We've sped up everything from shopping to television to food ordering to transport hailing, even turning on a light by voice instead of by switch. Once we get used to a new, faster way of doing something, we rarely look back. But we also rarely stop to consider if faster is necessarily better. Using those terms as synonyms is a false equivalency. Faster almost inevitably comes with a cost - be it financial, social, physical or psychological. And despite our best intentions, we don't always choose to reinvest the time we've saved particularly wisely.

Resistance is Fatal

"I cannot help fearing that men may reach a point where the look on every new theory as a danger, every innovation as a toilsome trouble, every social advance as a first step toward revolution, and that they absolutely refuse to move at all."

Alexis de Tocqueville

When Stores Stop Selling

If consumers aren't shopping as before, then stores can't expect to be about selling as before. 48% of US retail shoppers choose where and how to shop based on convenience rather than price. Humans no longer just buy from retailers. They buy direct from brands, they buy second-hand goods, they buy from other consumers on marketplace sites. They buy using their voice or their camera and they buy without involvement as they subscribe and replenish. They also let other entities do their buying for them.

While retailers expect brands to advertise and drive demand and footfall, few are equipped for their role in a journey where the physical retail store doesn't see the final purchase stage. In some sectors we face an uncomfortable truth - retail has outlived its purpose. Even if Amazon were to fade, there may be an inexorable trend away from certain physical retail as we know it for many types of products: a "natural" removal of inefficiencies, duplication and tradition from a sector that no longer serves the needs of its customers. Retail came about to bring products closer to people - to offer access to goods and services. Now, technology has removed the need for many kinds of physical retail.

The impacts of changes in consumption are not confined to the retail sector. There are widespread social consequences that make changes to the consumer economy of such critical importance. Changes in behavior and automation may lead to widespread layoffs. Retail's reach is so far that we are talking about social change, and even infrastructural change in how we design and zone our cities. Alongside the fairly obvious and predictable areas, there are also broader changes to consider - for example, if we shop in stores less and rely more on deliveries, we may see a reduction in car ownership. As the auto industry faces its own challenges from autonomy and electrification, a significant change in demand could further hasten its decline, bringing widespread redundancies.

Consumers, Technology and the Future of Retail

The next decade will see the end of retail as we've known it in modern times. The evolution in consumer behavior, combined with further transformative technological innovations, will lead to fundamental and irreversible changes. It's going to get easier for consumers and harder for retailers.

Today's consumer already expects to get what they want, when and where they want it, at the best price and with free delivery, agreeable returns policies and minimal environmental impact. When consumers start to experience the benefits of AI-assistants that will cater to their whims with even less effort, many companies will be unable to cope.

Brands and retailers need to take urgent action to address the challenges and position themselves to capitalize on the opportunities ahead. They can't do it alone, however. As well as partnering with technology providers, to bring about the needed changes, they will have to collaborate with regulators and policymakers, to help anticipate and respond effectively to the societal implications of the industry's transformation.

The impact of digital transformation on the retail workforce, the environment and communities will include some potentially negative implications that will need to be mitigated. Responsible, responsive leadership and collaborative action through public-private partnerships will be vital. The migration of more sectors to online, automation of existing physical retail, new shopping channels, new delivery channels and delegated shopping pose unprecedented challenges to brands and retailers. Paired with changes in consumer attitudes, expectations and environmental awareness, the retail sector is going to be one of the most changed in the coming years. Yet many retailers are on the ropes rather than the front foot, reeling from the changes described in the opening Chapters and far from ready for those outlined in later Chapters.

The impacts of changes in consumption habits will not be confined to the more obvious ones like store closures and the unprecedented changes to our shopping behaviors will reverberate around not only the boardrooms of brands and retailers, but also advertising agencies, financiers, landlords and regulators to name just some.

Many of the changes discussed here may initially appear as gimmicks, fads, or just the latest IT hype. For small retailers in particular, advanced technologies can feel far removed from the daily reality of trading. But something feels different about this wave of technology, coupled with the shifting purchasing power of new cohorts. Humans have irreversibly stopped shopping the way they used to. They are starting to replenish, starting to use technology to optimize, starting to delegate, starting to subscribe and rent. They're buying without shopping as purchasing moves from active to passive.

Retailers now face a greater challenge than they did with the emergence of online shopping and mobile in the last twenty years - if online was Act 1 and mobile was Act 2, the dramatic finale is the advent of AI in Act 3. Retail is already a 24/7, global, personalized endeavor. Brands and retailers need to be ready to meet customers consistently in numerous channels, on their terms. You need to care about their concerns, acting in line with their values whilst offering competitive prices and rapid service. Some retailers may choose to ignore many of the emerging trends and still prosper. But make no mistake, those will be the exceptional and the exceptions. Much of the shopping we're used to will be replaced by automated replenishment and pretail, with the remainder becoming more experiential and/or enhanced by technology. Mass retail as we knew it is dead.

For brands and retailers, a new era has begun: prepare to meet the next generation of customer – augmented humans and AI shoppers. Humans have stopped shopping in the old ways and consumers will never be the same again.

Appendix 1: Grocery & Restaurants

"The grocery and CPG industries are on the brink of change as the shift to digital technologies--combined with changes in consumer preferences--promise to reshape the sector going forward."

GroceryTalk 2019 Agenda

Of all the sectors of retail in which to consider the impacts of changing customers and changing technology, the food sector is among the most interesting. It's a massive industry, and poses unique challenges not found in any other sector; while fashion or electronics may go through rapid cycles of style or innovation, nothing approaches the complexities of food - from chilled and frozen to fresh ingredients and prepared meals, getting the right products to consumers in the right condition is a daunting challenge.

Just as with every other sector but even more intensely, local stores, supermarkets and restaurants are all experiencing the challenges of changes in consumer preferences, with age-old assumptions no longer valid. For example, consumers are tending to shop "little and often" rather than the traditional once-per-week journey to a large supermarket. The weekly shop in the same supermarket has been challenged by deliveries, discounters and more top-up convenience stores, as well as interest in farmers' markets.

Massive VC investment in start-ups that offer delivery on behalf of restaurants means that on-demand delivery of food is no longer limited to Pizza, with delivery now accounting for a substantial portion of the market as busy and affluent consumers no longer prepare their own meals.

Against this backdrop of change, there are also other factors, such as the rise of specialist dietary preferences (vegan, gluten free, etc.), as well as concern about the impact of the food supply chain on the environment (leading to demand for organic produce, plant-based meats, etc.), the growth of discounters and the application of technology at all stages of the chain, "from farm to fork".

In this Appendix, we'll explore how humans have stopped shopping for food in traditional ways and started consuming food sourced via new channels.

Grocery

"One in three UK shoppers say they spread their grocery spending more nowadays, so the store they use most often gets a smaller share than in the past. Combine this with the little and often trend that we found, and the danger for the large grocers is clear"

Shoppercentric StockTake 2020 Report[259]

No more one-stop-shopping

The age-old habit of shopping in the same supermarket for the same things on a regular basis is no longer the norm. 86% of shoppers use more than one supplier for their grocery needs.

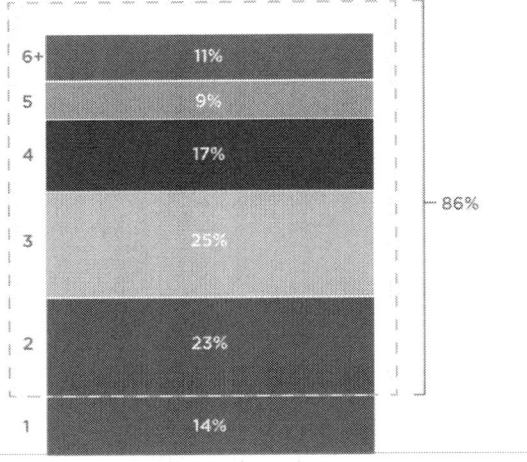

Figure 98 Just 14% of shoppers stick to a single supermarket. Source: Accenture[260]

Already over half of food shopping has been diverted from traditional supermarkets to other players. Supermarkets/grocers now have a 45% market share, representing an overall decline over the last 10 years, according to a 2015 Euromonitor study. Consumers now define convenience as shopping when and where suits them rather than it being in a single location.

According to a 2017 report from the USDA's Economic Research Service, Millennials shop at food stores less than any other age group, spend less time preparing food, and are more likely to eat carry-out, delivery, or fast food even when they do eat at home. Interest in shopping for groceries is at an all-time low - A Phononic[261] survey found half of Americans (50%) see grocery shopping as just something they have to do but don't necessarily want to. Another 12% went further, saying they'd be happy never to step foot inside a grocery store again. Three-quarters of Americans (76%) say it's likely that in five years that more physical stores will be offering ways to auto-replenish basics.

According to a Kurt Salmon survey, 44% of consumers do not even include a traditional grocery store in their consideration set for nonperishable grocery purchases - the dry grocery categories that were the original anchor for supermarkets are today the most likely product purchases shoppers are migrating to other channels, making the move to replenishment, posited earlier, more credible.

Changes to stores

We looked in Chapter 4 at some of the ways that grocery stores are changing to make the shopping experience faster - from guided shopping, scanning and even removing checkouts. Add the potential expansion of refill stations and the possible eventual reduction in shelf display of some large goods (such as detergent) as consumers move to replenishment. Take a step back and ask a fundamental question - does it make sense to setup grocery stores, with endless shelves, where people navigate, pick up 80% of the same items each week, queue, scan, repack, things? Grocery stores are already getting smaller - a notable effect of the digital grocery revolution is that grocers now have more stores, but those stores are getting physically smaller. On average, they have shrunk by 15% over the last decade. Some forecasts suggest that the grocery store of the future will probably be one-third or half of the size they are now but will be more customized in assortment to suit the local neighborhood - with that assortment being carefully predicted by AI.

Online Grocery Shopping

Only 3% of US grocery spending happens online at present. Compared with rates of up to 20% in South Korea and 8% in the UK, most Americans still purchase their groceries in stores. Shopping habits in the grocery sector are different than other retail areas. Consumers tend to be more loyal to their preferred supermarket and that behavior carries over to those that have tried food shopping online - 75% of online grocery shoppers say they are still shopping with the first retailer they tried for online grocery[262].

Walmart currently leads the U.S. online grocery market, well ahead of second placed Instacart. Amazon Prime Now is growing since the introduction of Whole Foods Market ranges, but it lacks reach compared to the almost nationwide scale of Walmart delivery.

There are signs of growth in online grocery ordering - Gen X shoppers in particular have risen from 29% in 2018 to 40% in 2019[263]. Across the generations, the in-store experience still matters for groceries, with 57% of shoppers reporting they do not purchase groceries online.

Online grocery shoppers are a demanding bunch; 52% of shoppers abandon their shopping cart when one/two or more items are out of stock. For those that do shop online or have tried it, according to the Luke Jenson, CEO of Ocado[264], the top 4 reported problems are:

- 26% ordered products missing
- 25% Incorrect substitutions
- 24% Out of date or short life
- 20% Late Deliveries

These customer-experience issues, alongside the challenging retailer economics for picking and delivery mean this is still an area where there's room for further innovation.

Despite the complexity of grocery orders, today's consumers still expect super-speedy service. In the UK, Sainsbury's has launched a special app, Chopchop, offering One Hour service, while Walmart's app touts "express orders in as little as an hour", available in 12 cities initially.

Aiming to increase the average basket value, online grocers are experimenting with additional services such as recipe-based shopping from firms such as Grocery Shopii[265], which automatically populates a shopper's cart with required items for selected recipes. This is both an attempt to the raise margins and also an attempt to encourage shoppers to continue to choose ingredients, rather than opting for prepared, delivered meal kits which reduce their dependence on the grocery store.

Order Picking

Operationally, selling groceries online profitability is difficult. Most experts estimate that it costs upwards of $10 to pick and fulfil each order, whereas delivery charges to the customer are typically half that amount. For retailers that don't have capital-intensive, dedicated automated fulfilment centers such as those offered by Ocado, the alternative remains paid human shoppers. This has led to complaints from customers in some supermarkets objecting to gig economy shoppers crowding the aisles attempting to fulfil online orders rapidly.

Picking and packing grocery orders for delivery is uniquely challenging. US online grocery Peapod says its average order contains 52 items which can range from heavy canned items and soft fruits to frozen and chilled items - all of which require separation and different treatment.

Kroger has announced a deal with UK firm Ocado to build as many as 20 automated grocery warehouses in the U.S. to help Kroger scale its e-commerce operation. Other retailers are turning to micro fulfilment centers (MFC) - small automated areas built within reclaimed existing store space rather than dedicated facilities that tend to be further from customers than existing stores. For example, Stop & Shop, owned by Dutch parent Ahold Delhaize, is building a 12,000-square-foot fully automated fulfillment center in the backroom of a store in Windsor, Connecticut, for deliveries in the Hartford area. As mentioned in Chapter 8, other firms are experimenting with "dark stores" - turning existing sites into pick up points, but with the order picking being done by staff rather than robots.

Delivery and Pickup

Once the complexities of picking an order are completed either by manual labor or by robots, the final phase of online shopping consists of getting the goods to the customer.

We mentioned in Chapter 8 about the growing popularity of pickup from store as this means the consumer can avoid navigating the supermarket and simply arrive to pickup their order, which may be more convenient than waiting for a delivery. In the US, at store pickup locations more than doubled in 2018 from 2451 in January to over 5,800 by December[266]. Around 13% of Walmart customers use curbside pickup.

A recent trend in grocery worth mentioning here, is the arrival of what were previously food delivery services to compete in this space. Companies that previously offered food delivery services from restaurants, are turning to supermarkets and convenience store orders as the next source of growth. Postmates, DoorDash and Uber Eats are partnering with grocery and convenience stores to offer their customer base access to deliveries.

Subscriptions & Meal kits

Going back to some earlier trends we mentioned concerning subscriptions and environmental concerns, the food sector is also seeing the impact of these shifts. Established meal kit firms Blue Apron and Hello Fresh are seeing startups like Platejoy, Fuel and Sunfare provide personalized meal plans and grocery delivery based on user's health goals, dietary needs and preferences.

Meal kits not only appeal to consumers in terms of convenience, but they may also offer benefits from an environmental point of view. Kits that provide precise amounts of ingredients can cut down on food waste - which is a major source of emissions - but only provide real benefits if the packaging they come in is recyclable and they are delivered in an environmentally efficient manner[267].

Restaurants

I want to talk now about restaurants - an adjacent sector to consumer retail - found in close proximity and sometimes mooted as a potential savior for main streets - with increases in casual dining and coffee shops potentially able to lure more people to the main street and plug some of the unsightly gaps in store fronts.

Although many will baulk at the emotive notion of the ritual of eating being corrupted by technology, we're likely to see more technology introduced into restaurants, even if only at the operational level, though there will be customer-facing innovation too. However, we're also likely to see a decline in the number or size of restaurants as home delivery becomes a bigger slice of the market.

Reservations

Reservations at restaurants have already moved largely online. Apps such as OpenTable, Resy or Google Maps offer an easy way to book a table for your preferred time with just a few clicks. Google's Assistant, via its Duplex AI voice synthesis technology, can even make a reservation for you at restaurants that only accept telephone bookings. It's noteworthy that one-third of customers won't consider a restaurant that doesn't accept online bookings, so even the most technologically averse restaurateurs need to adapt to changing consumer behavior.

In another shift towards convenience-driven experiences, it is now possible to not only make your reservation in advance but also to order your food in advance and have it ready for you as you arrive. An app called Allset, and a new feature from Uber Eats called Dine-In, allow you to order ahead from the menu, avoiding waiting time in your chosen restaurant. While the ability to order ahead and have the food ready just as you sit down might appeal to diners under time pressure, e.g. at lunch, there will, of course, be those who don't see perusing the menu and discussing meal choices with fellow diners as a 'friction' to be eliminated. As Uber Eats trials offering preorder for dine-in, leading restaurant reservations platform, OpenTable is now offering meal delivery from within its app, as the lines blur between reservations and delivery.

Robo Restaurants

Whether as a novelty factor, a doomed experiment or a genuine effort to increase efficiency or cope with worker shortages, a number of restaurants are looking at automating the dining experience.

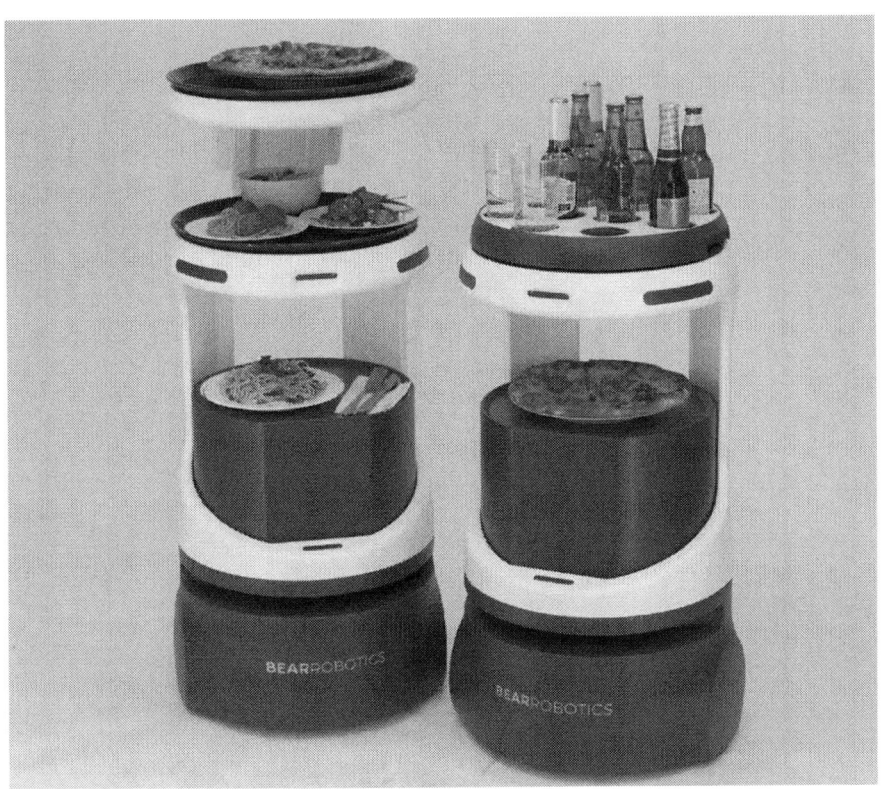

Figure 99 A food delivery robot. Source: BearRobotics[268]

For example, a Californian start-up has created a food service robot that can carry up to 30kg of food/crockery and it can work for 8-12 hours on a single charge, delivering food and drink to tables. The robot may be able to increase productivity by allowing a server to clear a table onto the robotic platform and have it return to the kitchen while the server moves on to the next customer. There are also potential uses in other settings such as nursing homes.

In China, one of Alibaba's Hema grocery stores in Shanghai features miniature robots that deliver orders to tables, while rival chain JD has opened the first of its X-cafes where everything from ordering, preparing, cooking, plating to serving is controlled by robots and artificial intelligence.

In an example of restaurant innovation that draws heavily on the ecommerce paradigm, Pizza Hut has added Amazon Locker-like "cubbies" for carryout orders purchased through the Pizza Hut website or app. Customers can then pick up their order from the locker without interacting with any Pizza Hut staff, eliminating the line, the wait and any conversation. Each cubby has a lining that keeps food hot and drinks cold.

Figure 100 A Pizza Hut pickup Cubby. Source: Pizza Hut

Restaurant Delivery - (When Humans Stop Cooking)

"Food delivery apps are starting to reshape the $863 billion American restaurant industry. As more people order food to eat at home, and as delivery becomes faster and more convenient, the apps are changing the very essence of what it means to operate a restaurant."

New York Times[269]

Contemporary consumers are cooking less than previous generations. The graph below shows the dramatic change that has taken place over the last few decades as spending on eating out has overtaken grocery budgets.

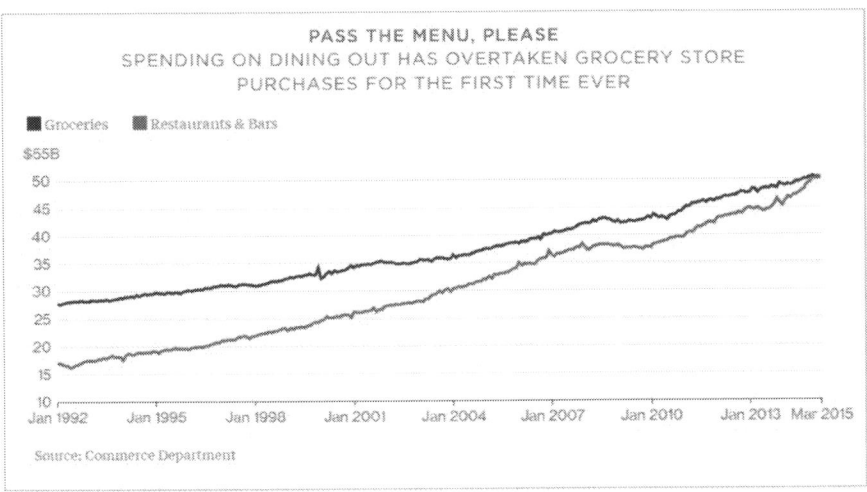

Figure 101 Restaurant spending overtakes Grocery spend. Source: US Commerce Department

Food delivery options used to be limited to Pizza and maybe your local Chinese restaurant. More recently, gig-economy platforms like Uber Eats, Postmates, DoorDash and Grubhub mean customers can order pastries from Panera, coffee from Starbucks, a burrito from Chipotle, a Big Mac from McDonald's among many others. Restaurants have based much of their recent growth on consumer deliveries and rely heavily on the big four delivery companies which combined have about 95% of the market.

This is leading to an uneasy relationship as delivery companies insert themselves between consumers and restaurants. They are eating into the already slim profit margins and can't always ensure that the food arrives to the customer in the condition that the restaurant would hope. Yet, as consumers adopt aggregation apps, restaurants that aren't on the platform may lose out.

In Europe too, food delivery apps such as Deliveroo, Just Eat and Uber Eats have led to an extra £400m in revenue for European restaurants[270]. UK based food delivery app, Deliveroo, has expanded its reach in the restaurant business further, by also offering "Pickup", where a Deliveroo customer can use the app to order their food, but then go and collect it instead of having a deliveroo person bring it to them. Making the service more of an "Orderoo", does still earn a commission but doesn't have any incremental costs, while keeping users who don't want or need to pay for delivery to remain loyal to the app, as well as arguably bringing incremental orders to restaurants.

Dark Kitchens

One of the most interesting impacts of changes in how modern consumers buy and consume meals is the emergence of the concept of dark kitchens (also known as ghost kitchens). Dark Kitchens are locations where meals are prepared for delivery only. Services such as Kitchen rents kitchen space in their facilities. With setup costs for opening a new traditional restaurant space easily running to half a million dollars and easily $10k per month rent, it's not difficult to see how food creators are considering renting dark kitchen space that comes with a $20k upfront fee and $5k monthly rental. Some facilities have one small kitchen producing for several brands, while others have larger spaces, with rented, booth-style kitchens serving the waiting DoorDash and Uber Eats drivers. In many cases, customers don't know if their order is coming from a traditional restaurant kitchen or from a shared dark kitchen.

As long as demand for food deliveries continues to grow, dark kitchens are substantially cheaper to operate than traditional restaurant locations, which incur staff overheads even while the premises are empty of eat-in customers. In one variation, restaurant chain Chipotle hasn't gone the dark kitchen route but added a second assembly line designated for delivery and takeout orders in its existing kitchens to maximize its space utilization.

In a sign of their growing power though, the food delivery apps can capture latent customer demand for a particular food type in a neighborhood and set up a dark kitchen to cater for it. For example, say that there's no Thai food delivery service in a particular area, but Uber Eats users nearby frequently search for Thai - then Uber Eats can look to rent local dark kitchen space and encourage a Thai service.

The "Groceraunt"

I'm not usually a fan of portmanteaus but in this case, there's little alternative to describe the hybrid stores trying to combine grocery shopping with restaurants. Faced with declining demand for ingredients, some grocers are responding by adding sit-down restaurants in store. Other retailers such as Lululemon and Crate & Barrel have already tested restaurants in stores to lure customers, and Alibaba's Hema stores in China offer in-store cooking by professional chefs.

Just as the size of grocery stores and many other retail premises are shrinking, the trend towards delivery may ultimately lead to smaller sit-in restaurants, as consumers eat out less often while still enjoying professionally prepared meals.

When Humans Stop Shopping

The upheaval in how people buy their food is another example of changing preferences and technological advances causing social and economic shifts. Along with the rest of the retail and consumer goods economy, the food sector is in the firing line as humans stop shopping the way they used to.

Appendix 2: Further Reading

If you're interested in reading further on this topic, here are some of the books I read as part of my research:

Amazon: How the World's Most Relentless Retailer will Continue to Revolutionize Commerce
Knights, Miya, Berg, Natalie

The New Rules of Retail
Lewis, Robin

Reengineering Retail: The Future of Selling in a Post-Digital World
Stephens, Doug, Pine, Joseph

The Shopping Revolution: How Successful Retailers Win Customers in an Era of Endless Disruption
Kahn, Barbara E.

Retail's Seismic Shift
Dart, Michael

Almost is Not Good Enough: How to Win or Lose in Retail
Jennings, Andrew

The Future of Omni-Channel Retail: Predictions in the Age of Amazon
Binnie, Lionel

Retail in the Age of i: A New Worldview for the Retail Industry
Hawkins, Gary

References

[1] Amazon Shareholder Letter, 2018
[2] Bureau of Labor Statistics, 2016
[3] https://cornerstonecapinc.com/wp-content/uploads/Retail-Automation_Stranded-Workers-Final-May-2017_corrected.pdf
[4] https://www.ft.com/content/86acdcd8-20a7-11e9-a46f-08f9738d6b2b
[5] https://www.bloomberg.com/opinion/articles/2019-09-07/movies-on-your-phone-screen-size-is-the-new-generational-divide
[6] https://www.forbes.com/sites/tommcgee/2018/08/13/retailers-adjust-to-surge-in-boomers/#7825a8635ab9
[7] https://www.loyalty.com/home/insights/article-details/loyalty-by-generation
[8] https://www.nielsen.com/wp-content/uploads/sites/3/2019/04/nielsen-boomers-report-082912.pdf
[9] https://www.thedrum.com/opinion/2019/06/24/baby-boomers-and-retail-how-re-engage-the-forgotten-generation
[10] https://www.emarketer.com/content/how-mobile-and-social-figure-into-gen-x-shopping
[11] https://www.centro.net/blog/generation-x-the-small-but-mighty-generation/
[12] https://www.nasdaq.com/press-release/retail-marketers-top-shopping-behaviors-for-gen-x-and-boomers-20190814-00675
[13] https://www.ft.com/content/194cd1c8-6583-11e8-a39d-4df188287fff
[14] Parment, A., 2011. Generation Y in Consumer and Labour Markets. Routledge, New York
[15] https://www.nielsen.com/ca/en/insights/article/2018/understanding-and-harnessing-Millennial-purchasing-power/
[16] https://www.cbsnews.com/news/walmart-strategy-walmart-is-now-targeting-Millennials/
[17] https://fortune.com/2019/09/17/procter-gamble-gillette-ad-carolyn-tastad/
[18] 3 New Ways to Work in an Era of Disruption
[19] https://adage.com/article/wp-engine/generation-z-digital-experience-human-experience/316487/
[20] https://retail-assist.co.uk/gen-z-vs-gen-x-vs-gen-y-shopping-habits-survey/
[21] https://www.thefuturelaboratory.com/blog/dear-brands-please-stop-selling-us-your-activism
[22] http://www.mckinsey.com/industries/consumer-packaged-goods/our-insights/the-consumer-sector-in-2030-trends-and-questions-to-consider
[23] https://twitter.com/DCoolican/status/1087896875322101760?s=09
[24] https://www.accenture.com/us-en/insights/strategy/brand-purpose
[25] https://www.bloomberg.com/opinion/articles/2018-10-29/why-fashion-brands-like-h-m-and-j-crew-are-going-green
[26] https://medium.com/bloomberg/brands-no-longer-want-your-loyalty-now-they-want-your-love-fc50a2850b83

[27] https://www.irishtimes.com/news/environment/how-climate-action-children-are-winning-over-parents-1.4025202
[28] https://www.retaildive.com/news/clouds-on-the-horizon-what-climate-change-means-for-retail/552791/
[29] https://www.drapersonline.com/news/fashion-hardest-hit-by-administrations/7039123.article
[30] https://www.dlapiper.com/en/us/news/2019/06/retail-sector-leadership-diversity-deficit-will-affect-future-competitiveness/
[31] https://internetretailing.net/mobile-theme/mobile-theme/2020-visions-the-year-of-the-conscious-consumer-and-customer-centric-personalisation-20732
[32] https://www.ellenmacarthurfoundation.org/publications/a-new-textiles-economy-redesigning-fashions-future
[33] https://www.cnbc.com/2019/08/28/best-buy-revs-up-supply-chain-ahead-of-the-holiday-season.html
[34] https://www.stern.nyu.edu/sites/default/files/assets/documents/NYUSternCSB_SustainableShareIndex_2019.pdf
[35] https://www.wsj.com/articles/big-brands-to-test-refillable-containers-11548316801
[36] https://www.thegrocer.co.uk/iceland/iceland-ended-loose-fresh-fruit-and-veg-trial-after-sales-fell-30/600000.article
[37] https://www.youtube.com/watch?v=l0DoQYGZt8M
[38] https://www.forbes.com/sites/michellegrant/2019/05/28/retailers-need-to-embrace-sustainability-in-western-europe/#15fe3c7b737c
[39] https://www.euronews.com/2019/09/20/french-supermarket-chain-to-remove-additives-using-phone-app-that-rates-products
[40] https://www.retaildive.com/news/disruptor-thredup-dive-awards/566185/
[41] https://www.businessinsider.com/teens-earn-money-fashion-depop-app-2019-4?r=US&IR=T
[42] https://www.bloomberg.com/opinion/articles/2019-09-15/china-learns-to-love-secondhand-goods?srnd=opinion
[43] https://techcrunch.com/2019/11/27/vinted-the-second-hand-clothes-marketplace-raises-141m-at-a-1b-valuation/
[44] https://www.thredup.com/resale
[45] https://www.wsj.com/articles/on-second-thought-traditional-retailers-make-room-for-used-clothes-11565947803
[46] https://www.economist.com/business/2018/06/07/rent-the-runway-is-taking-clothes-sharing-mainstream
[47] https://www.wired.com/story/just-rent-your-clothes/
[48] https://www.bloomberg.com/opinion/articles/2019-03-15/rental-clothing-is-the-future-of-fashion
[49] https://www.prnewswire.com/news-releases/more-than-80-of-shoppers-believe-theyre-more-knowledgeable-than-retail-store-associates-according-to-new-tulip-retail-survey-300423934.html
[50] https://www.signs.com/online-vs-in-store/
[51] https://www.marketingweek.com/2017/08/07/tom-goodwin-future-retail/

[52] https://internetretailing.net/themes/uk-leads-the-world-in-online-shopping-with-over-a-third-of-consumers-buying-online-multiple-times-a-week-20060
[53] https://twitter.com/benedictevans/status/1175464824781692928
[54] https://www.phononic.com/resources/food-and-beverage-innovations/sotf-2019-ebook
[55] https://www.shopify.com/blog/black-friday-cyber-monday-2018
[56] https://www.thinkwithgoogle.com/consumer-insights/omnichannel-shopping-journey/
[57] Amazon - How the world's most relentless retailer…Chp5
[58] Reengineering Retail - Doug Stephens Chp 1
[59] https://www.bbc.com/news/business-49349703
[60] https://eu.usatoday.com/story/money/2019/08/01/retail-flagship-stores-close-rent-online-shopping-skyrockets/1888004001/
[61] http://www.futuretimeline.net/21stcentury/2030.htm#shopping-malls-2030
[62] https://www.ft.com/content/070a7666-4028-11e9-9bee-efab61506f44
[63] https://twitter.com/NeilRetail/status/1079785924966445058?s=09
[64] https://www.cnbc.com/2019/08/13/we-are-in-the-middle-of-the-great-american-department-store-shakeout.html
[65] https://www.thinkwithgoogle.com/consumer-insights/online-in-store-shopping-search/
[66] https://hbr.org/2017/01/a-study-of-46000-shoppers-shows-that-omnichannel-retailing-works
[67] https://pressroom.ups.com/pressroom/ContentDetailsViewer.page?ConceptType=PressReleases&id=1565041068600-976
[68] https://www.thinkwithgoogle.com/advertising-channels/video/top-three-global-shopping-trends
[69] http://www.smartinsights.com/ecommerce/ecommerce-strategy/37-indispensable-ecommerce-stats-to-inform-your-2017-strategy/
[70] https://www.brightpearl.com/rise-of-the-review-culture
[71] https://markets.businessinsider.com/news/stocks/warren-buffett-huge-struggle-taking-place-in-retail-2017-8-1002295945
[72] https://www.thetimes.co.uk/edition/business/nikes-killer-blow-for-small-stores-5trqqhtxl
[73] https://www.theverge.com/2019/6/13/18663036/monzo-starling-mobile-banks-uk-report
[74] https://www.thetimes.co.uk/article/upstarts-are-putting-pressure-on-consumer-giants-and-it-shows-wp0629jqp
[75] https://www.iab.com/wp-content/uploads/2019/07/IAB-Disrupting-Brand-Preference_FINAL.pdf
[76] https://www.theguardian.com/business/2019/mar/05/long-read-aldi-discount-supermarket-changed-britain-shopping
[77] https://www.kantarworldpanel.com/en/grocery-market-share/great-britain
[78] https://www.retaildive.com/news/amazon-private-labels-target-wide-range-of-shoppers/525915/

[79] https://www.vox.com/podcasts/2019/1/16/18185512/glossier-ceo-emily-weiss-beauty-makeup-interview-podcast-recode-decode-kara-swisher
[80] https://edition.cnn.com/2019/02/19/tech/augmented-reality-makeup/index.html
[81] https://this.just.in/amazon-launches-private-label-cosmetics-in-europe/
[82] https://techcrunch.com/2019/06/18/youtubes-new-ar-beauty-try-on-lets-viewers-virtually-try-on-makeup-while-watching-video-reviews/
[83] https://medium.com/financial-times/retail-is-the-beauty-industry-amazon-proof-53dbcfcc1d0f
[84] https://www.digitalcommerce360.com/product/online-apparel-report
[85] https://www.telegraph.co.uk/business/2019/02/06/madecom-sales-soar-furniture-shoppers-shift-online/
[86] https://www.notarize.com/real-estate
[87] https://plc.autotrader.co.uk/press-centre/news-hub/market-report-september-2019/
[88] https://www.cnbc.com/2019/03/19/heres-why-retailers-should-be-scared-of-amazon-dominating-e-commerce.html
[89] https://www.comscore.com/Insights/Presentations-and-Whitepapers/2018/2018-State-of-the-US-Online-Retail-Economy
[90] https://www.npr.org/2018/06/06/615137239/what-americans-told-us-about-online-shopping-says-a-lot-about-amazon
[91] https://www.theguardian.com/business/2019/mar/07/almost-90-of-uk-shoppers-use-amazon-research-reveals
[92] Feb 2017 Ayden payments report
[93] Phononic's 2019 "Store of the Future" Report
[94] https://www.nytimes.com/2018/11/21/style/holiday-department-store-windows.html
[95] https://www.wsj.com/articles/wait-where-did-that-burger-go-diners-struggle-with-fast-moving-digital-menus-11567620271
[96] https://en.wikipedia.org/wiki/John_Wanamaker
[97] http://www.itif.org/files/2010-self-service-economy.pdf
[98] http://www.cbc.ca/news/business/marketplace-are-you-being-served-1.3422736
[99] https://www.theatlantic.com/magazine/archive/2018/03/stealing-from-self-checkout/550940/
[100] https://techcrunch.com/2018/11/15/walmart-and-target-embrace-in-store-mobile-checkout-for-the-holidays/
[101] https://stance.com
[102] https://twitter.com/laura_doonin/status/1103080051774414848
[103] https://internetretailing.net/themes/themes/what-sainsburys-is-doing-to-make-shopping-with-it-more-convenient-20524
[104] https://en.wikipedia.org/wiki/Radio-frequency_identification
[105] http://time.com/3880751/keedoozle-americas-first-automated-grocery/
[106] https://www.youtube.com/watch?v=eob532iEpqk
[107] https://youtu.be/NrmMk1Myrxc
[108] https://www.ibm.com/blogs/insights-on-business/ibmix/transforming-customer-experience-with-instant-checkout/

[109] http://www.convenience.org/Research/FactSheets/ScopeofIndustry/Pages/Convenience.aspx
[110] https://www.bls.gov/ooh/sales/cashiers.htm
[111] https://www.nytimes.com/2012/08/19/opinion/sunday/why-waiting-in-line-is-torture.html
[112] https://www.theguardian.com/money/2017/jul/12/cash-contactless-payments-uk-stores-cards-british-retail-consortium
[113] https://www.scmp.com/tech/apps-social/article/2186098/alipay-accepted-over-3000-walgreens-drugstores-us-amid-overseas
[114] https://www.wsj.com/articles/cash-plastic-or-hand-amazon-envisions-paying-with-a-wave-11579352401
[115] https://www.daimler-mobility.com/en/company/news/epayment-mercedes-pay/
[116] http://www.huffingtonpost.com/2014/10/20/apple-pay-will-make-you-s_n_6014870.html
[117] https://www.forbes.com/sites/cognitiveworld/2019/07/02/ais-increasing-role-in-customer-service/#4f4ffd5973fc
[118] https://www.alizila.com/at-alibaba-artificial-intelligence-is-changing-how-people-shop-online/
[119] https://www.ft.com/content/69c25116-1ac1-11e9-9e64-d150b3105d21
[120] https://aws.amazon.com/personalize/
[121] https://internetretailing.net/themes/themes/instagram-live-testing-checkout-begins-as-it-gears-up-to-exploit-what-deutsche-bank-analysts-say-is-a-10bn-opportunity--20104
[122] Thinkwithgoogle.com, August 2019
[123] https://www.pwc.ie/publications/2018/retail-consumer-report-2018.pdf
[124] https://www.theguardian.com/fashion/2019/mar/31/squaring-up-how-instagram-fashion-is-changing-the-way-we-shop
[125] https://blog.hootsuite.com/instagram-statistics/
[126] https://www.shopify.com/blog/instagram-marketing
[127] https://twitter.com/BigCommerce/status/1103072274209398784
[128] https://www.facebook.com/business/news/insights/how-instagram-boosts-brands-and-drives-sales
[129] http://seenconnects.com/
[130] https://www.thebloggerprogramme.com/
[131] http://www.pipersandler.com/3col.aspx?id=5751
[132] https://newsroom.pinterest.com/en/post/new-ways-to-shop-with-pinterest-0
[133] https://business.pinterest.com/en/shop-the-look-pins
[134] https://sproutsocial.com/insights/social-media-for-retail/
[135] https://www.slideshare.net/christinemoorman/the-cmo-survey-highlights-and-insights-report-feb-2019-143475387
[136] https://a16z.com/2019/12/05/video-first-ecommerce/
[137] https://twitter.com/BenedictEvans/status/760174699263385600?s=09
[138] https://slyce.it/wp-content/uploads/2015/11/Visual_Search_Technology_and_Market.pdf

[139] https://www.richrelevance.com/blog/2018/06/04/richrelevance-study-shows-americans-skeptical-voice-assisted-shopping/
[140] https://www.businesswire.com/news/home/20180822005090/en/21-Introduces-AI-Powered-Visual-Search-Navigation-Donde
[141] https://blog.aboutamazon.com/shopping/stylesnap-will-change-the-way-you-shop-forever
[142] https://pdfpiw.uspto.gov/.piw?docid=09858719
[143] https://www.hoxtonanalytics.com/
[144] https://www.telusinternational.com/articles/resources/compare-chat-vs-voice-customer-service/
[145] https://www.drift.com/wp-content/uploads/2018/01/2018-state-of-chatbots-report.pdf
[146] https://adlingo.com/
[147] https://techcrunch.com/2019/03/18/apple-business-chat-drives-in-seat-drink-ordering-at-quicken-loans-arena-in-cleveland/
[148] https://a16z.com/2019/09/06/china-is-cashing-in-on-group-chats/
[149] https://www.juniperresearch.com/document-library/white-papers/how-ai-can-revive-retail
[150] https://blog.calljoy.com/2019/04/phone-calls-the-heartbeat-of-small-biz-customer-service.html
[151] https://www.retaildive.com/news/consumers-like-chatbots-but-prefer-human-interaction/558940/
[152] Gartner, Market Guide for Virtual Customer Assistants, 11 July 2019
[153] https://www.nytimes.com/2016/03/10/technology/the-echo-from-amazon-brims-with-groundbreaking-promise.html?_r=3
[154] https://www.cnet.com/news/amazon-sees-alexa-devices-more-than-double-in-just-one-year/
[155] https://gds.blog.gov.uk/2018/06/27/building-the-gov-uk-of-the-future/
[156] https://www.pwc.com/us/en/advisory-services/publications/consumer-intelligence-series/pwc-voice-assistants.pdf
[157] https://internetretailing.net/payment/payment/more-than-half-of-consumers-happy-to-use-voice-to-pay-for-low-value-goods--but-most-shy-from-using-the-technology-for-larger-purchases-study-19963
[158] PWC Consumer Intelligence Series – Voice Assistants survey 2018
[159] https://medium.com/asos-techblog/why-were-using-google-assistant-to-make-asos-more-intuitive-2e43dc5446c7
[160] http://www.travelweekly.co.uk/articles/342061/easyjet-unveils-voice-recognition-flight-search
[161] https://www.voice2biz.com/shopify-voice-app/
[162] https://www.wired.com/story/amazons-dash-buttons-will-haunt-us-forever/
[163] https://www.joinhoney.com/
[164] https://joindrop.com
[165] https://www.wired.com/story/amazon-honey-security-warning/
[166] https://www.riaa.com/reports/2019-mid-year-music-industry-revenue-report-riaa/

[167] https://www.psychologytoday.com/us/blog/the-edge-choice/201207/the-way-we-spend-impacts-how-we-spend
[168] The Growth of Subscriptions, McKinsey
[169] https://www.forbes.com/sites/christinemoorman/2018/08/23/adobe-how-to-dominate-the-subscription-economy/#6b8c473f52e8
[170] https://www.livefeather.com
[171] https://www.cbsnews.com/news/feather-rents-and-swaps-furniture-as-your-lifestyle-and-tastes-change/
[172] https://techcrunch.com/2019/07/22/uber-tests-monthly-subscription-that-combines-eats-rides-bikes-and-scooters/
[173] https://mudjeans.eu/lease-a-jeans/
[174] https://www.vox.com/recode/2019/5/3/18511544/amazon-prime-oral-history-jeff-bezos-one-day-shipping
[175] Reengineering Retail - Doug Stephens, Chapter 3
[176] https://recurly.com/
[177] https://twitter.com/amywebb/status/1158900366387404801?s=09
[178] https://www.wsj.com/articles/stop-wasting-money-on-unnecessary-monthly-subscriptions-11557331377
[179] https://www.mckinsey.com/industries/technology-media-and-telecommunications/our-insights/thinking-inside-the-subscription-box-new-research-on-ecommerce-consumers
[180] https://www.wired.com/story/amazons-dash-buttons-will-haunt-us-forever/
[181] https://weplenish.com/
[182] https://twitter.com/EMI_MichelleG/status/1215413312126517248
[183] https://www.smarter.am/fridgecam
[184] https://techcrunch.com/2019/04/30/glovo-the-on-demand-deliver-anything-local-app-raises-169m-series-d/
[185] https://www.vox.com/2017/9/28/16377528/ikea-acquisition-taskrabbit-shopping-home-contract-labor
[186] https://trendwatching.com/quarterly/2018-05/the-future-of-retail/
[187] https://tech.instacart.com/deep-learning-with-emojis-not-math-660ba1ad6cdc
[188] https://www.fastcompany.com/90128248/how-stitch-fix-is-using-algorithmic-design-to-become-the-netflix-of-fashion
[189] https://fortune.com/longform/stitch-fix-data-algorithm-growth-katrina-lake/
[190] https://www.thinkwithgoogle.com/marketing-resources/experience-design/speed-is-key-optimize-your-mobile-experience/
[191] http://en.blogthinkbig.com/2016/03/21/3-themes-to-watch-in-2016-about-product-innovation/
[192] https://www.amazon.com/Intention-Economy-When-Customers-Charge/dp/1422158527
[193] https://www.thetimes.co.uk/article/next-trick-for-amazon-boss-jeff-bezos-is-the-end-of-shopping-c0w90mhsc
[194] https://trendwatching.com/quarterly/2018-05/the-future-of-retail/

[195] https://pdfs.semanticscholar.org/9b93/c6836e57b8f684abbb8a4f839bf81d50aa12.pdf
[196] https://qz.com/1304987/amazon-has-already-begun-automating-its-white-collar-jobs/
[197] https://www.cnbc.com/2019/05/05/amazon-can-already-ship-to-72percent-of-us-population-in-a-day-map-shows.html
[198] https://www.theindustry.fashion/almost-half-of-uk-online-clothing-shoppers-will-not-pay-for-delivery/
[199] GlobalData
[200] https://thefuturefedex.com/
[201] https://www.bbc.com/news/business-49633006
[202] https://twitter.com/PitneyBowes/status/1103069582791708673
[203] https://advisory.kpmg.us/content/dam/advisory/en/pdfs/2018/autonomy-delivers-final-secured-web.pdf
[204] https://envoy.com/deliveries/
[205] https://www.wired.com/story/how-amazon-cloned-neighborhood-test-delivery-robots/
[206] US Patent 010216188
[207] US Patent 010313638
[208] https://thenextweb.com/tech/2018/04/25/dji-launches-a-new-emergency-drone-program-in-europe/
[209] https://www.theverge.com/2018/1/18/16904802/drone-rescue-australia-video-ocean
[210] http://www.bbc.com/news/av/technology-40360164/the-defibrillator-drone-that-can-beat-ambulance-times
[211] http://coresight.com/research/us-online-grocery-survey-2019/
[212] https://www.thetimes.co.uk/article/more-stress-for-retailers-as-shoppers-click-but-dont-collect-cqmcss3p2
[213] https://www.wsj.com/articles/how-zara-is-defying-a-broad-retail-slump-1497467742
[214] https://www.grocerydive.com/news/walmarts-grocery-pickup-is-reaching-new-high-value-shoppers/555158/
[215] https://www.axios.com/fast-delivery-climate-change-amazon-walmart-target-40d0b733-ad06-4b88-9a07-5ac9b6a5c03b.html
[216] https://www.weforum.org/agenda/2018/02/delivering-packages-with-drones-might-be-good-for-the-environment/
[217] https://www.nature.com/articles/s41467-017-02411-5
[218] https://www.thinkwithgoogle.com/data/youtube-unboxing-videos-watch-time/
[219] https://edition.cnn.com/2019/07/15/business/fast-shipping-environmental-impact/index.html
[220] https://www.ft.com/content/2f7203dc-1b63-11ea-97df-cc63de1d73f4
[221] https://www.aboutamazon.com/amazon-fulfillment/
[222] https://www2.colliers.com/en/research/2017-Q4-US-Industrial-Market-Outlook-Report

[223] https://www.thetimes.co.uk/article/blackstone-bets-on-online-commerce-with-huge-warehouse-deal-7mfjw95pf
[224] https://www.wsj.com/articles/e-commerce-driving-bigger-demand-for-smaller-warehouses-cbre-says-11570701600
[225] https://www.propmodo.com/the-new-economy-runs-on-urban-logistics-centers/
[226] https://www.technologyreview.com/s/603229/the-robotic-grocery-store-of-the-future-is-here/
[227] https://ocadotechnology.com/blog/ocado-internet-of-vans/
[228] https://www.axios.com/in-china-a-picture-of-how-warehouse-jobs-can-vanish-d19f5cf1-f35b-4024-8783-2ba79a573405.html
[229] https://internetretailing.net/mobile-theme/mobile-theme/a-multichannel-world-how-european-retailers-are-responding-to-the-new-reality-of-mobile-first-retailing-19958
[230] https://www.alixpartners.com/insights-impact/insights/retail-viewpoint-many-happy-returns-for-retailers/
[231] http://news.pb.com/article_display.cfm?article_id=5881
[232] https://www.fastcompany.com/90378285/why-airbnb-target-and-walmart-are-betting-on-the-experience-economy
[233] https://vrscout.com/news/kelloggs-accenture-vr-eye-tracking
[234] Future Stores Conference, Miami 2019
[235] https://twitter.com/NeilRetail/status/1162400129606770688?s=09
[236] https://www.thedrum.com/news/2019/01/31/customers-want-service-not-sci-fi-high-street-retailers
[237] https://www.businesswire.com/news/home/20191114005024/en/Zebra-Study-75-Percent-Millennials-Abandon-In-Store
[238] https://greenamerica.org/report-STS
[239] https://www.thetimes.co.uk/article/big-stores-are-ikea-s-foundations-but-we-need-to-move-into-city-centres-3xffm3qv3
[240] https://www.ft.com/content/0b0c2780-5bf5-11e9-939a-341f5ada9d40
[241] https://www.cnbc.com/2019/12/19/how-amazon-changed-americas-malls-in-the-2010s.html
[242] http://www.cushmanwakefield.us/en/research-and-insight/2019/popup-palooza
[243] https://situlive.com/
[244] Google Data, U.S., April 2016–March 2017 vs. April 2018–March 2019
[245] https://jda.com/blueyonder
[246] https://medium.com/bloomberg/amazons-clever-machines-are-moving-from-the-warehouse-to-headquarters-e821582a9549
[247] https://www.thetimes.co.uk/article/lets-embrace-a-rebirth-of-the-high-street-not-mourn-every-lost-shop-7tj32s55j
[248] https://www.cnbc.com/2019/01/29/angela-ahrendts-heres-how-apple-store-staff-start-every-single-day.html
[249] https://internetretailing.net/strategy-and-innovation/hm-trims-store-opening-plans-as-shoppers-opt-to-buy-online-19835
[250] https://www.earnshaws.com/2019/12/archives/january-2020/redefining-retail/

[251] https://www.dallasnews.com/business/retail/2019/02/06/surveymore-half-us-retailers-said-just-surviving
[252] https://www.bbc.com/news/business-46640362
[253] https://www.amazon.com/Amazon-Relentless-Retailer-Continue-Revolutionize-ebook/dp/B07LCSY7QK
[254] Wedbush Securities
[255] https://www.ft.com/content/cf98680c-738f-11e7-aca6-c6bd07df1a3c
[256] https://www.accenture.com/t00010101T000000Z__w__/au-en/_acnmedia/PDF-52/Accenture-Strategy-DD-Painting-Digital-Future-POV-v2.pdf#zoom=50
[257] https://techcrunch.com/2018/12/27/amazon-walmart-india-e-commerce-restrictions/
[258] https://en.wikipedia.org/wiki/Roy_Amara
[259] https://www.shoppercentric.com/shopperstocktake2020
[260] https://www.accenture.com/us-en/_acnmedia/pdf-53/accenture-ksa-food.pdf
[261] https://phononic.com/wp-content/uploads/2019/03/Phononic-Store-of-the-Future-2019-eBook.pdf
[262] Google/Bain, U.S., Omnichannel Grocery, online grocery shoppers in the last 12 months, n=1,802, 2018
[263] https://www.fmi.org/our-research/research-reports/u-s-grocery-shopper-trends
[264] Luke Jenson, CEO, Ocado
[265] https://www.groceryshopii.com/
[266] https://www.digitalcommerce360.com/2019/03/27/the-growth-of-grocery-sales-is-online/
[267] http://www.webberenergygroup.com/publications/deliver-food-waste-model-framework-comparing-energy-use-meal-kit-delivery-groceries/
[268] https://www.bearrobotics.ai/
[269] https://www.nytimes.com/2019/08/14/technology/uber-eats-ghost-kitchens.html
[270] https://www2.deloitte.com/uk/en/pages/corporate-finance/articles/delivering-growth.html

.

Printed in Great Britain
by Amazon